LANGUAGE, THOUGHT AND COMPREHENSION

LANGUAGE, THOUGHT AND COMPREHENSION

A Case Study of the Writings of I. A. Richards

by

W. H. N. HOTOPF

Bloomington
INDIANA UNIVERSITY PRESS

Published in the U.S.A., 1965
by Indiana University Press
Bloomington, Indiana

© *W. H. N. Hotopf* 1965

Library of Congress catalog card number: 65-12278

Printed in Great Britain

TO MY WIFE

CONTENTS

CONTENTS

ACKNOWLEDGEMENTS

LARGE parts of this book have been read by Professors Ernest Gellner and D. W. Hamlyn, and shorter sections by Dr. Eva Bene, Professor Ronald Dore, Professor Donald MacRae, and Mr. James Thomson; I am deeply indebted to them for their useful comments and criticisms. They should not however be held responsible for the views expressed.

I would like to thank Mrs. Llewellyn and Mrs. Lorna Gadbury, who undertook the typing of the major part of the book, for their unfailing good humour, despite all the provocations of my handwriting.

NOTES

1. The following abbreviations will be used throughout this work in footnote references to books by I. A. Richards:

M. of M.	*The Meaning of Meaning*, 1st edition
P.L.C.	*Principles of Literary Criticism*, 5th edition
S. and P.	*Science and Poetry*, 1st edition
P.C.	*Practical Criticism*, 9th edition
M. on the M.	*Mencius on the Mind*
B.R.R.	*Basic Rules of Reason*
C. on I.	*Coleridge on Imagination*, 2nd edition
P.R.	*The Philosophy of Rhetoric*
I. in T.	*Interpretation in Teaching*
H.T.R.P.	*How to Read a Page*

2. The number in brackets after quotations in the text refers to the page number in the book there under discussion.

3. Italics in quotations are always those of the original author, unless otherwise indicated.

Chapter One

INTRODUCTION

THIS book is the outcome of many years spent in reading and critically appraising the writings of I. A. Richards. I have had two particular motives for doing this: first, an interest in theories about the influence of language upon the way in which we think; and second, a concern with how much we fail in communicating verbally with one another, and the reasons for this. Writing about Richards from these points of view should not result in a distorted picture, since these were themselves the fundamental motives of Richards' writings. But I should like to tell the reader what kind of work this is and why it has been written.

Let us start by considering the influence Richards has had. This has been strong in two areas in particular; that of education in proper thinking and comprehension of written material by improving our skill with words, and that of the appreciation of poetry. Much the most influential book in the first of these two fields was *The Meaning of Meaning*, his second full length work, which he wrote in collaboration with C. K. Ogden in 1923. The effect of this book was considerable: it has run through ten editions, the latest appearing in 1960; and it is still widely referred to. It aimed, as we may judge from its title, at having a wide appeal, but apart from its own particular qualities it was well positioned psychologically—written as a wave was gathering for its forward swoop—to be a great success. It popularised an idea, often put forward by philosophers, about the influence of language upon philosophical theories, and this idea was just starting a new life as a result of an attempt with a reformulated logic to create an ideal language. The new version had been proposed in 1918 by Russell in his lectures on *The Philosophy of Logical Atomism*[1] and in 1921 by Wittgenstein's *Tractatus Logico-Philosophicus*[2]. There was also a concern at the time with the propaganda

[1] I justify elsewhere this late dating of Russell's concern with the influence of ordinary language on philosophical thinking. There are only occasional and slight references to this in his earlier writings, which were much more concerned to put the blame for philosophical errors on the faults of classical logic, which in *The Principles of Mathematics* (1903), for example, was *contrasted* with ordinary language.

[2] Ogden, Richards' co-author in *The Meaning of Meaning*, both translated and sponsored the publication of Wittgenstein's *Tractatus*.

1

power attributed to the popular press, which had shown its strength in the congenial setting of the 1914-18 war. Fear of the strength of such propaganda, that was considered to work by manipulating various verbal devices, may have been part of the general reaction to the European trauma of the First World War which expressed itself in the markedly idealistic, war-abolishing rationalism that characterised the period. Holding beliefs and attitudes like these, and bringing to the problem a fervent belief in science as expressed in an enlightened behaviouristic psychology, whilst at the same time talking the language of mentalism; blending this with the methods of philosophical analysis and backing it up with a theory of language-magic, culled from the work of classical anthropologists (but backed, in the person of Malinowski, by the modern movement in anthropology), a theory moreover that was used to account both for Greek philosophy and the most up-to-date views of the Cambridge realists; the work united a wide range of intellectual fashions of the time, and contrived to be at once revolutionary and traditional. Testimony to the breadth of the book's influence was given by the references to it to be found both in works of scholarship and of popularisation. Many writings by logicians, philosophers, and linguists referred to Ogden and Richards' theory of signs and division of language function, though not generally in great detail, since, as we shall see, this work was not very systematic. Its effect was much more that of a stimulus. As its nearest and most influential successor we may take Charles Morris's *Signs, Language and Behaviour* (1946), which aimed at contributing "at this time the kind of stimulation that has been provided for several decades by C. K. Ogden's and I. A. Richards' *The Meaning of Meaning*",[1] but did it by being much more systematic and by being explicitly behaviouristic in the criteria it used to carry out what *The Meaning of Meaning* was a "pioneer attempt" to do, namely, "to distinguish the significa-tion of signs represented in its purest form in science from the kinds of signification characteristic of non-scientific discourse"[2]. In Morris's work we have a tidying-up and detailed working-out of the pro-gramme of *The Meaning of Meaning*, joined with the viewpoint of the Unity of Science Movement that had radiated outwards from the Vienna Circle, and was rendered genuinely consistent with the methodological outlook of present-day psychology. The influence of *The Meaning of Meaning*, together with that of Richards' next book, *The Principles of Literary Criticism*, was also shown on what, as far as attitude to method is concerned, may be regarded as the other wing of philosophical thinking, in Charles Stevenson's *Ethics and Language* (1944), which, testifying to Richards' influence, sports an epigraph

[1] *Signs, Language, and Behaviour*, p. vii.
[2] Ibid, p. 70.

2

from *The Meaning of Meaning* opposite its Preface, though this was, as we shall see, chosen as a result of a misunderstanding of its authors' meaning.

Popular testimonies to Ogden and Richards' influence came perhaps faster as a result of another shot in the arm from a book that obviously owed some of its stimulus to *The Meaning of Meaning*, Korzybski's geyser-like *Science and Sanity*, published in 1933. Unlike Richards, who has always worked in a university setting, Korzybski institution-alised his influence with some success in the General Semantics Movement. Stuart Chase's *The Tyranny of Words* (1938), the first in a series of smart popularisations of these ideas, hailed Korzybski and Ogden-and-Richards as twin heralds, and from within the movement Hayakawa, its leading propagandist, stressed their role as important precursors.[1]

Richards himself made comparatively little further contribution to these questions until *Interpretation in Teaching* (1938). This book was concerned with increasing prose language skills in order to improve communication and enhance our thinking power. The influence of this book, though by no means negligible amongst educational psycho-logists in Britain, seems to have been much stronger in America. It was itself a product of American educational concerns, since it was first presented as "a Statement on the Application of Theory of Interpretation to General Education [for] the General Education Board." Other evidences of American educationalists' concern with problems of language teaching at that time bear witness to Richards' influence. We may mention, for instance, *Reading in General Educa-tion*, (1940),[2] which was a report of the Committee on Reading in General Education of the American Council of Education; and *Language in General Education*, also published in 1940, this one being a report of the Language Section of the Committee on the Function of English in General Education for *its* parent body, the Commission on Secondary School Curriculum of the Progressive Education Association. The Commission believed, it was stated, that "increased facility in the understanding and use of language leads in the direction of realising democratic values" and that "many of the social, economic and cultural factors which profoundly affect men's lives" cannot be understood and coped with effectively "without a firm grasp upon verbal symbols and their ways".

Such emphases, reminiscent with all the capital letters I have had to write of Chuzzlewit's America, are in fact characteristic of Richards'

---

[1] Cf. *Language in Action* (1941), revised in 1949 as *Language in Thought and Action*.
[2] Edited by W. S. Gray. See particularly Gray's own contribution "Reading and Factors Influencing Reading Efficiency", and Zahner's "Reading Through Analysis of Meaning".

own, and the Committee responsible for the latter work places him foremost amongst their intellectual creditors, recognising a "debt . . . far more general than it has been possible to acknowledge through scattered specific references to his works". Individual books such as Hugh R. Walpole's *Semantics* were further attempts to adapt Richards more specifically to the classroom situation.

What must not be forgotten in all this is the part played by Basic English. Apart from all that Ogden, Richards' original partner, did from the administrative point of view to further the aims of *The Meaning of Meaning*, such as the editing of the International Library of Psychology, Philosophy, and Scientific Method, the founding of the Orthological Institute, the production of *Psyche* and those well-known essays in popular education, the *Psyche* Miniatures, Ogden's greatest achievement was the devising of this simplified natural language. According to Richards, this was another of the effects of *The Meaning of Meaning*, for it arose out of the discovery in their work on definition that "there might be some limited set of words in terms of which the meaning of all words might be stated"[1].

Ogden's interest in Basic English was mainly in its potential role as a universal language. For Richards, however, its main value up to the end of the last war lay in the exercise in linguistic skill which translating from ordinary into Basic English provided, a point of view he put forward in *Basic in Teaching: East and West* (1935), *Interpretation in Teaching, How to Read a Page* (1943), and *Basic English and Its Uses* (1943), and which also received mention in various books influenced by his teaching, particularly Walpole's *Semantics*. Since the war Richards has also concerned himself with the learning of a second language, whether Basic English itself, or some other language taught by pictorial means, an activity which has been institutionalised with the establishment at Harvard of the English Language Research Inc., of which Richards is the director.

When we turn to Richards' other main field of influence, that of the appreciation of poetry, we find there are aspects of it closely related to the educational concerns we have been documenting. In *Principles of Literary Criticism*, Richards applied to the analysis of ethical and aesthetic concepts the same method that had been used in the analysis of the concept of meaning, but his interests were always educational, and this was made most evident in his fifth book, *Practical Criticism* (1929), which reported the results of presenting poems to audiences of University students, and asking them, without their being told who the authors of the poems were, "to comment freely in writing upon them". Richards' direct methods of investigating poetic appreciation, so as to uncover faulty conceptions and procedures which interfered

[1] *Basic English and Its Uses*, p. 23.

4

with just judgment, have been very influential. "There is no doubt," according to a recent pamphlet produced by the Ministry of Education, "that [Richards' "pioneer work"] has been extremely influential in English Schools during the last twenty-five years. It has been misunderstood at times, and misapplied frequently, but, more than any other single influence, it has helped to change the spirit and method of study of poetry in grammar schools and therefore indirectly in all schools . . ."[1]. And to this we may add the tribute of an American critic: "I think presently the historians will be rating this book as one of the documents of major influence upon the thinking of our age."

The difference in attitude that these contrasting tributes show illustrates the different conceptions of their influence held by schoolmasters and university teachers. For the latter quotation comes from John Crowe Ransom's *The New Criticism* (1941), a book whose title became the motto of a new dynasty. "The new criticism," he wrote, "very nearly begins with [Richards]. It might be said also that it began with him in the right way, because he attempted to found it on a more comprehensive basis than other critics did." Here again Richards' influence appears to be greater in America than in England. It is true that he has been credited with some influence over T. S. Eliot. Some of the themes we find in *Principles of Literary Criticism* were however already present in various of the essays collected in *The Sacred Wood*, published five years earlier. Though both writers were responding to a stock of ideas that was to some extent common to them, we might well expect some reciprocal influence between the two.[2] Richards appears also to have influenced F. R. Leavis, whose books appeared much later, and whose tone in referring to Richards, with many of whose ideas he agreed, was up to 1933 courteous and friendly, but increasingly critical thereafter. Since Leavis' influence on literary criticism in Britain is fairly marked, we may perhaps attribute to this circumstance the smallness of Richards' apparent influence; smallness, that is, in number, for we always have Professor Empson to reckon with. And though Richards has been cast aside by Leavis and his followers, that does not of course mean that his influence has not been absorbed and passed on by them.

With the American critics, who have been organised under the heading of *New Criticism*, the case is different. Ransom, Tate, Burke, Blackmur and Cleanth Brooks, to mention some leading names, have

---

[1] *Language. Some Suggestions for Teachers of English and Others.* Ministry of Education Pamphlet No. 26. H.M.S.O., 1954, p. 145.
[2] Richards, as we shall see, rarely refers except in a critical way to the writings of contemporary critics, so testimonies as to influence amongst strict contemporaries tend to be one-way.

all at one time or another saluted him, and with their widespread influence in America, in universities, in literary criticism, goes some of Richards' too. Let synoptic works, telling of the New Critics and their affines, summarise for us. "The general pattern that emerges", writes S. E. Hyman, after giving, in *The Armed Vision* (1948) details of mentions of Richards, "is of Richards marking almost every serious critic working in our time". Likewise "The New Critics", Stallman's own contribution, to the comprehensive, illustrative survey he has edited,[1] ends with these words: "Our age is indeed an age of criticism. The structure of critical ideas and the practical criticism that British critics—Leavis, Turnell, Empson, Read—and American critics—Ransom, Tate, Brooks, Warren, Blackmur, Winters—have contrived upon the foundations of Eliot and Richards constitute an achievement in criticism the like of which has not been equalled in any previous period of our literary history."

Richards therefore is worth a book, for the sake of his ideas themselves and by reason of his contribution to the history of ideas. These two need not be the same, because what a man says is not necessarily what others understand him to say. If we were to generalise from our experience of how people have taken Richards, we might, instead of talking of the History of Ideas, talk of the History of Simplifications and Misinterpretations That Were Not Necessarily Unfruitful. I have come across very few writers, who have made critical comments in any detail, who do not betray some fairly important misunderstanding of Richards' position. And these are people professionally concerned with precision in language—philosophers and literary critics, who are themselves fostering the cult of close reading. One of my aims therefore is to set out what Richards meant as clearly as I can. In doing this, I shall concentrate on Richards' purposes, rather than on his details, and on the type of writing his is and how it should be taken, for some criticisms of Richards are like those of a man who stands close up to a Monet landscape and complains that the leaves have not been properly outlined. Though my book provides an exposition of Richards' views that aims at being more consistent with what he has said, and consequently defends him against certain criticisms that have been made, particularly those of the New Critics (Chapter VII), it exposes him at the same time to other criticisms. These I shall set out, partly in exposition of the books which, from the point of view of his general theory, are the most important (Chapters II-V), and partly in some chapters of appraisal after the exposition.

But my aims go beyond those of the exposition and appraisal of the thought of a writer who is an important figure in the intellectual

[1] *Critiques and Essays in Criticism*, 1930-1948.

history of our times. They are concerned with those two issues, mentioned at the start, on which Richards himself concentrates, that of our understanding of what others have written, and that of the role that language plays in thought. I have taken advantage of my detailed study of I. A. Richards to use his writings and those of his critics as case material for investigating these issues.

With regard to the first issue, I shall not only discuss Richards' own theory of comprehension, which treats comprehension very much as a function of attitude to language, but shall consider at length the misunderstandings to which his books have been subjected (Chapters VI and VII). I shall do this partly to illustrate the extent to which we fail to understand one another, but mainly to show how a different theory, one which lays more stress on our previous knowledge of the relevant ideas, provides a more fruitful analysis than Richards' theory does.

As regards the second issue, the part that language plays in thinking, Richards' position is similar in a number of respects to that of certain influential modern British philosophers (Chapters IX and X). The case study approach will enter here in two ways. If we wish to show how mistakes about language cause a theory to go astray, before carrying out such linguistic therapy we must be sure that we have understood a writer correctly. Our specimens of philosophers' failures to understand (Chapter VI) show this to be a considerable hazard. But I shall also consider the extent to which Richards' own errors can be accounted for in terms of the theories about the linguistic causes of error that he himself advances (Chapter X). We shall see that there is some evidence in favour of these theories, but that knowledge of these causes of error clearly does not prevent the errors from taking place, and, further, that such knowledge is insufficiently fundamental. So in my last chapter (Chapter XI), I shall attempt an explanation of Richards' theories in personality terms, or, to be more specific, in terms of his attitudes to the self and its relation with others.

One other purpose of this book may be mentioned. This, which grew out of considering Richards' theories and his practice, is that of revealing the anarchic consequences of too great emphasis upon self-expression in defiance, rather than through transcendence, of convention. Richards can be regarded as an apologist for certain trends in modern poetry and art to which have contributed in his case influences as diverse as the Freudian emphasis upon free association, the anti-normative attitudes of linguistics, and the over-individualistic psychology with which Richards operated. I hope to show that, by letting his theory influence his practice, Richards revealed, both in an excessive failure to communicate in his later books and in certain confusions of his thinking, the dangers of his course. We need to be

7

alert to this both because of his influence upon educational theory and because of the rather low level to which writing skills have fallen.

The interests of this book are interdisciplinary. This is because these were Richards' interests. We shall be concerned with ideas about education, literary theory, language, philosophy, and psychology. My own special discipline is that of psychology, and so I shall be particularly concerned with assessing Richards' wholesale application of psychological explanations within the different disciplines. But though Richards' explanations were psychological, his approach was philosophical. He believed it important that we should develop philosophical skills in every discipline. In this I believe he is right, so I have paid quite a lot of attention to his philosophical ideas. The other disciplines are less central.

Among the difficulties of an interdisciplinary approach is that of communication, and of the degree of detail with which one deals with the different disciplines. One is liable to fall between two stools in trying to maintain comprehensibility for the educated but non-professional reader and interest for the different professional readers. I may have written at an ellipsis-level which, in philosophy and psychology, is a little high for the non-professional reader. On the other hand, the professional reader may find the ellipsis-level not so much too low as insufficiently technical, detailed, and specific. But it is impossible, in a book of practical size, both to write in the close-meshed way that philosophers, for instance, do and to present Richards' views as a totality in the detail the purposes I have just been describing require. The latter needs must override all others, even though what is new in my intentions may make my choice of where to be detailed appear perverse.

Similar considerations apply as regards psychology. In applying the psychological viewpoint in the realm of these ideas, I must write more loosely, more openly speculatively, than psychologists, burdened by their scientific role, are wont to appear to do. By describing my approach as that of a case study, I hope to suggest that the clinical method may be applied in an area where the experimental approach has so far ruled. In expounding Richards' system of thought, in considering its aetiology as well as the miscomprehensions of his critics, the idea of applying content analysis, the next step in scientific strategy—quantification after systematic observation—has never been far from my mind. Though, having completed the case study, I would now feel much more confident of being able to apply a refined procedure to the test of a worthwhile question, the discrepancy between the articulation and comprehensiveness of the observations and what is yet practical with the procedure is still very great. But the functions of a psychologist are not limited to marching in the scientific procession towards further certain knowledge. Man is an animal who theorises psychologically. and the specialist training of a psychologist in a powerful empirical tradition ought to be able to sharpen and further articulate the experiences from which these inevitable theories come.

Chapter Two

THE MEANING OF
THE MEANING OF MEANING

I. MANIFESTO

WE shall start with Richards' second book. His first, *The Foundations of Aesthetics* (1922), also written in collaboration with C. K. Ogden, and with James Wood as well, is simply a brief description of a number of aesthetic theories with illustrations from the poems or works of the plastic arts that suit them best. Whatever part of it is relevant to our purposes is dealt with more fully in other books and will, if necessary, be mentioned in those connexions.

The Meaning of Meaning: A Study of the Influence of Language upon Thought and of the Science of Symbolism admirably illustrates, in its full title, its own flamboyance. Perhaps the best way of describing it is as a book written by two young men who pretend to be angry. It is an immensely high-spirited book. They attack almost everybody, and claim to solve a host of fundamental problems in philosophy, psychology, linguistics, and aesthetics, or, if not to solve them, at least to indicate the general lines upon which others might now proceed to their solution. Some of the brash positivism associated with youth reveals itself in their attitudes. It shows itself in great hopefulness, in impatience with uncertainties, in a belief in the practical importance of their mission. "Convinced as they are", they wrote in the Preface to the first edition, "of the urgency of a stricter examination of language from a point of view which is at present receiving no attention, the authors have preferred to publish this essay in its present form rather than to wait, perhaps indefinitely, until, in lives otherwise sufficiently occupied, enough moments of leisure had accumulated for it to be rewritten in a more complete and more systematized form" (xxx).[1] The authors revel in a display of learning. The book is a sort of polymathic orgy. We are prepared for this, again in the first edition's Preface, by their description of past work in the field they are to tackle.

Historical research shows that since the lost work of Antisthenes and Plato's *Cratylus* there have been seven chief methods of attack—the Grammatical (Aristotle, Dionysius Thrax), the Metaphysical (The Nominalists,

---

[1] For the meaning of bracketed numerals in this book, see Note 3 on p. viii.

Meinong), the Philological (Horne Tooke, Max Müller), the Psychological (Locke, Stout), the Logical (Leibniz, Russell), the Sociological (Steinthal, Wundt), and the Terminological (Baldwin, Husserl). From all these, as well as from such independent studies as those of Lady Welby, Marty, and C. S. Peirce, from Mauthner's *Kritik der Sprache*, Erdmann's *Die Bedeutung des Wortes*, and Taine's *De l'intelligence*, the writers have derived instruction and occasionally amusement. (xxviii).

The book is studded with quotations throughout—many of them bearing testimony on the part of a motley collection of writers to the great importance of language in the determination of thought. This well-known advertising technique is a marked feature of linguistic imperialism or, as I shall call it, 'linguism'. One has only to turn over the pages of *Science and Sanity* by Count Korzybski or that lively journal *Etc*, one of his progeny, to see this displayed. The chapter headings of *The Meaning of Meaning* are graced by epigraphs, often highly entertaining. This is one of Richards' gifts revealed throughout his books. We see this already at the start of the first chapter:

Chapter I

THOUGHTS, WORDS AND THINGS

> Let us get nearer to the fire, so that we
> can see what we are saying.
> *The Bubis of Fernando Po.*

The influence of Language upon Thought has attracted the attention of the wise and foolish alike, since Lao Tse came long ago to the conclusion—

> He who knows does not speak, he who
> speaks does not know.

Sometimes, in fact, the wise have in this field proved themselves the most foolish. Was it not the great Bentley, Master of Trinity College, Cambridge, Archdeacon of Bristol, and holder of two other livings besides, who declared: 'We are sure, from the names of persons and places mentioned in Scripture before the Deluge, not to insist upon other arguments, that Hebrew was the primitive language of mankind'? On the opposite page are collected other remarks on the subject of language and its Meaning, and whether wise or foolish, they at least raise questions to which, sooner or later, an answer is desirable.

Even for those days the tone—literary, scholarly, Common Room talk—was, I think, unprofessional, taking into account the nature of the subject they were dealing with.

But though academic, the effect is of great energy, which seems to be bursting out everywhere, in appendices, in summaries, in the garrulous table of contents, and, with later editions, in a whole string

11

of prefaces exultantly reporting further developments by each author of the programme *The Meaning of Meaning* initiated. Two stately supplements steam, as well as they may, in its choppy wake, one by Dr. Crookshank, *The Importance of a Theory of Signs and a Critique of Language in the Study of Medicine*, the other by Malinowski on *The Problem of Meaning in Primitive Languages*, well-known in its own right. The book with its great promise and its sketchy, at times slapdash, performance is almost more manifesto than scholarship. When the authors say, in their preface, that "they are, they believe, better aware of [their book's] failings than most critics will suppose", they are certainly right in their supposition. Where after all, beyond this preface, are their critics to get their evidence from? Nevertheless many insights glimmer behind their words, and the book anticipated certain philosophical developments by a number of years.

The key to the understanding of *The Meaning of Meaning* lies in our recognition of the immense importance the authors attributed to language in our thinking, or rather, to our attitudes to language.

All the more elaborate forms of social and intellectual life are affected by changes in our attitude towards, and our use of, words . . . . Only those who shut their eyes to the hasty readaptation to totally new circumstances which the human race has during the last century been blindly endeavouring to achieve, can pretend that there is no need to examine critically the most import-ant of all the instruments of civilization. New millions of participants in the control of general affairs must now attempt to form personal opinions upon matters which were once left to a few. At the same time the complexity of these matters has immensely increased (xxix).

The hundred-page-long second chapter, *The Power of Words*,[1] docu-ments this. "From the earliest times", the authors write,

the Symbols which men have used to aid the process of thinking and to record their achievements have been a continuous source of wonder and illusion. The whole human race has been so impressed by the properties of words as instruments for the control of objects, that in every age it has attributed to them occult powers. Unless we fully realise the profound influence of super-stitions concerning words, we shall not understand the fixity of certain widespread linguistic habits which still vitiate even the most careful thinking (32).

There follows a survey of verbal superstitions in primitive societies, in ancient civilisations, and in European society from the Dark Ages to the present day, leavened only by an account of early attempts at

---

[1] In later editions, the belief on the part of the authors that one of them (Ogden) had written a book called *Word Magic*, caused them to reduce this chapter to about a quarter of its original length.

Nominalist theories of signs, anticipating that of the authors,[1] from which it is interesting to note the name of Bentham is as yet absent.[2]

The author's omnibus way of characterising this is as "Word Magic"; they describe it as a *"superstition"*, which is *"barbarous"*, or *"mediaeval"*, or *"primitive"*, something whose "roots go down very deep into human nature", an "instinctive[3] attitude to words as natural containers of power, which has . . . from the dawn of language been assumed by mankind, and is still supported and encouraged by all the earlier stages of education" (225). They quote Frazer to the effect that "Superstitions survive because, while they shock the views of enlightened members of the community, they are still in harmony with the thoughts and feelings of others, who, though they are drilled by their betters into an appearance of civilisation, remain barbarians or savages at heart"[4] (33), and they speak of language as something that has survived rather than evolved, as the following rather extreme statement indicates—

. . . from the structure of our language we can hardly even think of escaping. Tens of thousands of years have elapsed since we shed our tails, but we are still communicating with a medium developed to meet the needs of arboreal man. And as the sounds and marks of language bear witness to its primeval origins, so the associations of those sounds and marks, and the habits of thought which have grown up with their use and with the structures imposed on them by our first parents, are found to bear witness to an equally significant continuity (34).

[1] Peirce's is the theory to which the authors give greatest credit, and they expound it at some length in an appendix. Some notion of the importance they attribute to their own contribution can be gauged from Ogden's punful, flippant fable, also given in an appendix, which concludes with emphasis upon the year of publication of *The Meaning of Meaning*. There he tells of how "when Homo came to study the parts of speech he wove himself a noose of Words" and "thus arose Church and State and Strife upon the Earth, for oftentimes Homo caused Hominem to die for Abstractions hypostatized and glorified." But "after much time, there appeared Reason" who advised Homo, "Go to now and seek the Doctrine of Symbolism which showeth that the bee buzzeth not in the Head but in the Bonnet." Homo, however, "hearkened not", but "all the while the noose was tightening and Homo began to grow inarticulate. Then had Reason compassion on him and . . . spake again softly: "Go to now, be a Man, Homo! Cast away the Noose of Words . . . Behold! the Doctrine of Symbolism which illumineth all things . . ." until finally, "There sang Reason and Man the Hymn 1923, "Glory to Man in the Highest for Man is the Master of Words"—nineteen hundred and twenty three."

[2] Only in later editions was a footnote introduced, referring to "the fundamental but neglected contribution of Jeremy Bentham".

[3] "Instinctive" here evidently means hereditary. Cf. the statement in Basic English in Richard's *Basic Rules of Reason* (*Psyche Miniatures*, 1933)—"We have, by the effect of teaching, and, it seems, possible, by birth, a strong impulse to take words to be the names of things—one thing, one name—one name, one thing . . ." (16-17).

[4] J. G. Frazer, *Psyche's Task*, p. 169.

This is not, as we might expect, a phenomenon whose strength declined with the growth of scientific ways of thought. On the contrary, "in some ways the twentieth century suffers more grievously than any previous age from the ravages of such verbal superstitions", nor is this confined, as Frazer held, to the unenlightened "members of the community", for "owing to developments in the methods of communication, and the creation of many special symbolic systems, the form of the disease has altered considerably; and, apart from the peculiar survival of religious apologetic, now takes more insidious forms than of yore" (38). Amongst their targets were those "analytic thinkers in fields bordering on mathematics, where the divorce between symbol and reality is most pronounced and the tendency to hypostatisation most alluring" (39). This is then backed up by that quotation-soiled affirmation of Russell's early Platonism from his *Principles of Mathematics*.[1]

Not only this but also the Realism, prevalent at Cambridge in their time, was regarded as the product of Word Magic. With thorough-going Nominalism they rejected the independent status of universals, concepts, and propositions, the existence of unanalysable qualities and relations, and the concept of judgment or knowledge as involving a direct and unique relation between a knower and objects of knowledge; Moore, Russell, Johnson and Wittgenstein are all the dupes of Word Magic, of the *same* instinctive superstition that caused primitive peoples to believe in the magic of names and the mysterious power inherent in certain words.[2]

We have concentrated on contemporary philosophers in order to bring out the extremism of Ogden and Richards' attitude, and also because it is with philosophers that the book is mainly concerned, in particular with the analyses they have put forward to establish the meaning of 'meaning'.

The reason for this concentration, as we shall see, is that Ogden and Richards believed that a popular understanding of the correct answer to the epistemological problems with which philosophers concerned themselves was the best means—because the most fundamental and therefore applicable to the widest range of situations—of counter-

[1] "Whatever may be an object of thought, or may occur in any true or false proposition, or can be accounted as *one*, I call a *term* . . . A man, a moment, a number, a class, a relation, a chimera, or anything else that can be mentioned is sure to be a term . . . A term is possessed of all the properties commonly assigned to substances or substantives . . . Every term is immutable and indestructible . . ." and so on. (*The Principles of Mathematics*, 1903, Vol. I, pp. 43-44.)

[2] "We may smile at the linguistic illusions of primitive man, but may we forget that the verbal machinery on which we so readily rely, and with which our metaphysicians still profess to probe the Nature of Existence, was set up by him, and may be responsible for other illusions hardly less gross and not more easily eradicable?" (35).

acting "the ravages of verbal superstitions" which were so prominent at the time. It would be wrong however to think that Ogden and Richards were only thinking of philosophical malpractices. Besides developments in mathematical logic, they also mentioned, as contemporary reasons for the urgency of the treatment,

> the possession by journalists and men of letters of an immense semi-technical vocabulary and their lack of opportunity, or unwillingness, to inquire into its proper use; . . . the extension of a knowledge of the cruder forms of symbolic convention (the three R's), combined with a widening gulf between the public and the scientific thought of the age; and finally the exploitation, for political and commercial purposes, of the printing press by the dissemination and reiteration of *clichés* (38-39).

Let us now consider in turn the actual ways in which the authors believe that attitudes to language affect thinking and communication and what remedies they propose.

2. DIAGNOSIS: LANGUAGE AND THE DISEASES OF THOUGHT

Five types of what we may call linguogenetic error are specially mentioned by Ogden and Richards. These are the "Phonetic", the "Hypostatic", and the "Utraquistic Subterfuges", Word Magic, and the confusion of referential with emotive meaning.

(1) The "Phonetic Subterfuge". This "consists in treating words which sound alike as though their expansions must be analogous. The most famous case is Mill's use of 'desirable' as though it must expand in the same way as 'visible' or 'knowable'."

(2) The "Hypostatic Subterfuge". "We must," say our authors, "if we are ever to finish making any general remark, contract and condense our language, but we need not hypostatise our contractions." They mention here not only superfluous entities introduced into philosophy but also such as are connected with words like "Virtue, Liberty, Democracy, Peace, Germany, Religion, Glory".

(3) The "Utraquistic Subterfuge". "It has long been recognised that the term 'perception' may have either a physical or a mental referent. Does it refer to what is perceived, or to the perceiving of this? Similarly, 'knowledge' may refer to what is known or to the knowing of it. The Utraquistic subterfuge consists in the use of such terms for both the diverse referents at once. We have it typically when the term 'beauty' is employed, reference being made confusedly both to qualities of the beautiful object and to emotional effects of these qualities on the beholder" (134). This subterfuge, the authors claim, "has probably made more bad argument plausible than any other

15

controversial device which has been practised upon trustful humanity" (239).

These types of error are called 'subterfuges' because it is the authors' wish to draw attention to various tricks of controversy. It is quite evident, however, that they also regard them as effects which can come about without any dishonest intention on the part of those debating. As they say, somewhat ingenuously, of the Phonetic Subterfuge in the case of Mill, "the subterfuge is to be charged against language rather than against Mill" (239). The status of these types of linguogenetic error is a subordinate one. The 'subterfuges' are introduced in a section entitled "Rules of Thumb", which comes after the presentation of their theory of signs, upon which, as we shall see, they mainly rely for remedying linguogenetic error.

(4) Word Magic. This, which we will remember was again and again referred to in the opening section as responsible for so much in all societies and in all ages, is what the authors are mainly concerned with. They described it as "the superstition that words are in some ways parts of things or always imply things corresponding to them" (19).[1] This clearly includes the Hypostatic Subterfuge. Basically what this "superstition" does is to prevent us noticing that words are *instruments*, and that therefore their relations with things are indirect, depending for their full understanding on knowledge of their user's purposes. For this reason it also comprehends "the curious instinctive tendency to believe that a word has its own true or proper use, which",

[1] Malinowski in his Supplement gives a psychological explanation of the genesis of Word Magic, both in primitive societies and in societies like our own, in terms of his functional theory of language. In his view, a child comes to find that the sounds it makes fulfil various functions, such as bringing food or particular people to him, having uncomfortable things removed from him, and so on. This is all the more important because it is one of the few instruments the child has for controlling the environment. "In all the child's experience, words *mean*, in so far as they act and not in so far as they make the child understand or apperceive" (487). It is the same with language in primitive society. Words have meaning only in the "context of the situation". For instance, "a word, signifying an important utensil, is used in action, not to comment on its nature or reflect on its properties, but to make it appear, be handed over to the speaker, or to direct another man to its proper use" (488), and other language-games are also mentioned, such as words in connection with action, with narrative, and with ritual. "Thus, when a savage learns to understand the meaning of a word, this process is not accomplished by explanations . . . but by learning to handle it. A word *means* to a native the proper use of the thing for which it stands, exactly as an implement *means* something when it can be handled and means nothing when no active experience of it is at hand . . . The word therefore has a power of its own, it is a means of bringing things about, it is a handle to acts and objects and not a definition of them" (488-9). Similar usages of language are recognised in our society, so that both from this and from childhood experiences the notion of this direct relationship between words and things arises, the notion, that is, of Word Magic. In 1923 the facts of use, rather than the proper name theory of language, were thought to have led to a wrong theory of language.

the authors add, "we have seen has its roots in magic" (225), a belief later described by Richards as the "Proper Meaning Superstition"[1]. It follows that the "Utraquistic Subterfuge" can also be included under this general explanation, for according to this, we neglect that a word has more than one meaning, which enables us to shuttle to and fro to suit the purposes of our argument.

(5) The confusion of referential with emotive meaning. Among the effects of failure to make this distinction in theory of language, the authors referred (i) to attacks on reason and logic in favour of feeling and intuition on the part of philosophers like Bergson,[2] which were further confused by failing to distinguish different meanings of such words as 'truth' and 'knowledge'; (ii) to subjective factors in theory-making and accepting, such as the emotive components of meta-physical theories, which lead us wrongly to accept them as referential accounts and to feel that such a theory as their own is inadequate; and (iii) to the notion of *unique, unanalysable* concepts, belief in which they explained as due to the particular "emotional aura" of a word which, though unique, did not mean that the reference was unique also.[3] This last theory of linguogenetic error was another of the weapons they used against current Realism. It was another answer to Moore, whose theory of the unanalysable nature of 'good' they took as example, thus finally clearing the way for Richards' naturalistic theory of value in *Principles of Literary Criticism*.

3. DIAGNOSIS: LANGUAGE AND THE DISEASES OF COMMUNICATION

The Meaning of Meaning proceeds from a major concern with theories of language as a source of error in thought, to a major concern with communication. One source of this was failure to distinguish between emotive and referential uses of language which led, in the authors' opinion, to a good deal of fruitless controversy, but the main trouble was the "Proper Meaning Superstition". Given their psychological theory of meaning, an associationist one as we shall see, and given that "the past histories of individuals differ" (230), it is "extremely

---

[1] *The Philosophy of Rhetoric*, 1936, p. 11.

[2] Cf. their comment "the chaos to which uncritical reliance upon speech has reduced this topic . . . is by itself a powerful argument for the prosecution of the inquiry into Symbolism" (380).

[3] I do not think Ogden and Richards are consistent here. Reference can be unique just as much as emotional association; in fact, as we shall see, they themselves consider it so. Therefore Moore's theory, which is the one they attack, can be as easily explained in these terms as in the others. Indeed, to regard Moore's theory as due to an implicit recognition that a word has a particular use, not to be explained away by reductive analysis, would now be considered by many a merit rather than a drawback. Cf. N. Malcolm in *Philosophy of G. E. Moore*, ed. P. A. Schilpp (1942).

unlikely that any two references will ever be *strictly* similar" (189). This does not make communication impossible, provided the "two references have sufficient similarity to allow profitable discussion" (189-190); nevertheless "we ought to regard communication as a difficult matter, and close correspondence of reference for different thinkers as a comparatively rare event" (226). But, it is not just a matter of differences about shades of meaning, for "it constantly happens that one word has to serve the functions for which a hundred would not be too many" (235). This is because, "with sciences in their initial stages, before they have developed into affairs for specialists, and while they are still public concerns, the resistance to new terms is very great", probably, Ogden and Richards suggest, because of "the lack of emotive power which is a peculiarity of all technicalities". This is one "cause for the extravagant ambiguity of all the more important words used in general discussion" (236). The other is the process of "metaphorical shift" in the history of words, according to which any two or more senses of a given word may have no meaning in common since they derive from different aspects of their original, a conception similar to that which Wittgenstein later used the phrase, "family resemblances", to describe,[1] and for the treatment of which, as we shall see later, Ogden and Richards recommended a similar cure (see p. 31 below). Two other reasons for difficulty in communication that should be mentioned, perhaps not unrelated to one another, are the shorthand nature of much of our communication, and the fact that language, having evolved from speech, requires for its supplementation gesture and tone, which are necessarily absent from written language.

To illustrate their thesis that lack of awareness of these varieties of meaning results in communication failures, Ogden and Richards have a chapter in which the dull thudding noise that throughout the book has syncopated with the bugle flourishes and rattling drumsticks of their rhetoric now executes a virtuoso solo and is seen to originate from the banging together of many heads. What we have here is an exhibition of uses of the word 'meaning', taken from articles and symposia (including the "Meaning of Meaning" Symposium in *Mind*, 1920-21, Vols. 29 and 30) to substantiate Ogden and Richards' assertion that "the resort to such a term in serious argument, as though it had some accepted use, or as though the author's use were at once obvious, is a practice to be discredited" (273). Though the chapter is entitled *The Meaning of Philosophers*, others are included; "so helpful a term", they write, "is equally in demand as a carminative in ecclesiastical controversy, as a *vade mecum* in musical criticism, as an indication of the precise point where doctors differ, and as a

[1] *Philosophical Investigations*, 1953, Sect. 67.

lubricant for the spinning-wheel of the absolute relativist" (296); psychologists and psycho-analysts, "historians of philosophy and childhood, Reformers, social and grammatical—all have their own uses of the word, obvious yet undefined" (300).

4. CURE: CULTIVATING THE CORRECT AWARENESS

Among those who concern themselves with the distortions that the language we use can cause to our thought, two types of remedies circulate. One of these is altering our language, when used for philosophical purposes, of which we can take Carnap as an example; the other is alerting its user to its systematically misleading properties. This is the attitude of Ayer in *Language, Truth, and Logic*[1] and, of course of Linguistic Philosophers. These remedies I would describe respectively as 'changing the instrument' and 'changing the user'.

Ogden and Richards are convinced user-changers. They reject changing the instrument on the stock ground that, for anything other than the sciences dealing with "the simplest aspects of nature", "the stage of systematic symbolisation with its fixed and unalterable definitions has not been reached" (224). This follows of course from the world-saving nature of their educational ambitions. In one of a series of water images, *à propos* Frazer's picture of the superstition and barbarism "honeycombing . . . the ground beneath our feet", they say, "only . . . by foregoing the advantages of this or that special scientific symbol system, by drinking of the same unpurified stream, can we share in the life of the community", and continue, "If the clouds of accumulated verbal tradition burst above us in the open— in the effort to communicate, in the attempt at interpretation—few have, as yet, evolved even the rudiments of a defence." (34). But just as occasional references to "the vernacular" by the instrument-changers indicate a bias, despite their protestations that they are not concerned with language in its everyday uses, so I think are there many signs in *The Meaning of Meaning* of a partiality for language just as it is. Apart from their enjoyment in using it, their emphasis upon "the plasticity, facility and convenience" of ordinary language, there is a constant hostility against '*artificiality*',[2] with which they

---

[1] Cf. his remarks *à propos* Russell's head-shaking over ordinary languages as a medium for philosophical communication, in his preface to the 2nd edition (1946), p. 23.

[2] In this connection Ogden's choice of Basic English—a natural language however much pruned instead of an artificial one—as his candidate for a universal language, is surely significant. Cf. I. A. Richards *Basic English and its Uses* (1943), Chapter I, where Ogden's choice is justified in terms of a language's effectiveness being a consequence of its use.

stigmatize current theories of meaning of their day. They also criticise the dissatisfaction with language which they attribute to Wittgenstein[1] or Bergson, and the plain man's "It's all a matter of words" cynicism.[2]

Awareness is the authors' solution, and to this purpose they instruct the user in two ways, in theory and in practice. The former we shall consider here; the latter in our next section.

That instruction in the right theory should be important follows of course from the authors' diagnosis of the malady, namely, that the trouble is due to the inherited and educationally fostered wrong beliefs about language. And just as the wrong views are due to barbarous superstitions in whose toils the leading philosophers of the day were enmeshed, so the right view is to be found in one source and one source only, Science. In this book Science is the shining white to Word Magic's black; they are hero and villain, the clash of whose arms resounds on page after page.

The science the authors appeal to is psychology; not introspectionist psychology, but a true "scientific" psychology, one basically derived "from observations of other people". Though in 1923 the day was yet to come when "more accurate knowledge of psychological laws will enable relations such as 'meaning', 'knowledge', 'being the object of', and 'cognition' to be treated as *linguistic* phantoms . . ., their place being taken by observable correlations" (326—my italics), they considered psychology already sufficiently well advanced for it to be no longer necessary for "the science of Symbolism" to "remain in abeyance". And they certainly had considerable hopes of its future. Because of this the authors content themselves with adumbrating their theory of signs and symbols, the so-called *Context* theory of meaning. In describing this, we shall for a little while have to be rather technical.

The theory is an associationist one which, true to their desire to

---

[1] ibid., Appendix A, p. 399.

[2] Not that Ogden and Richards, any more than instrument-changers, entirely abjure the other type of cure. In the *Rules of Thumb* section (pp. 238-243) to which we have already referred, they brand certain groups of words; such as "Irritants", that is, words liable to evoke emotion irrelevant to the purpose of the discussion, e.g. 'Real', 'Thing', and 'Phenomenon' (to take their own examples); and "Degenerates", words which mislead "because of the multiplicity of their associated references", for which they recommend an "Index Expurgatorius from 'Appearance' to 'Reality' or as near Z as possible" (242). Their attitude to "Meaning" was similar and this was the purpose of their impressionistic exhibition in *The Meaning of Philosophers* chapter. But to judge by their examples, both in that chapter and in the *Rules of Thumb* section, their hostility to branded words was mainly due to the metaphysical associations of these words. And it would be difficult to find a more slippery term, if we are to judge by their use of it, than 'reference', which is one of the words the authors wish to substitute for 'meaning'. (see p. 307 below).

20

banish "linguistic phantoms", they present in causal[1] terms, it being important for them that psychological theories should use the same terms as the natural sciences and not require a special language of their own.[2] Their theory is, as we shall see, a centralist theory like Tolman's, rather than a peripheralist one like Hull's,[3] showing the characteristic bias of such theories in stressing interpretation rather than in pursuing the will-o'-the-wisp of behavioural actualisation, a circumstance which fits in with their reluctance to trust in artificial language.

According to their theory, whenever an object, which has been experienced together with or just before another object, causes us to think of that other, then it acts as a *sign* of the other. These objects are said then to form a context; supply one part of the *context*, and thought of the other follows. This thought, being directed to another object, is described as *referring* to this other object. In their technical language, it is a *reference*. Though it is quite natural, in virtue of their past association, to describe the relation between sign and reference as a *causal* one, Ogden and Richards often talk as though they accept what in psychology is called a substitution theory of learning, according to which learning basically consists in one stimulus substituting for another in calling out the same response. Thus, in their paradigm of the scrape of a match stick which is a sign for the appearance of a flame, they describe the relevant expectation as a thought which is "directed to" the future and is "directed to" flame; and by "directed to", they understand "similar to *what has been caused by*." In other words, what in this case is caused by hearing the scrape is a thought which is similar to past ones caused by seeing flames and experiencing temporal succession. This analysis is obviously influenced by the Pavlovian theory of conditioned reflexes, which is also a substitution theory. According to this theory, the conditioned reflex is regarded as the same as the unconditioned one, only it is elicited by another stimulus. An alternative view, which points out behavioural differences between the two 'reflexes', suggests that the conditioned 'reflex' is the consequence of an expectation[4] and different in kind from the unconditioned one.

[1] The authors in fact intend a correlational account, emphasizing that they deny any causal account of the push-pull variety. ". . . in this preliminary account we are merely using causal language as an expository convenience for the sake of its brevity and its verbs" (138).

[2] Whenever Ogden and Richards emphasise scientific *versus* non-scientific approaches, it will generally be found that they are making this point about language. In this respect, they anticipate the standpoint of the Unity of Science movement.

[3] See footnote to p. 47 below.

[4] My criticism is similar to that of Max Black in 'Ogden and Richards' Theory of

Another example of Ogden and Richards' use of a substitution theory is shown when they describe "recognitions, inferences or thinkings" as "members of certain recurrent psychological contexts", and assert that "an interpretation is itself a recurrence". But these in fact all *depend* upon contexts and are not therefore to be identified with them. Despite their constant criticism of the theories of others on the grounds of artificiality, their own is somewhat artificial too.

Their sign theory, which they apply to perception, and which as they indicate in a brief chapter can solve all the old epistemological problems that the paradoxes of perception give rise to, is also extended to language. "Symbols" they call a class of signs that "men use to communicate one with another and as instruments of thought" (30). Symbols have the special feature that not only can they cause references, as all signs do, but they can also be caused by them. How, psychologically, this is done they do not indicate, seeming to be unaware that since communication is purposive, the initiation of it must be psychologically more complex than the simple model of sign interpretation they use suggests.[1] Their aim, however, is only to indicate some kind of empirical solution to the problem of meaning. "Something along these lines" is what they are saying, and they illustrate it cursorily by advancing from a genetic account of object words to an account of different types of logical form, adding characteristically, "the detailed investigation of such contexts is a task to which sooner or later psychology must address itself, but the methods required are of a kind for which the science has only recently begun to seek. Much may be expected when the theory of the conditioned reflex, due to Pavlov, has been further developed" (66, 6th edn.). Certainly there is no lack of more systematic schematizations, though none, I think, yet does justice to the need to recognise that linguistic responses are purposive and not automatic.

One of the purposes of their psychological model was to make readers more aware that the same word is unlikely to have the same meaning, to cause, that is, or to be caused by, the same reference, because the contexts in which it occurred will be different from one person to another. Therefore no two people's references are identical. We have already referred to this belief when dealing with Ogden and

---

[1] Ogden and Richards do not just mean that when signs are caused by references, they are called symbols. They are clearly concerned that they should be used for the *purpose* of communication, and presumably, though this would clearly be still harder to delimit, for the *purpose* of thought.

Interpretation', *J. Phil.*, 39, 1942 (reprinted in *Language and Philosophy*), though Black, in accusing them of assimilating expectation to perception, neglects the feature of temporal succession, which, for Ogden and Richards, was an important part of their analysis. On Black's general misinterpretation of *The Meaning of Meaning*, see pp. 151-158 below.

Richards' attitude to communication. There is no reason, of course, why the contexts should not lead to references of "sufficient similarity to allow profitable discussion", but it is clear that the authors think it will result in a great deal of variation. Richards, as we shall see later, was always concerned with emphasising the individuality of linguistic experience. This is perhaps a consequence of his concern with literature.

The authors also thought, as we have seen, that the same word will have a number of different meanings for the same person; in other words, it will be for him a member of different contexts. But they did not show how this could be so in terms of their theory of signs. All along in their theorising, they acted as though each symbol has only one meaning for each person. This was perhaps a simplifying assumption, necessary for them to make the particular points they wanted to make.

Another of the purposes of the model was to defeat Word Magic, to show that, far from it being the case that there is any direct relation between words and things, the relationship is always indirect, for between words and things there comes the slippery mind. References, thoughts, events in the central nervous system—whatever we like to call them—cause or are caused by words. They are intervening variables, standing between words and 'things'. Hence the *triangle of reference* with which Ogden and Richards popularised their conception. But more is involved than merely to stress that between the words and what they refer to, there is the individual experience, the cerebral event. There is also the conception of words being used as instruments. "Language", they say, "though often spoken of as a medium of communication, is best regarded as an instrument" (196). As an instrument it has to be "a ready instrument"; therefore "the handiness and ease of a phrase is always more important in deciding whether it will be extensively used than its accuracy" (16). This is another reason why it is not possible to tell directly by what references particular symbols were caused. Very likely they are shorthand for something that would have to be spelled out at greater length. The consequences of the realisation of this for expectations of ease of communication are obvious.

As for the tendency to hypostatisation, awareness of the instrumental nature of language and of the fact that it is often abbreviated expression should counteract any very simple linguistically determined entities. What entities are admissible was in fact determined by the authors' bald assertion, "the only entities in the real world are propertied things which are only symbolically distinguishable into properties and things" (309), "the most important argument" for which is "the natural incredibility of there being such universal

23

denizens of a world of being" as " 'character', 'relation', 'property', 'concept' etc." (154). Therefore words for properties and universal words, as well as logical words, were not classed as symbols at all, because not accountable for in terms of the context theory of meaning. They were "linguistic accessories", which could be part of a symbol ('symbol' was used both for object words and true declarative sentences, distinguished as simple and complex symbols respectively). They were also regarded in the light of instruments, as "conveniences in description, not necessities in the structure of things". "This is shown", Ogden and Richards went on to say,

by the fact that various alternatives are open to us in describing any referent. We can either use a grammar of 'substantives' and 'attributes' (nouns and adjectives), or one of 'Events' and 'Objects', or of 'Place' and 'Referent', according as we favour an Aristotelian outlook, or that of Modern Physics, or a pictorial exposition of the views here advocated. To discuss some questions in any other spirit than that in which we decide between the merits of different Weed killers is to waste all our own time and possibly that of other people (199-200).

There are many affinities between the approach of Ogden and Richards and that of Russell. In some respects one might describe theirs as a psychological translation of Russell's logical extensionalism. But though psychological, they follow Russell (and Bradley) in rejecting Mill's purely psychological analysis of meaning. Their key-word, 'refer', ensures that theirs is a relational theory; realism is, as it were, built-in. Judgments are basic for them, though, in contrast to Russell, they conceive every use of a symbol as a judgment—an existential judgment, as will become clearer when we consider their analysis of false statements. They also anticipate later developments in philosophy in their heightened awareness of, and the great stress they lay on, the actual conditions of use of language as a corrective against faulty theories. This is suggested by their description of language as an instrument and their reminders concerning the way language is actually learned. But though, in this respect, they anticipate Wittgenstein in his later incarnation, they do not, like him, do this in order to stimulate the reader into awareness of the different *uses* to which different words may be put. They stuck to what Ryle would call a proper name theory of meaning, though I think the fact that it was a sign-theory better explains its weaknesses and omissions.[1]

To do justice to Ogden and Richards, we have to recognise the extent to which they were individual. Different philosophers during the last fifty years have had different touchstones of reality—ostensive definability, verifiability, use, capacity to yield deductively statements

[1] Cf. Chapter X, pp. 288-291 and 300-302 above.

that are empirically testable, and so on. Ogden and Richards' touch-stone—one they were always fingering—was the actual psychological conditions that caused an individual utterance. Use of this—and they were not always consistent here—led them to deny that we ever actually talked nonsense. It was also the means by which they rejected many theories that seemed fanciful because remote from common-sense ways of talking. Let us see how this touchstone operates in connection with specific issues.

Their theory of meaning was set out in one of a number of "Canons of Symbolism" that they drew up, namely, the "Canon of Actuality". According to this, "A symbol refers to what it is actually used to refer to; not necessarily to what it ought in good usage, or is intended by an interpreter or is intended by the user, to refer to" (201). They called this "the most important sense in which words have meaning" (325-6). The emphasis, as we pointed out before, is upon interpreta-tion. This applies to the speaker just as much as to the listener. What a person thinks he is saying is not necessarily what he is saying. "Introspective judgments like other judgments are interpretations" (326). Ogden and Richards illustrate this in connection with psycho-analysts. In discussing the psychoanalyst's use of 'meaning', they say

> When he discovers the 'meaning' of some mental phenomenon, what he has found is usually a conspicuous part of the cause, and he rarely makes any other *actual* use of the word. But by introducing theories of unconscious wishes, 'meaning' in the sense of something unconsciously intended, and by introducing 'universal symbols', kings, queens, etc., 'meaning', in the sense of some intrinsic property of the symbol, may easily come to be what he believes himself to be discussing (325, my italics)[1].

This same actualising tendency is also shown in Ogden and Richards' treatment of negative facts. They "solve" the problem of truth by stating that if a reference actually has a referent, then the

---

[1] It takes a lot of reading of *The Meaning of Meaning* to realise that the use of "actual" in this quotation is not just for emphasis. Consider, as another example of this psycho-*logical* extensionalist solution of philosophical problems, the following:
"We are now in a position to grapple with the difference between definitions and ordinary assertions. "Gorillas are animals" and "Gorillas are affable" are unlike one another in the respect that the first appears to be certainly true as soon as we understand it, while the second may be doubted. From "This is a gorilla" it follows directly that "This is an animal", but not that it is an affable one. If we look for a distinction in essential connection between animality and gorillarity on the one hand, and gorillarity and affability on the other, we shall make but indifferent use of our leisure. But if the difference be sought in its proper place, that is, between or in the references, it will be found that the definition *actually* used in the first case includes animal, so that in speaking of a gorilla we have spoken of an animal and are therefore able to refer again without diffidence to what we have already referred to; while affability was not so included. The relevant definition, in fact, is the one *actually* used" (211: my italics).

reference is true. Now the reference may be symbolised by a sentence. If this reference is true (or "adequate", to use their technical term), then there *is* a referent, and the true sentence is a single, albeit complex, symbol. This is laid down by Ogden and Richards in the first of their Canons of Symbolism, "One Symbol stands for one and only one Referent". If however the sentence is false, then it consists of a set of symbols and symbolic accessories, whose relationship amongst themselves is not that which exists amongst the individual referents to which the symbols refer. It is not necessary to assert the existence of negative facts. A false sentence is said to be composed of a number of *true* symbols, each of which has a referent. Ogden and Richards' point is that any object word must, by definition, have a referent, even if only a very general one, and therefore the object word will be "true". "Thus, if we say 'This is a book' and are in error, our reference will be composed of a simple indefinite reference to any book, another to anything now, another to anything which may be here and so on [and] these constituents will all be true" (6th ed., 72).

It might look as though this commits them to a belief in universals and imaginary objects. But they have an escape hatch in their third Canon of Symbolism, "The referent of a contracted symbol is the referent of that symbol expanded". This recognises the point we made earlier about the instrumental nature of language resulting in our often speaking in an elliptical, "shorthand" way. "When a disputed symbol is encountered . . . [we should] expand it, if possible, to its full form—to such a form, that is, as will indicate the sign situations behind the reference it symbolises."[1] "Instances of this expansion", they add, "occur continually in all scientific discussion" (192). According to this excellent prescription, which was the pragmatic motive behind Russell's reductionist analysis and was exemplified in Moore's passionate hunting of the problem,[2] a sentence like "Hamlet is mad" is "a contracted symbol needing to be expanded before it can be discussed." "Hamlet was mad on the stage" or "in my interpretation of the play" may be expanded symbols for what is referred to" (93). This clearly gives Ogden and Richards considerable scope in

[1] The need for this procedure is also implied by the Canon of Actuality. Black's belief that "this rule would require us, in case of dispute concerning interpretation . . ., to ask what cerebral events in the past have been similar to the cerebral event which occurred in the course of the act of interpretation in question" (Black, ibid, p. 194), is an example of the peculiar interpretation to which his overstressing of Ogden and Richards' passing mention of engrams led him. The Canon of Actuality warns us that a person's meaning is never as transparent as current conceptions of meaning lead us to suppose. This does not however mean that the authors believe that in any individual case it is in practice exactly determinable.

[2] Cf. his ten successive formulations of the question to be answered in 'The Nature of Reality of Objects of Perception', *Proc. Arist. Soc.*, 1907-8.

dealing with the problem of the ontological status of imaginary objects. Similarly, when we find them referring in connection with the object word 'green', not to any potential universal like 'greeness' but to 'green things', we can see how obedient the expansion of symbols is to the ontology they prefer.

Strictly speaking, since Ogden and Richards allow that sensations may be referents, the Canons of "Expansion" and "Actuality" mean that no statement that is used in a particular situation can ever be false. They introduce the Canon of Actuality whilst discussing the statement, "My pipe is alight", when in fact it is out. They point out that the *actual* referent may have been "some feeling and not burning tobacco". The statement was therefore shorthand and could be "expanded" to "my pipe feels as though it were alight". (103, 6th edn.) Although this consequence, that by their analysis no actual statement can ever be false, was not intended by the authors in this book, Richards in his later works in effect frequently accepts it.

Because of their emphasis upon actualities, which is due to their fear of the dangers of abstraction, Ogden and Richards often give the impression of advancing empirical solutions of philosophical problems.[1] Certainly they have difficulty in thinking in terms of the hypothetical. The status of their Canons of Symbolism, for instance, is ambiguous. These six Canons, three of which we have already mentioned and of which Aristotle's "Laws of Thought" constitute a fourth, are described as "rules or conventions of symbolism" (6th edn., 246), as "postulates [or] regulative presumptions without which no system of symbols, no science, not even logic could develop." Ogden and Richards add that "modern mathematicians . . . either tacitly assume these Canons, or when confronted by difficulties due to their neglect, introduce *ad hoc* complexities into their systems" (6th edn. 87), of which they give as example Russell's Theory of Types. They claim further that "the observance of these Canons ensures a clear prose style" and that when they "are fully set forth in the forms implied by systematic discourse, the solutions of many long-standing problems are found to be *de facto* provided" (6th edn., 246).

On the other hand, the Canons are also described as being "as essential to all discourse as chemistry to physiology, . . . or psychology to aesthetics" (6th edn., 246). Here evidently what is being assumed is not certain *postulates*, but knowledge of certain *facts* which are relatively more basic. The Canons are described as "deriving from the nature of mental processes", and in fact they are, with one exception, all presented in declarative sentences, as the reader will have noticed in the case of the three we have already mentioned (see pages 25 and 26). The exception is the Canon embodying Aristotle's Laws of

[1] Cf., for instance, Ramsey's review of *The Meaning of Meaning*, in *Mind*, 1925

Thought, "No complex symbol *may* contain constituent symbols which claim the same 'place' " (6th edn., 105, my italics).

What Ogden and Richards are implying is that the problems which the systematic setting forth of the Canons will solve, which they say include those of "Truth", "Universals", "Negative Facts", and "Round Squares", are ones which depend upon a proper understanding of how symbols are learned. The inadequate solutions they describe, generally in such terms as "highly artificial", are merely verbal ones, which no one could possibly remain satisfied with if he were really alert to the relations between words, ourselves and things. As for the ambiguity in their formulation of the status of the Canons, this looks like careless writing but, as we shall see later in Richards' case, it is more likely to be deliberate—at all events, unashamed.

One more aspect of Ogden and Richards' theory needs to be considered, namely, that relevant to errors in thought brought about by confusing referential with emotive language. This can be dealt with quite briefly. Contrary to the general view, Ogden and Richards had *two* different distinctions in mind. 'Emotive' writing could refer to the purpose of the writing or to the psychological conditions of its production.

According to the first distinction, referential or, as they sometimes call it, 'symbolic' writing is writing that aims only at informing the reader; emotive is that done for the sake of its effects on the reader. This is what the authors had in mind when making such widely quoted statements as "[a poem] tells us, or should tell us, nothing" (270) and "The best test of whether our use of words is essentially symbolic or emotive is the question—"Is this true or false in the ordinary strict scientific sense?" If this question is relevant then the use is symbolic, if it is clearly irrelevant then we have an emotive utterance" (259).[1] "*Symbolic* statements", they say, "may indeed be used as a means of evoking attitudes, but when this use is occurring it will be noticed that the truth or falsity of the statements is of no consequence provided that they are accepted by the hearer" (my italics). Most use of language, they hold, is either emotive in function or has a mixed function; the exception is "scientific statement, that recent new development of linguistic activity"[2] (227).

But writing can also be distinguished according to its causes. ". . . in speaking a sentence we are giving rise to, as in hearing it we are confronted by, at least two sign-situations. One is interpreted

---

[1] The reading of these statements should stress 'tells', 'relevant', and 'use'. Quite frequently the last sentence, which is vital for explaining its predecesscr, is omitted in quotations from the book.

[2] This has some similarity to a *denial* that a proper name theory of meaning would be adequate for most uses of language.

from symbols to reference and so to referent; the other is interpreted from verbal signs to the attitude, mood, interest, purpose, desire and so forth of the speaker, and thence to the situation, circumstances and conditions in which the utterance is made" (356). A word may be *associated* with an emotion or feeling by a speaker so that, when he speaks it, it is no more than a sign (provided he does not have the intention of communicating, of presenting it so that it will be taken as a sign); or it may be associated with a thought or a perception, in which case it will be a symbol. The word or sentence may be part sign, part symbol, as when our choice from synonymous alternatives is determined by attitudinal factors, or it may be purely emotive, as the authors thought sometimes happens with words like 'good' and 'true', when what is said in controversy has no other effect than to incite approval or disapproval.[1]

Three kinds of emotive function are distinguished.[2] These are the expressing of the writer's attitude to his audience, the expressing of his attitude to what he is writing about, and the expression of his intentions in writing, later referred to respectively as *tone*, *feeling*, and *intention*. This classification is of relevance whether it is the *purpose* of the writing or the causal sign-situation that is being referred to. As Ogden and Richards put it, "each of these non-symbolic functions may employ words either in a symbolic capacity, to attain the required end through the references produced in the listener, or in a non-symbolic capacity when the end is gained through the direct effects of the words" (359). The other function, the symbolic one, which, unlike the emotive ones, could only be served by words having references as their causes, comes to be referred to as *sense*.[3] The rather passive role the authors seem to assign to the language-user might be explained on the assumption that their major interest was an educational one, namely improvement in comprehension.

---

[1] This point has been widely misunderstood as indicating that Ogden and Richards were early proponents of an emotive theory of ethics. There seem no grounds for this. See pp. 161-164 and 174-176.

[2] A fourth, "support of reference", we omit because of the uncertainty of its role in the system. In *The Meaning of Meaning* it refers to signs of ease or difficulty in recall, but not to the degree of certainty or doubt about the reference recalled. This does not seem a very important distinction to make, and no reference is made to it in later treatments of the different non-symbolic functions in *Practical Criticism* or *Mencius on the Mind*. There is, however, mention in *The Philosophy of Rhetoric*, p. 50, of a function in language of indicating "the confidence I have in the soundness of the remark". But that would seem to refer to the degree of certainty or doubt about a reference.

[3] Cf. *Practical Criticism*, 1929, pp. 181-2.

5. CURE: THERAPEUTIC EXERCISES

Ogden and Richards' main remedy for counteracting the evil effects of Word Magic on thinking and communication was to practise the technique of multiple definition. Two things were involved. First, emphasising that there are a number of different meanings of various important words and that our knowledge of what these are would make us more cautious in interpretation and less liable to error; and, second, instructing the reader in how to work out these meanings for himself. To the latter object, Chapter VI, "The Theory of Definition", is devoted. What the authors seem to be selling is a sort of 'Analysis for Everyman',[1] except that, instead of limiting themselves to a single meaning as is suggested by phrases, such as Moore's "as the word is *naturally* used", they are, as we have seen, ardent advocates of the belief that *many* meanings are in common use. What in fact they do is both kinds of analysis, concentrating on the one meaning for arriving at truth, on many meanings for improving communication. An inconsistency lurks here, to which I shall refer again later, but which might be described by calling them, to invert a phrase they themselves use, "relativist Absolutists".

The instructions for defining laid down by the authors abundantly indicate the "pragmatic basis" they claim. "The starting-point must be familiar", and this, for them, "can in practice only be guaranteed when it is either something with which we are directly . . . acquainted . . . , or something with a wide and vague extension involving no ambiguity in the context[2] in which it is used" (214). This is then connected with the definiendum by means of a number of easily understood relations, varying from the simple (e.g. such relations as similarity, and causal, spatial, or temporal relations) to the complex. For the authors cause for optimism is to be found in their belief that the former are few in number, an optimism which provided the impetus for Ogden's later creation of "Basic English"[3] with its great

---

[1] Cf. the effective popularisation of this some ten years later in Joad's "It depends what you mean by . . ." performances in the Brains Trust.

[2] Here 'context' seems to be used in its ordinary and not in their technical sense. Richards continued to use the word in both senses until in *Interpretation in Teaching* (1938), his eighth book after *The Meaning of Meaning*, after referring to misunderstandings of his thesis, he introduced the word 'setting' for the ordinary use of 'context', thus preserving the latter for his technical purpose. As he pertinently, but not apparently penitently, said, "It is the half-technicalised words—and this includes the whole vocabulary of philosophy, criticism and the allied subjects—that make even the most careful readers and writers scratch their heads in despair" (p. 133).

[3] Cf. I. A. Richards, "Recollections of C. K. Ogden", *Encounter*, September 1957 Vol. IX, No. 3, p. 12.

reduction in number of verbs. Complex relations, which could be reduced to simple relations, were however admitted in instruction about defining, on pragmatic grounds. If, that is to say, there was a good chance of their being successfully employed as far as communication was concerned, then the economy brought about by their use made them well worth while.

Having given instructions in the theory of definition, the authors then demonstrate its application. "At the beginning . . . of any serious examination of . . . subjects" (like beauty, truth, or meaning) "we should provide ourselves with as complete a list as possible of different uses of the principal words" (236) ". . . *without* seeking for a common element". And "the next step is to order these uses with a view to discovering which main routes of identification have been adopted for the referents concerned" (232). This yields (inevitable phrase!) "a map", which is valuable because "it is extraordinarily difficult in such fields to retain consistently what may be called 'a sense of position' " (237). This is illustrated in the cases of the words 'beauty', and 'meaning', the former of service because it enables the authors to point to cases in which the emotive function of statements in which it figures is prominent,[1] the latter, following the chapter on *The Meaning of Philosophers*, indicating the *variety* of usage those philosophers were considered to have manifested unknowingly in their practice. In the case of both words the 'meanings' listed are in fact the different theories that have been held in these fields. They are very briefly[2] presented in terms of the relations indicated in the chapter on *The Theory of Definition*—theories in terms of the unanalysable nature of the quality or relation concerned (oddly taken as an example of definition in terms of the relation of similarity), theories in terms of causation of psychological conditions, and theories in terms of complex relations. We find a contrast here with present-day trends, for, instead of *showing* varying uses in order to correct or to banish theory, Ogden and Richards show the various theories in order to correct usage. What they are in fact saying is that it is impossible to use a general word without having loyalty to a theory,

---

[1] This is not to say they regard 'beauty' any more than 'good' as 'emotive words', as Toulmin and Baier (*Mind*, LXI, 1952) in their theory of "the Great Divide" in the functions of words as either descriptive or emotive suggest, or as Frankena (*Language, Thought and Culture*, ed. P. Henle), in following them, asserts. I don't think Ogden and Richards regard any words as either emotive or referential; it is only to the uses or occasions of words that these terms apply. Sixteen different referential definitions of 'Beauty' are listed in *The Meaning of Meaning*. Although Richards' own definition of 'beauty' is in terms of the effects of beautiful objects upon their perceivers, this does not at all mean to say that he thinks the *word* is emotive.

[2] Nowhere is the absurdly high ellipsis level at which this book is written, bearing in mind its purposes, more apparent than in this section.

the important point being not to confuse theories in one's successive uses of a word. In *The Meaning of Meaning* they concentrate on 'meaning', but in the earlier *The Foundations of Aesthetics*, as well as in the subsequent *Principles of Literary Criticism* by Richards alone, 'beauty' and related terms are considered in more detail. In both these books, as well as in that at present being considered, these presentations of different ways of looking at the world are combined with an evaluative attitude towards them. In part the alternative theories are criticised on grounds of contamination by Word Magic, as hypostatising non-existent entities or tempting others to do so, or as being insufficiently thorough analyses. Both these latter charges, for instance, are made against what they describe as the Traditional theory of meaning carried out in terms of connotation and denotation, for which, in *certain* uses of those terms, they substituted the notions of reference and referent, but, because they were Nominalists, with the psychological mode of operation *insisted on* rather than taken for granted.

The alternative theories are not, however, to be explained away completely like this. Nevertheless, they are considered inferior. As Ogden and Richards put it, *theirs*, i.e., that expressed by the Canon of Actuality, is "the most important sense in which words have *meaning*" (325-6, my italics). I would guess that what they mean is that the concept they are concerned with is the most *general* one in the field of communication, one which has applicability to all instead of only to *some* communication situations. But, as I suggested earlier, they are not concerned, like Moore, only with removing possible misunderstandings before coming to grips with the central problem of analysis. For them the former activity is as important as the latter or, if it is not yet so in *The Meaning of Meaning*, it becomes so in Richards' later writings. The paradox of the search for certainty leading to greater uncertainty, which Russell resolved by successive solutions but which led Moore to intensify his doubt, made Richards even more of a Hindu. Nevertheless his writings are to the end normatively orientated. I think he is always a relativist Absolutist, and this perhaps is the reason why he and Ogden never called their book "The Meaning*s* of Meaning". And if, with ironical intent, one is tempted to do this for them, Richards would welcome it, for, as we shall see, he did not consider that the fertility of ambiguity was confined to verse.

Chapter Three

THE SCIENCE OF SYMBOLS
APPLIED TO LITERATURE

THE Meaning of Meaning, as we pointed out, was a manifesto which launched a programme: as edition followed edition, the authors reported in new prefaces to these editions what they had done further to implement this programme. Let us have a quick look at these prefaces. In that to the second, they report on two books by Ogden, one of which, *Word Magic*, seems never to have materialised, so that its promise to "present the historical and philological apparatus by the aid of which alone our current linguistic habits may be explained", despite its renewal in every edition after the second, remains unfulfilled. The two books by Richards were *Principles of Literary Criticism* (1925), described as providing "for the emotive function of language the same critical foundation as is here attempted for the symbolic", and *Science and Poetry* (1926), which "discusses the place and future of literature in our civilization. The authors go on to say in their preface,

these additions still leave much of the new ground opened by *The Meaning of Meaning* to be explored. Chief among these desiderata are the development of an educational technique whereby both the child and the adult may be assisted to a better use of language, the investigation of the general principles of notation with its bearing on the problem of a universal scientific language, and the analytical task of discovering a grammar by means of which translation from one symbol-system to another could be controlled.

Characteristically, the authors claim "these are projects which demand an Institute of Linguistic Research with headquarters in Geneva, New York, and Peking".

In the third edition, they feel they are able to report the satisfaction of these "desiderata", Ogden's Basic English[1] claiming to meet the second and third, and *Practical Criticism*, "an educational application of Chapter X" of *The Meaning of Meaning*, the first. They add that Richards' experience "as Visiting Professor at Peking (1928-30) makes

[1] Cf. Volume IX and X of *Psyche*, 1928-30. There is also the *Psyche* Miniature *Basic English* (1930), which elsewhere the authors describe as "an application of Chapters V and VI ["The Canons of Symbolism" and "Definition"] of the present work to the problem of a universal language" (p. iv, 6th ed.).

the need for further work upon all these questions appear still more urgent", and the preface to the next edition reports a fruit of that visit, *Mencius on the Mind* (1932), which "examines the difficulties which beset the translator and explores the technique of multiple definition", a technique "further elucidated in *Basic Rules of Reason*" (1933). In addition to these books by Richards, they reported *Coleridge on Imagination* (1934), "a new estimate of Coleridge's theory in the light of a more adequate evaluation of emotive language", and two works by Ogden, *Bentham's Theory of Fictions* and *Opposition*. Finally, the preface to the 6th edition reports briefly some articles in *Psyche* by Ogden and *Interpretation in Teaching* (1938) and *How to Read a Page* (1943) by Richards.

The books by Richards do not quite constitute all he has written. In addition, we should mention *The Philosophy of Rhetoric* (1936), *Basic in Teaching: East and West* (1935), and *Basic English and its Uses* (1943). There is also *Speculative Instruments* (1955), which is a collection of Richards' articles, and a few teaching handbooks and translations into Basic English. Of Richards' books, we shall consider in detail only five: *Principles of Literary Criticism*, *Coleridge on Imagination*, *The Philosophy of Rhetoric*, *Interpretation in Teaching*, and *How to Read a Page*. They will show sufficiently well how the programme outlined in the Prefaces to *The Meaning of Meaning* has, at least from Richards' point of view, been carried out.

Principles of Literary Criticism forms with his next two books, *Science and Poetry* and *Practical Criticism*, a compact group. They are concerned with the value to be derived from the arts, particularly poetry, but since such value can only be enjoyed if the artistic products are correctly interpreted, they are also concerned with combatting faulty theories which interfere with such interpretation. The first book sets out the theory; the second, a *Psyche* Miniature, popularises it; and the third applies it. We can deal with their combined message by considering the first in detail and drawing upon the other two for a few additional points. We are concerned with them not fundamentally because of their contribution to literary criticism as a specialist subject, but because the theory of value worked out in them underlies Richards' teaching activities. According to these books, poetry is the highest source of value there is, and correct reading of good poetry is the key to self-realisation. In later books these claims come increasingly to be made for philosophy, and Richards' attention is turned back to the understanding of prose. But we cannot understand the importance the latter has for him, unless we understand the significance of the former.

I. INTRODUCING "PRINCIPLES OF LITERARY CRITICISM"

Though Richards has a love of heights, no other book of his is showy like *The Meaning of Meaning*. This perhaps was Ogden's contribution. Richards' books on literary criticism are, in my view, his most interesting, and the *Principles* his best book. Partly this is because of his great gift for poetry but not for philosophy, where he has too much lingered. But partly also it is due to the fact that the *Principles* concentrates more on its theme and is less scarred with digressions than Richards' other books. It shows signs of being more carefully written[1] and covers a wider range of cogent articulated ideas. Its chapters are splendidly short—suited to our spans of apprehension. Later books tended more and more to note form. *Principles of Literary Criticism* has the concentration of notes but maintains the courtesies of consecutive presentation.

But though there are many contrasts with *The Meaning of Meaning*, the two books are obviously products of the same mind. *Principles of Literary Criticism*, we find, applies to artistic theory the same treatment as *The Meaning of Meaning* had applied to the question of meaning. It is similarly, though not so drastically, iconoclastic in its treatment of aesthetics, as its opening salvo, a chapter called *The Chaos of Critical Theories*, at once makes clear. It denies, too, a special separated-off aesthetic realm as its predecessor had denied a special mental realm, and it counteracts that sense of artificial abstraction many writings on aesthetics aroused in Richards, by the same corrective of spelled out psychological extensionalism. Thus what a poem is is treated in the same kind of way as what meaning is—in causal terms. Different definitions are reviewed, according to the spirit of multiple definition, but Richards' own is put forward as "by far the most convenient, in fact . . . the only workable way of defining a poem; namely, as a class of experiences which do not differ in any character more than a certain amount, varying for each character, from a standard experience . . . [which is] the relevant experience of the poet when contemplating the completed composition" (227). This is like defining the meaning of a sentence in terms of references or thoughts it symbolises, but more than references are involved, because there are also the feelings and emotions that caused these signs or contributed to these symbols. Therefore the definition is in terms of the wider term, "experiences".

For Richards certain features characterised the highest artistic experiences more prominently than they characterised any other experience—variety with harmony, the feeling of being intensely

[1] Cf. Richards' remarks in the Preface and his concluding note at the end of the last chapter.

alive yet dispassionate, and, though unillusioned, free. He did not wish these to be mysteries, but wanted to show them consistent with the world we know. This was part of his desire to face up to reality which bad art, he believed, with its too emphatic contours, hid from us. The value of these experiences, therefore, must be demonstrated in such a way that they could be shown to be central to all our activities. We must confront aesthetics frankly, too, by showing the theory of it *in principle* amenable to science, which he did by sketching a *possible* psychological analysis. Criticism, we might say, had come to suffer what poetry during the nineteenth century suffered from, being 'poetical',[1] and his critical attitude was part of the revaluation of poetry[2] with which in England we associate in particular the names of Eliot and Leavis. But though he intended by "the science of symbolism" to banish from literary criticism all its fairy entities, he seems in one respect to have been in agreement with those he opposed. This is in his wish to deny a utilitarian function to art, expressed in his denial that there is any material message in poetry, in his separation of referential and emotive purposes. "Seems to have been in agreement" because probably a more important motive was, as we shall see, his hostility, like D. H. Lawrence's, to intellectualism, and his insistence on accepting the truth of one's feelings. All this set him a nice problem. But before embarking on our account of how he tried to solve it, there is one more point to be made. Though there is much talk of science here and elsewhere in Richards' books, this is anti-magic in intent and not a manifestation of scientism. In *The Meaning of Meaning*, instead of following the "scientific" line of turning our language into a calculating machine, he and Ogden stressed the cultivation of awareness for developing *skill* in thought and interpretation. And of *Principles of Literary Criticism* the message was this. Since much that is of the greatest value to us as individuals is as yet far beyond the reach of science, here represented by psychology, it is the experience of the most highly ordered people, that is to say, poets, that can do us most good, provided we get rid of mind-stunting misconceptions that prevent our receiving the poet's communications. "Only the simplest human activities", Richards writes, "are at present amenable to laboratory methods". "Such more complex [aesthetic] objects as have been examined [in the laboratory] have yielded very uncertain results, for reasons which anyone who has ever *both* looked at a picture or read a poem *and* been inside a

---

[1] Richards in fact links the two, saying of the aestheticism he was attacking that its "effects upon literature and the arts have been noticeable, in a narrowing and restriction of the interests active, in preciousness, artificiality and spurious aloofness" (18).

[2] See, for instance, *Science and Poetry* and his criticism of the early Yeats.

psychological laboratory or conversed with a representative psychologist will understand" (8). It cannot possibly be held against Richards, as some have maintained,[1] that he tried to make of literary criticism a *science*.

2. RICHARDS' THEORY OF VALUE

The morality Richards wants is one "which will change its values as circumstances alter, a morality free from occultism, absolutes and arbitrariness, a morality which will explain, as no morality has yet explained, the place and value of the arts in human affairs." This is to be found in a naturalistic ethic. "When we say that anything is good, we mean that it satisfies, and by a good experience we mean one in which the impulses which make it are fulfilled and successful, adding as the necessary qualification that this exercise and satisfaction shall not interfere in any way with more important impulses" (58). There are two points to be noted about this statement. First, Richards' basic units are the different impulses and their satisfaction, not pleasure. "Every activity", he says, "has its own specific goal" (96). "Pleasure and unpleasure . . . are at most delicate signs of how our activities are thriving", but "signs which need a very wary interpretation" (97), their intensity, for instance, being not directly related to the extent of the long-term success of the activities; and when they *are*, as a result of past experiences, goals of activity, then they may be self-defeating.[2]

The second feature of Richards' statement is the phrase, "more important impulses". Though he nowhere states that impulses are equal Richards implies that they may be taken as such. Accordingly, he defines the importance of an impulse in terms of "the extent of the disturbance of other impulses in the individual's activities which the thwarting of the impulse involves". "A vague definition", he comments, "but therefore suitable to our present incomplete and hazy knowledge of how impulses are related" (51). Examples are given to show what he means. Many of our physiological needs, which are necessary for life, require for their satisfaction "complicated cycles of instrumental labour". They thus "involve as conditions a group of impulses, whose satisfaction becomes only second in importance to physiological necessities, those, namely, upon which communication and the ability to co-operate depend".[3] "But", Richards continues,

---

[1] E.g., R. P. Blackmur, in *Language as Gesture*, p. 390.

[2] This of course could be taken into account by a utilitarian theory of ethics, since the paradox of psychological hedonism is psychological, not logical.

[3] The part which communication-needs, Richards' key emphasis, play in his theory of human nature is worth remarking.

"these, since man is a social creature, also become more directly necessary to his well-being". "Impulses", therefore, "whose exercise may have been originally only important as means, and which once might have been replaced by quite different sets, become in time necessary conditions for innumerable quite different performances" (49). This is not quite, I think, another version of Gordon Allport's theory of the functional autonomy of motives,[1] as to a quick reading it might appear, as a theory that any new functional activity is likely soon to serve *other* functions as well, which are furthermore hierarchically interrelated in ways determined by the prevailing social organisation. This is then used to cope with such paradoxes of a naturalistic ethic as self-sacrifice of various kinds. "Acts", Richards says, "which will debar [a man] from his normal relations with his fellows are often avoided, even at the cost of death. Total cessation of all activities is preferred to the dreadful thwarting and privation which would ensue" (49-50). Included among these activities could presumably be asserting or denying a naturalistic ethic. Much of value has as its ground "humane, sympathetic, and friendly relations between individuals." "Unfair or aggressive behaviour, and preoccupation with self-regarding interests to the exclusion of due sensitiveness to the reciprocal claims of human intercourse, lead to a form of organisation which deprives the person so organised of whole ranges of important values" (53).

The interrelation of these impulses, from the point of view of their fulfilment, imposes on us a need to order them one with another. Some have to be renounced, gratification of others has to be postponed, judgments have to be made about their relative priorities. This procedure, which takes place as we grow up and which, as Richards points out, has to take into account the realities of the society in which we live, and so may be described as socialisation, results in "systematisations of impulses". These systematisations may differ in their efficiency, that is, in value. As Richards says, "every systematisation . . . involves a degree of sacrifice, but for some the price to be paid in opportunities foregone is greater than for others. By the extent of the loss, the range of impulses thwarted or starved, and their degree of importance, the merit of a systematisation is judged" (52). Thus, "the debauchee and the victim of conscience alike have achieved organisation whose price in sacrifice is excessive" (52-53), and "the most valuable states of mind . . . are those which involve the widest and most comprehensive co-ordination of activities —the least curtailments, conflict, starvation and restriction" (59). Characteristically, Richards believes that "no one systematisation can

[1] *Personality*, 1937, Chapter VII. Cf. also R. S. Woodworth's influential *Dynamic Psychology* (1918), which had been published not many years before Richards' book.

claim a supreme position. Men are naturally different and in any society specialisation is inevitable. There are evidently a great number of good systematisations and what is good for one person will not be good for another . . . With different conditions different values necessarily arise" (60). Moral value, just as value in the arts, can be achieved by a *variety* of means. Richards' is a catholic theory. It illustrates a constant feature of his thinking, an alternating emphasis on plurality and unity—*plurality* in recognising many different meanings for every word, in regarding value as a function of number of separate impulse-satisfactions, in accepting that there are many different good systematisations, and that art is various and, as we shall see, not to be encapsulated within a single formula: *unity* in there being one best meaning, in organisation being necessary if a large number of impulses are to be satisfied, and in there being a single criterion by which the variety of systematisations and works of art may be judged equal.

We come now to a twist in Richards' theory which in most accounts of it seems not to have been noticed. Our co-ordinating of our impulses increases, at least during our early life. "A growing order is the principle of mind" (50). Richards would have this continue as long as we live. He regarded it not only as a result of learning, but also as a direct consequence of certain experiences—"we pass as a rule from a chaotic to a better organised state by ways which we know nothing about" (57). This means that experiences can be valuable in *two* different ways—by virtue of the number of impulses directly satisfied and by virtue of the increased capacity for co-ordinating impulses in the future that results from the experience. Indeed Richards sometimes talks as though *only* the latter were important. "It is not the intensity of the conscious experience, its thrill, its pleasure or its poignancy which gives it value", he says in one place, "but the organisation of its impulses for freedom and fullness of life" (132). Richards is not denying that present satisfaction of impulses has anything to do with value, only that the effects of the experience on our *future* capacity to satisfy them is what matters most. "Even the most intense delight may indicate only a local success and the activity be generally detrimental, [so it is a] sign which needs a very wary interpretation" (97). Richards' relative emphases are typical and indicate the strenuousness of his attitude to art and how different it is from any conception such as the storing-up for our happiness of numbers of precious moments.[1] For Richards, the interrelation of impulses extends far into the future. The greater value of some

---

[1] "Too great insistence upon the quality of the momentary *consciousness* which the arts occasion has in recent times been a prevalent critical blunder" (132), he writes and mentions the Epilogue of Pater's *Renaissance*.

impulses than of others, and the capacity of some people to be better judges of value by virtue of the finer and more complex systematisations they had achieved, does not constitute a surreptitious reintroduction of qualitative differences in value, as some have held,[1] for they are entirely explained in terms of interferences and organisation of roughly equal impulses. I say "roughly equal" because, as we pointed out before, nowhere does Richards actually assert that they are equal. But it seems from his treatment that, in comparison with their interaction with one another, any differences must be of negligible importance—they are like the individual notes in a symphony.

3. THEORY OF VALUE APPLIED TO ART

But how does Richards apply his theory of value to art? Whilst steering his tricky course between the Scylla of Art for Art's Sake and the Charybdis of Utilitarian theories of Art, Richards called upon Shelley, "another aristocrat, equally a supreme artist" to rebut Tolstoy (not, be it noted, that worshipful aristocrat Plato).

The whole objection of the immorality of poetry rests upon a misconception of the manner in which poetry acts to produce the moral improvement of man. Ethical science arranges the elements which poetry has created, and propounds schemes and proposes examples of civil and domestic life: nor is it for want of admirable doctrines that men hate, and despise, and censure, and deceive and subjugate one another.

But poetry acts in a diviner manner. It awakens and enlarges the mind itself by rendering it the receptacle of a thousand unapprehended combinations of thought. Whatever strengthens and purifies the affections, enlarges the imagination, and adds spirit to sense, is useful (quoted on pp. 66–67).

We may look upon *Principles of Literary Criticism* as an attempt to chisel this doctrine into the marble of positivism.

Works of art represent, for Richards, satisfactions of impulses. Their value is particularly high, not only because in them many impulses are satisfied, but also because in the satisfying of these impulses capacity for future satisfaction is increased. In connection with art, too, Richards talks as though the latter were much the more important contribution to value. The means by which works of art achieve a high degree of value, reckoned in terms of both the present and the future, is by ordering our impulses.

[The artist is most distinguished from the ordinary person] in the range, delicacy and freedom of the connections he is able to make between different elements of his experience (181).

[1] For instance, Manuel Bilsky in his criticism of Richards' *Theory of Value*, in *Phil. Phen. Res.* XIV, 1954 (see p. 165 below).

His experiences . . . represent conciliation of impulses which in most minds are still confused, intertrammeled and conflicting. His work is the ordering of what in most minds is disordered (61).

Richards wields this criterion in judging relative value in literature.

There are two ways in which impulses may be organised; by exclusion and by inclusion, by synthesis and by elimination. Although every coherent state of mind depends upon both, it is permissible to contrast experiences which win stability and order through a narrowing of the response with those which widen it. . . .

. . . A poem of the first group is built out of sets of impulses which run parallel, which have the same direction. In a poem of the second group the most obvious feature is the extraordinary heterogeneity of the distinguishable impulses. But they are more than heterogeneous, they are opposed. They are such that in ordinary, non-poetic, non-imaginative experience, one or other set would be suppressed to give as it might appear freer development to the others (249–50).

The latter are valued more highly than the former, not only because they enable a greater range of impulses to be satisfied, but also because the organisation is more stable. The former can be more easily parodied and made a victim of irony, for irony "consists in the bringing in of the opposite, the complementary impulses; that is why poetry which is exposed to it is not of the highest order, and why irony itself is so constantly a characteristic of poetry which is" (250).

On similar grounds, tragedy is exalted, and Aristotle's analysis conveniently assimilated. "What clearer instance of the 'balance or reconciliation of opposite and discordant qualities' can be found than Tragedy? Pity, the impulse to approach, and Terror, the impulse to retreat, are brought in Tragedy to a reconciliation which they find nowhere else, and with them who knows what other allied groups of equally discordant impulses" (245). "This", Richards adds, "is the explanation of that sense of release, of repose in the midst of stress, of balance and composure, given by Tragedy, for there is no other way in which such impulses, once awakened, can be set at rest without suppression" (246).

And on these grounds, too, impersonality as a feature of aesthetic experience is also accounted for.

The equilibrium of opposed impulses, which we suspect to be the ground-plan of the most valuable aesthetic responses, brings into play far more of our personality than is possible in experiences of a more defined emotion. We cease to be orientated in one definite direction; more facets of the mind are exposed and, what is the same thing, more aspects of things are able to affect us. To respond, not through one narrow channel of interest, but simultaneously and coherently through many, is to be *disinterested* in the only sense which concerns us here (251).

There follows an appraisal of the virtues of disinterestedness: its relation to detachment and impersonality, the greater objectivity we achieve, and the greater engagement of our personalities, virtues often commended in art or in religion. All these evaluations follow, by way of elucidatory comment, Richards' reference to what epitomises his standpoint, Coleridge's theory of imagination, which caps five other 'definitions', presented according to the multiple definition technique; "That synthetic and magical power [that] . . . reveals itself in the balance or reconciliation of opposite or discordant qualities . . . the sense of novelty and freshness, with old and familiar objects; a more than usual state of emotion, with more than usual order; judgment ever awake and steady self-possession with enthusiasm and feeling profound or vehement" and "the sense of unusual delight . . . with the power of reducing multitude into unity of effect, and modifying a series of thoughts by some one predominant thought or feeling".[1]

Such then, is the way in which Richards justifies the value of art, and relative value within art, by means of a naturalistic ethic. His initial belief that "when we say that anything is good we mean that it satisfies" (58) is the weakest point in his argument, showing a need for Multiple Definition, for I should have thought this was only true for certain non-moral meanings of 'good'.[2] But we are concerned here more with description than with criticism, even, we might say, with phenomenological description of Richards' arguments. Granted his initial postulate, is his view of art consistent with his theory of value? To regard art as the product and potential cause of a greater variety and complexity of experiences ordered with regard to one another than is the case with any other type of experience, seems to me a not implausible notion, though not one I would myself favour as being useful, even were it to be more explicitly formulated. But accepting also this view of Richards', is there not rather a big gap between the being able to have a wide variety of experiences together and the being able to satisfy together a wide variety of differing needs? Just as do many textbooks of psychology, Richards, in outlining his theory of value, distinguished between physiological needs and social ones. In other words, he grouped them in pretty coarse categories, the kind that are imposed on us when we wish to talk about man in general. But does not talking in this way give the impression of pre-existing needs, which men have in varying degrees on different occasions, so that they go around, like animals, seeking their satisfaction? What sort of model is this for the enjoyment of art? One is tempted, one might almost say, mesmerised by current conventions,

[1] Quoted on p. 242.
[2] See Section 2 of Chapter VIII below: also pp. 286-288.

to reply in terms of certain *aesthetic* needs. But this of course is what Richards denied. Among other things it would be much too *general* an answer. Richards conceived of a large number of different individual needs being satisfied. But how is one to get from anything so large-scale as 'human needs' to anything so small and particular as all the things that happen to us when we read a poem correctly? In formulating this difficulty I have used the word 'need', because it is in terms of words like this, and 'motive', and 'purpose', and 'desire', that naturalistic theories of ethics would be presented in psychological fashion. But the main word that Richard uses is, as we have seen, 'impulse', and it is by a most skilful exploitation of the meanings of this word that he resolves the difficulty we have described. As an illustration of possible relations between language and thought as well as an exemplification of the theory of language Richards was *later* to develop, it will be worth examining his use of 'impulse' in a little more detail.

Richards has macroscopic and microscopic uses of 'impulse', and thus uses it to bridge the gap between general classes of needs—the way we talk when outlining naturalistic theories of value—and the particular "experiences" (a favourite word of his) we have in art. Here is the key quotation:

> The process in the course of which a mental event may occur, a process apparently beginning in a stimulus and ending in an act, is what we have called an impulse. In actual experience single impulses of course never occur. Even the simplest human reflexes are very intricate bundles of mutually dependent impulses, and in any actual human behaviour the number of simultaneous and connected impulses occurring is beyond estimation. The simple impulse in fact is a limit, and the only impulses psychology is concerned with are complex. It is often convenient to speak as though simple impulses were in question, as when we speak of an impulse of hunger, or an impulse to laugh, but we must not forget how intricate all our activities are (86).

The "convenience" of the macroscopic use is one of which Richards frequently avails himself. This indeed is how he uses it when he first uses it on a large scale, that is, in presenting his psychological theory of value. In two of his first three uses, it occurs in these phrases— "their impulses, their desires, their preferences, the things they esteem . . ." (45), and "the impulses, desires, and propensities of the individual" (46). The synonyms cue how 'impulse' is to be taken in the rest of the chapter, where, with one exception, it always occurs on its own. But in the later chapter, from which the key quotation given above comes, matters are very differently arranged. This chapter introduces the psychological theory which Richards adumbrates to suggest that his theory is in principle testable by the methods of science. This we shall describe later. What concerns us here is that in that chapter, 'needs', 'desires', 'interests', are frequently mentioned, alone and *never* in conjunction with 'impulses'. What we *do* find some paragraphs after the key quotation are the following uses of 'impulse' —"Only that part of the cause of a mental event which takes place through *incoming (sensory) impulses* or through effects of past *sensory impulses* . . ." and "only those movements which the nervous system is specialised to incite, which take place through *motor impulses* . . ." (89—my italics). This suggests that the microscopic use of 'impulse' is a quite different one, namely a *nerve* impulse, a passage of electrical and chemical change along the length of a nerve fibre. This view is supported when we find Richards using a schematic diagram of nerves so as to indicate the temporal succession of sensation, tied images, free images, references, emotions, and attitudes which the words of a poem will arouse, and describing the vertical lines which represent the nerve fibres as being "intended to represent, schematic-ally, *streams of impulses* flowing through the mind" (124, my italics). The use to which Richards puts this identification of two meanings of 'impulse' is revealed when he goes on to say "these impulses are the weft of the experience, the warp being the pre-existing systematic structure of the mind, that organised system of possible impulses" (124).

It would be tempting to suggest here that Richards has used his own "Phonetic Subterfuge", and that the reasoning by which he arrives at the conclusion, given his theory of value, that artistic experiences are the most valuable ones, is based upon a common term which is not in fact common, there being two different senses to 'impulse'. But it is difficult to make precisely this charge stick, because it is difficult to see why artistic experiences should satisfy *more* impulses than any other experience. And anyhow the notion of satis-faction is inapplicable to nervous impulses.

What we do get is the suggestion of impulses as being concrete, episodic, and minute. "The problem of morality", he says, with regard to his theory of value "becomes a problem of organisation, both in the individual life and in the adjustment of individual lives to one another, and is delivered from all non-psychological ideas, from absolute goods and immediate convictions, which incidentally help greatly to give unnecessary stiffness and fixity to obsolescent codes" (58-59). "What value is", he adds later "and which experiences are most valuable will never be understood so long as we think in terms of those large abstractions, the virtues and the vices" (61). Instead we should recognise "that value lies in the 'minute particulars' of response and attitude", a matter in which "the artist is an expert" (61), as indeed the critic should be too. But, as we have seen, Richards uses the same word to refer to "large abstractions" and minute events, so he is able to combine large theoretical significance with a stress on actual experience as the touchstone of value.

Further, identifying 'impulse' with 'nervous impulse', which enables him to affirm that "in actual experience simple impulses of course never occur", makes it easier to deny that difference in value between individual impulses is of any importance in calculating value. There is little present evidence of any difference between nerve impulses. What matter for our sensations or perceptions are the number, kind, and position of the nerve fibres, along which the impulses come. This means that a purely quantitative utilitarian theory becomes plausible, as well as suggesting that it is the *organisation* of these nervous atoms that matters psychologically. The emphasis upon ordering, that is so important a part of Richards' theory, is strongly supported by neurological models. "No individual", he says, "can live one minute without a very intricate and, so far as it goes, very perfect co-ordination of impulses. It is only when we pass from the activities which from second to second maintain life to those which from hour to hour determine what kind of life it shall be, that we find wide differences" (51-52). He then describes these different systematisations we referred to in presenting his theory. Or again in trying to persuade the reader that "a growing order is the principle of the mind", he refers to the differences "between moments when we do with our bodies more delicate and dexterous things than seem possible, and moments of clumsiness, when we are 'all thumbs', have no 'balance' or 'timing', and nothing 'comes off' " (50). Richards then adds

These differences are differences in momentary organisation, differences in precedence between rival possible systematisations. The more permanent and more specifically 'moral' differences between individuals grow out of differences such as these and correspond to similar precedences between larger systems (50–51).

4. WHY POETRY IS GOOD FOR US

We have pointed out that, in Richards' theory, value is not only determined by the number of impulses an experience satisfies, but also by the effects of the experience upon our future capacity for impulse satisfaction. Each new achievement by an artist increases his future capacity to have still further achievements of impulse-ordering in the future, not just in the arts but in any sphere, since, as we have seen, the impulses art satisfies are not special 'aesthetic' ones but are of the kinds which enter into non-artistic activities also. Furthermore, these effects of an artistic achievement on the future are not limited to their creator, but can be transferred to any spectator, whose own impulses are satisfied in the contemplation of the work of art in question.

The artist, Richards writes, is able to "make states of mind accessible to the many which otherwise would be possible only to the few"; and "We pass as a rule from a chaotic to a better organised state . . . typically through the influence of other minds. Literature and the arts are the chief means by which these influences are diffused" (57). Faith is placed in transfer of training.

> Few people . . . will dispute the assertion that transference of ability frequently occurs although the mode by which it comes about may be obscure. When very widespread and very fundamental impulses are implicated, where attitudes constantly taken up in ordinary life are aroused, this transference effect may be very marked. Everybody knows the feeling of freedom, of relief, of increased competence and sanity, that follows any reading in which more than usual order and coherence has been given to our responses. We seem to feel that our command of life, our insight into it and our discrimination of its possibilities is enhanced, even for situations having little or nothing to do with the subject of the reading (235).

Much of course depends upon who the "few people" are who do the disputing. But Richards did not leave the situation quite as blank as this psychologically. The *Principles of Literary Criticism* contains an extension of the psychological theorising of *The Meaning of Meaning*.

This takes the form of laying much more stress on purpose in cognition. This is shown in two ways. Firstly, in stating that "stimuli are only received if they serve some need of the organism" (87) and secondly, in regarding every mental event as resulting in some action. The first is not worked out consistently in the book at present under consideration, though it assumes more and more importance later on. It is with the second that we shall mainly concern ourselves. The action in which mental events result is often no more than slight innervations of muscle of the kind that characterise preparation for action. These Richards calls 'attitudes', and their effects in consciousness are considered part of what we understand by 'emotion'[1] or 'feeling'. Therefore "emotions are primarily signs of attitudes and owe their great prominence in the theory of art to this" (132). Now psychologists have been familiar with the notion of motor 'sets' or attitudes since the work of the Würzburg psychologists at the turn of the century, though these have been conceived as preceding an experience rather than following it. In the pervasive role Richards ascribes to innervations of the musculature he is more to be compared with American psychologists like Washburn, proponents of the motor

---

[1] The other part was "a diffused reaction in the organs of the body brought about through the sympathetic systems" (101). Richards clearly accepted the James-Lange theory of emotion.

theory of consciousness, who may be looked upon as precursors of the Behaviourists in the sense that they threw away the bath water, so that all Watson needed to do was to dispose of the baby. What is important, though, is the role attitudes play in Richards' system. "This incipient activity", he writes,"stands to overt action much as an image stands to a sensation" (108). He then argues that just as we can work out the solution to intellectual problems in our heads, so we can work out the solution to emotional problems in our bodies. And, just as in the former case, doing it in our heads or on paper is more economical, speedier, and often much more practical than trying to solve the problem with overt behaviour in the actual situation, so is it also with emotional problems. There is a striking similarity between Richards' conception of attitudes and that advanced by Clark Hull a few years later of 'fractional anticipatory responses'. The difference is that for Hull they are the behaviouristic equivalent of ideas, whereas for Richards they constitute an extension by analogy from the realm of thought into that of emotion. What it suggests is that the dichotomy of thought and emotion we get in *The Meaning of Meaning* is presented as one between thought and action in the *Principles*. So we have the rather incongruous combination, a typical piece of Richards cake, both had and eaten, of a centralist theory for thought and a peripheralist one for emotion.[1]

But what are the "emotional problems" with which Richards is concerned? It seems they are always ones of organising into a unity a number of diverse responses. This of course follows from the belief that everything we experience, we experience because of some need to whose satisfaction the ensuing activity is directed, and from the belief that these activities may interfere with one another. In works of art, masters' solutions are enshrined. What better works than these for practising on? To their stimuli we attitudinally respond, organising our responses more and more effectively, just as we do in the learning of any game involving motor skill. What is novel and suspect in Richards' theory may perhaps best be brought out if we see that it is

---

[1] 'Centralist' and 'peripheralist' are labels used by psychologists to distinguish between those theorists who believe that associations may take place and problems therefore be solved in the brain (i.e. *central* nervous system), the musculature being the executive which acts on the information and orders given; and those who believe thinking is covert activity and therefore *peripheral* to the central nervous system. According to the second, complex processes of learning and problem-solving are in principle capable of being studied directly by detecting muscular movements; according to the first, they must be *inferred* from the movements. Perhaps, strictly speaking, both have to be inferred, but it is clear that much more interpretation will have to be done with the first than with the second, and this has important methodological implications. Cf. E. Hilgard, *Theories of Learning*, Chaps. 1 and 12, particularly pp. 331-334.

47

not, say, the *playing* of tennis he enjoins for increasing our capacity to play tennis or cricket or other skills making commensurate demands on our ability to organise movement;[1] it is the *watching* of tennis being played—so long as it is being played by first-class players and the game is *properly* watched. The latter qualification is necessary for the implicit reproduction of the right muscular responses, or rather patterns of muscular responses.[2] *Proper* empathy is practising at its most economical. Works of art are also most economical because they are composed of signs and symbols of complex activities. This also makes them much more accessible. And they are most efficacious because the shorthand activities they signify and symbolise are the highest exhibits of order there are. Richards' model is of something like emotional intelligence that can be trained by practice in any of its manifestations and will reveal its new power in any other.[3] It would, however, have been more in keeping with Richards' outlook if he could have accepted that belief of Gestalt psychology, to which he was otherwise favourably disposed, that confines transfer of training to insight into general principles, where these applied. His failure to do so is, I think, due to his urgent need to keep apart reference and emotion, a need for which he produces his justification at the end of the book.

Before turning to this justification, let us glance at how Richards' theory of attitudes ties up with his theory about impulses. According to our key quotation (see p. 43 above), "the process in the course of which a mental event may occur, a process apparently beginning in a stimulus and ending in an act, is what we have called an impulse" (86). The confusion of logical category that haunts Richards' work is evident here. He should really say that the "act" represents the realisation of the impulse, if we mean by an impulse, macroscopically considered, a desire. But if the act is no more than incipient, preparatory to overt activity, can it really be considered a fulfilment of an impulse? If we answer no, then I think we must say that Richards was operating the "Phonetic Subterfuge" with 'impulse'. To avoid this, Richards would have had to regard the act as more than merely preparatory. This, as we have seen, he has done. For the act is taken as a substitute for what it would have led to. Groups of impulses

[1] Cf. his remark "A step in mathematical accomplishment, other things being equal, facilitates the acquisition of a new turn in ski-ing", ibid., p. 234.

[2] That the pattern is more important than the specific impulses out of which it is composed, a concept characteristic of Gestalt psychology, is suggested by his belief that divergent readings of the same poem were compatible with agreement about its value. ibid., Chapter XXVI.

[3] Richards in fact refers to the theory of the general factor in intelligence (*P.L.C.*, p. 234), though he does not refer to the fact that belief in this is based upon a denial of its trainability.

receive in the well-ordered person a kind of fantasy gratification. But they never get beyond this, because, as we shall see, art or philosophical thought continues to represent the most valuable experiences to which we can attain, and much of this value consists in the achievement of ordering which brings yet more complex thought and emotion within our ken. Therefore, though Richards may be exonerated from the charge of using the "Phonetic Subterfuge", the price that has to be paid is committal to the view that, though all the World may be a Stage, we never get beyond a Dress Rehearsal on it.

5. POETRY IS NOT SCIENCE

Richards' writings are thick with ideas. We have tried to indicate these in our exposition even at the risk of overloading it. Partly this is because we shall wish to refer to these later. But partly also it is because we wish to show how much his theory seems to be a description of his practice. With his ideas he is like a juggler, and it is quite a breathless business seeing how many of such impulses he can enjoy at once without committing obvious contradictions. As examples of the multiplicity of his thought, we may mention the combination of a naturalistic ethic, working with equal units which, by emphasising formal virtues such as harmony and ordering, enables him to raise poetry above pushpin and justify fashionable values within poetry; and this is made more plausible by being given a hypothetical basis in psychology, which in turn leads him to gain further support for his system of relative value by appeal to the general factor of intelligence, to the superiority of covert thought compared with overt action, and to the economic, because symbolic, nature of artistic representation.

This combination of many different arguments in a loose association, which gives rise to some very general assertion, can be seen very clearly in the case he advances for keeping separate the emotive from the referential *function* of language in considering poetry. It is particularly important to consider this because of the extent to which Richards' position has been misunderstood. We will postpone consideration of actual misunderstandings till Chapters 6 and 7. Here we shall describe his argument only. Just as in *The Meaning of Meaning*, here also Richards asserts that poetry gains its effects to an important extent from the *meanings* of the words used. "Many arrangements of words evoke attitudes without any reference being required *en route*. They operate like musical phrases." Though he says this—and he certainly dropped this belief almost completely later on—he goes on to say, "But *usually* references are involved as conditions for, or stages in, the ensuing development of attitudes . . ." (267 —my italics). It follows that understanding the meaning of what is

49

thus presented is an important part of proper reading of poetry,[1] a point quite missed by those who express surprise at *Practical Criticism's* concern with understanding of referential meaning.[2] What Richards is concerned with emphasising is that the poet's purpose was different from that of the scientist. The poet isn't writing to inform. The truth, in the sense of the correctness, of what he said was not the vital consideration. Of course, as we have seen, Richards believed that writing that was purely referential in function was very rare. Most writing in philosophy, psychology, aesthetics (including therefore *Principles of Literary Criticism*), and the social studies was *mixed* in function. The point about poetry was that it was purely emotive, only concerned with the harmonising of the personality, and this extreme position is perhaps the main weakness of Richards' theory.

Why should Richards have put forward this point of view, which regarded negatively—the poet's is not the scientist's function—seems so trite? Richards has been interpreted in terms of stock propaganda positions, as 'a Romantic', 'a psychological critic', 'an anti-intellectual', judgments which have then to be reconciled with the same critics' attacks on him for overstressing the role of science. But really there are many ordinary, commonsense reasons for Richards' position. Indeed he is always much closer to the common man and his difficulties and very much less specialist and refined than those who criticise him. There is such a contrast here, for instance, between Richards and Empson, who in *The Structure of Complex Words* searches for the football of Richards' meaning with a magnifying glass. What *is* confusing about Richards is the number of different, not always well-assorted, reasons he relies on.

[1] Cf. a comment like the following: "The ambiguities due to erratic reading are as important for criticism as others, and practically more troublesome" (207); or Richards' comments on how to read Swinburne—"The mere *sense* without any further reflection is very often sufficient thought, in Swinburne, . . . for the full response" (my italics). "Little beyond vague thoughts of the things the words stand for is here required"—in contrast with Hardy, where he suggests that not only "sound and sense", but the bringing of the words "into intelligible connection with one another" (129) is necessary for the full effect, a procedure clearly requiring considerable precision in reading. Many other examples could be taken to show how unlikely it was that Richards, even granted normal human inconsistency, should have thought the sense often unimportant in the reading of poetry; indeed, in the above example, it plays a part even in reading Swinburne.

[2] Even Empson seems to make this mistake when he suggests that Richards "dropped the idea that a writer of poetry had better not worry about the Sense . . . because he had subjected himself to so much reading of bad criticism by his students in these 'protocols,'" (*The Structure of Complex Words*, 1951). Richards never held the "idea" attributed to him. To make it right one would have to substitute 'literal Truth' for "Sense". Richards showed clearly already in *The Meaning of Meaning* his belief that misunderstanding of what people wrote was very widespread.

In considering what these reasons are, we shall draw also on his next book, the *Psyche* Miniature, *Science and Poetry*[1] (1926), for this book is solely concerned with this question, source of many misunderstandings which Richards made some effort to correct in a second edition, produced in 1935.[2]

At the start there is his psychological theory. He makes the quite commonplace point that, in addition to considering the senses and the environment, we also have to take into account a person's needs, and these may vary independently of the information coming in from the external environment. Consequently to understand a person's perceptions and beliefs we have to consider his needs as well. A functionalist theory of perception and belief of this kind is familiar to psychologists. Science, Richards continues, allows for or removes these distorting effects of our wishes and fears. Its success has been such that our old "Magical View" of the world can no longer be easily maintained in Western society. It has resulted in what Richards, in *Science and Poetry* where he develops this theme, called a "Neutralisation of Nature". Richards considers this also to apply to our views of ourselves, though he often writes of how little progress science has yet made in this respect. However, there can be little doubt that many of our private views were, from epistemological and ontological standpoints, inconsistent with the scientific outlook,[3] and this of course was the reason why Richards wrote about meaning, art, and value in the way he did. Now these old magical views, since they satisfied our needs, were of value to us. They provided us with occasions for complex emotional play, valuable for the development of our feelings. Loss of them threatened us with emotional starvation, or with one-sided exercise of more trivial impulses, with effects all the worse in view of the break-up of tradition, the development of specialisms, etc. For religion had concerned itself with central positions on the chess-board of our emotions, and religion was a main victim of science's advances. Those who sought to withstand this by hostility to science, or by developing private mythologies, like Yeats or Lawrence, or by retreating into the world of childhood, like

---

[1] A case might be made for saying that *Science and Poetry*, taken by itself, might justify the belief that Richards was indifferent to the sense of words in poems. But it would obviously be wrong to take this book by itself in considering an important theoretical point like this.

[2] Richards also added a few paragraphs in which, as well as in a footnote or two, he modified slightly what he had originally stated, in the light of developments in his thought fully reported in *Coleridge on Imagination* and later books.

[3] In the second edition of *Science and Poetry*, Richards, following on the development of his ideas in *Coleridge on Imagination*, agreed that any scientific world view was mythical too. But this was the consequence of his Pragmatism and did not mean any flight from empiricism.

Walter de la Mare, were separating themselves dangerously from the main streams of contemporary life, were cutting themselves off from much potential experience, and therefore denying themselves important chances of full development, which for Richards was the greatest crime on the artist's calendar.

The answer to this dilemma lay for Richards in recognising that what was valuable in the beliefs of the past was not the legitimate concern of science at all. Our emotional development is independent of our achievement of scientific objectivity and knowledge; having the latter does not mean having the former, nor is the converse true. The best source of their value today lies in the arts and the experiences they can arouse. The statements made in the arts, which use language, can more easily be recognised as not assertions about the nature of the world we live in. Their purpose, we might say, is aesthetic, remembering however that in Richards' view aesthetic experiences, though distinctive, are not different in kind from some non-aesthetic experiences. Of course sometimes in the arts, and generally in religion and metaphysics, such statements are taken as if they were assertions. In *Science and Poetry*, Richards referred to them as "pseudo-statements", a term which recalls Carnap's "pseudo-object sentences", suggested some seven years later in *Logical Syntax of Language* (1933). But unlike Carnap, who considered such statements to be formal sentences in material disguise, Richards, who obviously recognised that they might be nonsense, literally interpreted, did consider that some of them might be false,[1] and we know from what he wrote in the *Principles* and in the second edition of *Science and Poetry* (p. 65) that they might be true, too. They are "pseudo" in the sense that their final purpose is not that of reporting on how things link up with one another, i.e. conveying information for its own sake.[2] Taking them as though they were and so either rejecting them as false, or dismissing them as nonsense, or nodding one's head and saying "How True!" are all equally mistaken reactions.

The distinctions Richards was trying to make were rendered more

[1] "Mathematicians . . . find the alleged statements to be *false*, which is one reason why some mathematicians cannot read [poetry]". (*Science and Poetry*, p. 56—I have reversed the order of statement and clause).

[2] Richards defined a pseudo-statement as "a form of words which is justified entirely by its effect in releasing or organizing our impulses and attitudes". He would have been better advised to call them 'pseudo-assertions', or indeed to have dropped the word 'pseudo-' altogether, since, by reason of its frequently pejorative connotation, this has led many, who were unable to use Richards' contextual guidance, to think he was saying something derogatory about statements in poetry. Cf. for instance Stanley Hyman, who describes it as "implicitly pejorative" (*The Armed Vision*); or Wimsatt and Beardsley, who claim it is "for Mr. Richards a patronizing term by which he indicated the attractive nullity of poems." ("The Affective Fallacy" in *Critiques and Essays in Criticism 1920-1948*, ed. R. W. Stallman).

difficult by perfectly legitimate uses of 'true' and 'knowledge' in connection with art. But these, he maintained, were different uses from those employed in connection with assertion, reference and science. When we talk, for instance, of the 'truth' and 'knowledge' of the *heart*, we are using different words, homonyms of those we use when talking of the head. These other uses refer to the just balancing and sequential ordering of emotions, such as when we talk of a happy ending striking a *false* note. One reason for confusion is that there is often a common emotional element to sudden scientific insight and intense poetic experience. It is this that leads to Revelation theories of art. But the *feeling* of revelation, conviction, and significance does not guarantee truth in the referential sense. Such "belief feelings" can be induced by drugs, and scientists and philosophers have testified to how misleading they can be—present with a false insight, absent with a genuine discovery. Their detachability from genuine discoveries Richards characterised by calling them "objectless beliefs". The best description, in his view, that had been given of them, was Coleridge's description of the Imagination. His major theoretical development, which we shall find in *Coleridge on Imagination*, was to regard this experience as in fact one of knowledge. When this happens we shall find the separation of emotion from reference to be no longer central to his position.

Richards has always believed in our being honest without rationalising deception about our emotions, which means, amongst other things, being able to feel them at all. The theme was one which, amongst contemporary writers, was prominent in the novels of E. M. Forster and it was also of course an axiom of Freudian therapy. There were many manifestations of it in the *Principles* and in *Science and Poetry*. One of these was the stress on the reader's feeling the sensory aspects of the language used in poetry. Another was the warning against the danger for literature, through failure to realise its difference in function from that of science, of substituting a formula or doctrine associated with certain emotional effects, to bring about these effects, instead of creating them in the reader "by the more difficult means peculiar to the arts" (275). This doctrine, possibly related to D. H. Lawrence's of the essentially destructive nature of the individual will, is itself admirably illustrated by Lawrence's own frequent attempts to argue and repetitively assert it instead of creating it. Linked to this is perhaps also Richards' hostility to "message-hunting" in, for instance, Shakespeare's plays—"a damaging . . . mode of interpreting the phrase, 'a criticism of life' " (229), and an intellectual response serving to ward off emotional encroachment. Richards' attitude is also very widely manifested in what he says about how we should read poetry—*acceptance* of the sounds, words, and statements for the sake of their effects upon us as opposed to the "questioning, verificatory way of handling" the poem's references. I see no reason for construing Richards' meaning here so as to hold him guilty of recommending completely uncritical, standardless acceptances. Then again there is Richards' desire to confront our situations as they really are; the view that only by freedom from illusion would we be able to respond creatively. Hence the value of tragedy, the badness of bad art, the weakness of religious statements believed in today as scientific ones were.

These themes are illustrated in Richards' remarks on "The Poetry of T. S. Eliot", an appendix he added to the second edition of the *Principles* in 1926. Eliot's poetry, by virtue of "the unobtrusiveness, in some cases the absence, of any coherent intellectual thread upon which the items of the poem are strung" (289), should have been particularly well suited for showing that poetry should be read in a different kind of way from expository prose. Richards says of it:

> If it were desired to label in three words the most characteristic feature of Mr. Eliot's technique, this might be done by calling his poetry a 'music of ideas'. The ideas are of all kinds, abstract and concrete, general and particular, and, like the musician's phrases, they are arranged not that they may tell us something, but that their effects in us may combine into a coherent whole of feeling and attitude and produce a peculiar liberation of the will. They are there to be responded to, not to be pondered or worked out. This is, of course, a method used intermittently in very much poetry, and only an accentuation and isolation of one of its normal resources. The peculiarity of Mr. Eliot's later, more puzzling, work is his deliberate and almost exclusive employment of it (293).

The wrong approach makes the poetry obscure, as illustrated by Middleton Murry's criticism of *The Waste Land*—"The reader is compelled, in the mere effort to understand, to adopt an attitude of intellectual suspicion, which makes impossible the communication of feeling" (291). As Eliot himself wrote later, a "difficulty" of modern poetry—and he might have included modern painting too—is that "caused by the author's having left out something which the reader is used to finding; so that the reader, bewildered, gropes about for what is absent, and puzzles his head for a kind of 'meaning' which is not there, and is not meant to be there".[1]

Nothing in what Richards says implies that the construing of the *sense* of the words of the poem is unimportant, and he would not have called it "music of ideas" if he had thought so. And when in the same year he wrote in *Science and Poetry* that Eliot had effected in *The Waste Land* "a complete severance between his poetry and *all* beliefs", he is referring to Eliot's not using insecure general beliefs or doctrines

[1] *The Use of Poetry and the Use of Criticism*, 1933.

in the poem for the sake of their effects upon our attitudes. He does not mean that *knowledge* of what these are is unnecessary. The understanding of allusion in *The Waste Land* is as necessary to successful reading of the poem as, in *The Divine Comedy*, the capacity to "imaginatively reproduce the world outlook of Aquinas, and certain attitudes to women and to chastity, which [today] are even more inaccessible" (222). *The Waste Land* accepted the "neutralisation of nature", which science had brought about by dispelling the Magical View, and which Richards identified with Hardy's view of the universe as "indifferent" to us. Eliot worked with our feelings, not attempting to link them up and explain them but accepting, as the "way to the only solution" of the difficulties of our present position, Conrad's advice—"in the destructive element immerse".[1] It is only when Richards claims that Eliot, by this means, gave to his readers "a clearer, fuller realisation of their plight, the plight of a whole generation, than they find elsewhere" (295), that we can claim that he is no longer being consistent. All these different points we have mentioned —the distorting effects on perception and belief of our needs, the way in which science, as it were, *describes* rather than explains the world we live in, the expressive functions that religion fulfils, the harm that comes from too literal an approach to poetry, the temptation to use formulas instead of working on the reader by the poet's individual deployment of language, and so on—all these can reasonably be connected with one another in support of Richards' thesis. But there are other reasons which Richards adds, which it is more difficult to fit in, and which give the impression that Richards uses almost any argument he can think of provided there is *some* association with his thesis, as though the main consideration was quantity. We will mention four of these. One of these is important, the others rather peripheral, but we mention them partly because they have caused particular difficulty in the interpretation of Richards, and partly to illustrate this very characteristic tendency of his thinking.[2]

The first of these reasons I call important because I think it may have had much to do with Richards' putting forward the theory he did. Richards wanted to treat the arts as a whole, not just poetry alone. He was therefore influenced by the movement, then in full cry, to deny the necessity of accurate representation to good painting. In particular, he had to account for the high value attributed to so

[1] Richards favoured his critics with a more extended quotation from *Lord Jim* in the second edition of *Science and Poetry*—"A man that is born falls into a dream like a man falls into the sea. If he tries to climb out into the air as inexperienced people endeavour to do he drowns . . . The way is to the destructive element submit yourself, and with the exertions of your hands and feet in the water make the deep, deep sea keep you up".

[2] See pp. 101-104 where this tendency is illustrated and discussed further.

formal an art as music. He may have exploited the ambiguities of 'impulse' here, for we find him writing of "the immense scope for the resolution, interanimation, conflict and equilibrium of impulses opened up by the extraordinary complexity of musical sounds and of their possible arrangement" (173). Though I think Richards' view that formal features of the arts may produce emotional effects that can also be elicited by non-aesthetic stimuli a plausible one, I think it also presents him with temptations to win easy successes. We see this, for instance, when in writing of "those works of art which most unmistakably attune [us] to existence", Richards asks: "In the reading of *King Lear* what facts verifiable by science, or accepted and believed in as we accept and believe in ascertained facts, are relevant?" In answering "None whatever", he adds, "Still more clearly in the experience of some music, of some architecture and of some abstract design, attitudes are evoked and developed which are unquestionably independent of all beliefs as to fact" (282). The weak point here, I think, is the suggestion that the latter works "attune us to existence", by associating them with an example of tragedy, which he had previously argued had a cathartic, illusion-dissolving effect on us by virtue of what was *presented*—which of course had nothing to do with scientific certitudes.

The second of the reasons we mentioned above was that there was no point in verifying "statements" in poetry, not because such an approach would prevent the right attitudes developing, but because the statements were unverifiable. They were unverifiable by reason of "the natural generality and vagueness of all reference which is not made specific by the aid of space and time" (128). In other words, poets don't make statements of that degree of specificity which science requires in order that the statement may be experimentally tested!

Thirdly,

the emotions and attitudes resulting from a statement used emotively need not be directed towards anything to which the statement refers. This is clearly evident in dramatic poetry, but much more poetry than is usually supposed is dramatic in structure. As a rule a statement in poetry arouses attitudes much more wide and general in direction than the references of the statement (273).[1]

Presumably we do not respond simply to the limited dramatic situation literally interpreted, we universalise it.[2] This is one of those points that were too obvious for Richards' critics to apprehend.

[1] The sentence which follows, "Neglect of this fact makes most verbal analysis of poetry irrelevant", should not be taken as Ransom (*The New Criticism*, p. 34) takes it, as though the first two words were missing. Richards thought "most verbal analysis" was wrong, not that it was unnecessary.

[2] This may be linked with a point frequently made by Richards in later writings:

The fourth reason was expressed in a statement which has caused much trouble: "for emotive language the widest differences in reference are of no importance if the further effects in attitude and emotion are of the required kind" (268). This cannot mean that it does not matter how one reads. It refers, I think, to Richards' recognition, elaborated in his chapter on "Divergent Readings", that though different readers may disagree in their interpretation of, say, Hamlet's character, "with all allowances it seems certain that widely different interpretations have seemed to good critics to result in the same peculiarly high value of tragedy" (209). "Usually", Richards suggests,

> there is some genuine source for the agreement [as to value, which is] to be found in some common character of the experiences. What this common character is may be difficult to discover. It may be merely the rhythm, or the cadence of some phrase, or the form of a sequence of references. But sometimes, if it is a more obvious part, such as a description or metaphor, a discussion between critical readers, who are aware that their experiences differ, will bring it to light (208–209).

In other words, in so far as the attitudes are elicited by means of reference, then the references of different readers may differ widely *provided* the attitudes they occasion are equally complex and well-balanced in the different readers. An ingenious point, but scarcely one, I should have thought, that comes from experience.

Richards has been pretty widely accused of inconsistencies in his argument in the *Principles*. I have tried to present his theory to show that it has nothing like the inconsistencies attributed to it. The trouble is that his language is not always easy; he uses words loosely and does not express himself at all explicitly, thus illustrating in his own practice features that his theory said were universally true. Nevertheless his prose is far less difficult than much of the poetry it is his critics' profession to value. Richards, as we have already pointed out, is a thinker of markedly catholic tendencies. His theories are, one might say, much more *disjunctive* than his critics have taken them to be. Just as he attributes many different meanings to words, or thinks that there is no *one* feature which marks great art—paintings, poems, music can be great for all sorts of different reasons—, so he has *two* different senses of 'emotive' language, according to whether

"Every myth is a projection of some human situation, of some coordination of human feelings, needs and desires [and] the scope of its relevance . . . must be limited. . . . What we know, as science, that we must act upon, under pain of imminent danger to our lives if we do not . . . But our response to poetry is restricted and conditional . . ." (*C. on I.* 174-5). "This fundamentally important difference between the myths of natural science and the myths of poetry [lies] in the unrestricted claim upon our overt action of the former". (ibid. 178).

emotions and attitudes are function or cause. And so also he believes that in poetry words may *either* have an immediate emotive effect *or* have one only in consequence of the reference they bring to the mind.

But one or two contraries in his thought still remain. One of these is the way in which he talks of purely referential language, in the sense of language that is caused only by references, as opposed to purely emotive or mixed language, where, either wholly or in part, our language is caused by our needs. Since by his functional view no mental event is unmotivated, *all* use of language must be in the service of our needs, and therefore, from the point of view of cause, there can be no such thing as purely referential language. Since this is an inconsistency running through Richards' writings, I shall postpone consideration of it till later (see pp. 245-252).

The other inconsistency in Richards' theory about the relation between poetry and reference can be revealed by confronting these two quotations with one another:

> . . . clear and impartial awareness of the nature of the world in which we live and the development of attitudes which will enable us to live in it finely are both necessities, and neither can be subordinated to the other. They are almost independent, such connections as exist in well-organised individuals being adventitious (282).

> Knowledge *is* . . . an indispensable condition for the attainment of the widest, most stable, and most important values (177).

"Knowledge" in the second quotation must include what Richards means by "clear and impartial awareness of the nature of the world in which we live" in the first, but, if knowledge is "indispensable" for the "attainment" of the highest values, how can it be said to be "almost independent" of our having the latter?

The "sign-situation" from which the first statement derives is, I think, Richards' recognition that scientists do not necessarily, as a result of their scientific knowledge, develop the "attitudes which will enable [them] to live . . . finely", and that those with scarcely any scientific knowledge may do so, and will have done so in the past when there was far less "knowledge". This is certainly a widely held opinion.

The "sign-situation" for the second statement is Richards' belief that nowadays the highest value can be attained only if we give up comforting illusions such as religion provides; we must accept the "neutralisation of nature". But this of course is a consequence of our scientific knowledge. Richards seems to have thought of knowledge in terms of *positive* information, but to know that something is not true is also knowledge.

This inconsistency shows us that, though Richards claims that works of art derive their value only from the exercise of the attitudes and the *formal* transfer of the ordering of these to other situations, they may also act by making us more aware of the true nature of the world we live in. They communicate the poet's not being illusioned.

> . . . in the full tragic experience there is no suppression. The mind does not shy away from anything, it does not protect itself with any illusion, it stands uncomforted, unintimidated, alone and self-reliant (246).

This awareness, which, as Richards said in *Science and Poetry*, was vital for good poetry today, involves *information*, however much the information is ineffective unless emotionally realised. Insofar then as communication of content is important, we have a justification of art by *material* transfer. We shall find in Richards' later books an increasing reliance on this justification for what he does, without however any slackening off in his use of formal transfer as well.

6. A NOTE ON "SINCERITY"

The practice Richards' theory resulted in found expression in his next book, the well-known *Practical Criticism* (1929), where he reveals the kind of answers he got when he submitted to an audience, predominantly of University students, a set of poems for them to appraise in ignorance of who their authors were, a book he claims with some justice as a "record of a piece of field-work in comparative ideology", a study undertaken "with a view to advancing our knowledge of . . . the natural history of human opinions and feelings" (6), particularly one might add of stereotypes, ever the objects of his attack. His aim however is, as always, a normative one, and his book attempts to show how the poems should be read and to orient the reader correctly as to theory, thus illustrating, as most of his books do, the twin remedies against linguogenetic error—practice, and instruction in theory. The main stress in the work is on communication. This involves perception, but perception is affected by belief. Therefore the wrong beliefs or theories have to be corrected, the right ones fostered, which means, among other things, stressing the difference between referential and emotive language, whether functionally or genetically considered, and bearing in mind the different emotive factors, sense, tone, and intention, so that the reader is alert to the right shades of expression. Correct theory alone is not enough. ". . . no theory, no description, of poetry can be trusted which is not too intricate to be applied" (302), writes Richards, referring again to Blake's "Virtue resides only in minute particulars". Only indirectly, by their effects on feeling, can poems be judged. This requires a sort of global judgment, which we may guess is all the more necessary since the poems, if good, involved the satisfaction of so many impulses delicately balanced against one another. Hence "the choice of our whole personality may be the only instrument we possess delicate enough to effect the discrimination" (302). We have to work hard, intelligently and perseveringly at concrete instances, such as *Practical Criticism* provides, to achieve that ordering which makes us susceptible to the poem's order, so that we may experience the poem in such a way as to undergo furthur growth.

Let us put Richards' evaluation of what he is doing in his own words:

> If there be any means by which we may artificially strengthen our minds' capacity to order themselves, we must avail ourselves of them. And of all possible means, Poetry, the unique, linguistic instrument by which our minds have ordered their thoughts, emotions, desires . . . in the past, seems to be most serviceable. It may well be a matter of some urgency for us, in the interests of our standard of civilisation, to make this highest form of language more accessible. From the beginning civilisation has been dependent upon speech, for words are our chief link with the past and with one another and the channel of our spiritual inheritance. As the other vehicles of tradition, the family and the community, for example, are dissolved, we are forced more and more to rely upon language (321).

This condition of being able to profit from a poem Richards described as 'sincerity', taking the concept from the *Chung Yung* of Confucius, to which in his first book, *The Foundations of Aesthetics*, he and his co-authors had approximated their aesthetic doctrine. He quotes Confucius: "He who possesses sincerity is he who, without an effort, hits what is right, and apprehends, without the exercise of thought." This intuitive power, the product of many exercises previously carried out, which enables one to respond harmoniously, is also described in the *Chung Yung* as "that whereby self-completion is effected" (284). The notion of self-completion, which plays an important part in Richards' thought, is to be understood in terms of his theory of value. By definition, the more of one's impulses one can satisfy without mutual frustration and interference, the more one realises one's potentialities, the more one becomes oneself. Richards postulates "a tendency to increased order" derived "from the fundamental imbalance to which biological development may be supposed to be due", "the strain put upon [the organism] by life in a partly uncongenial environment" (286), which, as we saw, requires for its resolving better and wider systematisations. Sincerity is described as "obedience to that tendency", which "takes effect unless baffled by" such things as "fixations of habit that prevent us from continuing to learn by experience, or by ideas too invested with emotion for other ideas that disturb them to be formed" (286), and so on. The cultivation

of sincerity involves the removal of obstacles to successful communication. That is why, in *Practical Criticism*, Richards lays so much
stress on communication. As he puts it,

> the whole apparatus of critical rules and principles is a means to the attain-
> ment of finer, more precise, more discriminating communication . . . When
> we have solved, completely, the communication problem, when we have got,
> perfectly, the experience, *the mental condition* relevant to the poem, we have
> still to judge it . . . But the later question nearly always settles itself (11).

What he believes is that the effect of a valuable experience, expressed
in the poem, can be the *cause* of a like valuable experience, if we have
the poem in correct focus. This, as we have seen, is not to say that the
two experiences are necessarily closely similar as regards the actual
impulses concerned, only that the *relations* of the responses, a manifestation of the valuable ordering, are.

However the suggestion in the above quotation that the judgment
"nearly always settles itself", Richards' belief that "good reading, in
the end, is the whole secret of 'good judgment' ", is not quite as
simple as it might appear on the surface. For the full benefit to be
derived, it is essential that a *choice* should be made. "Mere acquiescent
immersion in good poetry can", Richards admits, "give us . . . much
that is valuable . . . But the greater values can only be gained by making
poetry the occasion for those momentous decisions of the will". He
perhaps intended this doctrine of committal to have an empirical
justification. We have already quoted his remark about "the choice
of our whole personality [being] the only instrument . . . delicate
enough to effect the discrimination". "Only . . . by collecting all our
energies in our choice", he says elsewhere, "can we overcome [the]
treacheries within us" (305). It is not just a plea for the necessity of
concentrating. It is a requirement which to an extent follows from his
doctrine that the value of a work of art depends on the number of
impulses it fulfils, and on the increased potentiality for ordering
experiences in the future. The better a poem, the more impulses it
satisfies, or, put in another way, the more of the personality it
involves. But clearly Richards held that an act of choice was itself
also something involving much of the personality, at least when
something fairly important was being decided. The decision, he says,
"must be an essential not an arbitrary choice, one which expresses the
needs of the being as a whole, not a random gust of desire or the
obstructing capacity of some dead member" (302). And when we
have made our decision, "when an old habit, which has been welcom-
ing a bad poem, is revivified into a fresh formation, or a new limb
which has grown to meet a good poem wakes into life", he wrote,
using the 'growth' imagery that played a more and more important

part in his thought, "the mind clears, and new energy wells up; after a pause a collectedness supervenes; behind our rejection or acceptance . . . we feel the sanction and authority of the self-completing spirit" (304). Revelation, it seems, is creeping back.

Chapter Four

TRANSITION

THE next book it is important to consider in detail is *Coleridge on Imagination* (1934), but, before we come to it, let us have a brief glance at the two books that followed *Practical Criticism*. These are *Mencius on the Mind* (1932) and *Basic Rules of Reason* (1933). In certain respects they are anticipatory of, and complementary to, *Coleridge on Imagination*. Coleridge and Confucianism were both major influences upon Richards. Confucius' doctrine of Equilibrium and Harmony and Coleridge's theory of the Imagination were, each in turn, in *The Foundations of Aesthetics* and *Principles of Literary Criticism* respectively, largely equated with Richards' own theory concerning the nature of the most valuable experiences. *Mencius on the Mind* and *Coleridge on Imagination* represent much more detailed attempts to wrest from these sources further elaborations of Richards' own theories.

But Coleridge looms larger. As we shall see, two lengthy quotations from Coleridge start and end the book on Mencius; the second of them points straight to *Basic Rules of Reason*, a fact reflected in its very title. Let us hasten through these that we may finally come to grips with Richards on Coleridge.

I. TRANSLATION AND MULTIPLE DEFINITION

Twenty-one years after *Mencius on the Mind* was published, Richards wrote of some of the difficulties that attended the writing of it.

> The book was written hurriedly, in a whirl of lecturing on *Ulysses* and on *The Possessed*, during a first teaching visit to Harvard. It was worked up from notes made between Tsing Hua and Yenching, under the guidance of divers advisers, and written out with much of the feeling one has in trying to scribble down a dream before it fades away.[1]

Hence, though "it stammered away persistently, . . . what it was trying to say never, *as a whole*, got said". Richards adds, "I have some doubts whether any whole was in any steady way in the mind of the sayer." It is a relief to be told this and hence to be absolved from one's

[1] "Towards a Theory of Translating" in *Studies in Chinese Thought*, ed. Arthur F. Wright (1953), reprinted in *Speculative Instruments*, pp. 17-38.

difficulties in making much of it. It is tentative, "glimpsing possibilities" to a confusing degree, indecisive to an extent unusual even for Richards.

In the Appendix are given "passages of psychology from Mencius" in Chinese characters with a literal word-for-word English translation immediately below. In his first two chapters Richards comments on the passages section by section, suggests alternative translations, muses on the arguments employed. This is the first example of a technique he was to use continuously in later books—commenting point by point on the meaning of a passage chosen for exhibition which itself dealt with matters with which Richards was concerned. In this case it is Mencius' theory of personality which, "historically and in its influence upon humanity, ranks with the most important constructions of 'the shaping spirit of imagination' " (xv). This theory, confusing though Richards' account of it is, sometimes bears marked resemblance to Richards' own.[1] Similarly, the absence, according to Richards, of any theory of cognition in Mencius, enables Richards to question the traditional Western conception of it as potentially neutral, though he does not in fact reject it—at least not at the time. The split in his mind on this matter is nowhere more evident than here.

By taking Chinese, so often used as a linguistic exemplar, Richard is also able to magnify effects he considers exist in English, but tend to be neglected. "It is the extreme case which shows us—better than the average case—how interpretation of all language which is not governed by an explicit logic proceeds. And more of our language than we suppose is of this kind" (7). At the same time by taking a language thought to use different concepts and a different system of relationships from our own, Richards is hoping to make the reader conscious of what he had been taking too much for granted as a sort of absolute. So, following his stress in *The Meaning of Meaning* on concept words as "linguistic accessories", whose choice should be determined by functional convenience (see p. 24 above), he tries to show how Mencius makes use of none of our customary logical distinctions. This raises the question whether we do not distort his meaning in employing our own logical machinery in analysing it. But not only does Mencius not require any of our "elaborate apparatus of universals, particulars, substances, attributes, abstracts, concretes, generalities, specificities, properties, qualities, relations, . . . classes, individuals, . . . objects, events, forms, contents etc.", he also "gets

---

[1] Cf. for instance, this from Richards' discussion of the concept of *hsing*—"we can see that . . . [Mencius'] conception of *hsing* was in terms of activity or incipient activity—an activity which, if permitted, tended always to be self-development. *This tendency to self-development—to the fulfilment of the mind—was what he meant by its goodness*". (*Mencius on the Mind*, 71).

along . . . with nothing definite to take its place" (89). Richards refers to the vagueness, the indefiniteness, of Mencius' writing, suggesting that often the answer to this question—which of alternative translations is the correct one—is that the original contains a blend of them, and that the elements blended have never in fact been *separately* conceived. The thought in this sense is pre-analytic, but not valued the less for that.

A more direct way of describing the indefiniteness of Mencius' writing is to say that it, like most Chinese writing, lacks as clearly articulated a syntax as our own. The method of expression is one more commonly used in poetry: that is, the meaning is highly condensed by relying on a considerable degree of implicitness, and interpretation depends to quite an extent on the interpretation of other passages in the same text, often equally indefinite themselves. Indeed Richards adds that Mencius' "aims seem often to be those of poetry rather than of prose philosophy" (7). This is suggested to him by some of the apparent inconsistencies in the argument, some of the baffling failures of disputants in the dialogue to make obvious points in argument, and the fact that they do not seem interested in detecting logical flaws in the arguments used. Mencius' intention, Richards thought, as one possible interpretation, may have been dominantly "suasive", that is to say, with justifying an agreed code of behaviour rather than in arriving at the truth. "Chinese thinking (in the instance of Mencius)", wrote Richards, "operates within an unquestioned limit and seeks a conception of the mind that will be a good servant to the accepted moral system rather than one which is primarily accordant to the facts" (59), and "the very absence in Mencius of anything which we can recognise as a theory of knowledge is strong evidence in this direction" (61).

The means of winning an understanding of Mencius—or of other writers, particularly when of different philosophical habits to ourselves —lies in the exercise of Multiple Definition, which, introduced, as we saw, in *The Meaning of Meaning* and used on occasion in the books in between, holds once again the centre of the stage, since it is presented in the final chapter as adumbrating the solution to the problems raised in the consideration of Mencius' meanings. Once again important general words are considered, such as 'Beauty', 'Truth', 'Knowledge', 'Order', and 'Principle', their definitions presented very much in terms of different philosophical theories,[1] but with the addition, in

---

[1] Cf., for example, his treatment of 'Truth' in terms of Correspondence theories, Coherence theory, "Coherence Idealism", "Methodological Pragmatism", "Politico-ethical and voluntaristic-metaphysical pragmatisms", etc. But Richards is not talking of ordinary use, which he considers would be a vague blending of some of the senses he distinguishes. *Ibid.*, p. 102.

the case of some of them, of their attitudinal intents, 'gestures', as Richards calls them, to distinguish these from 'senses'. The aim, once again, is to make the reader aware of the different possible senses the words he is reading might bear and of their emotional intentions, whether advertent or not. "What is needed", writes Richards, "is greater imaginative resource in a double venture—in imagining other purposes than our own and other structures for the thought that serves them" (92).

Richards stresses too the interrelations of senses, suggesting that *different* clusters of concepts may on different occasions be using the *same* sets of words. Dictionaries are criticised as enshrinements of the *ad hoc*. The influence of Coleridge is evident here too, for the book is sandwiched between two quotations from Coleridge's writings; the first criticising dictionaries, schemes for "conveying the *meaning* of each term, that might perhaps have answered at the Tower of Babel during the interval between the confusion of Tongues and the Dispersion of the Speakers"; the second proposing "a Dictionary constructed on the only one philosophical principle, which, regarding words as living growths, affects, and organs of the human soul, seeks to trace each historically through all the periods of its natural growth and accidental modifications. . . . A work which executed from any one language, would yet be a benefaction to the world", for it would aid "in the exposure and detection of those ambiguities [which provide] the best means of making men sensible of the faulty and relaxed state of their intellectual powers and functions". Multiple Definition Richards puts forward, with ambitious modesty, as "a plan for a technique", a first step to such a "general method for handling the distinctions required in a systematic way" that dictionary-making needs, for "any considered lists, however imperfect, whose procedure was explicitly stated in discussable form would help enormously towards the preparation of better lists . . . and, however defective, . . . would be of immediate assistance" (124).

The peroration of *Mencius on the Mind* prepares us for the topic of *Basic Rules of Reason*. This, a *Psyche* Miniature written in Basic English, applies the Multiple Definition Technique to eighteen words chosen so that he can discourse briefly on a variety of philosophical issues. Whereas till now the main emphasis in the technique of Multiple Definition had been on communication, with this book its value in checking linguogenetic error comes to the fore. The Phonetic and the Utraquistic subterfuges of *The Meaning of Meaning* are not referred to in Richards' later writings, at least not by name. They were attempts to make distinctions *within* the general category of mistakes due to a single word having different meanings. In *Basic Rules of*

Reason, Richards is concerned only with the general category it-self. "The trouble we have in giving order to our thoughts almost all comes from taking one thought for another through the use of one word for two thoughts" (10-11). Particularly it comes from confusing definitions with assertions. In accordance with his functional theory of language, he insists on freedom of definition. What Richards claims happens is that advancing a theory, say, about poetry, is in fact presenting a new definition, a view implicit already in the use of multiple definition in *The Meaning of Meaning.*

It is not however necessary in the avoidance of error to subject *all* words to the multiple definition procedure. Following the hints dropped in his criticism of dictionaries and in his functional theory of logical categorisation, we should not be surprised to find Richards concentrating on certain key words alone. "A great part of logic", he wrote, claiming the authority of Bentham and Peirce in support of his view, "becomes the theory and right use of the senses of our chief words—*those upon which the ordering of the senses of our other words is dependent*" (10—my italics). "The senses of these chief words—and their ways of working with or against one another", Richards added, explaining the book's title, "are the rules of reason", for "the process of putting our thoughts into a system, so that if some of them are taken we have then to take others, is *reasoning.*" Since reasoning is his aim, his interest in this book is confined to reference—in Basic English, *thought*—and the purpose of the ordering of our thoughts is "to make them come into agreement with things, to make them give us a truer picture, a representative map or instrument for guiding our acts, so that men may give effect to as great a number of their desires as possible."

2. AN EXEMPLARY PREFACE TO "COLERIDGE ON IMAGINATION"

We come now at last to *Coleridge on Imagination,* the book in which Coleridge's influence over Richards came to a head. As a result of a more thoroughgoing consideration of Coleridge's theories, a major development in Richards' own thought took place. Some critics, for instance, Mr. John Crowe Ransom and Mr. Allen Tate (see p. 207 below), have considered this book introduced a revolutionary change in Richards' thought. I believe this view is an exaggeration. It is true that there was some change in Richards' epistemological views, and that he also changed somewhat in his attitude to Coleridge's belief that Imagination gave knowledge. However he continued to reject metaphysical doctrines as such, maintaining what he called a "Materialist" standpoint. It is more accurate to say that what

Richards did in *Coleridge on Imagination* was to develop his theory and to elaborate parts of it that had been left vague.

An idea that plays a prominent part in *Coleridge on Imagination* is that of distinguishing between actual experiences, which Richards described in Coleridge's words as "facts of mind", and the abstractions, generally theories, we derive from them. Much stress throughout his book was laid on the danger of mistaking abstractions for facts. Abstractions were useful, indeed inevitable, but they could do a lot of harm if we forgot that they were only abstractions.

Now this position is very similar to that he adopted in *The Meaning of Meaning*. The only difference, and this has confused his critics, is that he has changed his terms, a practice he frequently shows as book follows book. Forgetfulness of abstraction is the new form taken by Word Magic, of which much less mention is made from now on, and referral to "facts of mind" is the same as the insistence, in *The Meaning of Meaning*, on discovering the original sign-situation, when trying to determine the meaning of a word that is being used. This was connected, it will be remembered, not only with the denial of the existence of universals and the suggestion of uniqueness of meaning ("no two persons' references will be the same"), but also with the stress on the shorthand, abbreviated nature of many of the sentences we spoke or wrote.

The distinction between abstractions and "facts of minds" is crucial to understanding Richards' attitude to Coleridge in the book we are now considering. Richards rejected Coleridge's metaphysical doctrines, regarding them as instances of the mistaking of abstractions for facts. But he valued Coleridge's theories because they were concerned with fundamental questions. The "facts of mind", that considering these theories properly would cause him to have, were particularly important ones. He opposed Eliot's suggestion that "what was best in [Coleridge's] criticism" came not from his philosophy so much as "from his own delicacy and subtlety of insight as he reflected upon his own experience of writing poetry."[1] Richards thought the insight could not be separated from the philosophical speculation, quoting Coleridge's own reference to the dependence of "observation" on "meditation", to "eyes, for which [meditation] has predetermined their field of vision and to which, as to its organ, it communicates a microscopic power."[2] It was to this that Richards was referring when, again using Coleridge's words, he called theories "speculative instruments." For Richards, the purpose of *Coleridge on Imagination* was the presentation of the "derived instrument" that he constructed out of the experiences Coleridge's "speculative instru-

[1] *The Use of Poetry and the Use of Criticism* (1933), p. 80.
[2] *Biographia Literaria*, II, p. 64. (Shawcross' edition).

ments" gave to him. Coleridge's instrument had been constructed to study the "deep and general change [that] was occurring in man's conceptions of himself and of his world" (2), and it is evident from the last chapter of *Coleridge on Imagination*, "The Bridle of Pegasus," that Richards wanted to use his own derived instrument, not only to render literary criticism more powerful, but to effect similar ambitious purposes to Coleridge's.

At the start of his book, Richards made a lot of play with the fact that the philosophical position he was adopting was the opposite of Coleridge's own. Referring to some remarks by Coleridge and by John Stuart Mill in his essay on Coleridge, he suggested that "two opposite-seeming types of outlook" pervaded philosophy but were in fact "complementary to one another", being "in their endless antagonism . . . a necessary conjoint self-critical process." As we shall see, the point he has in mind is that, given a certain issue, there are two sets of abstractions such that, combined, they completely describe the "facts of mind" of which either is a partial reflection. But one cannot consistently write about a philosophical issue except in terms of one or other of them. We cannot express in words without abstracting and our abstractions, if consistent, will only be partial truth. So Richards says:

> I write then as a Materialist trying to interpret before you the utterances of an extreme Idealist and you, whatever you be by birth or training, Aristotelian or Platonist, Benthamite or Coleridgean, Materialist or Idealist, have to reinterpret my remarks again in your turn (19).

In saying this, Richards is demonstrating his concern about our always being aware of our abstracting. And in putting it in *this* way, rather than simply saying, "My object is to understand Coleridge", he reveals his own obsession with philosophy which, as a consequence of his thinking in this book, came to occupy him more and more in his last three major books.

So much by way of preface. What we have had to say to explain Richards' approach will be elaborated in the course of describing the book. As so often with Richards, his practice is an exemplification of his theory. My preface, for its proper understanding, requires the reading of what it prefaces.

3. A ROMANTIC CONTRAST: IMAGINATION V. FANCY

In *Coleridge on Imagination*, Richards frequently quotes Coleridge, and himself often echoes him, as making distinctions between two types of mental activity, which are of differing value. The one is vital, creative, manifesting deep feeling, the other mechanical, dead, empty, without ground, or at best merely utilitarian, a servant to the other. They enter not only into poetry but also into philosophy, indeed into all thought. Imagination is the first of these, and Fancy the second. Richards' aim, as usual, is to give a psychological account of these two processes. In attempting this, I think he is attempting something worth while, that has been widely neglected by psychologists. But about his execution of this task I have many reservations.

The distinction between Fancy and Imagination is presented as like that between a mixture and a chemical compound. In the former, the mental elements, though associated in new ways, do not, as they do in the latter, change. In Coleridge's words, the Imagination "dissolves, diffuses, dissipates, in order to recreate; or where this process is rendered impossible, yet still at all events it struggles to idealize and to unify. It is essentially *vital* ... Fancy, on the contrary, has no other counters to play with, but fixities and definites ... Equally with the ordinary memory the Fancy must receive all its materials ready made from the law of association."[1] Coleridge added that Fancy was operated by "that empirical phenomenon of the will, which we express by the word CHOICE", and that the images in Fancy "have no connection natural or moral, but are yoked together by the poet by means of some accidental coincidence." One would expect by contrast then that, with the Imagination, the images would well up from the unconscious, all more or less naturally connected with one another.

That something of this kind is the case is suggested by Richards when, in an attempt to examine Imagination as "fact of mind", he carries out a detailed analysis of some lines of poetry, said to exemplify the two kinds of process. He takes the same lines from *Venus and Adonis* that Coleridge himself gave as instances. We shall not concern ourselves with what he says about Fancy, except when necessary by way of contrast, since our interest is in his psychological theory of the Imagination. The example of Imagination he gives are the following lines, which refer to Adonis' leaving of Venus:

Look! how a bright star shooteth from the sky
So glides he in the night from Venus' eye (82).

We will reproduce Richards' comment in full:

Here, in contrast to the other case [of Fancy], the more the image is followed up, the more links of relevance between the units are discovered. As Adonis to Venus, so these lines to the reader seem to linger in the eye like the after-images that make the trail of the meteor. Here Shakespeare is realising, and making the reader realise—not by any intensity of effort, but

[1] *Biographia Literaria*, I, 202.

by the fulness and self-completing growth of the response—Adonis' flight as it was to Venus, and the sense of loss, of increased darkness, that invades her. The separable meanings of each word, *Look!* (our surprise at the meteor, hers at his flight), *star* (a light-giver, an influence, a remote and uncontrollable thing) *shooteth* (the sudden, irremediable, portentous fall or death of what had been a guide, a destiny), *the sky* (the source of light and now of ruin), *glides* (not rapidity only, but fatal ease too), *in the night* (the darkness of the scene and of Venus' world now)—all these separable meanings are here brought into one. And as they come together, as the reader's mind finds cross-connexion after cross-connexion between them, he seems, in becoming more aware of them, to be discovering not only Shakespeare's meaning, but something which he, the reader, is himself making. His understanding of Shakespeare is sanctioned by his own activity in it. As Coleridge says: "You feel him to be a poet, inasmuch as for a time he has made you one—an active creative being" (83–84).

An interesting phrase of Richards' here is "the self-completing growth of the response." Many times[1] Richards refers to a sort of effortless, exhilarating, continuing activity of the mind, which is set off by some instance of another's imagination. He seems to take it as a hall-mark of the Imagination, sanctioning it by describing it as "living" and "growth".

The phrase also suggests that Richards is referring to some *whole*, just as he did in the statement that "all these separable meanings are here brought into one." The differentiation between Imagination and Fancy requires this distinction for it is in terms of a whole that "the links of relevance between the units" are relevant. To be able to blend into the whole, "interanimating" one another, the "units", however conceived, whether "images", "notions, feelings, desires or attitudes" (79), must be capable of "dissolving", of being "modified". In Fancy, on the other hand, the units do not fuse. They are separate conceits, such as those used in "A lily prison'd in a gaol of snow" to express Venus' taking of Adonis' hand. "The links between them are accidental"; that is to say, there may be some links but they "are here irrelevant and merely distracting."[2]

---

[1] For example, in phrases like these—"A reach and repercussion to this meaning . . . consiliences and reverberations between the feelings then aroused" (82), "later ramifications and reverberations of effects due to our simultaneous and successive apprehensions" (89), "we are invited to stretch our minds, and no one can flatter himself that he has now finished the process of understanding . . . [the phrases] carry, at first unnoticed, secondary and tertiary co-implications among their possibilities of interpretation." (93-94).

[2] In view of Ransom's assertion that nobody is "better entitled" than Richards "to the honours of being [the] discoverer" of the importance of "irrelevance in poetry", it is interesting to note that for Richards the distinguishing mark of the Imagination is very much in terms of relevance (see pp. 214-215 below).

71

4. THREE FUSIONS

The idea of *fusion*, of unity as opposed to separateness, is applied by Richards in three further ways. Apart from the fusion of the "units" of the poem with one another, he emphasises the fusion of perception with feeling, of a word's sound with its meaning, and of the reader's whole personality with the experience he is having. In briefly describing these, we will mention some distinctions Richards makes that we shall refer to again later.

The first fusion, that of perception and feeling, Richards describes not in connection with art, but in connection with the way a person sees the world or, as he in his book on Coleridge calls it, "Nature". Richards carries out a Multiple Definition of "Nature" in which he distinguishes four senses. Since we shall have to refer to these frequently, we had better list them briefly at the start, explaining them in more detail later.

Sense I   "The influences of whatever kind, to which the mind is subject from whatever is without and independent of itself" (157). This sense, which seems to correspond to Kant's "things-in-themselves", contrasts with the others, all of which are *conceptions* of Nature (Sense I).

Sense II   The conception of Nature in which our feelings are projected into it.

Sense III   "A selection of II including only such . . . as are perceived by all men alike, allowance being made for variations in the conditions of perception . . . This is the world of our practical everyday experience whose laws are verified every minute of our lives."

Sense IV   "A still narrower selection from II including only such of them as are required at any stage in the theoretical development of Physics for the purpose of giving an account of Nature in Sense I" (158).

Sense II is the one that particularly manifests the fusion of perception and feeling, though, following Coleridge, Richards attributes this to the *Secondary* Imagination, as opposed to the *Primary* Imagination, which is responsible for Sense III. This is very confusing of him. However, there is no doubt that whenever he talks of the Imagination, it is to the Secondary Imagination that he is referring, and we will pay no further attention to the Primary Imagination, which he neglects and which might just as well be Fancy.

Richards puts his distinction between the two different conceptions of Nature (Senses III and II) in the following words:

"The Primary Imagination is normal perception that produces the usual world of the senses,

72

That inanimate cold world allowed
To the poor loveless ever-anxious crowd,

the world of motor-buses, beef-steaks, and acquaintances, the framework of things and events within which we maintain our everyday existence, the world of the routine satisfaction of our minimum exigencies. The Secondary Imagination, reforming this world, gives us not only poetry—in the limited sense in which literary critics concern themselves with it—but every aspect of the routine world in which it is invested with other values than those necessary for our bare continuance as living beings; all objects for which we can feel love, awe, admiration . . ." (58).

Nature (Sense II) in being highly valued, reminds us of what Richards wrote earlier about the value of religious and metaphysical views of the Universe, before the development of science made the holding of these a danger to sincerity. Now, in referring to the potentialities of science, Richards writes that to realise these potentialities we need "wisdom". In contrast to the scientist's Nature (Sense IV), "wisdom requires a different co-ordination of our perceptions, yielding another Nature for us to live in—a Nature in which", Richards adds, echoing his earlier statements about the satisfaction of our impulses, "our hopes and fears and desires, by projection, can come to terms with one another" (169-170). But Richards' view has not altered fundamentally, for he still holds that the "myths", which are different ways of conceiving Nature (Sense I), need to be believed "in a very restricted sense."

If every myth is a projection of some human situation, of some co-ordination of human feelings, needs, and desires, the scope of its relevance and therefore of its proper influence upon action must be limited (174).

The second type of fusion that characterises the Imagination is that between a word and its meaning. Richards carries out a multiple definition of 'word'. According to this, the senses ranged in what he calls a scale of comprehensiveness from "words taken as bare signs [to] words into which some part or the whole of their meaning is projected" (109). This scale of comprehensiveness Richards takes as a paradigm for other words like 'Poem', 'Language', 'Symbol' and, as we shall explain later, 'Nature' itself. He describes "the projection of its meaning into a word [as] an instance of Imagination", comparing it directly with the projection of feeling into perception, and suggests

. . . most poetry which is markedly imaginative will naturally be read as though its meanings were inherent in the words; and some of the poetry of Fancy, on the other hand, will be best read otherwise—with a clear and recognized distinction between the words and the meanings we take from them (110–111).

Elsewhere, in more characteristic terms, he distinguishes between words "taken as conventional signs" and words "read as living inexhaustible meanings" (108). By "meaning" here we are to understand not only references and "thoughts", but also feelings and attitudes.

Richards' paradigm, the definition of 'word', is confused, and we must pause for a moment to consider this. He distinguishes four definitions altogether, of which the first two correspond to Peirce's token and type distinction.[1] The fourth, which we have just described, includes meaning as well. But of these only the first two seem to be definitions of 'word'. In the last, Richards is not referring to *definitions* nor to the word, 'word'. As the quotations in the previous paragraph should show, he is clearly concerned with individual words, like 'apple' and 'truth'; he does not, in these "definitions", talk about what 'word' means so much as about how we "take" words or what "our attitude to words" is.

The third type of union that for Richards characterises the mode of Imagination is that of the whole personality in the experience it is having. We are totally absorbed in our experience; in the words of Coleridge that Richards was fond of quoting, it "brings the whole soul of man into activity." In this way it contrasts with the Fancy, of which "the commonest characteristic effect . . . is the coolness and disengagement with which we are invited to attend to what is taking place" (82). Richards describes Associationist theory, according to which Fancy alone is said to work, as one in which

. . . a state of mind is represented as a cluster or composition of revived impressions fished up from a mental storehouse and arranged around a sensation given to a passive mind—the whole offered like a deck of cards to a self or will standing over against it and able at best to approve or veto or rearrange it. . . . (69).

The fusion of the personality in the experience does not however mean that we *lose* ourselves in the experience. One of the characteristics of the experience for Coleridge was "steady self-possession". And, when he wrote of "the coalescence of subject and object in the

---

[1] i.e., 'word' as referring to the individual occurrences, as when we talk of an article being 5,000 words long, and 'word' as referring to a class of occurrences with the same form, which is the sense we would probably have in mind if we asked how many *different* words there were in the article just referred to.

act of knowledge", he extracted from this "fact of mind" that one may then achieve the "heaven-descended [command] KNOW THYSELF" by, as Richards put it, "at the same time and in the same act becoming aware by the INNER SENSE of what we are doing" (46).

Richards contrasts with the model of the mind he attributes to the Associationists Coleridge's conception of it "as an active, self-forming, self-realising system", which "strives to realise itself in knowing itself", and himself frequently describes the exercise of the Imagination in poetry in similar terms, though concentrating on the "self-forming" activity, rather than on "knowing oneself". The last three sentences of his description of the Imagination, quoted on page 71, are instances of this.

Richards does not, however, confine the operation of the Imagination to poetry. He extends it, we may say, to any mental activity that deals with important issues that may legitimately arouse deep feelings in us, notably philosophy. *Coleridge on Imagination*, Richards' last book that is mainly on poetry, is transitional in the sense that it begins to be concerned with philosophy and prose, which largely took over in the last three major books. It is transitional also in the sense that, though much concerned with Coleridge's idea about the effects on self-development of self-awareness during moments of Imagination, Richards still writes as though it were something like the satisfaction of a wide variety of desires that determines the value of an experience. As we shall show in Section 7, it is only the language that changes. He talks much more in terms of "personality" and "self". But this seems to be a way of referring to occasions where a wide variety of important feelings and values are involved and act in the mode of Imagination, that is to say, they are concentrated, the experience being one of unity. The advantages of actual awareness of the experience at the moment it is happening is something he only develops when he is dealing with philosophy.

The question of the relationship of the self to its experiences is a central one for Richards, and our understanding of the relation of his later to his earlier books, as well as of the basic aims of the later ones, depends upon our understanding of his theories on this. It is necessary to go into some detail. I shall deal, first, with the "facts of mind" upon which the notions of involvement and separation of the self from its experience depend; second, with Richards' treatment of Coleridge's theory of "the coalescence of the subject and object in the act of knowledge"; and, third, with his reasons why exercise of the Imagination should result in self-development and self-realisation.

5. SYNTAX AND THE SUBCONSCIOUS

The "facts of mind", upon which I believe Richards mainly depends in considering the self's involvement in or separation from its experiences, are ones concerned with the question of amount of conscious control. The mode of Fancy, we saw, was one where the "impressions [were] offered like a deck of cards to a self or will standing over against it [which is] able to approve or veto or rearrange [them]". It is natural to contrast this with the situation where we do not seem able by conscious exercise of the will to bring about what we want to. We have instead to wait for it to *happen* to us. Richards quotes Coleridge as saying,

> Association depends in a much greater degree on the recurrence of resembling states of feeling than on trains of ideas.
> Ideas no more recall one another than the leaves in a tree fluttering in the breeze propagate their motion one to another (68).

This is reminiscent of another saying of Coleridge Richards was particularly fond of, "Are not words, etc., parts and germinations of the plant," suggesting something that is preordained, that develops to fulfil its nature, like the unfolding leaf- and flower-buds of a tree, all of which of course serve functions for the total organism and are interdependent, thus providing a model for the Imagination.

The emphasis upon unconscious factors is frequent with Richards. In the *Principles*, for example, he wrote: "Little by little experience corrects [our mistakes in judgment] . . ., not through reflection—almost all critical choices are irreflective, spontaneous, as some say—but through unconscious reorganisation of impulses. We rarely chauge our tastes, we rather find them changed."[1] This is reminiscent of the conception of *sincerity* he later developed in *Practical Criticism*, of which he wrote:

> A direct effort to be sincere, like other efforts *to will ourselves into action*, more often than not frustrates its intention.[2]

A similar attitude was shown in *Science and Poetry*, with regard to poetic composition:

> The choice of the rhythm or the epithet [is] not an intellectual matter . . . but [is] due to an instinctive impulse seeking to confirm itself, or to order itself with its fellows. For the motives which shape a poem spring from the root of the mind. The poet's style is the direct outcome of the way in which his interests are organised. That amazing capacity of his for ordering speech

---

[1] *P.L.C.*, 198.
[2] *P.C.*, 283, (my italics).

is only a part of a more amazing capacity for ordering his experience . . .
Poetry cannot be written by cunning and study, by craft and contrivance . . .
Characteristically its rhythm will give it away . . . moving rhythm in poetry
arises only from genuinely stirred impulses.[1]

But is Richards, in linking the Imagination with the Unconscious,
really reporting "facts of mind"? It is widely recognised that many
original conceptions, works of art or scientific discoveries, are not
to be commanded by the self, but have to be waited for, frequently
after much hard, conscious work on them has been done[2]. "Growth"
is not a bad image to use to describe this phenomenon. But this should
not make us lose sight of the fact that this is a universal phenomenon,
not limited to original creation, but entering widely into the acquisition of skill, and shown even in memorising, where, under certain
circumstances, the passage of a period of time may result in better
recall.[3] Richards however vacillates. In his general psychological
theorising, he seems to recognise the universality of this factor. But
when he is boosting Imagination, he is inclined to make a mystery of
it, treating it as something many people, including Coleridge for part
of his life,[4] may be without. But he gives no indication of how, in
psychological terms, other than by its manifestations, it may be
differentiated. And to appeal just to these manifestations is, as
Richards is often under suspicion of doing, to rely on a circular
argument, as in the old Faculty error.

The part played by consciousness in connection with the working
of the Imagination is not however limited to a consideration of the
Unconscious; the degree of conscious control is also relevant, though
here again the phenomenon seems to be much more widespread than
any attempted confinement of it to the Imagination would suggest.
It is well known, for instance, that Freud found that urging his
patients to try to remember something was self-defeating, and that the
analytical practice is for the patient to lie relaxed on a couch, saying
what comes. Right at the other end of the scale, it is recognised that
threshold judgments in psychophysical experiments are best made

---

[1] S. & P., 39-40.

[2] Cf., for example, *The Anatomy of Inspiration* (1942) by Rosamond Harding.

[3] Growth in the nervous system has actually been postulated in some psychological
theories. Cf. G. S. Snoddy, *Evidence for Two Opposed Processes in Mental Growth*,
1935. Another model is used if we say that what happened in the meantime was
unconscious learning. The most influential explanation, stemming from Hullian
learning theory, is in terms of the interaction of excitatory and inhibitory forces
within the central nervous system, these being conceived as having different durations,
so that the apparent learning achievement varies according to the time at which it
is manifested. This, being the most articulated, has been the most fruitful of experiment. By the same token, it may have been the greatest scientific time-waster.

[4] C. on I., 59-60.

when the stimuli to be judged are not responded to with full conscious attention. There is good evidence, too, that the acquisition of a skill consists in the cultivation of the capacity to respond with lessened attention to the stimuli that matter, as well as to the movements we make in response to them.

Richards has, maybe, these facts in mind when he from time to time recommends, and quotes Coleridge as recommending, a relaxed, non-problem-solving approach to poetry. But he also appears to be opposed to clarity and definiteness in the poetry itself. Before looking closely at what he says, let us consider two other ideas psychologists have made use of.

According to the Gestalt psychologists, our nervous system responds to stimuli in such a way as to cause us to perceive things in as regular and patterned a way as the external stimuli allow. The controlling influence of these external stimuli depends both on the conditions of perception and the nature of the stimulus. The influence is weak, or as the Gestalt psychologists put it, the external forces are weak, when, for instance, the lighting is poor, we only glance moment-arily at something, or the stimulus itself is faint. Under these circum-stances, we are more likely to see things in a patterned way. One example of this is the way in which, when reading a book, we may catch a pattern in the corner of our eye, which is formed on the opposite page to the one we are reading. When we look at the page directly, the pattern disappears. But we can trace it out by noting some regularity in the way in which the print is aligned on the page. Similarly, putting the eyes out of focus, blurring the image which is before us, may be necessary to detect a pattern in it. An experience may often need to be made fainter, by being made less recent, in order for it to be more organised. We often cannot order properly in our mind a topic we have closely studied until some days have gone by; only then may we be able to see it in perspective. Similarly with our attempts to see an order that we may have created in attempting to solve some problem; though in both these cases it is necessary no doubt to postulate some intervening activity. The main point is that, according to the Gestalt view, we may expect, under certain circum-stances, that a lessening of direct attention or reduction in definiteness will favour ordering.

The other idea comes from Dynamic Psychology, and is concerned with our feelings and emotions as well. According to this, quite apart from our degree of conscious control which is lessened under drugs or when asleep, the less definite and complete the external situation, the more we shall perceive it in accordance with our needs, fears, and desires. Thus projection tests work with ink blots, vague and am-biguous pictures, single words, and incomplete sentences. Though here again we must qualify by adding that these are effective to the degree that they are suggestive. Just vagueness or incompleteness is not enough. Here however there is no question of any superior ordering.

Richards seems to combine these two ideas. He argues that "the absence of syntax is a favourable condition for Imagination", because when we are presented with words not arranged in a sentence structure such that they can have only one meaning, "we are free to combine the parts as we please." This he thought

explains why languages whose syntax we do not understand sometimes seem inherently poetical: *e.g.* literal, word for word translations from 'primitive' tongues or from Chinese; why ambiguous syntax is so frequent in Shakespeare; and why, in much of the modern verse which derives from Mr. Ezra Pound, it is easy to mistake a mere freedom to interpret as we will for controlling unity of sane purpose—that is, purpose integrated with and relevant to our lives as wholes. . . . (91).

Later Richards quoted Coleridge's claim that

The older languages were fitter for poetry because they expressed only prominent ideas with clearness, the others but darkly . . . Poetry gives most pleasure when only generally and not perfectly understood (214).

Here he took "not properly understood" as referring to poetry with "ambiguous syntax", and described Rupert Brooke as a less good poet on the grounds that "the ideas and other components [of his verse] . . . are all expressed with prominence."[1]

All this has implications for the way in which we should read, though Richards' own account is "dark" enough. He recognises with regard to the earlier poems of Eliot, for example, that "something resembling" "the detective intelligence, or the Cross-Word Puzzler's technique, [which] are not [in themselves] proper methods in reading poetry", may be "a suitable mode of preparation for reading" (215) such poems. But those who did use "something resembling" this technique, "found that what they thus discovered—though its discovery may have been necessary for them—was no essential part of the poetry when this came to life." "But apart altogether from this play of extrinsic explicit conjecture", Richards continues,

---

[1] Richards also quotes Coleridge on how "by deep feeling we make our ideas *dim*", and referred to Coleridge's "acute remarks . . . about the pernicious effect of the 'despotism of the eye'." (54). He approved too of Coleridge's remarks about how metre produces its effects "by the quick reciprocations of curiosity still gratified and still re-excited, *which are too slight indeed to be at any one moment objects of distinct consciousness*, yet become considerable in their aggregate influence. As a medicated atmosphere, or as wine during animated conversation, they act powerfully, *though themselves unnoticed*" (117 (Richards' italics)).

there is another way of 'looking into' abstruse poetry a receptive sub-mission, which will perhaps *be reflected* in conjectures but into which infer-ences among these conjectures do not enter. For example, the differences between the opening lines of the first and last sections of Mr. Eliot's *Ash Wednesday*:
Because I do not hope to turn again
and
Although I do not hope to turn again
in their joint context and their coterminous sub-contexts, will come into full being for very few readers without movements of exploration and resultant ponderings that I should not care to attempt to reflect in even the most distant prose translation. And yet these very movements—untrackable as they perhaps are, and uninducible as they almost certainly are by any other words—are the very life of the poem. In these searchings for meanings of a certain sort its being consists (216).

What we have here is a further elaboration of Richards' point in the *Principles* about how "the questioning, verificatory way of handling [the references in poetry] is irrelevant," expressed now in terms of that hall-mark of the Imagination, the "growth of the response". There is, Richards says, with "the best poetry . . . nowhere to arrive, no final solution." In contrast with this,

Poems which have a destination, a final solution—whether it be the enunciation of a supposed truth, or suasion to a policy, or the attainment of an end-state of consciousness, or some temporary or permanent exclusive attitude to the world, to society, or to the self, have only a subordinate value (213–214).

Though Richards now recognises the existence of, and accords some value to, poems which seek to inform, instruct, or edify, it is evident, I think, that he regards them as *abstractions* from "facts of mind" in comparison with "the best poetry", which is more consequent on these facts of mind, and more likely to cause similar ones in the reader, if he read properly.

I have considered in some detail Richards' attitude to the psychology of what we may call "creative writing" and "creative reading" because we find him showing a similar attitude to prose. It is suggestive that in *Mencius on the Mind*, he already contrasted Chinese syntax favourably with the "explicit sentence forms" and "explicit logic" of the West, distinguishing between "those with a taste for clear, precise views . . . [who] will accuse [Mencius] of not knowing what he wants to say" and those for whom, like Mencius, "a thought [may be] present whose structure and content are not suited to available formulation, [so] that these successive, perhaps incompatible, statements partly represent, partly misrepresent, an idea independent of them which none the less has its own order and coherent reference."[1]

[1] *M. on the M.*, 8.

In *Interpretation in Teaching* we shall find him making similar remarks. For instance, attacking the "usage theory" about grammar, according to which we should follow general usage in our writing, he declares in that book that this view

> goes best with the assumption that fully formed thought seeks words with which to utter itself, and that the attention and clear thinking which are requisite are concerned with distinguishing which thought we have and with picking the right word for it.

This is contrasted with the view Richards holds,

> That most thought forms itself in and through experiments with the language that is to utter it, and that a step between the choice of a word and the shaping of a thought is not easily marked[1].

We shall also find Richards emphasising the importance of the process rather than of the conclusions, the journey and not the destination, in prose, as he had done in poetry. Thus in *Interpretation in Teaching*, we shall find him saying:

> In some writing, non-controversial technology, for example, only the outcome matters. In most interesting discussions, certainly in all these discussions about language, in criticism, psychology, logic, rhetoric and grammar, the other sort of argument [the process of interpretation in action], is the all important thing. With most of them we never settle finally just what is said.[2]

There is a hint of anti-rationalism in Richards' outlook, a danger of mystery-mongering. He himself sometimes followed remarks, like those we have quoted above, with appropriate warnings. His own practice, for which his theory may have acted as rationalisation, but which became more extreme after the development of this theory, does not in fact seem to have escaped these dangers. They are manifested in his not being very successful in communicating with his readers, particularly in his last books. As for his thinking, we have already seen from the random assortment of his arguments concerning the function of poetry in the *Principles*, as well as from the illicit conclusion he derived by confusing different senses of 'impulse', the damage it can do. We shall shortly come across a further example of this.

6. "COALESCENCE OF SUBJECT AND OBJECT"

The case against bringing full conscious attention to bear, when trying to breed a new order within oneself, can easily be overstated.

[1] *I. in T.*, 276-277.
[2] *I. in T.*, 249.

81

We need in fact constantly to be aware and to check what we are doing. Sometimes Richards seems to recognise this. We have seen how in *Practical Criticism* he wrote of the importance of making an explicit, conscious decision about a poem (see pp. 61-62 above), and, in *Coleridge on Imagination*, he makes further reference to this. But the language he uses—as when he writes, "the judgment that a passage is good is an act of living" (140)—betrays him. He is obsessed by the abstract notion of the self. Instead of considering the specific purposes of such judgments, he seems to recommend them only for the reason that they are good for us.

But now we must consider a further aspect of awareness during experiences of the Imagination that may be related to Richards' emphasis on making a conscious decision about a poem. This is Coleridge's "postulate of philosophy", upon the realisation of which, namely, the having of self-knowledge, any person's capacity for philosophy, for 'knowledge' in a special sense, and for the exercise of Imagination, depended. In describing what Richards makes of this, I shall not concern myself with the accuracy of his account of Coleridge's philosophy.

As Richards pointed out, Coleridge's epistemology derived from Kant's. Therefore he believed that "nothing of which we are in any way conscious is *given* to the mind. Into the simplest seeming 'datum' a constructing, forming activity from the mind has entered" (57). Richards appealed with some justice to "modern psychology" for support of this view, attributing this activity to the Primary Imagination. Of course, we can correct phenomenal experience (Nature, Sense III—see the Multiple Definition on page 72 above) by co-ordinating experiences of the same object that take place under different conditions, or we can use different senses (touch correcting vision and so on), or employ different measuring instruments. This would give us the world of science, (Nature (Sense IV)). Richards, however, and this is one of the main changes from his earlier books, describes it as a "myth", though elsewhere he attributes myths only to the Secondary Imagination, which projects our feelings, emotions, and desires, thus giving us Nature (Sense II). Why should Richards call the scientific view a myth? Characteristically, he has two different reasons which are not of the same logical order. The first is: "as [the scientist] investigates [the world] the picture he frames of it changes, and . . . it is this changing picture that is the myth" (178). Here Richards seems to be referring to the hypothetical nature of scientific theory. The second is that we can never know what Nature really is —"we can say nothing . . . and think nothing . . . without producing a myth" (181). Nature (Sense IV) is not Nature (Sense I, i.e. things-in-themselves). But of course the latter is of quite a different logical category. What Richards is saying boils down to the assertion that a cause is not to be identified with its effects.

Returning to Coleridge's postulate, the way in which we can "know ourselves" is through this constructive factor in perception. In perceiving things, if we are aware of what we are doing in the act of perceiving, we shall know something about ourselves too, because the perception is a creation of our own. But we, in our turn, are made by the Nature that is "without and independent of [us]", so we are it, as it is us. Subject and object "coalesce" because

The subject (the self) has gone into what it perceives, and what it perceives is, in this sense, itself. So the object becomes the subject and the subject the object. And as, to understand what Coleridge is saying, we must not take the object as something given to us; so equally we must not take the subject to be a mere formless void out of which all things mysteriously and ceaselessly rush to become everything we know. The subject is what it is through the objects it has been (57).

I have presented Richards' argument prosaically because he claims his is a Materialist interpretation of Coleridge's view and appeals to "modern psychology" to support him in his view of the constructive nature of perception. The chapter in which Richards presents these views is wayward even for him, and confusing to the reader with its constant warnings against misunderstanding. I think Richards is ill-advised to use Coleridge's actual words about the coalescence of subject and object, since he attributes to Coleridge a literal belief in this, but denies one for himself. It is difficult to see from Richards' account alone how anything of value can come from this realisation of Coleridge's postulate. However, in a later chapter, Richards gives one detailed example of its operation in the case of Coleridge himself. From this he generalises to the conclusion we mentioned at the start, namely, that apparently contrary epistemological positions are in fact (of mind) not opposed to one another. Let us examine his example.

Richards raises the question which of two alternative views of Nature Coleridge in his poetry held, the "Realist" or the "Projective", which were identified with Nature in Senses I and II, respectively. His actual description of the two doctrines, however, suggests that the first is rather more complicated than might be expected from his description of "Sense I".

(i) The mind of the poet at moments, penetrating 'the film of familiarity and selfish solicitude', gains an insight into reality, reads Nature as a symbol of something behind or within Nature not ordinarily perceived.
(ii) The mind of the poet creates a Nature into which his own feelings, his aspirations and apprehensions, are projected (145).

As opposed to other answers to this question, Richards argues, first, that both views are true, and second, that Coleridge's poetry reflects his knowledge that this was so.

Richards thinks they are both true presumably because, as a "Materialist", he accepts that there are material objects, that *esse* is not *percipi*. On the other hand, he also holds, as we saw, that the only Nature we can *experience* is of our own making. He states further that he only means the doctrines are true in the *emotional*, not the scientific, sense. However, he proceeds to argue, inconsistently with this, that their *appearance* of being contradictory is due to "systematic linguistic illusions, arising in the course of the translation *from* the fact of mind *into* philosophic terminologies" (147).

The particular "systematic linguistic illusions" Richards has in mind are the variations in comprehensiveness of meaning that a group of words can have, for which, as we showed earlier, the multiple definition of 'word' acts as paradigm. Just as the different meanings of 'word' are said to be capable of being placed on a scale of comprehensiveness, so also with 'Nature'. "Nature in Sense I", Richards writes, "contains the minimum of meaning." Nature in Sense II, "as the inclusive myth, if it would be not abstractly conceived but concretely imagined, . . . could contain all meanings " (181). Senses III and IV are of course intermediate.

Examining lines from Coleridge's poetry, Richards shows how extremely difficult it is to say which view Coleridge believed in, because words in his poems, like 'Nature' and 'thought', can be interpreted so as to suggest either view. Richards takes this as indicating the truth to his actual experience of Coleridge's words. Commenting on the poem *Dejection*, after examining with similar conclusions *The Aeolian Harp*, Richards writes:

> As before, we cannot say if we take the poem as a whole, that it contains the one doctrine rather than the other. The colours of Nature are a suffusion from the light of the mind, but the light of the mind in its turn, the shaping spirit of Imagination, comes from the mind's response to Nature:
>
> > To thee do all things live from pole to pole
> > Their life the eddying of thy living soul.
>
> . . . This ambiguity (or rather, completeness) in Coleridge's thought . . . give[s] us a concrete example of that self-knowledge, which . . . was for him, both 'speculatively and practically', the principle of all his thinking (152).

Finally, Richards generalises his argument about Coleridge. Quoting Coleridge's belief that the "highest problem of philosophy" is "Whether ideas are regulative only, according to Aristotle and Kant: or likewise constitutive, and one with the power and life of nature, according to Plato and Plotinus", he argues:

... I have tried to make the position acceptable that these rival doctrines here derive from different arrangements of our vocabularies and are only seeming alternatives, that each pressed far enough includes the other, and that the Ultimate Unabstracted and Unrepresentable View that thus results is something we are familiar and at home with in the concrete fact of mind (184).

After these tell-tale capitals we are ready for a parable from Confucius, containing the words of the Yellow Emperor, "who knows speaks not, who speaks knows not. Therefore the sage teaches a doctrine which is without words." The truest we can achieve is with ambiguity. Perhaps we can adapt another well-known quotation. "Wovon man nicht sprechen kann, darüber muss man zweideutig reden."

The theory we have just described indicates some of the dangers that writing in the mode of Imagination brings, particularly perhaps in that, by writing in the way he does, obviously not concerning himself about any logical tidiness, Richards puts one at a moral disadvantage. One has to resist a strong sense of behaving inappropriately if one wishes to pick holes in his argument. But since a major purpose of mine, as it was of Richards, is to consider the causes of faulty thinking, I shall nevertheless do this.

What Richards seems to do, as Plato did, is to compound a mystical with an epistemological theory. It is not just a question whether we have to postulate universals to account for recognition, for instance, in our ordinary perception, but whether we attain to a vision of Reality. We have already noted this in the difference of his formulation of the "realist" doctrine from what is implied in "Sense I" of 'Nature'.

The mind of the poet at moments, penetrating 'the film of familiarity and selfish solicitude', gains an insight into reality, reads Nature as a symbol of something behind or within Nature not ordinarily perceived (145).

This view is obviously true of Coleridge's poetry, but why drag in general epistemological theories?

Then there is a category error in Richards' notion of a scale of comprehensiveness applying to his senses of 'Nature'. "Nature (Sense I)", the *cause* of our perceptions as opposed to our perceptions themselves, is, as we pointed out earlier, of a different logical category from the other sense. The same sense of 'comprehensive' cannot apply to it as to the others.

The trouble seems to have been the "paradigm" multiple definition of 'word' which, it will be remembered, was also applied to 'symbol' and 'language'. We will not quibble about the application of the notion of "scale of comprehensiveness" here. Clearly what Richards meant by the least comprehensive sense of these was a sense in which we refer only to a physical object or event, apart from its meaning—not to "things in themselves", which was the "least comprehensive sense" of 'Nature', but just to things we have not yet learned the meaning of. Richards seems to have applied this to 'Nature', forgetting the difference in "least comprehensive sense" between the two. Consequently, the "realist" view becomes one in which we see things without yet knowing what they are, just as we might see the *words* of a language we have not yet learned. Hence Richards' remarks about "reading Nature as a symbol", about the "realist view" being one "according to which Nature is a language" (159), and hence, too, his compounding of a mystical with a general epistemological doctrine.

7. IMAGINATION AND VALUE

We have described many of the "facts of mind" and some of the arguments Richards advanced in connection with his belief that exercise of the Imagination resulted in self-development. It is time we completed our exposition of his argument.

At the end of our discussion of the *Principles* (page 59), we distinguished between "formal" and "material transfer" as the means by which the benefits of poetry could extend beyond poetry. The former, in the shape of our increased capacity to organise our impulses so as to satisfy a larger number at once, was what Richards meant to rely on. However, as we pointed out, he did sometimes surreptitiously rely on material transfer as well. What we shall now find is that Richards in his later books made more and more use of material transfer, but that at the same time he characteristically continued to use formal transfer as a justification, too. What we shall now do is first of all to describe how much Richards' case for poetry depends upon formal transfer and then turn to the part played by material transfer. Our aim is not only to reveal his theory but also to connect what he said in *Coleridge on Imagination* with what he said in earlier or later books. This is relevant to certain interpretations of Richards that have been made (see Chapter 7, Sections 7 and 8). We will postpone to Chapter 8, Section 1, the evaluation of this theories of formal and material transfer.

(a) Formal Transfer

To see the extent to which Richards in *Coleridge on Imagination* was relying on the same reasons for expecting benefit from works of art as he was in the *Principles*, we have to show that his change of language did not necessitate any change in theory. His change of language can be seen if we compare the quotation from *Science and Poetry* we made some pages back (pp.76-77) with one to the same effect from *Coleridge on Imagination*. In the former, he talked of "the choice of rhythm being due to an instinctive impulse seeking . . . to order itself with its fellows", of its being "the direct outcome of the way in which [the poet's] interests are organised", and of its arising "only from genuinely stirred impulses". In the latter, he simply says, "the organisation of language into metre [is] a part . . . of the self-organisation of the mind that is uttering itself" (118). What has happened is that he now talks about the order, rather than about that which is ordered, and then identifies the former with the "self". This is used from then on as shorthand for what he spelled out in more detail in the earlier books. It is as though, having worked out his theory, he no longer felt the need to refer to it all the time in terms of the words he originally used.

The abbreviation seems to have been due to the influence of the Chinese, and was first used in *Practical Criticism*. The quotations from Legge's translation of Confucious that he gave when elaborating his concept of *sincerity* do very much, by use of the word 'self', particularly 'self-completion', suggest a holistic psychological view. Richards started his commentary[1] by taking "self-completion as our starting-point". "The completed mind [is] that . . . in which no disorder, no mutual frustration of impulses remained." He postulated "*a tendency towards increased order* . . . which takes effect unless baffled" by the various impediments to "learning by experience" that we mentioned, when discussing *Practical Criticism*, and which the cultivation of sincerity by study should remove. This ordering is in relation to an environment. Increased order means increased adaptation to the environment. "By self-completion the superior man would"—and Richards quotes Confucious again—"effect a union of the external and the internal," or as Coleridge would have put it, "[bring about] a coincidence of subject with object." Richards next construed the phrase, "one's own true nature", though in so circular a manner as to make one giddy

Any response . . . which embodies the present activity of this tendency to inner adjustments will be sincere, and any response that conflicts with it or inhibits it will be insincere. Thus to be sincere is to act, feel and think in accordance with 'one's true nature', and to be insincere is to act, feel or think in a contrary manner (289)[2].

[1] *P. C.* 285-289.
[2] The reader will become giddier still if he reads on and notes that, "If we seek a standard for a new response whose sincerity may be in doubt, we shall find it in the very responses which make the new one possible." (298). And, Richards continues, if we are not sure about "these instrumental responses" in their turn, we can judge

From all this, it is evident that when Richards in his later books writes about "self-development," "self-forming," "self-realising," and "self-completing," he can still be using the theory of value he developed in the *Principles*. And he does in fact right up to the end continue to see value in terms of the satisfaction of the greatest possible number of our impulses.

Similarly, we may note how in *Practical Criticism* Richards abbreviated a point he made in psychological detail in the *Principles*. There, in connection with his idea of emotions as signs of attitudes, he talked of the greater accuracy in sensory judgments that is often achieved, "not by attentive optical comparison . . ., but by the general emotional or organic reaction which the colours evoke when simply glanced at."[1] In the later book, he followed up his remark, that "value in poetry turns nearly always upon differences and connections too minute and unobtrusive to be directly perceived. We recognise them only in their effects,"[2] by saying that "the choice of *our whole personality* may be the only instrument . . . delicate enough to effect the discrimination."[3] Clearly he is here referring to "the general emotional or organic reaction" of the earlier book. The choice, he goes on to say, is "an essential not an arbitrary choice, one which expresses the needs of the being as a whole, not a random gust of desire . . .". And later, in *Coleridge on Imagination*, he makes such remarks as, "the judgment that a passage is good is an act of living", or asserts that through the "greater mythologies," like religions or political creeds,

> our will is collected, our powers unified, our growth controlled . . . [and] the infinitely divergent strayings of our being . . . brought into 'balance or reconciliation' (171–172).

What now can we say about the *additional* arguments, advanced in *Coleridge on Imagination*, for considering experiences of the Imagination to be self-developing and self-fulfilling as regards their effects? According to one argument, we will remember, the poem is something of an ordered nature that happens to us, if we give ourselves up to it, allowing the self-ordering to take place within us. This is in contrast to something in which the self is not *involved* because it is itself in entire conscious control of the operation, as in the solving by application of certain rules of a routine algebraic problem. But surely all one can really say, if one wishes to talk in terms of wholes, is that the

---

[1] *P.L.C.*, 99.
[2] *P.C.*, 301.
[3] *P.C.*, 302 (my italics).

---

their sincerity by comparing them with yet other responses, such as our distaste for a bad smell, when we should be fairly sure that our response is genuine.

poetic conception "forms" and "realises itself". This is the "fact of mind", however much one may feel "steady self-possession with enthusiasm and feeling profound or vehement", or feel that "one's whole soul" has come "into activity". By "self-forming", then, Richards is obviously implying the successful operation of the "tendency towards increased order". In default of further reasons, he must still be using the formal transfer theory of the *Principles*.

But what about Coleridge's self-awareness in the act of Imagination? Unfortunately, the only example Richards gave of this was, as we saw in the previous section, one where the self's relation to Nature was the subject being considered. In so far as further insight into this is revealed to the reader by these poems, so that there is some enhancement in his adaptive capacity, then this is a case of material, and not formal, transfer. In other words, the self-forming, that comes from the self's awareness of itself embroiled in its experience, is limited only to poems specifically dealing with this.

(b) *Material Transfer*

Two ideas played an important part in Richards's use of material transfer for proving that exercise of the Imagination was good for us. These were Coleridge's conception of "Good Sense", and Richards's conception, also supported by Coleridge, of theories as "speculative instruments", to which one "experimentally submitted" oneself for the sake of the experience.

Coleridge's conception of "Good Sense" (or "Taste" or "Sanity"), was similar to Richards' of "sincerity", as can be seen from Coleridge's description, which Richards quotes:

> If it be asked, by what principles the poet is to regulate his own style? . . . I reply: . . . By the principles of grammar, logic, psychology! In one word by such a knowledge of the facts, material and spiritual, that most appertain to his art, as, if it has been governed and applied by good-sense, and rendered instinctive by habit, becomes the representative and reward of our past conscious reasonings, insights, and conclusions and acquires the name of TASTE (126).

Richards however, in adopting Coleridge's term, no longer confined its operation to preparing us for the better understanding of poetry alone. He regarded its development as something that will save us from over-literal belief in "mythologies", in which he included religious and political creeds. These, since they are "projections of some human situation", are "limited [as regards] the scope of their relevance and therefore of their proper influence upon action" (174). Richards says,

89

an extremely general misunderstanding and misuse of myth and a confusion of it with the special myths of science, has been characteristic of humanity ... We have to ... appeal to an *ideal of sanity or integrity or sincerity in the mind, to its growing order in response to the Universe* (Nature, Sense I) (175, my italics).

Now it should be noted that "our growing order in response to the Universe" is evidently not scientific knowledge, to which we would normally refer to explain our increased adaptation to our environment. On the other hand, it is not the order described in the *Principles*, that is, our ability to satisfy a number of impulses at the same time, for, if sincerity is achieved by *study* of "the principles of grammar, logic and psychology", then it is at least in part achieved by properly responding to language whose function is informative. What then is the status of this kind of order in Richards' system?

The answer is that it is the kind of knowledge that we get through personal experience which we cannot yet make explicit and control, as we can scientific knowledge. This is where Richards' other notion, that of theories as speculative instruments, comes in. Theories are valuable, not in just being intellectually apprehended, but in so far as they lead us to experience personally the "facts of mind" from which they come. Richards is clearly applying to the realm of intellect the way of thinking he applied to art. He uses the same phrase, "experimental submission", with regard to both. And clearly Coleridge's emphasis upon being aware of what one is doing at the moment one is doing it, is relevant here in a way it does not seem to be relevant in connection with poetry. Richards constantly shifts from one to the other, from poetry to learning by study or the reverse, through absent-mindedness, or, wishing to make important assertions, through mistaking his abstractions for "facts of mind".

An important reason for Richards' assimilation of the experience of reading poetry to that of study was his emphasis upon the activity of the mind in both. In the former, we have noted how much weight Richards laid upon the reader being active whilst reading poetry. For instance, towards the end of the long passage describing the activity of the Imagination, with which we started this discussion (see pp. 70-71 above), Richards wrote about how, in finding "cross-connexion after cross-connexion", the reader "seems . . . to be discovering not only Shakespeare's meaning, but something which he . . . is himself *making* [so that] as Coleridge says, [he becomes] a poet . . .—an *active creative* being" (my italics). And in his next book, Richards provided an additional reason for the absence of syntax in the best poetry: "In all interpretation we are filling in connections, and for poetry, of course, our freedom to fill in—the absence of explicitly stated intermediate steps—is a main source of its powers"[1].

Similarly, because of his belief that perception was a constructive process, Richards could describe knowing as a kind of "doing". Now "doing" implies purpose, and purpose, for Richards, always meant emotion. The "facts of mind", which consideration of theories should lead us to experience, should as true facts of mind be unitary, the feeling and sensation not abstracted from one another. These theories were the more important, the more the issues with which they dealt concern the whole of us. Richards tried a definition of freedom as "action according to its own laws". Distinguishing these laws in order of complexity, he held that "a man would be free . . . if his acts were determined by laws of appropriate complexity" (62). This is going to lead Richards in his last book to say that in so far as a man is doing this—"the whole soul of man in activity", the personality fused with the experience—he is acting according to his "nature", and the greater the extent to which he does this, the more he is "realising" his nature, achieving, as a result of the silent reorganisation that follows learning, a more complex order.

In his last book we shall also find Richards returning to Coleridge's "postulate", according to which, in the attempt to "know" ourselves, we "make" ourselves. There, in interpreting Plato's theory of knowledge, he distinguishes what he calls "degrees of knowledge" by means of the metaphor of distance between the known and what is known. This metaphor appears to be another way of referring to degree of abstraction, that is to say, of separation between the word and what it refers to, between thought and feeling, between the personality and the experience it is having. When "this metaphorical distance . . . close[s] down to nothing . . . the mind then knows its own activity—KNOWING becomes BEING", and when "most things most come together to determine our action . . . we most truly DO. It is then that we most truly ARE and KNOW, and accordingly then 'Nature' is 'true being'. Whatever man *does* in the course of this self-realisation he does naturally—i.e., he is moving towards his nature." We may add that he described 'realise' as having two senses—" 'to see clearly' and 'to become actually' "—and commented "This is one of the innumerable suggestions in language that BEING and KNOWING are somehow one"[2].

---

[1] *P.R.*, 125.
[2] *H.T.R.P.*, 178-179.

8. GOLDEN PAST, PLATINUM FUTURE:
ONLY THE PRESENT IS LEAD

In the last chapter of *Coleridge on Imagination*, Richards returns to the theme of *Science and Poetry* by considering once again the condition of our society today. He proposes the rhetorical question— whether Coleridge's " 'philosophic' approach to criticism" and consequent insights can help us today—and of course discovers that the answer is 'Yes'. His position is similar to what it was before, except for a greater tendency, when he makes a positive statement, to safeguard himself by adding, as a qualification, its contradictory. He thus follows the example he attributed to Coleridge, only writing in prose, not poetry. But since much more emphasis is laid upon the positive statements than upon their contradictories, I will ignore the latter, save for an occasional footnote, concentrating rather upon the effect that Richards' writing makes.

During the past four centuries, Richards argues, there has been an increasing loss of "order". This is due to a break-up in the "homogeneity of the intellectual tradition", characterised by

the growth of Science and History, our changing attitudes to Authority in all its forms, to the Bible, to Tradition (as a body of truth to be received because of its source), to custom (to be accepted because established), to parental opinion (220).

This process, which Richards regards as due to the "inevitable growth of human awareness", is reflected in

the widespread increase in the aptitude of the average mind for self-dissolving introspection, the general heightened awareness of goings on of our own minds, merely *as goings on*, not as transitions from one well-known and linguistically recognised moral or intellectual condition to another (220–221),

which found expression particularly in prose, such as Joyce's *Ulysses* or the novels of Virginia Woolf.[1]

The task of "reconstituting a less relaxed, a less adventitious order for the mind" Richards lays at the door of "contemporary poetry"[2],

---

[1] Richards is surprisingly unfair to Joyce, as the bracketing of him together with Virginia Woolf suggests. To refer to "the composition of whole books with meanings of a structure which in poetry is found only in phrases or single lines . . ." in connection with the many-structured *Ulysses* suggests very much a judgment in terms of theories *abstracted* from other sources and applied automatically to another work without considering *its* special purpose.

[2] A different attitude to poetry is shown by Richards in his previous chapter. There he describes poems as "minor myths" in contrast to "the greater mythologies", *viz.*, religious and political creeds. The former can help us with the latter, for "an account of the [psychological] origin and function of myths is more conveniently tested in lesser examples" (176).

arguing, very much in the style of the *Principles* and *Science and Poetry*, that "there can be no question of a return to any mythologic structures prevailing before the seventeenth century" (225). Richards, now fortified by his new view of science also being a myth, repeats some of the arguments of his earlier books:

while any part of the world-picture is regarded as not of mythopoeic origin, poetry—earlier recognised as mythopoeic—could not but be given a second place. . . . [But] if we grant all is myth, poetry, as the myth-making which most brings 'the whole soul of man into activity', and as working with words, 'parts and germinations of the plant' and, through them, in 'the medium by which spirits communicate with one another', becomes the necessary channel for the reconstitution of order (228)[1].

The new poetry of Yeats, Eliot, Auden, and Empson, upon which Richards pinned his hopes, will not however be very effective unless we are able to read it properly. But this capacity is itself "disordered" by the same "great diversity in our current intellectual tradition", that causes the general loss of order, as well as additional factors such as the decline in the use of "rigorous translation exercises in the schools" and the large amount of "shoddy reading material in our daily intake of printed matter" (193). The effects of all this are not apparently limited to the average man. "Twentieth century criticism", Richards writes, "has been marked . . . by the betrayal of general inability to read anything with safety on the part of most of those who have anything to say" (195), and he takes as his text a specimen of criticism from the *Criterion*, whose misreadings he subjects to detailed analysis. Commenting on our reading skill in the past, Richards writes:

Intellectual tradition tells us, among other things, *how literally* to read a passage. It guides us in our metaphorical, allegorical, symbolical modes of interpretation. The hierarchy of these modes is elaborate and variable; and to read aright we need to shift with an at present indescribable adroitness and celerity from one mode to another. Our sixteenth- and seventeenth-century literature, supported by practice in listening to sermons and by conventions in speech and letter-writing which made 'direct' statement rare to a point which seems to us unnatural, gave an extraordinary training in this skill. But it was skill merely; it was not followed up by theory (193–194).

As our skill has since diminished, it is to theory that Richards now appeals for salvation. "Our remedy", he writes, "is the dangerous one of analysis"—"dangerous" because of abstractionism, because of the temptation to "take the divisions we make as established insurmountably in the order of things".

[1] Two sentences later Richards argues that "the mind has never been in order", that previous ages in this respect were in fact the same as ours. In doing this, he contradicts the tenor of the argument he developed over the previous 35 pages.

When he comes to illustrate his remedy, however, it does not seem to amount to much more than a reasseveration of this danger. The attitude to beauty that Richards stressed in his first three books and in *Practical Criticism*—that beauty has many forms of which different aesthetic doctrines are the consequences but that there is no possibility of reducing them all to one, except in terms of the effects on the true interpreter—this same attitude is now revealed in his treatment of different poetic structures. These structures are unique expressions of the "self-organisations of the minds that were uttering themselves in poetic composition". Failure to appreciate them is due to one-sided allegiance to aesthetic theory, as well as a limited "attitude to language, to [the] different ways in which words are used, and in which they are assumed to work" (197). Since these theories and attitudes differ fundamentally in different critics—Richards instances T. S. Eliot and F. L. Lucas—there is a communication gap between them far greater than any that existed between critics in the past.

In particular, Richards takes up the problem of the relation between the "prose sense" of a poem and its total meaning, taking Housman's lecture, *The Name and Nature of Poetry*, as his stalking-horse. Richards holds that, generally speaking, you cannot separate the "prose sense" from the rest of the poem and say that the effect of the poem depends upon it. On the other hand, you must not say, as Housman, or indeed as Richards himself had done, that the meaning of the words is sometimes of no importance. It always has an effect, though the nature of this differs from poem to poem: the effects are due to subtle interactions between the meaning of the different words, the mode of the Imagination obviously being implied. In this connection, Richards emphasises again that in the "best" poems it is not the message, or the product, that matters, so much as the process.

We may sum up Richards' view about improving the ordering of our reading, so that we may benefit by modern poets' reconstitution of our lost order, in a sentence. It consists in making the reader aware that poetry is an ordering and that this ordering is more or less unique to every poem. This summary sufficiently expresses the rather empty though involved impression that the last chapter of *Coleridge on Imagination* makes on one. I have not done it entire justice because I have omitted the actual examples—one poem by Blake, and some stray lines by others—that Richards uses with some effect. But there is not much exemplification, and the main impression left on the reader is that these are examples of not much more than the fact of organic interrelatedness and the consequent dangers of analysis, of attempting to separate the "*what*" from the "*how*", the "*means*" from the "*ends*", or the "*way*" from the "*whither*".

So much for what *poetry*, and our better reading of it, can do for us. Only once more, in his chapters on metaphor in *The Philosophy of Rhetoric*, shall we find Richards returning to this theme. Otherwise it will be "Good Sense" in Richards's extended version of this, our "growing order in response to the Universe", that will provide our salvation. Language will take over from poetry.

> Our world and our life have grown and taken what order they have for us through separated meanings which we can only hold together or keep apart through words (230).

Though we have lost the Golden Age, there is the platinum Dawn that Science promises:

> With Coleridge we step across the threshold of a general theoretical study of language capable of opening to us new powers over our minds comparable to those which systematic physical inquiries are giving us over our environment. The step across was of the same type as that which took Galileo into the modern world. It requires the shift from a preoccupation with the What and Why to the How of language (232).

Chapter Five

LANGUAGE AND THE SOUL

WITH the task envisaged at the close of *Coleridge on Imagination*, Richards' last three books,[1] *The Philosophy of Rhetoric*, *Interpretation in Teaching*, and *How to Read a Page*, were concerned. It is easy to read them as being concerned merely with problems of grammar and literary theory; with, for instance, developing a more fundamental conception of metaphor, or with the educational task of improving reading ability by exercises in interpretation and definition, or with attacking certain current notions, such as the Usage theory or the various prescriptions of Grammarians. This is indeed their main matter, but the style in which they are written, the images used, and a number of allusive comments, eye-catching like glints in quartzite paving-stone once we think of looking, suggest the aspiration that bears them. Our wrestle with *Coleridge on Imagination* has extracted from it that this is not mere rhetorical euphoria, but a theory of value, personality, and learning, according to which what Richards does, the way he does it, and the very great value he puts on it, are all interrelated. What we get now is a return to the aims of *The Meaning of Meaning*, but regarded as much more weighty now that the development of the whole personality is seen to be involved.

I. "THE PHILOSOPHY OF RHETORIC": INTERANIMATION AND METAPHOR

Much of what *The Philosophy of Rhetoric* (1936) covers is repeated in the much longer *Interpretation in Teaching*, and we shall deal with some of this in discussing the latter book. *The Philosophy of Rhetoric* by its form, unusually for Richards free from interpolations and

---

[1] It is not worth describing in detail *Basic in Teaching: East and West* (1935), which Richards wrote between *Coleridge on Imagination* and *The Philosophy of Rhetoric*. It suggests that Basic English should be used by the Chinese in any attempt to understand Western thought, since their own language (*vide Mencius on the Mind*) has such entirely different presuppositions. The advantage of translation exercises with Basic for students in the West is to counteract the decline in our skills referred to in *Coleridge on Imagination*. What Richards writes about the deficiencies of Western education and the virtues of Basic is dealt with again and in more detail in *Interpretation in Teaching*.

demonstrative exercises, owing to the occasion of its writing,[1] does however bring out with particular clarity what Richards' outlook is like. In describing once again his Context theory of meaning, Richards reverts to an associationist explanation. But he placates Coleridge by using organic images rather frequently and attacking Locke.

As opposed to a view which explains our apprehension of universals in terms of the induction of what is common to a set of particulars, Richards accounts for particulars by the refining down of universals, believing after Pavlov that stimuli are initially generalised, so that only by the accumulation of negative instances do we come to discriminate more and more particulars. Richards does not deny that general ideas may be arrived at by a process of synthesis, he is only concerned with saying that there is in effect no such thing as a particular. He expresses this by denying we ever have sensations, there are only perceptions. In other words, we always classify. Or, put in another way, "all thinking from the lowest to the highest . . . is sorting" (30). Richards is attacking bricks-and-mortar models, whether of our perception of the outside world as being built out of basic units of sensational complexes or of our understanding of complex meaning as being determined by the meanings of individual words, assumed to be fixed and definite. From "the primordial generality and abstractness of meaning" more particular meanings develop by a process of individuation.

The theorem holds that we *begin* with the general abstract anything, split it, as the world makes us, into sorts and then arrive at concrete particulars by the overlapping or common membership of these sorts (31).

Richards then gives an example which shows that there is no change in his explanation from the one with which we are familiar in *The Meaning of Meaning*.

This bit of paper here now in my hand is a concrete particular to us so far as we think of it as paperish, hereish, nowish and in my hand; it is the more concrete as we take it as of more sorts, and the more specific as the sorts are narrower and more exclusive (31).

But though formally there is no change, the emphasis is different. It is on *generality*. Abstraction is harmful only in so far as we may be unaware of its universality. It is inevitable in our use of language.

. . . when we mean the simplest-seeming concrete object, its concreteness comes to it from the way in which we are bringing it simultaneously into a number of sorts. The sorts grow together in it to form that meaning. Theory here, as so often, can merely exploit the etymological hint given in the word 'concrete' (35-36).

[1] It is based on a course of public lectures, "The Mary Flexner Lectures on the Humanities", that Richards gave at Bryn Mawr College in America.

Such de-concretising operations make words much more sensitive, more easily permeable, as Lecture III, "The Interanimation of Words", tries to show. Words vary in meaning according to their contexts, whether in Richards' technical or in the ordinary sense of the word. Richards includes in this the whole background of our language as we have learned it, taking the case of "expressive morphemes" like 'fl-', in words like 'flash', 'flicker', 'flare' and 'flame', and suggesting that their expressiveness is not due to any quality of the sound itself but rather to the association the other words, starting with 'fl-', may unconsciously provide whenever we use any *one* of them. Indeed, he goes on to suggest that this association may result in the use of the morpheme in the coinage of new words, so that the expressiveness of the morpheme is due to its use rather than the use occasioned by the expressiveness.[1] From this Richard advances to the notion that there may be other interdependencies between the words we are using and others we are not but have "in the background of the mind", pointing out the relevance of this to translating and to the effect of words in poetry. The whole of a language by his reckoning may be an associative system, and

as the movement of my hand uses nearly the whole skeletal system of muscles and is supported by them, so a phrase may take its powers from an immense system of supporting uses of other words in other contexts (65).

A word then in its meaning is subject to a great variety of influences, and though it may be that the actual stabilities of the contexts which operate "hide from us this universal relativity or, better, inter-dependence of meanings" (10), Richards generally writes as if it were *instability* that was the norm, so that we have to train our powers of microscopic observing.

This emphasis of Richards' on the way words are influenced by their settings is no doubt influenced by Gestalt psychology. Thus he describes a word as "always a cooperative member of an organism" (69), and refers to the evidence from perception for the dependence of colour or size on its setting. Also he uses similar images to those of the Gestalt psychologists. We have already mentioned the bricks-and-mortar one; more common is that of a mosaic. Yet Richards' view is rather different from the Gestalt one, largely because it is association-ist. Thus what he means when he adopts the Gestalt psychologists' saying that there is no such thing as sensation is very different from what Köhler or Koffka meant. Further, there is in the Gestalt Theory more emphasis on stability. The saying that the whole is more than the sum of its parts means in effect that many alterations in the parts

[1] Richards provides no evidence for this, though I should have thought the plausibility of his idea could be relatively easily determined.

make no difference to the whole; the structure withstands it. Richards' model on the other hand is that of a *jelly* in which the movement of any part sends a shiver through the whole.[1] ". . . in most ordinary discourse the individual words . . . cooperate with the other words to carry jointly a total meaning for the whole sentence. Change the sentence and they are no longer doing the same work. And in many sentences it is very difficult to decide just what they are doing, because other sentences in which they are doing just the same are not easily to be found".[2] Richards lays little stress on structure,[3] much more on relativity, interdependence, and possibility. Evidently this is a consequence of the emphasis on generality; it is an aspect of Richards' de-concretisation. If "concrete particulars" are the consequences of sorting operations, then they may vary as we decide to do the sorting one way or another. "And thereby we re-discover that the world— so far from being a solid matter of fact—is rather a fabric of conventions, which for obscure reasons it has suited us in the past to manufacture and support" (41-42). There are also interesting references to Berkeley. In commenting on his proposal to treat meanings in a way that "has its analogues with Mr. Whitehead's treatment of things", Richards remarks that "no one to whom Berkeley has mattered will be very confident as to which is which" (12), and quotes Yeats' lines

> God appointed Berkeley who proved all things a dream,
> That this preposterous pragmatical pig of a world, its
>   farrow that so solid seem,
> Must vanish on the instant did the mind but change its
>   theme.

Richards' outlook is also manifested in connection with literary theory. Thus, a true Coleridgean, he opposed the fashionable emphasis on the use of concrete, individual images in writing. Quoting, without benefit of interpretation, Hulme—"The great aim is accurate, precise and definite description" and "[the language of poetry] is a visual concrete one. It always endeavours to arrest you, and make you continuously see a physical thing, to prevent you gliding through an abstract process"—Richards asserts, on the contrary, that "the language of the greatest poetry is frequently abstract in the extreme",

---

[1] For the Gestalt psychologists, this would only be one of many possible types of field situation.
[2] *I. in T.*, 261. Cf. the similar point made about the uniqueness of different contexts in *The Meaning of Meaning*, (pp. 17-18 above).
[3] Cf. Max Black's reference to the "intrusive and pervasive dissolution of structure" characteristic of Richards' later thought, fairly acknowledged by Richards as an "admirably discerning and penetrating phrase". (A Symposium on Emotive Meaning, *Phil. Rev.*, 57, 1948).

and attacks, as Coleridge did on metaphysical grounds,[1] the taking of seeing as a model for understanding.[2] Words "have very much more important work to do" than to arouse sensations, for "language, well used, is a *completion* and does what the intuitions of sensation by themselves cannot do. Words are the meeting points at which regions of experience which can never combine in sensation or intuition, come together. They are the occasion and the means of that growth which is the mind's endless endeavour to order itself" (131). So, as opposed to "The patient toil of scores of teachers [which] is going on every day, in courses about the appreciation of poetry, into the effort to make children (and adults) visualise where visualisation is a mere distraction and of no service" (130), Richards will advance as an educational aim in the teaching of English the multiple defining of the most *abstract* words, because these are the most *general* and enter therefore into the greatest number of activities.

Indeed this aversion to the concrete, the definite, and the clear-cut is everywhere manifested by Richards. We have already referred to his negative attitude to syntax, because it fixes and controls, reducing the number of alternative meanings possible, and we have shown that this attitude is evident in his own practice. We have spoken of the high degree of ellipsis in his own writing, his 'something along these lines' way of saying things, which one suspects sometimes allows him to avoid coming to grips with the hard problems. Similarly, in *Practical Criticism*, his comments on the more valuable poems are generally oblique. It is as though, for *all* his attempts to increase its sensitivity, language itself cannot do justice to the most valuable states of mind, something that becomes the more significant, the more knowledge in its turn comes to be identified with a *state of mind* (see page 91 above). What he says about ambiguity is probably a recognition of this. Perhaps the fact that he has a lot to say and wants to say it quickly, his desire for large practical impact, means that he has to avoid the concrete and definite. The poetry of Coleridge which Richards quotes is likewise a good example of expressing complex general feelings and beliefs. Yet in *The Rime of the Ancient Mariner*, Coleridge has himself shown how the concrete and definite can be used to express such complexities. I can think of few concrete images that Richards uses. One example which comes from *Principles of Literary Criticism*—"The wheeling of the pigeons in Trafalgar Square may

[1] In *Coleridge on Imagination*, Richards refers to Coleridge's attack on the "despotism of the eye" under which "we are restless because invisible things are not the objects of vision".

[2] Richards in fact accuses Hulme of confusing the literal and metaphorical senses of 'see', and it is, amongst other things, to prevent this kind of linguogenetic error that 'see' is multiply defined in *How to Read a Page*, pages 180-185.

seem to have no relation to the colour of the water in the basins, or to the tones of a speaker's voice or to the drift of his remarks"— has, I think an invented quality and could certainly be further individualised. To deny that exact statement is the be-all and end-all of poetic aspiration does not mean that no images should be used. The only exception I can think of to this general characterisation of Richards lies in his ear and memory for quotation. His epigraphs make excellent and unusual reading. Of course, it might be said this fits in with his *literary* approach. His role is that of the middle-man, advertising 'Poetry is Good for You', provided, no simple matter, it is taken the right way. Yet the generality of his level of reference, on the intellectual side as well, suggests that we have to do here with a personality characteristic and that his anti-concrete attitude does not therefore just follow from the argument he advances.

Another area which shows Richards' attack on the concrete is that of metaphor. Since Richards' views about metaphor form an important part of his theory and provide opportunity for illustrating a number of features of his thought, we will go into this in some detail. Richards starts off by criticising eighteenth-century theories on metaphor, described as "the traditional approach", particularly as presented by Lord Kames. The theories are criticised largely for limiting the scope of metaphor, but also in one way or another for limiting its freedom by logical or what might be called representa-tional criteria. Indeed what we have said about Richards' opposition to Hulme arose out of a similar difference of opinion about the scope of metaphor, and in *Interpretation in Teaching* certain specimens of modern teaching with regard to mixing metaphors or overdoing them are also attacked. That metaphor should *not* be limited by considera-tions of logic or representation, or be confined simply to decoration or the fulfilling of emotive purposes, or be conceived simply in terms of resemblance between, to adopt Richards' technical terms, the vehicle and the tenor (the image and what is being imaged),[1] follows for Richards from the fact that metaphor is "the *omni-present prin-ciple of language*" (92, my italics). This is because it is involved in all thinking. "Thought is radically metaphoric ... since meaning only arises through the *causal contexts* by which a sign stands for ... an instance of a sort. To think of anything is to take it *as* of a sort ... and that 'as' brings in ... the analogy, the parallel, the metaphoric grapple

---

[1] Richards would not like this way of putting it because he is hostile, from *The Meaning of Meaning* on, to theories which describe understanding in terms of images, mainly I think because of his belief in the necessary primacy of the general over the concrete, and his belief that thought was not confined to what could be conceived by the senses.

or ground or grasp or draw by which alone the mind takes hold."[1]

In thus stretching his use of the word 'metaphor', one would have thought Richards was neglecting his own counsel always to pay attention to the purpose for which a distinction was made. Indeed he has later to return to the usual use of the word, explaining in a footnote, "to give the fully extended sense to the term 'metaphor' on all occasions would be inconvenient. For other purposes we do need to distinguish metaphor from what is not metaphor—without however forgetting the likeness of all modes of thinking, to stress which I have been stretching the term here. Only when metaphor (in narrower senses) is seen as a special type of the mode of operation of all languages (and all signs) does a study of it become really fruitful".[2] This claim we shall examine in more detail later, but certainly one reason for his extension in the meaning of 'metaphor' is to make it in its narrower meaning appear much more important. What I want to do before this is to focus attention on the other things Richards says about metaphor, which serve to emphasise its multifariousness.

First, Richards identifies metaphor with projection. "The processes of metaphor in language, the exchanges between the meanings of words which we study in explicit verbal metaphors, are superimposed upon a perceived world which is itself a product of earlier or un-witting metaphor" (108-109), for "our world is a projected world, shot through with characters lent it from our own life" (108).

Secondly, Richards takes up the case of so-called dead metaphors. For him, they are not dead but sleeping and can always be woken into life; indeed he implies they may be working independently of the writer's awareness. This belief of Richards follows from his point about all thinking and therefore all language being metaphorical, and in the sentence we quoted from him a page back, referring to ". . . the parallel, the metaphoric grapple or ground or gasp or draw by which alone the mind takes hold", he was purposely using words designed to bring this out, pointing out however that if he had talked in terms of 'cognition', 'attention', 'apprehension', and 'intellection' instead, this would still have been true. Richards does in fact occasionally justify an interpretation of a word in terms of its etymology; we have already come across two examples of this[3]. "Historians of language", he writes elsewhere,

---

[1] *I. in T.*, 48-49.

[2] *I. in T.*, 50.

[3] The words 'realise', and 'concrete' on pages 91 and 97 above Cf. also his remark, referring to other of "the innumerable suggestions in language that BEING and KNOWING are somehow one", about "the etymology of 'conception'—that best of metaphors by which we describe the formation in us of an IDEA . . ." (*How to Read a Page*, 179). Two other examples are 'discern' and 'perceive', (ibid., 86.) Also 'interpret' (*Interpretation in Teaching*, viii).

have long taught that we can find no word or description for any of the intellectual operations which, if its history is known, is not seen to have been taken, by metaphor, from a description of some physical happening. Only Jeremy Bentham, as successor to Bacon and Hobbes, insisted—with his technique of archetypation and phraseoplerosis—upon one inference that might be drawn; namely, that the mind and all its doings are fictions. He left it to Coleridge, F. H. Bradley and Vaihinger to point to the further inference; namely, that matter and its adventures, and all the derivative objects of contemplation, are fictions, too, of varied rank because of varied service (91).

Thirdly, Richards means by metaphor the models we use in thinking about things. His own organic psychological model is an obvious example, just as are the mechanical models of the mind's working he was attacking, or mechanical models of the world, such as are attributed to classical physics. He writes:

In philosophy, above all, we can take no step safely without an unrelaxing awareness of the metaphors we, and our audience, may be employing; . . . And this is the more true, the more severe and abstract the philosophy is. As it grows more abstract we think increasingly by means of metaphors that we profess *not* to be relying on. The metaphors we are avoiding steer our thought as much as those we accept . . . And in philosophy . . . I would hold with Bradley that our pretence to do without metaphor is never more than a bluff waiting to be called (92).

Finally, Richards also describes as evidence for metaphor being "the omnipresent principle of language," (i), the mere fact that all our words in "ordinary fluid discourse" are constantly shifting their senses, that is, mean different things at *different* times, and, (ii), "to cover all cases where . . . we compound different uses of the word into one" (116), that is to say, where we mean different things at the *same* time.

This congeries of cases, not all consistent with one another, to which Richards wishes to apply the concept of metaphor, is a further example of the process we noted in the *Principles* and illustrated with regard to the variety of arguments for not treating poetry as giving information (see pages 49-59). It illustrates the mode of reasoning that the Imagination in Richards' conception of it favours. The holding of a particular opinion, in this case that metaphor is much more widely used in language than literary theorists realise, acts as a sort of associative magnet to other views having some similarity to this. Consequently the theory often seems to be overdetermined in the sense that a number of reasons are advanced for it which are not necessarily connected and may indeed be inconsistent with one

103

another. In this sense, Richards is very like Freud,[1] who baffles the reader by his fecundity in thinking up ever-new explanations of clinical phenomena he has already explained in a particular way.

What use does Richards make of his more exalted conception of metaphor? One thing he does is greatly to subtilise the reading of metaphor. He points out that a metaphor may work, not by any resemblance between vehicle and tenor that may be concretely representable, so much as by a common attitude or feeling with regard to both; that sometimes it may be the contrast, rather than the similarity, which contributes most to the effect; that the relative emphasis that should be paid on different occasions to tenor and vehicle, could be imagined as on a scale. "At one end the tenor is in the forefront and the vehicle in the background; at the other the vehicle is in front and the tenor behind. In the middle case, tenor and vehicle are equally prominent, neither is subordinated to the other. This mid-case is often described as 'a fusion', or 'identification', between them, with an implication, as a rule, that this is a specially desirable state of affairs, above all in poetry."[2]

In particular, Richards wants to distinguish between the relation of vehicle to tenor on the one hand, and the relation of these two combined to *their* total meaning, or effect on the reader, on the other. He believes that we can mean by 'metaphor,' however we conceive it, *either* the vehicle, i.e. the image, *or* the combination of tenor and vehicle. Presumably one would be talking about the latter whenever one compared the effect of a metaphorical with a non-metaphorical way of putting things. The reason why Richards is concerned with distinguishing these two particular senses is that he thinks much theorising about metaphor is mistaken, through these senses being confused. He argues this about Hulme, interpreting Hulme's remarks (see page 99) about the necessity for accuracy and precision, as the "truism" that "the metaphor (the whole thing, tenor and vehicle together) should mean what it should." The demand for any "supposedly needful accuracy between vehicle and tenor" (132) is quite another thing, and owes what plausibility it has to an unconscious confusion of the two senses, an argument that he elaborates at greater length in *Interpretation in Teaching*. What is unusual in this case is that Richards does not content himself with multiple definition but actually invents some

---

[1] Richards in fact compares his "theorem" about ambiguity with Freud's and claims that his "goes further, and regards all discourse—outside the technicalities of science—as over-determined, as having multiplicity of meaning" (39).

[2] *Interpretation in Teaching*, page 121. Richards rejects the 'fusion' image as unnecessary, but a reference to *Coleridge on Imagination* suggests that he regards this image as denying a view that he believed in, namely "that fancy and imagination were two distinct or widely different faculties".

technical terms. It is, I think, the only occasion in which he has attempted to deal with ambiguity in this way.

But Richards' concern with metaphor has more exalted purposes than just literary theory. The consequences of the confusion of its meanings, he argues, enter "into the ways we envisage all our most important problems" (134), particularly for example, "the question of belief". In what sense, for instance, are we to believe the Bible, or the *Divine Comedy*, whose description by Eliot as "one vast metaphor" Richards approvingly quotes? Richards' answer is that:

> There are at least four possible modes of interpretation to be considered . . . And the kinds of believing that will be appropriate will as a rule be different. We can extract the tenor and believe that as a statement; or extract the vehicle; or, taking tenor and vehicle together, contemplate for acceptance or rejection some statement about their relations, or we can accept or refuse the direction which together they would give to our living (134-135).

It is evident that he is using "metaphor" here for the same purposes as he used "fictions" for in *Principles of Literary Criticism*, "pseudo-statements" in *Science and Poetry*, and "myths" in *Coleridge on Imagination*. Just as he made more important the myths of poetry, religion, and metaphysics by stating that all apprehension is myth, so now he makes the metaphors of poetry, religion, and metaphysics vital issues, because all thinking and all language is said to be metaphorical, both of which views he fortifies by references to Bradley's belief in the unavoidability of fictions. In some ways his treatment of metaphor is, as far as his analyses of poetry are concerned, like his treatment of myth, except that in the case of the former he deals with smaller units. But otherwise his treatment of the 'prose sense' in poems of different structure in *Coleridge on Imagination* is very much the paying of attention to the relations of vehicle and tenor and to their combined action. Certainly the aim is the same.

A further example of that over-determination principle we referred to occurs when we find, as an additional reason for the importance of metaphor, the psycho-analytical concept of transference regarded as yet another instance of it. Here indeed we get an explicit claim for Richards' exercises to assist in psychotherapy,

> A 'command of metaphor' . . . can go deeper still into the control of the world that we make for ourselves to live in. The psycho-analysts have shown us with their discussions of 'transference'—another name for metaphor—how constantly modes of regarding, of loving, of acting, that have developed with one set of things or people, are shifted to another. They have shown us chiefly the pathology of these transferences, cases where the vehicle—the borrowed attitude, the parental fixation, say—tyrannizes over the new situation, the tenor, and behaviour is inappropriate. The victim is unable to see the new person except in terms of the old passion and its accidents. He reads the

situation only in terms of the figure, the archetypal image, the vehicle. But in healthy growth, tenor and vehicle—the new human relationship and the family constellation—co-operate freely; and the resultant behaviour derives in due measure from both. Thus in happy living the same patterns are exemplified and the same risks of error are avoided as in tactful and discerning reading.

The general form of the interpretative process is the same, with a small-scale instance—the right understanding of a figure of speech—or with a large-scale instance—the conduct of a friendship (135-136).

"But," he adds, "the literary instance is easier to discuss and more accessible to investigation," therefore

it seems modest and reasonable to hope that a patient persistence with the problems of Rhetoric may, while exposing the causes and modes of the misinterpretation of words, also throw light upon and suggest a remedial discipline for deeper and more grievous disorders; that, as the small and local errors in our everyday misunderstandings with language are models in miniature of the greatest errors which disturb the development of our person- alities, their study may also show us more about how these large-scale disasters may be avoided (136-137).

For all the careful modesty of expression shown here, it does seem to indicate once again the simplicity of the model Richards is working with, that is, the vehicle that is carrying him around. The model is one of *degree* of organisation. The different kinds of organisation, equal as regards complexity, are not distinguished. *What* is organised is not treated as so relevant. Therefore *transfer*, as we saw when considering *Principles of Literary Criticism*, has unlimited scope, and Man can be saved by the right kind of education, one which by the economical means of symbols will make Man's structure correspond to that of the Universe. Fittingly, Richards closes his book with a quotation from the *Timaeus*:

Harmony, having her courses kin unto the revolutions in our Soul, hath been given by the Muses to be a helper to the man who, with understanding, shall use their art, not for the getting of unreasonable pleasure—which is commonly esteemed the use of Music—but for the ordering of the circuit of our Soul which hath fallen out of Harmony, and the bringing thereof into concord with itself . . . Now unto the Divine Part in us the motions that are kin are the Thoughts and Circuits of the All. These must every man follow, that he may regulate the Revolutions in his Head which were disturbed when the Soul was born in the Flesh and by thoroughly learning the Harmonies and Circuits of the All may make that which understandeth like unto that which is understood, even as it was in the beginning; and, having made it like, may attain unto the perfection of that Best Life which is offered unto men by the Gods, for the present time and for the time hereafter (137-138).

2. "INTERPRETATION IN TEACHING", OR THE TRIVIUM SHOULD NOT BE TRIVIAL

To the problems of education and the practices involved in it, Richards turns in his next book, *Interpretation in Teaching* (1938). This book, according to Richards, "came into being under the . . . stimulus of the General Education Board, as a Statement on the application of Theory of Interpretation to General Education". The book was "written for teachers and concerns the layman only in the degree to which he recognises that in the matter of the conduct of our native language we are all our own pupils". It is a sort of *Practical Criticism*[1] applied to prose, reporting the results of presenting a number of passages, which raised various theoretical issues about use of language, to groups of University students, extracts from whose answers are given by way of illustration. Three areas are covered, those of Rhetoric, Grammar, and Logic, which Richards described as "the first three liberal Arts, the three ways to intelligence and a command of the mind that met in the Trivium" (3). It is Good Sense, or Sanity, the mind's order, that we are after, something which, it will be remembered, Coleridge wished to achieve by the not so very different "principles of logic, grammar, psychology". Richards' target is the books used in teaching logic, rhetoric, and grammar at a fairly elementary level. He appears to have made an informal survey of those books and to have found them in many ways wanting. Many of the exercises are concerned with passages taken from these books, and what Richards wants is that his subjects should see through the errors taught by his contemporaries.

Partly, in the exercises, Richards is concerned with a problem which always held his interest, that of comprehension.

I shall offer evidence, in plenty, that passages of ordinary everyday prose of no unusual difficulty whatever, needing no special information or training or any experience which is not commonly assumed to be inevitable, were wildly and inexplicably misread, not by a few stray souls from India who may have been in the audience, but by so many seemingly qualified persons that we can assume no one to be exempt from such aberrations (24).

He appeals further to "every candid teacher . . . [who will know that] the majority of his pupils at the end of all their schooling understand remarkably little of what they hear or read" (v) and is therefore likely to accept his evidence from university students' failures. If we

[1] There is in fact a reference in *Practical Criticism* (page 329) to "some further experiments with the paraphrasing of fairly simple figurative and semi-allegorical passages", which he hoped to report "in a future work".

remember too his strictures against modern literary critics, mentioned towards the end of our consideration of *Coleridge on Imagination*, it will be evident that the communication problem is for him a very big one. But Richards also claims that his results reveal a very large amount of error in *theory*, and in judgment under the guidance of theory, in respect of each of the headings with which the book deals. With regard to this, Richards oscillates, I would say, rhetorically, between two standpoints. According to the one, for all our clumsiness and insensitivity in theorising, we have very considerable skills, which we shall still further improve if we can "translate more of our skill into discussable science"; according to the other, our skills are in fact at a very low level owing to all the misconceptions we hold, which are themselves due to the faulty theories propagated by books used in teaching today.

He brings forward once again arguments on the necessity for learning theory by practising it; it is indeed the aim of his book to show how this can be done by means of exercises such as he presents. One might in fact call this book a case-book to accompany the brief theoretical survey that *The Philosophy of Rhetoric* carried out. Richards has many interesting things to say for teachers in it. Valuable, for instance, is the chapter, "General Attitudes Preventing Approach", where he tackles the problem, with which most teachers must be familiar, of pupils avoiding coming to grips with the problems set, or, as he calls it—and this, as we have seen plays an important part in his theory of poetry and of knowledge—"the remoteness of thought from its subject matter". The best way of tackling this, he suggests, is to show examples of it to the pupils themselves, and Richards then provides documented evidence of various "types of remoteness" such as private fantasy, "the hobby-horse rider", "the fence-sitter", or "the dealer in homely 'common-sense' parallels". Here, as elsewhere in the book, Richards exemplifies the practice he recommends, of publishing "case-histories" in educational journals, describing "plainly and candidly actual procedures followed by teachers in correcting or discussing the composition of their pupils, and detailing the explanations they venture to give of their corrections" (74), instead of all the "repetitive discussions of principles" with which such journals "bulge" at present. With regard to some of his exercises Richards admits, what is always very much to be expected of his approach, that the problems presented were too difficult, at least for the time allowed, and I think it a defect of his approach that he did not interview his subjects to find out further about their answers. He distinguished his approach from that of educational psychology by attacking the latter, suggesting that the labours of psychologists should be confined to research and that teachers would be much better off without it. For Richards, it meant "the replacement of insight into the learning process by a rote acquaintance with the jargon of the subject and its typical formulations", thus providing "an excellent example of the disease of abstractionism with which [educational practice] is perenially afflicted" (11). I cannot help feeling Richards is inconsistent here, judging psychology by the abstractions of possibly bad text-books rather than by the experiences from which such abstractions come. In all his psychologising about perception, thinking, and feeling in their general aspects, one feels the want of detailed, intensive experiencing, in contrast, for instance, to what he says about poetry.

If we turn now to what Richards reports under each of his headings, we can deal rapidly with the first one, Rhetoric, for his concerns here, the different functions of language and, particularly, metaphor, involve theories we have already dealt with fully enough. The two passages he presented to his subjects were each taken from well-known books on English prose style and both criticised examples of metaphorical writing in ways with which Richards himself disagreed. The kinds of misapprehension on his subjects' part that Richards dealt with can best be given in his words. Basically, there was the "assumption that metaphor is only suited to dim, vague, mysterious, inexplicable, intangible, and indefinite matters" (59).

If we add the notions that metaphor is not a serious way of thinking, that metaphors are merely decorative, not structural, in thought, that they are fanciful and, unless used by Poets (and perhaps even then), flimsy, frivolous, irresponsible and unreliable: add in too the associations of the word 'concrete' (hard, solid, heavy, detailed, business-like, suitable for foundations, brute fact) and those of 'abstract' (thin or hot air, remote, empty, invisible, intangible, not to be grasped, sublime, remote) this common assumption or prejudice is not difficult to understand. That it is deplorable and disastrous, that it hinders its victims in acquiring control of an immense range of the most important uses of language and modes of thought, that it deprives them of powers which they badly need, will, I take it, require little showing (60).

Here he evidently does not think existing skills are very great, but believes that by means of the correct theory of metaphor, if practised through judging the metaphors of others and inventing parallel ones of one's own, reading, writing, thinking and living may all grow better, showing a reassociation of sensibility.

3. GRAMMAR AS AUNT SALLY

When we come to the next section, that on Grammar, we find Richards at his most destructive. Indeed, one might call *Interpretation in Teaching* his most destructive work since *The Meaning of Meaning*,

for not only has he, as with *Practical Criticism*, the protocols of his
subjects, with all their errors to deal with, but he also faults many
theorists of his own or past times. He does not simply criticise those
he disagrees with, but presents them as exhibits, though handling
them, when they are not anonymous and not dead, with courtesy,
mitigating his criticism with praise of their worth. It is perhaps his
emphasis on vigilance and awareness that is responsible for this very
critical impression one derives from him. But it is striking how much
he attacks both the past and the fashionable present, whether in
philosophy, in literary theory, or in linguistics, and how, with the
exception of Ogden and perhaps, in his later work, Whitehead, he
seems without allies, as individual in this sense as D. H. Lawrence,
who also stressed so much unique emotion. Richards' heroes are
certain great figures of the past. Coleridge, of course, though even he
was not free from Richards' watchfulness, some of his writings being
taken as exhibits for detailed criticism in the book dealing with him.
Only figures so great and so distant as to be almost legendary—or
should we say very ambiguous?—are free from criticism. Such are
Plato and Aristotle with whom, in his final book, Richards ended in
firm partnership, and such of course his favourites of China.

So when Richards comes to deal with grammar, remembering his
awareness of flux and his hostility to the definite, we are prepared for
the knock-about that follows. "The proposal I make in [this] section",
he writes, "is . . . that as a school subject we replace Grammar by a
study of what Grammar is". This leads immediately to Richards'
third exercise, "a sort of animated cocoanut-shy for our pupils",
consisting of "an exhibition of some of the odd arbitrarinesses and
mistakes of grammarians" (175), which he took "from a mixed
collection of school books and Handbooks for Teachers", explaining
there was "no special significance in the choice [for] there is no lack
of similar examples, similar models of criticism. My difficulty is to
refrain from putting in a bookful"[1] (177).

Richards starts like his and the whole section is studded with
examples of things even the most distinguished grammarians have
said which Richards attacks. The kinds of things they are accused of
are neglecting contextual factors in their analysis of constructions,
uncritical acceptance of usage as a norm, and regarding their classifications and distinctions as absolute rather than as related to
particular purposes. These are specific issues, but by implication it is
suggested that these grammarians are arbitrary, confused, and super-

[1] Richards considers this way of introducing a course on grammar as "excellent
pedagogy". "Formal descriptive grammar", he writes, "generates a resentment
against the grammarian, which is traditional in the subject. I believe that this resentment can be made use of . . ." (175).

ficial. For one thing, they approach the subject macroscopically, dealing with generalities—true on the average, but disturbing for every case of actual detailed interpretation, and misleading because the limits of the application of their statements are not made clear. Their main fault is that they do not approach their subject philosophically, that is to say, that they do not "attend critically to its methods and assumptions" (vii).

Let us consider the three charges brought against grammarians that we have just mentioned.

(i) Richards' first charge against the grammarians is one very familiar to Linguistic Philosophers today. He takes examples of sentences where there has been dispute between grammarians as to their correct construction. In so far as a grammarian, as in Richards' examples, criticises a given construction on the grounds that it changes the meaning of the sentence, it is of course easy for Richards to point out that the meaning depends upon the *use* of the sentence, and this is not given us by merely presenting the sentence in print. It follows that there is no *one* correct construction of any sentence.

A common undiscussed assumption is that for every sentence in a language such as English, an account (in the strictest view, *one and only one* account) can be given, in terms of a limited number of primitive ideas, which is *the correct grammatical account* of its construction. The analogy supporting this assumption is perhaps an analogy with that vague and philosophically hazardous assumption that if we knew enough about the laws of Nature we should find that they could all be stated in terms of a limited number of ideas or axioms. Another analogy might be drawn from the attempts made recently by logicians to derive all mathematics from an initial set of primitive propositions or operations (187).

(ii) The use which is being made of a sentence is not the only factor that has to be taken into account in analysing its construction. There is also the grammarian's purpose in carrying out the analysis. Richards' second charge against the grammarians is that they fail to realise that grammar is studied for many different purposes. This results in their using for one purpose grammatical classifications that have been devised for another.[1] It also makes them think of their classifications as absolute features of language.

Richards carries out a sort of multiple definition of grammar with the aim of showing how many different purposes it is carrying out.

---

[1] I think Richards' is an important point because many subjects are only unitary in the sense that they have been institutionalised. Such institutionalising often results in the application of norms derived from one purpose, which has powerful supporters, to other purposes to which they are less appropriate. It is nevertheless indicative of Richards' attitude that this relativist position is adopted only with regard to grammar and not with regard to philosophy or logic (see pages 9-10, *Basic Rules of Reason*).

He distinguishes between such purposes as, for instance, that of "providing a machine by the aid of which a language may be taught", that of "giving a psychological analysis of the different mental processes . . . supposed to accompany the use of different words and sentences", and that of "providing apparatus by which languages can be compared as regards [various aspects]" (190). The last he seems to consider the "main task" of Grammar and one that chiefly determines the distinctions that are made. These distinctions are however of no use for *his* aim, which is "to aid training in interpretation by which our use of language, both active and passive, might be improved" (190). What the grammarians' distinctions "would tell us about our *use of words*" is something which, in one sense, "we knew, practically, almost all about . . . already" (192). Richards indeed argues that traditional grammar should not be taught at all in the schools except in his negative and destructive sense, or in so far as the conundrums its analyses unwittingly pose, such as whether a given question is factual or purely a matter of definition, provide valuable exercise for schoolboys' or schoolgirls' wits.

It may of course sometimes be necessary to refer to classes of words, but Richards will evidently have nothing to do with formal classes. He suggests that teachers might offer their pupils a very simple fourfold classification of words in terms of the different things they do. Such classes might be "*names pointing to things*, whether material or fictional; *quality* words, by which we further determine what we are pointing to, whether as having a quality or as the object of our feelings; *names of the key acts* in terms of which complex meanings having to do with change may be built up; and *names* of directions in which things are put in motion" (201). "These", Richards adds, "are the categories which Basic [English] offers, in place of the traditional noun, adjective, verb and preposition with which to open up better modes of training in interpretation" (201). One superiority that is claimed for this classification over previous attempts to define in material terms the different parts of speech is based upon its being instrumental rather than mentalistic in approach. It is, we might say, a highly schematic and rather conventional attempt to classify words according to *use*. "Manual acts" (Richards is referring here to the key position played in Basic English by Ogden's 18 verb-operators) "and not Locke's 'clear and distinct ideas' or any other products of cogitation" are "the necessary key terms" because, it is suggested, they are in the ontogenetic sense primary, and therefore, by virtue of a contingent association, simplest of analysis.

Throughout the whole fabric of our meanings the pattern they set persists as essential structure, however much linguistic cross-connections, through metaphor, compression and repeated substitutions, may overlay it. And that in part is why Basic with so few words is able to render the essentials of any English sentence—though frequently neither its feelings nor its sensory charge (202).

(iii) The last aspect of grammar that Richards proposes for destructive study in the school is "the doctrine of usage". Richards' fourth exercise is a passage from Campbell's *The Philosophy of Rhetoric* where Campbell attacks Swift for believing that there were certain absolutes of grammar.

"It is not the business of grammar," the passage begins, "as some critics seem preposterously to imagine, to give law to the fashions which regulate our speech. On the contrary, from its conformity to these, and from that alone it derives all its authority and value." (213, quoted from Campbell).

This Richards presented to his subjects "with . . . an invitation to discuss it as doctrine and as argument." He used the results to demonstrate the many odd, confused and mistaken notions subjects carried from their schooldays about the reasons for our linguistic norms.[1]

Some excerpts from another "book fairly representative of the main tradition in school and college teaching", Gardiner, Kittredge and Arnold's *Manual of Composition and Rhetoric*, are then put into the stocks, and subjected to persistent, often rather captious, criticism. Richards has two main points to make. One, that to define usage in terms of the practice of "the *best* writers", as these authors do, is to beg the question. Two, that since we use language for various purposes it is these that should receive primary consideration.

'*Why* is this sentence right and that sentence wrong, or this arrangement of words better than that?' are questions all want to ask. We damp curiosity when we insist that they must just learn *which* is right. And to fob them off with an answer in terms merely of *usage*, 'It's right because good writers write so! That's *why*!' is a quick way of destroying just that movement of the mind which would be of the most value to it (175).

For this reason the usage doctrine is

on the whole, the most pernicious influence in current English teaching, doing more than all other removable errors together to inhibit the course of self-critical and profitable reflection about the conduct of thought in language (174).

[1] Richards is hardly fair with his subjects. He gave them another exercise together with this one, and only three quarters of an hour was allowed for both. Most of his subjects chose to do the other exercise first, and "the comments on Campbell are mostly short, show evidences of fatigue and content themselves frequently with the first thoughts that came" (215).

Richards' stand on this issue is important and welcome in view of the repeated reassertion of the doctrine of usage by linguists today in a form that seems to deny anybody's right to try to influence the way in which we use language. It is here that Richards' insistence on the philosophic approach most applies. But here also unfortunately we come up against his anti-concrete attitude. Only in *The Philosophy of Rhetoric*, and then rather tortuously, sacrificing definiteness to a sort of super-sensitive balancing act with abstracts, does Richards consider the requirements we make of language. His emphasis in the book now being discussed is so destructive as to give the impression that any kind of normative attitude is wrong; there is so much emphasising individualistic awareness of 'what actually is' that he seems to play into the hands of the usage theorists. In *The Philosophy of Rhetoric* (page 70), Richards writes, the "criteria of words— precision, vividness, expressiveness, clarity, beauty, are representative instances of them—are misleading and unprofitable to study unless we use them with a due recognition of [the] interdependence among the words we use them to describe . . ." In *Interpretation in Teaching*, in taking some similar criteria advanced "within the limits of good usage" in Gardiner, Kittredge and Arnold's book, Richards is only concerned with this negative, critical standpoint,[1] confining the positive aspect of his point of view to such cryptic remarks as "the standard [by which we should judge language] . . . resides in us, as the active principle of communication, and is manifested in our developed skill with words" (278)[2].

Essentially what Richards is saying is that, though the Usage doctrine was a revolt against blind authority determining how we should write, he himself is against the Usage doctrine for similar reasons. Both are cases of an external sanction being imposed, resulting in copying, imitative behaviour. A true Protestant, he believes the criterion to reside within us. The usage theorists were at fault because in their treatment they constantly sounded as though

---

[1] I think it is poor pedagogy so much to emphasise what is incorrect, and a mistake, in *introducing* a different idea, not to be fairly specific in one's examples. Richards is bad at getting down to his readers' level, or in judging just by what amount he should be above them. Or perhaps one should say that in his later books he does not emulate the quality he admires in the greatest works of art, appeal at many different levels.

[2] For instances of the application of his anti-usage view, see his attack on the blurring of the meaning of 'infer' and 'disinterested' in "Notes toward an Agreement between Literary Criticism and Some of the Sciences" in *Speculative Instruments* (1955). Some of the things Fowler says in *Modern English Usage* are also just. Cf., for instance, his comparison of present-day English and American usages of the impersonal pronoun, 'one'. What Fowler says in preferring the more recent English practice seems to me interesting and plausible. He does not however produce evidence for this and other of his assertions, and sometimes this is needed.

words had fixed meanings, for it was in terms of these that what usage was said to be was determined. Theirs was a "macroscopic treatment", true enough perhaps if we interpreted the word's "definite meaning" as "a wide range of different meanings", but different from the microscopic approach that was concerned with these different meanings themselves, "choice between which may entail all the differences between good and bad reading and writing" (266), and which were constantly being increased as with "new settings" we "forced new meanings".

But, it may be asked, if the macroscopic treatment was true when properly interpreted, why does Richards attack *it* rather than the misinterpretation of it? He introduces his discussion of it by saying that "the usage controversy can be made to yield insight into a type of interpretative situations", namely one of "cross-purposed disputes", the "type . . . which arises when a traditional, macroscopic or distant treatment is challenged by the elaborated distinctions of a relatively microscopic analytic study" (265). This seems to suggest that, despite the hard things Richards says about it, he really accepts the theory. It differs from and does not really contradict his own view.

Three things can be said about this. Firstly, that, because of his theory of interpretation, Richards' attitude to any theory is ambivalent, since it is always open to him to say that it derives from certain 'facts of mind' and that the words it uses have different meanings from those used by the people who would contradict the theory. Secondly, Richards evidently believes that the proponents of the usage theory misinterpreted it themselves. And thirdly, as we have seen, he is always in favour of a more microscopic approach and presumably believes that only this, which gives us a view of the fluidity and sensitivity of language, can help us in reading and writing. And certainly it is this microscopic approach concerned with word-meanings that he puts forward as the *positive* grammar that should be taught in our schools. He defines grammar, whose purpose for him, we will remember, was "to aid training in interpretation . . .", as "for *our* purposes, nothing but *the study of the co-operation of words with one another in their contexts*" (16). Let us see what this positive conception of grammar involves.

4. ONLY MICROSCOPIC GRAMMAR IS GOOD

Richards' fourth exercise, where his subjects have to comment on the passage from Campbell, apart from showing the confused notions they hold about language, reveals something else that appears to have surprised and even shocked Richards:

With an almost perfectly straightforward very lucid and forcible piece of debater's prose, an appreciable proportion of the readers failed at certain points to make out *in the least* what was being said (215).

Richards decided that the main reasons for this were that they were misled by the Proper Meaning superstition or read sentences in isolation from the rest of the passage, failed, that is to say, to perceive the dependence of a word's meaning on the larger units of which it formed part. To counter this failing, Richards provided a detailed analysis of what Campbell was doing with his main words in the first paragraph of the passage, part of which we shall describe so as to provide an example of Richards' "microscopic" approach in action.

The first use of the word 'grammar', in the passage from Campbell, Richards described as one

we must frequently make, at the beginning of a discussion, of words with challengeable and disputable senses—that is of nearly all words but those for concrete things and acts. It is the use of a word prior to fixing any specific sense for it; a sort of reservation we make with it—without having settled yet, for the company or even necessarily for ourselves, who is going to be the passenger (247).

This use Richards dubbed the "Mesopotamian use", after the story of the old woman who "found great support in that blessed word 'Mesopotamia' ", the point being that nobody knew "what she meant by the blessed word".

This technicality is a device for drawing attention to the process by which, as we read on, the meanings we are already trying out, in some degree, for the words, hang in suspense, alternate, merge in, lapse—in a score of ways respond to (as they reciprocally prepare) the following meanings. Few words keep to a Mesopotamian use for more than a very brief moment, and we may have to make an effort to get back to it, when we need to. Some passenger, more or less definite (in several of the senses of 'definite'), almost at once occupies the berth: and we cannot too much realise how complex these dramas between rival tenants, all of whom hold tickets they believe to be valid, sometimes are. The Conductor goes by what the other passengers think, and they change their minds. As for the Engine Driver, well, the train only travels so far as the passengers agree about something! Thus two very different things may be called 'the argument'. One is this drama, the process of interpretation in action. The other is a resultant of it—what finally we take to be what the statements say, when we have settled, if we ever do, what that is—which then gives a definite meaning to each key-word. A key-word is one which thenceforward (unless the writer shifts it or the reader muddles) carries, packed up as part of its meaning, something that has been said with its aid in the passage (248).

Richards' analysis of Campbell's passage reaches its climax with his assertion that Campbell had been caught in "the great snare of

116

language", that is, "the confusion between a definition and a statement that is not about the use of words". This, as we know, is a
favourite linguogenetic error with Richards, and he gives other
examples of it in this book. In Campbell's case, he points out that
Campbell's view of grammar—"a collection of general observations
methodically digested" rather than, what "some critics seem preposterously to imagine" an authority that "gives law to the fashions
which regulate our speech"—was in fact inconsistent. By the very
usage doctrine that Campbell was advocating, the "preposterous"
meaning of 'grammar' was correct, so that Campbell was in fact
proposing to change usage. Neither Campbell nor his readers—for
hardly any of Richards' audience had any real qualms about the
doctrine Campbell was advancing—were aware of those shifts in
meaning which enabled such a thing to happen. "There is nothing,
alack! unusual about such a manoeuvre in argument. Logically, it is
fatal; rhetorically it is often triumphant." "The peculiar half-way-
between, looking both-ways, position", that the unconscious combin-
ing of an empirical assertion with a definition brings about, "gives
[the statement] both its seeming truth and its seeming content, its
plausibility and its air of saying something" (256).

Richards then restates his view about what happens in reading,
putting it into general form by the use of symbols, and emphasising
the importance of setting. It is here he suggests his jelly model of
language. ". . . In most ordinary discourse the individual words have
no constant, separable, definite meaning. They cooperate with the
other words to carry jointly a total meaning for the whole sentence.
Change the sentence and they are no longer doing the same work"
(261). Both as writers and as readers we have to watch carefully what
is happening all the time, something which the usage view discourages,

for if we feel usage is looking after and regulating the 'significations' of
words, we are inclined to feel less distinctly that we are giving a word its
meaning (arranging by the setting how it shall be understood) and are more
apt to assume that it comes to us with a normal and already settled meaning
. . . Similarly the usage-indoctrinated reader tends to take it as backed up so,
without looking to see just which of the countless usages is doing the
backing (256).

"Only the context", Richards says, "can tell us, if anything can, that
this identification of the meanings of a part of the sentence and of the
rest of it has occurred" (263)—that is to say, whether in a particular
instance we have to do with a definition or a statement.

I have quoted in some detail what Richards writes about his positive
substitute for grammar in order to emphasise it and to reveal more
concretely its nature. It is an approach much influenced, as I have

already suggested by his view of poetry. There is, for instance, "the drama of interpretation". It is a drama for him because, as we shall see when we come to consider *How To Read a Page*, he thinks reading should be accompanied by an interior dialogue in which the alternative meanings are constantly questioned and argued about. It is this, "the drama over the berths", rather than the actual outcome (the other sense of 'argument' in the passage quoted above), that "is the all important thing . . . in most interesting discussion, certainly in all, these discussions about language, in criticism, psychology, logic rhetoric and grammar". The connection with the valuable activity of the imagination in poetry and its effect on growth is evident.

But another effect of his study of poetry is shown in the emphasis upon setting. In *The Meaning of Meaning*, stress was laid upon context, upon tracing what was said back to the actual sign-situation of which it was an abbreviation. Richards did not mean that any genetic psychological investigation should in fact be carried out, only that we should *realise* that for complete understanding this would be necessary. But *now* the emphasis upon the shiftiness of words is less on the grounds of the individual user's history than on those of the interdependency of everything. This view, as we saw, was prepared for Richards by Coleridge both in his philosophy and, specifically, in the distinction between Imagination and Fancy; it was then applied in general to language in *The Philosophy of Rhetoric*. Testimony to the importance of 'setting' is made by Richards' adoption of this word in the book we are now considering to save it from being confused with his use of 'context'. He implies that such confusion was due to poor reading by reviewers of his previous book. But there can be no doubt that since *The Meaning of Meaning* he constantly used 'context' in its ordinary sense. Indeed I think he still does in the present book, as the statement quoted the page before, that only "the *context* can tell us" whether a given sentence is a definition or not, suggests.

To increase readers' awareness of these fluctuations of meanings with different settings, Richards appeals once again to Basic English, suggesting that some exercises should be carried out in it. These are translations of passages from ordinary English into Basic, and the matching of, or inventing of parallels for, sentences which use the same word in different successive senses, by sentences using another word. Partly, Richards thinks that since Basic has a smaller vocabulary, its words will have to play a larger number of roles; translation into these will intensify our awareness of multiple meaning. Further, he thinks that it will be more difficult to shirk analysing the meaning than in translation where such restrictions do not operate. "An alert questioning of the whole intention of the original must be maintained throughout. Routine, word-for-word translation—of the de-coding, mechanical type—soon fails in Basic—through not making sense", for "there is hardly ever a safe, mechanical, single word equivalent, or a regular phrase equivalent, for even the most frequent English clichés" (203).

Fundamentally, *Richards loves Basic* because of the analysis of the language the construction of it involved. We have already referred to his remarks on the *primacy* of 'manual acts' and how, on his metaphoric view, these provided the vehicle for other acts, particularly those of the mind. Thus using Basic should heighten our awareness of the omnipotence of metaphor. The versatility of its key words gives insight into structure. ". . . Basic, since it has to exploit its few words to the most varied advantage, turns them and twists them and gives us good reason to see what they will and will not do", so that "learning to write in Basic, under the disguise of a game, is an exploration of the most important devices of English syntax. . . . Basic deserves its name, because its constructions and vocabulary are the foundation of the language" (208). This theme is destined, we shall see, for development in Richards' next and last book.

This completes what we have to say on the Grammar section of Richards' book, but before we go on to the section on Logic, let us consider for a while some of the assertions Richards has been making.

5. BUT WAS RICHARDS RIGHT?

We will start with a fairly obvious point. Richards suggests that it is unnecessary to teach formal grammatical analysis in our schools because it is something we already know in our use of language. Clearly he means that this knowledge is implicit. But we have already seen that a major purpose of the book, indeed of Richards' whole approach, is to recommend instruction in theory, of which we already show a high degree of implicit knowledge, on the grounds that *further* advances in our skill require it. Why then should the kind of information that systematic grammatical analysis provides be avoided in the teaching of English? Presumably because it is formal; that is to say, does not deal with *meanings*. I should have thought however that if syntax needs to be taught, then there needs to be some neutral way of referring to words. To identify a word as a noun or a verb is to identify, in general, its formal properties. Without doubt there are better grammatical classifications, but the traditional one is superior to any that classifies words in terms of use, because such classes have no exact and simple relationship with any formal classes[1]—or perhaps one should say, its exceptions are more easily

---

[1] Richards himself makes this point in discussing the relation of logic and grammar.

memorised than those of any material classification that is precise enough to be practicable.

Richards may of course not mean his recommendation about not teaching traditional grammar to be taken literally. He might rephrase his objection as one against too great concentration on grammar in schools at present. But I think his bias is very evident. Grammar, in part, is stated to be either irrelevant or ridiculous. The latter charge is often put forward in a way that offends against his own canons of interpretation. It is a feature of his exercises that only short passages can be presented for criticism. When his intention is hostile, it is very easy to give an impression of arbitrariness by this device. By omitting the historical and theoretical context, Richards makes the grammarians look like muddled pedants.[1] Similar considerations apply to the "cocoa-nut-shy" with which he starts the section. The exhibits he presents are criticisms of the grammatical construction of short extracts. I believe the comments he makes are just, but, except in the case of a perverse criticism of a beautiful piece of observation by Ruskin, the examples he gives are trivial. Indeed, with this one exception, *all* the pieces of writing he defends against grammarians in this book are undistinguished, and not such that they could not be improved.

Richards' attitude can perhaps best be shown by considering one of his examples. We will not take those of his "cocoa-nut-shy" because these belong more to the section on rhetoric, since it is the metaphors that are chiefly criticised. But in the last chapter of the section, a passage from J. S. Mill's Inaugural Lecture at St. Andrews University, presenting grammar as "the most elementary part of logic", is examined, and the opening sentence considered as "an illustration of the control of the setting over interpretation" (281). The sentence reads,

Even as mere languages, no modern European language is so valuable a discipline to the intellect as those of Greece and Rome, on account of their regular and complicated structure (280).

It is the setting, Richards claims, that tells us that "the regular and complicated structure" refers to Greek and Latin and not to any "modern European language". He will have nothing to do with any suggestion that the grammar of the sentence might have been better.

[1] One example of this is Richards' critical treatment of a statement by Jespersen concerning the status of relative clauses when used as "primaries", as in 'Who steals my purse steals trash'. Jespersen argues that the relative clause, and not some "imaginary *he*", is the subject in this example. Richards accuses him of confusing (i) a definition with an assertion, and (ii) a psychological statement with one about the structure of language. But surely what Jespersen is doing is rejecting an analysis that attempts to bolster up a theory by the *ad hoc* device of an assumed ellipsis.

"The pedants with whom we began this Part could doubtless complain of the sentence as faulty in form, and ask us to rewrite it:

Even as mere languages, those of Greece and Rome, on account of their regular and complicated structure, are a better discipline to the intellect than any modern European language (282).

Though Richards agrees that this "would certainly throw less responsibility on the setting", he rejects it on the grounds that "it would alter Mill's emphasis". Obviously it is the 'jelly' model that is operating again, according to which any alteration—and better ones than his Aunt Sally are conceivable—brings about a change. It suggests the attitude to reading that comes from poetry, one that ignores the greater element of redundancy, the less close-knit structure, we generally have in prose. We are reminded also of his attitude to syntax, which we remarked on in *Coleridge on Imagination*, an attitude that would scarcely regard grammatical prescription in a favourable light. It is in this section indeed that Richards makes the statement about writing that we have already quoted (page 81).

This attitude of Richards combines in its effect with another, namely, his fear of being definite, which prevents him from being at all explicit about the criteria which should govern our use of words (see page 114 above). Here we are reminded of what he said in *Practical Criticism* about judging poetry—"no theory, no description . . . can be trusted which is not too intricate to be applied". Or, as he puts it at the end of his section on Grammar in the book we are now examining, the first moral "that I find in the discussions of this Grammar Section [is] . . . that old one again, that the pupil must . . . be his own adviser" (293). But the consequence of this is that, just as with the usage doctrine, "Whatever is, is right", the only difference being that "what is" is likely to be much more complex and idiosyncratic than it was with the usage doctrine. And this of course serves to make Richards' view, that we need to cultivate our skills of interpretation, all the more right.

6. LOGIC AT SCHOOL

The section on logic differs from the other two in the sense that, logic not being a conventional school subject, there is no mention of books used specifically in teaching English at school[1]. But Richards believes that a consideration of logic is required by the other two sections. It is important, for instance, to distinguish grammar from logic. Mill's Inaugural Lecture provides Richards with a splendid specimen to

---

[1] Two books seem however to have been specially considered. These are J. N. Keynes' *Formal Logic*, and Susan Stebbing's *A Modern Introduction to Logic* (1930).

effect the transition from the former to the latter subject, since Mill virtually claims that Greek and Latin in their syntax embody universal logic and therefore provide valuable teaching matter in the school.

The connection of logic with rhetoric is suggested by Richards' definition of logic as "the Art or discipline of managing our sortings" (16). Because "all thinking is sorting", it will be remembered, thinking was for Richards "radically metaphoric", though, in the section on Rhetoric, Richards in fact concentrated on metaphor in the usual sense of that word.

Some figures of speech can be translated into relatively non-figurative language with ease, others only with difficulty and some perhaps not at all. Such translation exercises . . . are an invaluable device for redirecting attention to what is being said and how it is being understood. They lead naturally and insensibly into Logic. I might equally say that Logic, for our purposes, is just a more thorough inquiry into these translations. For example, if we try to say what is said in one metaphor by means of another metaphor . . . we find ourselves really studying in the most practical and immediate way the process of *abstraction* itself. And to ask whether or not a parallel, e.g.

> Meaning is an arrow which reaches is mark when least encumbered with feathers

really supports the view it is introduced to state, or whether it weakens it unnecessarily, is a better exercise in argument than any that formal instruction in the syllogism provides (15).

What Richards says here indicates how well he can tolerate ambiguity. The exercise he mentions is described with others and documented by the subjects' protocols in an appendix. Whether it is to be treated as Rhetoric or as Logic is left indeterminate.

Having committed himself to having a section on logic, Richards, is faced with the question—What out of all that logic offers should he choose for his ends in teaching the theory of interpretation?

Most logic-teaching has failed in the past because the students have had to learn a doctrine before they realised, in their own experience, how interesting and important the questions were that the doctrine was trying to explain. I shall, therefore, be studying here the presentation of only a few typical logical problems, and the presentation rather than the problems themselves or their treatment (301).

Not surprisingly Richards concentrates on definition. He tackles it in three ways.

(i) He starts off with an exercise, which in effect asked the subjects to detect when a sentence embodied a definition and when a statement. This confronted his subjects with the issue that so much concerned Richards, namely, the confusion of a definition with an assertion, of which, we will remember, he accused Hulme in the section on Rhetoric, and Jespersen and Campbell in the Grammar section. The exercise appropriately enough involved a multiple definition of a *logical* word, 'is', the subjects being required to "distinguish between the uses of 'is' in [six different sentences], and say which, if any, [they] take to be true by definition". Richards was able to show from the answers to this exercise that many subjects believed both that there was a correct use of 'is' and that one of the sentences probably exemplified it. The subjects were not very good at detecting which of the sentences was in fact a definition, but judging by their comments it looks very much as though many of them had not understood (see page 145 below). Richards in fact referred to "several [subjects] who took 'true by definition' not as applying to the sentences as wholes but to some supposed true or 'correct' use of is" (306). Richards makes a lot of this, but I think this would not have happened if he had simply asked in a straightforward way which of the sentences was a definition. Richards then listed eight different uses of 'is' and suggested that there were in addition "a large number of minor jobs" it could do, and that in any occurrence of the word it was probably fulfilling several different uses simultaneously.

(ii) Richards then writes about "logical machinery" and "its uses", very largely from the point of view of definition. His approach is somewhat old-fashioned and, as he says, "highly simplified", showing a marked preference for dichotomous classification.

He starts off with "a sketch of an . . . exposition of some of the more important uses of the chief terms we may employ in analyzing meanings" (347). These terms are presented dichotomously as being concerned either with "what we are talking of" or with "what we are saying about it"—with an "it" and the "sort" we put it in—, and include such pairs as "subject, predicate", "substance, attribute", "particular, universal", "class, characteristic". Richards emphasises that the words for one or the other purpose are not exact synonyms, and promises a "natural history classification of their varied uses in ordinary speech and thought", but disappointingly this yields little more than a pageful ringing connotational changes, such as

Attribute . . . has often a strong suggestion that what is thought, or said to be so, is not so, or may not be (from 'attributed to Shakespeare', and so on) and sometimes an equally strong 'of course' gesture ('to bear a club is an attribute of Hercules; being Hercules, he has his club, of course'). This can go further to suggest that a thing's attributes are what make it what it is, that is, are among its defining properties" (361).

He distinguishes the terms 'connotation' and 'denotation', and, in doing so, talks about the difference between 'concrete' and 'abstract names', something which enables him to repair a deficiency (like the belief that metaphors were always concrete) that he felt was particularly marked in the subjects' answers in the exercises in the Rhetoric section.

One might think that the very simple structure implied in these distinctions would not recommend itself to Richards with his functional emphasis. It is surprising too that he should now seem to accept the "traditional account" of meaning in terms of connotation and denotation that *The Meaning of Meaning* wished to demolish. Richards however is none the less alert to the dangers of this. He still refers to the operation of Word Magic, and though no longer a Nominalist, is very much on his guard against a purely language-engendered Realism. He makes indeed a sweeping condemnation of "elementary Logic" because, "by the way it talks about terms and by the choice of examples", it "does little or nothing but encourage" us to "mistake the forms of speech for the forms of thought", to take as "an account of some very fundamental facts about language and how it works [what is no more than] a tricky set of suggested definitions to be used only for certain purposes of analysis" (374). Logicians, in other words, are accused of the same kinds of things grammarians were accused of.

Apart from general theoretical arguments, in which he distinguishes (another dichotomy) logical from descriptive words, and, on the same lines as Wittgenstein and Carnap, warns his readers against asking 'What is . . .?' questions about universal words in the way we ask them about object words, Richards deals with the dangers of misleading talk in two ways.

The first of these is "defensive excursions illustrating how [these terms] should *not* be employed and trying to say why" (347). These are lengthy and confusing digressions in which extracts from the books of Jevons and, particularly, J. N. Keynes, dealing with the relationship between abstract and concrete names, denotation and connotation, "things" and attributes, are subjected to considerable critical comment. As in the Grammar section, Richards recommends this as a pedagogic exercise, though I would have thought this would result in training in attack, in heresy-hunting rather than in understanding, amongst his students.

Even at the time Richards was writing, the logicians he was attacking were somewhat of the past. But then so, perhaps, was the "logical machinery" he recommends. He does however refer to more modern logicians, and it is interesting to notice how much more respectful Richards' tone is with them than with the Grammarians or the more old-fashioned logicians. His attitude is that what they are doing, the simplifications they inevitably employ, are relevant to their purposes,

124

but these are not his. Nor of course will he have anything to do with logical symbolism or with any solution to the confusion of grammar with logic which works by "deriving our syntax from logic". Richards is only concerned with ordinary language, in which "we apprehend, and respond to, far more connections in the discourse than anything but an intolerably prolix analysis . . . can display" (257).

> . . . the logical use of words, with single constant senses that are the same for each recurrence, maintained unchanged through a series of sentence manipulations, . . . is no more like our usual ways of talking than the goose-step is like our strolling gait (256).

Somewhat contrarily, he criticises Russell's theory of descriptions in so far as it aimed at preventing anybody from believing that, "because we can talk of a thing, it therefore must 'exist' to be talked of". "But did anyone who was not stuck fast in an injudiciously technicalised set of words ever suppose anything of the sort? In interpreting ordinary fluid language with full settings there is no need for these ingenious devices" (332). Awareness of the different meanings of 'is', he suggests, is all that we require. This is indeed one of those occasions when one feels that Richards has created a theory which enables him to criticise or praise anyone he wishes according to his passing desire. A writer may be faulted; or he may be saved by an interpretation that refers back to the 'facts of mind' from which his statement derives. In this case, logicians are taken to be at fault, but in other places Richards himself warns the lay reader against equally unlikely errors. Richards is balancing on an unstable log that one moment flatters our intuitive skills, another, tut-tuts our clumsiness. At one moment, he is shocked at how badly we read, and at the next, he is asserting that "we are all, at times, consummate practical logicians".

Richards' second way of dealing with the dangers of misleading talk, which these last remarks have anticipated, is dealing in a microscopic way with particular examples, which he recommends the reader to practise.

> every sentence we reflect upon brings up questions about the choice of a logical form for it, and . . . *that* can never be settled apart from its purposes and occasions. Thus, . . . every sentence can be made a lesson in logic; and the best sentences for that purpose are not those of philosophy but those of everyday life, for with them we are all, at times, consummate practical logicians. To control our skills a little more constantly is all we need (367).

It is because of his concern with ordinary language that Richards so frequently, from *The Meaning of Meaning* on, criticises theories as artificial or arbitrary. Naturalism, rather than realism, is what he values. Nevertheless the specimen sentences whose logical form he considers—'Diogenes is wise', 'Chalk is white', and 'Shakespeare wrote a good poem'—do not have a high degree of verisimilitude. The purpose of his procedure is once again to show that the analysis will vary according to the meaning of the words, and what they mean is a function of our purpose in using the sentence containing them. Thus 'poem' in his last example must be taken as having different meanings according to the purpose of the literary critic making that statement—"social, suasive, literary, comparative, analytic, scientific . . .". Literary criticism, like grammar, has different purposes, and, as with grammar, much unnecessary controversy comes from their being crossed. "Undoubtedly", therefore, "it would be healthy for literary studies, if the different logical forms of 'Shakespeare wrote a good poem', appropriate for different purposes, were more widely recognised" (369).

But the logical form we give to a sentence or to a word not only varies with the writer's purposes; it can also vary according to how we "like to take it", that is to say, according to the setting we like to assume for it. Richards' approach here is the same as that he adopted with regard to grammatical analyses of sentences. One example he gives is that of whether we take a proper name (like 'Diogenes' in 'Diogenes is wise') as a "pure proper name", or whether we "take it as more than a mere name, as carrying with it a further description" (362). This is reminiscent of Richards' earlier distinction concerning whether we take a word as the mere printed mark or sound, or whether we take it "as containing in itself a part or whole of the meaning we give to it." Another example is provided in his view that any sentence, containing what he calls the 'is' of "connection", can be taken as a class-membership sentence, one of predication, or as relational. "If we like, that is, if we find it helpful, we can take any word or phrase as covering a certain field of things"; "if we like, instead, we can take our words as being handles to properties"; and "if we like, we can take a third way of explaining what IS does here. We can take it as a mark of relation" (325). For instance, we can take 'chalk is white' not as predicating a colour of chalk, but as stating that it is a member of the class of white things, or we can take the sentence as relational, because we are thinking of the various conditions which are implied, such as the state of health of the percipient, the conditions of illumination and so on. Likewise we can think of 'chalk' more or less abstractly or concretely, rather than tying these distinctions (with Richards' logicians) to "whether a word is put as a subject or as an attribute in a sentence" (380).

These examples illustrate well the subjectivity of Richards' approach when he takes up logic again. They also show how he continues to make do with a structurally rather barren and rigid set of distinctions for dealing with meaning in ordinary language by suggesting that there is an infinity of intermediate positions between any two members of one of his dichotomous pairs, any of which positions the *same* expression may at any time occupy. The combination of individuality with poor articulation is highly characteristic.

(iii) The third way in which Richards tackles definition in his Logic section is by dealing with the process itself. This he does in his significantly titled last chapter, "Freedom in Definition", of which it might be said that this was practically all it was about.

Richards starts off promisingly:

> The flounderings of the protocols show how frequently people do not know what they are talking about: in this sense, that they cannot separate *the properties which determine the thing they are talking about* from other properties which may or may not belong to it *without* its being thereby any less itself. They wobble in a fatal indecision as to which exactly of the things they happen to know about a thing they will include *in* it, and constantly use accidents, or inessential properties, as defining 'its very nature'. The process, then, of clearing up their views must be that of giving them increased power to form new and better arranged *things* to think about (382).

Anyone who has taught a social science and has had any sort of philosophical training must agree with Richards on this. Our expectations, however, are to be disappointed. Richards concludes the paragraph we have just quoted from with these words:

> Or, rather, of making them recognise that what they mean by a word is within their own control—not given them inexorably by the language. And that in their choices here they create the things they are talking about.

What follows is largely a tussle with Miss Stebbing, who was guilty of "doubting" "whether the giving of typical examples [i.e. 'ostensive definitions'] can be *rightly* regarded as a process of defining"[1] (386). This, since she also referred to "what is ordinarily meant by definition", was attempted "*legislation*", and of course condemned. Richards argues *per contra* that we should accept, as definitions, "ostensive definitions", since this would help to prevent the logician's "definitions . . . from remaining merely a circular system of more or less complex equivalent symbols" (388). Indeed, he recommends extending the meaning of 'expression' in "equivalent expression" "to include any act whatever that may be found (in a given setting) a useful way of indicating the sense of a word" (389), a recommendation similar in intention to his suggestion that the Basic English word classifications in terms of *acts* should be used instead of the traditional ones. In this

[1] Quoted by Richards (italics supplied) from L. S. Stebbing, *A Modern Introduction to Logic*, (1930).

way Richards demonstrates his view that, subject to the needs of communication, we are free to use words as we wish, and that a definition is not a statement, but "an invitation, a request, or, on occasion, an imperative", though in his treatment, one might add, very much the first of these three.

This concludes my summary of Richards' Logic section. I find it the most disappointing of all the sections, largely because, through teaching, I have most experience of the needs that have to be met here. Certainly, the pessimistic view Richards has of our general lack of ability at handling abstract words that his protocols gave him, is a true one. But his, despite its length, sketchy account, his poorly articulated somewhat conventional conceptual scheme, his over-emphasis on microscopic observation of the *individual* detail, the absence of a sense of significance, reduce considerably, it seems to me, the value of his positive contribution.

Partly, perhaps, these characteristics, which are present in all his writing, are a matter of temperament. We have from time to time commented on how difficult Richards often is to understand, odd, particularly in view of his mission. Richards himself frequently shows some awareness of this, defending himself with such comments as, "it is the prime difficulty of the whole undertaking that the thoughts we most need are those that are hardest to elicit" (vi). But it is in this book, where he attempts direct contact with the targets of his endeavours, that he most reveals the gap that separates himself from them. Though the protocols of his subjects reveal in detail widespread inability to talk about language in a theoretical way, one is also struck by the extent of his *surprise* at the degree of confusion the protocols show. He often overestimates what his audience can do, presenting them with exercises that were too difficult; there is quite a degree of misunderstanding of the *instructions* for his exercises; his subjects frequently show they are wrestling with problems of a more elementary nature than the questions he in his writings has been concerned with; and there seems also to be evidence of his subjects' having misunderstood what he had been lecturing to them about. It is Richards' way to find virtue in confronting this and to renounce hope of short-cuts to the solution of the problems presented. But with all his emphasis on empiricism and experiencing, is there not an inconsistency—particularly in view of the importance he attributes to these matters —in his failure to work again at the less successful exercises, to interview the subjects as indeed he himself recommends, and in the light of this to alter and develop his exercises, so that he could have more faith in them before passing them on to teachers, and so that he could have communicated more of the expertise he himself might have gained in working on them?

Richards' books read as though, for them to have their energy, there has to be a marked element of spontaneity in the writing of them. There is something of a fling in Richards' writing, and, as such, it is exhilarating. One does not want to clip his wings, but to provide more power to his flight. Need for freedom is one of the keys to understanding Richards. It explains, I believe, not only his refusal to be imprisoned in an office life of fact-collecting, but also his looseness of form. His hostility to grammatical prescriptions, to writing in *conformity* with 'usage', his description of any attempt to amend syntax to the form of logic as "regimentation into uniformity," of the "logical use of words" as "the goose step", his stressing of *freedom* in defining—"the more optative our view of definition, the more humane Logic becomes"—all these tell their tale. It is true that the circumstances of the time at which he wrote the book may have caused him to accentuate this emphasis. "Today's battle for the cultural domination of the world is being conducted upon strategic principles implied in the rival answers to the last questions", he wrote at the end of the Rhetoric section, referring to the questions he had been discussing there, adding that "Neither Hitler nor Mussolini have underestimated them" (170). And in the brief codas at the end of the other two sections, also, there are references to "the ruling madmen", to the "factual manipulations and indoctrination [that] so hold the field today". Perhaps the urgency was such that there was no time for more patient and laborious methods. But I do not think such an excuse can altogether explain what Richards does. There are always references in his books to the world's condition, and his emphases are the same throughout. We have only to compare, for instance, his stress on *choice* in deciding the merit of a poem with his equal stress on *choice* in definition, to see that this is his native language. But it can be argued, as I shall attempt to do later, that there is some *excess* in his freedom-needs.

7. "HOW TO READ A PAGE", OR WORD BY WORD

Richards' experience of his subjects' protocols, as we saw, impressed him with the extent to which bad reading existed. We are therefore prepared for the title of his last book, *How To Read a Page: A Course in Effective Reading with an Introduction to a Hundred Great Words* (1943). The title is a parody of Mortimer J. Adler's *How To Read a Book* (1940) with its introduction to a "Hundred Great Books", the point of the parody lying in Richards' stress on the microscopic approach, which inevitably requires concentration on smaller units.

The first part of the book contains a 'page' or two from Aristotle and Whitehead which are exercises for the reader to practise reading on. The topics they deal with are those of perception and abstraction, processes themselves involved in the very reading of the passages. The reader is practising them as he reads them, but for full benefit to be derived from this he must, Richards stresses once again, pay attention to what he is doing. To assist him in this, Richards adds a translation of the passage into Basic English and comments, comparing translation with original, on key points. The passages are, as may be expected, very difficult (though perhaps not so difficult as the second part of the book itself) and Richards admits this, excusing himself on the ground that these provide the best practice and that "it is the difficulties of reading we are studying". "It is the hard sentences and hard paragraphs which can do us good, as readers; our mental gums need strengthening" (78).

This contrasts with the current approach to the teaching of comprehension. One has only to think of the neat gobbets of factual writing of which most comprehension tests are composed to be aware of the difference. There is something to be said for Richards' criticism, though not, I believe, for his practice, which exhibits an astonishing unawareness of what can be expected, *from the start*, of the average student. His freedom, in comparison with that of designers of comprehension material, he owes partly to his willingness to recognise that there is no one certain and correct interpretation.

With the pages which on a long view have mattered most to the world . . . we may reasonably doubt whether there is one right and only right reading. These greatest sayings of man have an inexhaustible fertility. Different minds have found such different things in them that we would be very rash if we assumed that some one way of reading them which commends itself to us is the right one (11).

Whatever the value of this view, there can be little doubt that it is their desire to be objective and to quantify that limits the scope of comprehension tests at present.

In conformity with his approach, Richards cuts across "the conception of comprehension" of "the massed professional teachers of the reading art", by opposing their concern with increasing speed of reading. "Most of us" he says, "read too fast rather than too slowly", and "anything that is worth *studying* should be read as *slowly* as it will let you, and read again and again till you have it by heart" (42). Richards adds for good measure that reading aloud, subvocal reading, or reading so as to produce "images of the speech movements and of the sound of the words" (40)[1], are often of assistance to better understanding, as well as reacting by "anything from ejaculations,

---

[1] Much psychological evidence suggests in fact that there is no difference between this and subvocal reading.

130

delighted or derisory, to an analytic commentary" whilst the reading is going on.

Reactions such as these on the reader's part are designed to assist that continuous activity in the mind that led to Richards' praise of the imagination. Learning depends on doing, for, though "bad theory does lead to bad reading, . . . good theory will not necessarily produce good reading" (19). But, as we know, Richards' expectations from improved reading were much larger than those that normally exercise educationalists in their work on comprehension. The greater our mastery of words, for Richards, the greater our total good. Words were the means by which we could adjust to the complexity of reality. And the passages used for exercises, as well as additional ones on the related topic of learning, although concerned with our traffic with the world through our senses, were all applied by Richards to the learning of the meanings of words as well. Just as he defined 'Nature' after the paradigm of 'word' in *Coleridge on Imagination*, so here he transposes a passage from Whitehead on how we abstract from our projective view of Nature (Nature, Sense II—see page 72 above) the emotionally neutral view subserving science (Nature, Senses III or IV), into one on how we abstract the "Proper Meaning" from words which in the concrete circumstances of actual use vary, according to the user's purposes, from this "Proper Meaning". As Richards said in *The Philosophy of Rhetoric* (page 12) "the way I propose to treat meanings has its analogues with Mr. Whitehead's treatment of things", adding, "no one to whom Berkeley has mattered will be very confident as to which is which". This theme, on which we have already said something, is the major one of *How To Read a Page*. The systematising of sense impressions into universals[1] with which the passage from Aristotle deals, and "the growth of these connections with one another" in the soul, is what by means of multiple definition of some of his "A Hundred Great Words" Richards wishes to bring about in the reader.

These multiple definitions are the subject of the second part of this book, but before describing these, it is necessary to go into a little more detail about what Richards' purposes are in making them. He wants of course to combat the 'Proper Meaning' theory, because this view leads to misreading and misthinking. The main reason why words vary in meaning is, as we have seen, the different purposes of their users. But purpose, which has always to be taken into account in interpreting, may itself mislead us, the readers, by causing us to

---

[1] For Richards this view is not incompatible with his stress on thought and perception being abstract that he developed in *The Philosophy of Rhetoric*. The point here is that though we from the first respond according to 'universals', our *recognition* of what is common to a number of experiences still has to be achieved.

misinterpret in order to fulfil certain needs of our own. Richards gives an example of such misreading in an attack by Collingwood on McDougall's exposition of the concept of trial and error learning. Collingwood's misreading is presented as an example of "desire overruling reason", an instance of

the immemorial warfare of the head and the heart which rages everywhere, from that high abstract plane on which it enters into the discussion of itself to the most concrete matter of choosing to give one or other of two meanings to a word (73).

"In every pulse of the reading process", Richards adds,

intellect and will come together and what the outcome shall be is constantly the reader's problem (73).

Richards sets himself against the irrationalism which, in *Coleridge on Imagination*, he identified with abstraction in the sense that it involved overgeneralising through failing to observe the range of relevance of a given myth. What should reign is Reason. But, Richards asks

what is our view of this Reason which fights with pressure groups among the desires which try to make us misread? Have we a view of it and can we improve it by watching Reason at work in our reading?

In answer, he tells the reader to wait.

All the rest of this book will be the endeavour to reach such a view. This is not a matter to be settled in a preface, but the most important of all questions, that on which every other one turns. For it is about the ἀρκή, the first principle or archproblem, upon which depends not only how we will read but what we who read will be (75).

And so back to theories and the practising of them, exercise in reading the passage from Whitehead with its message of the inevitability of feeling, emotion, or purpose in our experience and behaviour, and then to the defining of the most important of the Hundred Great Words, brief notes on important philosophical issues, until we come to the final trio, 'Reason' itself, 'Purpose' and 'Work' by means of which Plato's conception of the Good is explained.

These last five chapters of the book, which present the multiple definitions, provide a sort of repetition of the suggestively titled *Basic Rules of Reason*. Most of the words defined, however, are different. The reason for this lies partly in Richards' acceptance of Platonism, as he interprets it, and partly in his acceptance of the analysis of Basic English as to which the most important words are. Let us deal with this latter first.

The two criteria Richards uses in deciding which are his hundred great words are:

1. They cover the ideas we can least avoid using, those which are concerned in all that we do as thinking beings.
2. They are words we are forced to use in explaining other words because it is in terms of the ideas they cover that the meaning of other words must be given (22).

The second of these criteria is the same as that used in choosing the 18 words *Basic Rules of Reason* dealt with, and indeed these words are to be found amongst Richards' hundred. But the words out of the hundred that are specially chosen for multiple definition in this book are different. Apart from some abstract words that come at the end of *How To Read a Page* and which are chosen because they are the most important for the philosophy of Plato and Aristotle, the words chosen are verbs—a new departure for Richards—which Ogden had shown could be reduced to 18 in number, perhaps the greatest economy he effected in Basic English.[1] One might say that Richards' criterion for choosing these verbs, ('make', 'get', 'give' 'love', 'have', 'seem', 'be', 'do', 'see') was linguistic as opposed to the philosophical 'criterion' that obviously operated in *Basic Rules of Reason*. Their "extreme versatility and ambiguity", "the position of their ideas as the very hinges of all thought", followed, for them, from "Mr. C. K. Ogden's vast researches into the substitutability of English words".

When it comes to the actual defining of them, however, Richards' interest seems to be mainly in referring, in note form, to various important philosophical issues of the past. 'Love', is presented in terms of two meanings, 'eros' and 'agape', which gives rise to a brief homily on the Platonic and the Christian conceptions of it. By describing this in terms of 'Get' or 'Give', the link between the different words defined is demonstrated. A similar duality in meaning in 'love' is detected by Richards in the sexual as opposed to the theological uses of the word.

That one word with such varied possibilities behind it should span so vast a range of interest and activities is perhaps the single linguistic fact which has made most difference to human history (156).

[1] Cf. Richards' *Basic English and Its Uses*, pages 50-52. It should be mentioned, however, that 300 "Names of things" can be verbalised according to the rules of Basic English, by adding "endings in 'ing' and 'ed' " to them. Therefore its boast that its entire vocabulary of 850 words can be written down on a piece of notepaper because of this reduction in verbs is not to be taken quite literally. However, the great frequency with which one or other of these verbs occurs in sentence after sentence is, I think, what is mainly responsible for giving Basic English its simple 'Reading without Tears' quality.

'Have' provides the occasion for a short discourse on the virtues of private property for individualism. 'Make' ("Beauty makes beautiful things beautiful") and 'See' mainly prepare the way for Plato's theory of Ideas, though with the former there is passing mention of the concepts of cause, logical entailment, and law. 'Be', defined as in *Interpretation in Teaching*, leads to warnings against three kinds of ambiguity; definition and statement, 'mere statement' versus 'statement with belief' (to understand you do not have to believe, only to entertain or 'experimentally submit yourself'), and the different senses of existence which will differ according to how one "sorts" in thinking.

What Richards says in connection with this is as fine a statement as any of his relativist Absolutism, his all-incorporating, having-it-all-ways desires. We should not, he writes, necessarily be satisfied with any one ontology. As in his reasoning about mediocre art and stereotypes in *Principles of Literary Criticism*, he asserts that by "claiming to know *what is what* we may make the attainment of order, coherence, stability and power easier", which, he adds is true

whichever answer we so take—phenomenalist, mechanistic material, idealist, Platonic, Christian, or Vedantic—*though the Christian answer is the most central, rejects least, and unites the most conflicting components* (172) (my italics).

"But", Richards goes on,

there is a price, however little it is in comparison with the price we pay for having no stable view at all. These views are jealous goddesses. If we are faithful to one, our devotion gives us an unbalanced knowledge of possibility. If and as we change our attachment we find this out. These views are rather eyes than things seen, so much do they settle what shall be visible (172).

It is implied by Richards that our *un*awareness of the way in which "the IS of existence changes its sense with the philosophy it serves" is at least in part responsible for this limitation. Philosophy in this book has the role of poetry in earlier books, and the ability "to enjoy the use of all philosophies" is clearly similar to that achievement of order by poetic training that makes possible the simultaneous satisfaction of multifarious desire.

Finally, with 'do' we deal with the question of free-will and responsibility. "DO", as Richards says, "is the great replacer among verbs". So it is important by his criteria, for "its characteristic behaviour reflects that of innumerable other words, among which *act, agent, responsible, free, cause, reason, choice* are of prime importance" (173).

This leads up to the thesis that in the highest kind of knowledge there is no distinction between what knows and what is known. Once again the changes are rung on 'do', 'know', 'be', and 'make'. We have already quoted from what he says here in our discussion of these matters in *Coleridge on Imagination*. But whereas in that book Coleridge was the hero, and the philosophy that which had been transmuted in Coleridge's mind from Kant and Schelling, now it is Plato powerfully supported by Aristotle whom the limelight holds. "What now seems clearer to me", Richards wrote in his preface to the second edition of *Coleridge on Imagination*, in 1949, "is Coleridge's accord, at his best, with *The Republic*." So, in this book, ideas or universals are identified with the meanings of words. It is the relations between realities that give language its stability, not a social contract such as is implied by the Usage theory. That notion is of a building up from "fixities and definites", words listed in dictionaries. Instead Richards emphasises *interdependency*. Groups of words have comparable shifts of meaning, such as we have noted with 'word', 'symbol', 'myth', 'poem', and 'nature'; 'do' and the words it understudies; 'experience', and " 'mind', 'observation', 'attention', 'knowledge', 'feeling', and 'consciousness', which systematically vary in meaning in corresponding ways" (21). The "systematising of sense impressions", to which the translation exercise from Aristotle refers, Richards interprets as "the coming into the soul of universals and the growth of their connections with one another there, [for] it is these connections which stabilise them" (36). Or again,

the universals which good reading calls for concern the wide general ways in which minor universals of less scope may and may not fit together. What counts most is not familiarity with the senses of words taken separately but knowledge of their interdependencies (107).

A comparison is made with the interdependencies within a visual field of stimuli seen from different angles, any of which we can interpret, so as to know how the complex would appear when viewed at right angles to the line of vision. The point presumably is that with reading, were we equally skilled, we would interpret the *interdependent* words appropriately, imputing similar shifts in sense to each of them. Corresponding to this we find much use of images from weaving or knitting. "The soul just is the universals which knit together all it knows" and "its knowledge (compare the metaphor in *cognition*, [is] that knitting together" (36). "A language is a fabric which holds itself together . . . [one] which, for the most part brokenly and confusedly but sometimes with startling and heartbreaking clarity . . ., reflects the fabric of universals which is our world"[1] (51). That the reflection is generally "broken and confused" is, I suppose, due to the variety

[1] Cf. *Practical Criticism*, page 220, on "the very curious and interesting order [that] may be sometimes glimpsed" behind "the notation" we use for our feelings.

135

of meanings words have, so that we need to practise multiple definition, so that, by means of it, the soul grows to have the same order
as reality has. *"In* the things the mind knows . . . and *in* the mind
itself (enabling it to repeat its acts) is a structure." This we may learn,
"but what we then learn is not the ways of our minds (except incidentally); it is what truly is: The order of the IDEAS" (201). What
Richards means here is that it is not *only* the ways of our minds that
we learn. After all, the soul is also the order of Ideas. As he says
elsewhere:

> Understanding comes through active thinking. We are not wax which
> takes impressions from an alien world. We are so intimately interrelated with
> it that it is impossible to say where we stop and it begins; or whether we are
> more its work than it is ours (184).

And in completest knowledge knower and what is known are one, so
that in realising what is, we realise ourselves. "We understand nothing
except through understanding ourselves and understanding ourselves
is understanding these words" (186-7).

"These words" are the last "Great Words" he deals with. 'Mind',
'Thought', 'Idea', 'Knowledge', 'Reason', 'Purpose', 'Work'. To show
respect, we have given them capitals, but it is fair to add Richards'
epigraph for the first of the two chapters defining them—". . . I do
not want to talk that language of spiritual aspiration which is nothing
but words"[1]. We have anticipated much that he says in these chapters;
indeed we have poached from them in doing so. The main things he
does are to set up his interpretation of Plato's theory of knowledge,
by means of a criticism of Locke's, on the excuse of clearing up one
of the ambiguities of 'Idea'; to distinguish, amongst other meanings
of 'Knowledge', four different grades of it, based upon Plato's
distinctions, and to treat 'Reason' in a parallel way—the main point,
in the case of each word, being to lecture cursorily on the most
elevated of these senses—; and to recommend, in his treatment of
'Reason', 'Purpose' and 'Work', Plato's theory of the Good in terms
of which the problem posed by the partiality of purpose in reading
and writing is finally solved, the theoretical answer being given when
the reader had been given the fullest chance of *practice*. For

> On a huge hill,
> Cragged and steep, Truth stands and hee that will
> Reach her, about must, and about must goe;
> And what the hills suddennes resists, winne so.[2]

---

[1] From T. S. Eliot's *Towards a Christian Britain*. Richards has come closer and
closer to Eliot in his later writings. The line now dividing them is as thin as the
horizon line.

[2] From Donne's Satyre III, quoted on page 97.

The highest type of Knowledge is described, following Plato, by contrast with the knowledge of the sciences. It is distinguished from them by not being departmental. It is the consequence in us of the analysis of concepts, which may be common to a number of sciences and which each takes as analysed. This was a modern enough notion of the purpose of philosophers, and one acceptable enough to Richards with his programme of Analysis for Everyman. 'Reason' is treated similarly. "In the sense which goes with the highest mode of knowledge, REASON is the dependence of all knowledge upon one principle. Only as viewed through or with that would all become reasonable" (210) and, referring to Plato,

The REASON which rules in the most inclusive study of all—Dialectic is the name he gave it—is by him expressly distinguished from reason in the sciences . . .

Each science, for its own purposes, simplifies by abstracting, . . . It is this which separates them. If the body of knowledge they together compose is to be seen as a whole, these abstract simplifications must be put together again. Moreover, each science takes these abstractions as its starting points "without troubling to give any account of them, to itself or to others, simply believing they are clear enough to anyone. They start out from these assumptions and go on from them in an ordered way, till they come to the end for which they started . . . And in this (in the sciences) the soul is forced to use these starting points; it does not go on up to a first principle because it is unable to escape from and get up higher than these starting-point bases". But, in Dialectic, "The things reasoning takes as bases are not taken by it as unquestioned starting points, but as helps or steppingstones, as something to give a footing, or as springboards, by which it is made able to go up to that which is no such base which needs to be taken, but is the first principle of everything. And after getting to that, it takes again a grip of the first things dependent on that, and so goes down again to the outcome. (*Republic*, 511) (215-216).

Many things come together here.

To be a good Dialectician—a good reasoner in this superdepartmental inquiry—he must not only be able to "see very different sorts of things (e.g. Ideas and atoms) together"; he must be able "to ask questions and answer them." Thought here is internal dialogue, a process which examines itself. This is connected with Definition. He must be "able to give and audit a full account of what may be meant in a discussion" (*Republic*, 532). This amounts to being able to say what he is talking about, and being able to find out what others are talking about—in other words, to a mastery of definition. The Dialectician is an expert in knowing what he himself and others are talking about, and whether their professed definitions, set forth in the same words maybe, are in fact the same or not. To fit the departmental studies together, he has to see whether, for example, "matter" and "observe," as the physicist is now using them, mean the same as the similarly spelled words the psychologists use and so on. (217)

Multiple Definition is what Plato cares for. "Thought here is internal dialogue, a process which examines itself" hints at the Imagination. As Richards says, Coleridge's "co-ordinating imagination is a close analogue, if no more, to the synoptic activity of 'the true music of dialectic'."[1] Dialectic reasoning is carefully distinguished from arguing and controversy.

> It works not through contention and debate, which are modes of verbal *fighting*, but through displaying clearly the relevant differences and connections between the things we may be saying. It is the art of exhibiting and respecting the divisions between the Ideas (the sense of words) which are needed for the purpose of the discussion and of remaining undistracted by the innumerable irrelevant others; it is the art to which all readers aspire (221-222).

This is clearly related to that internal dialogue which Richards recommended to his readers as worth cultivating when reading, and to the "drama of berths" that he tried to describe in *Interpretation in Teaching*. There is a suggestion of an activity that should go on of its own accord like growth, not something that is the consequence of an act of will separated in experience from what we do, or something that involves force like "verbal fighting". Again and again, Richards says things which suggest this. We have already referred to his statement, in the book we are at present considering, that "the pages which on a long view have mattered most to the world . . . have an inexhaustible fertility . . . [for] they are the great exercisers of the spirit" (11-12). To this we might add his comment on a remark by Emerson that "a man might have, if he were fortunate, some hundreds of reasonable moments in a long life."—

> The great pages are the most constant and dependable sources of "reasonable moments", if we mean by them moments when we know more completely what we are, and why we are so, and thus "see into the life of things" more deeply than in our everyday routine of existence. Such reasonable moments are the highest aim of reading. In them we do more than communicate with our authors—in the humble sense of communicate. We partake with them of wisdom (15).

One consideration that might weigh against this identification of Reason with Imagination is that of the position of feeling, attitude, or emotion. Little mention is made of these in Richards' description of Dialectic or reasoning. But since he is talking about the interrelatedness of all "knowledge" in his 'highest' sense, he should be talking about experiencing in which there is no abstraction of

---

[1] Preface to the second edition of *Coleridge on Imagination*. Note how evasive, how *un*concrete, Richards' statement is. He uses words in his philosophy like an Impressionist paints.

either reference or feeling alone, the experiencing whose value he argued in his treatment of poetry. On the other hand, passages such as he quotes from Aristotle which, given proper communication, result presumably in "reasonable moments", do seem to differ very much, in the exercise they provide for the emotions from passages from Shakespeare or the book of Job. The generality or absence of separation that results from the analysis or definition of words, which are common to separate sciences, seems to be a purely intellectual matter, different from that generality where feelings are not excluded as irrelevant. There are two kinds of growth, it will be remembered; that which results from practising theories which brings about an increase in ordering capacity, and that which results from a poetical experience being communicated, which communication can only be successfully achieved through having attained this earlier increase in ordering capacity. In both cases, growth follows from the kind of intense, concentrated experience that was described in *Coleridge on Imagination*. Perhaps in *philosophic* poetry the two may be the same, and this is why a consideration of Coleridge made the identification possible. But if this is so, it would seem that Richards' concerns here changed from the time he wrote *Principles of Literary Criticism* and *Practical Criticism*, with the high valuation put there, for instance, on tragedy. There is a tendency to pay more attention to the thought than to its expression. This is a particularly severe charge to bring against Richards, who of all people is alive to such distinctions. Yet surely great philosophers may write badly and yet produce "reasonable moments" in their readers? In *The Meaning of Meaning*, Richards recognised that what is written may often bear a very indirect relation to the sign-situation which gave rise to it. The former may be a very abbreviated version of the latter. In *Principles of Literary Criticism*, writing was being considered that expressed with great sensitiveness the sign-situations which gave it birth, so much so that in *Practical Criticism* Richards was saying in effect that, if the words were properly read, then a similar sign-situation—the object-correlate of the language—would be aroused in the reader. It would seem that in Richards' attempted synthesis, which was assisted by his theory of direct experience as being necessary to learning—mere theoretical learning being no more than skin-deep—, the relation between experience and language on the *writer's* part was overlooked.

One factor that may have contributed to this confusion was the increasing attention Richards paid to *purpose*, in the sense of the purposes underlying our use of words. It is necessary to go into this in order to understand Richards' definition of 'reason' "in the highest sense" and what he meant when he talked of "our view of this Reason which fights with pressure groups among the desires which try to make us misread" (75). The answer is given in defining the meanings of 'purpose' and 'work' and, through these, though it is not a word included in his official list, of 'good'. "Whatever [man] does is purposive to some degree . . . Yet another way of saying this: he is always seeking GOOD" (227). It is still the theory of value of *Principles of Literary Criticism*. The *greatest* good will be achieved if man acts according to his nature. That is, if he seeks to have knowledge in the highest sense of the term, or, as we might put it, if he achieves the greatest degree of ordering; because then he will be able to satisfy the greatest number of desires, now and forever.

Reason, 'dividing at the joints', discovers that a man is what he can do, that his end or purpose is to realise his fullest being by doing what he can do best, and that best here means that which most conforms with that order through which alone a man can DO anything, or BE at all. As Socrates says in the *Phaedo* (99), 'It is the binding power of good which really holds things together' (232).

The world has an order and we must act as best we may in accordance with that order to achieve the greatest good, something which requires recognising also our interdependence one with another. Seeing this means seeing how the conflict of heart and head should be resolved. Being reasonable does not mean not acting according to desire but acting in such a way as to realise our desires most fully.

But how does this Aristotelian view apply to reading? Richards' answer to the question he posed earlier in the book, "What should guide the reader's mind?", is

Our awareness of interdependence, of how things hang together, which makes us able to give and audit an account of what may be meant in a discussion—that highest activity of REASON which Plato named 'Dialectic' (240).

Similarly in summarising a page from the *Nichomachean Ethics*—"a last page we may take as an exercise in our power to read"—he writes

In everything which has parts, every part has a certain WORK TO DO in relation to the whole. It is a good or bad part as it does that work well or ill. When we KNOW something in the deeper sense of *knowing what it is*, we see how its various parts make it up and the WORK they do in making it up. This is what REASON in the parallel sense, discovers. Moreover, this WORK is their PURPOSE in the whole; it is the way in which they are means to the being of the whole. And again this work is the reason why the whole has that part. Thus, to say anything is GOOD, in this sense, is to say that it does its WORK with regard to some whole.

The application of this to the words in a page, and to the meanings which a reader gives them, will be evident. A good reader would be one who exerted and obeyed in his reading the same principles which, if he exerted and obeyed them in life, would make him blessed and happy (229-230).

It is *purpose*, entering into all reading and all writing, as it does into our other activities, that appeared now to be Richards' stand-in for the feelings and emotions, whose co-presence is necessary for the highest knowledge, and therefore for Reason in its most elevated sense. This is perhaps the route by which Richards came to speak of a page of Aristotle's philosophy in similar terms to those to which he spoke of the operation of the Imagination in lines of Coleridge's poetry, going now not so much by the shorthand as by the order of Ideas that occasioned it.

But, we may ask, reflecting on what Richards has said, is it after all anything more than saying that to read properly we must not be biassed, giving way to partial desires, as Collingwood did in his hostility to experimental psychology? Is it more than what might appear on "the usual postcard's worth of crude common sense"? The answer is that it is philosophical; that is to say, it is a view that illustrates itself by being in harmony with basic assumptions in terms of which it is justified. It is *involved* in them. Here is the Chinese box effect in Richards' thinking, something to which he sometimes explicitly refers. For instance, commenting on one of the passages from Whitehead in which the word 'involves' occurs:—

We will do well to give this word 'involves' all its meaning here: 'rolls up in itself, spirally; gathers in, embraces, includes' ('My love involves the love before'—Tennyson); the peculiar returning-on-itself motion of a snake; the old mathematical sense of multiplication by itself; the philosophic sense in which a higher form involves lower forms as its conditions; even the mystical sense in which the Sufi exclaims, "I am the wine whose vine is its jar" (84).

The notion is one that Richards constantly refers to in the image from the *Chung Yung*, "In hewing an axe handle, in hewing an axe handle, the pattern is not far off".[1] We can learn by self-awareness, as we use our skills. To recognise the interdependence of word-meanings, then, is not an arbitrary theoretical point we have to understand in order to read properly, but a truth of the world that follows from the way in which we perceive it. The world is such that there are more and less developed orders of universals (word-meanings) within us, to which stands in direct relationship our capacity to satisfy our desires. By learning about words through practising and being aware of our experience without self-intrusion or disjointed effort, we grow more capable of receiving communications which, if we are aware of our experience without self-intrusion or disjointed effort, will make us

[1] Quoted in *Practical Criticism*, page 284.

141

grow more capable of . . . and so on. Of course there are different philosophies produced by sages of different traditions. Are there not therefore different best orders? But we could have these different orders if we "created" a mediating philosophy, i.e. a yet higher order.

The mind that could do that could enjoy the use of all the philosophies, as we enjoy the use of all our senses, would be the perfect Dialectician . . . and would know another world than any we know (173).

We aspire towards Reason, and reading expresses what we have achieved and further assists our aspiration, if we are aware in practice of how Reason operates in the passage and in ourselves.

These interdependencies of word-meanings that are the interdependencies of our ideas, which can grow ever more harmonious in the sense of agreeing at higher and higher levels with the world that can satisfy our impulses, provided that this world, which is to so large an extent social and therefore consisting of interdependencies of people, is itself harmoniously ordered. But though people are dependent on one another, and fullest development can only follow acceptance of this "each man's GOOD is an END in itself" and a society's "GOOD is realised only through theirs". Society has "no purpose apart from the well-being—the full development through their proper WORK—of its members and future members" (232). "The greatest evil is injustice, things out of place and therefore against one another—in a mind, in a nation, and in the World State" (242).

Reading justly, then, Richards invests with significance. He requires states of mind that are not narrow or limited; he wants an immense awareness. But one may wonder whether, for awareness to be so extensive, a formula is not required making it possible for us to be conscious of everything important at once, a palpable state of mind, that is to say, that stands-in for something else. Plato leads Richards from images of growth back to those concepts of harmony which nourished his early thoughts on art. But philosophy is less particular than poetry and the music of the spheres is dull music.

Chapter Six

COMPREHENDING COMPREHENDING
(I)—PHILOSOPHERS

HAVING completed our account of Richards' basic theories and their changes with time, we can turn to the first of our major preoccupations, the problem of comprehension. Since we shall use for illustration other writers' comprehension of Richards, this and the next chapter will also serve to bring out more clearly what Richards' theories were. It will enable us to consider critically how far our interpretation is correct by comparing it with the interpretation of others.

I. HOW FAR DO WE UNDERSTAND ONE ANOTHER?

From *The Meaning of Meaning* on, Richards' belief that completely successful communication in words was difficult and rare was evident in nearly every book he wrote. It is a continuous concern in *The Meaning of Meaning* itself, of which the chapter on "The Meaning of Philosophers", in particular, is entirely devoted to an impressionistic sketch of communicative chaos; it is the main theme of *Mencius on the Mind*, and figures largely in *Coleridge on Imagination*. Two books, which act like models for dictionaries, being full of multiple definitions of key words—*Basic Rules of Reason* and *How To Read a Page*—are very much concerned with better reading. Of bad reading, *Practical Criticism* and *Interpretation in Teaching* claim to provide evidence in detail from subjects' protocols, whilst each of Richards' last four books provides a number of demonstrations of faulty interpretation by philosophers, linguists, and literary critics.

As we saw, however, Richards did not *always* talk in this way. A certain amount of ambivalence was shown, not only in his occasional oscillations from deploring our failures in communication to praising our natural skill, but also in the fact that he went on writing in the same way as before. One would have expected that his writing would have become simpler; instead it became, if anything, more complex, though this was probably a consequence of his changed theory of knowledge. If we were to appeal to the experience of others, I think we should find very much the same ambivalence in attitude. On the one

143

hand, we have the complaints of teachers, in particular educational psychologists, concerned with improving the standard of comprehension amongst university students; the evidence of all those who have to use language as an instrument of research in measuring attitudes or personality, or in public opinion polling; the manifest desire on the part of experimental psychologists wherever possible not to use language as the experimental response, a factor which played an important part in the development of behaviourism; and the experience of those who have given talks or written books as to how these have been interpreted by reviewers and critics. Richards himself frequently comments on how his books have been misunderstood. "Who has written a careful book on [for instance, "economics, philosophy, criticism, social theory"] without having privately to admit that all his reviewers have misread him?"[1] And though book-reviewing may not fairly represent general standards of reading, such evidence as Moore's or Russell's comments, on being confronted with a score of critical articles on their philosophy to which they had to write an answer, as to the extent to which they had been misunderstood is certainly impressive testimony.[2]

On the other hand, for many of us complex communication by speech or writing is our daily bread, and there are powerful forces against anything like a full realisation of the extent to which we fail. Those who investigate questionnaire-wording or public opinion polling, for instance, generalise, on the basis of very *narrow* evidence, that only on issues that are relatively unstructured, that is, where the respondents have not thought a lot about their opinion and come to definite conclusions, is wording likely to be a serious source of error[3], which is certainly a comforting belief. Others working on compre-

---

[1] *I. in T.*, 219.

[2] *The Philosophy of G. E. Moore* (1942) and *The Philosophy of Bertrand Russell* (1944), both edited by P. A. Schilpp. The expression of their comments by the two men shows characteristic differences. With Moore, statements that he had not held this or that opinion attributed to him appear in the course of *A Reply to My Critics*, separated from each other often by lengthy consideration as to what a given critic had meant, if at all determinable, and with full recognition on Moore's part that his own expression might also have been at fault. Whereas Russell, according to his editor, declared that "over half [the] authors [of the critical articles] had *not* understood" him, a fact which he found astonishing, and all the more so because "of his concern to write clearly . . .". Wittgenstein's two prefaces to his books (*Tractatus Logico-Philosophicus* and *Philosophical Investigations*) are also profoundly pessimistic about his chances of being understood.

[3] H. Cantril and D. Rugg, *Gauging Public Opinion*; G. Gallup, "Sociometry," 1941, IV; L. Cronbach, "Educat. Psychol. Measurement," 1946, VI. The article last mentioned deals with 'response sets' in questionnaires. However, these are in fact interpretations of the questionnaire-designer's intentions derived from the instructions, questions asked, and situation within which the questionnaire is presented; in other words, they indicate how the language used is comprehended.

hension tests may point to these as evidence of successful understanding, forgetting the relative simplicity of the test material and of
the questions asked, always the price of objectivity.[1] There are also
certain general attitudes in accordance with which we may blame our
audience, ourselves, or the medium, ordinary language, for failures in
communication of complex material, thus preserving the image of an
ideal reader, an ideal writer, or an ideal language. Above all, we hide
from ourselves the extent to which in our society we interact instead
of communicating, by lending meaning to the words we hear, a
process like rationalisation which, adapting a well-known psychological term, we might call *false closure*. Only when conventional
forms are not employed, as in certain modern art and poetry, do we
get to any extent a failure of this process, which expresses itself,
however, less in a request for meaning, as in a denial, masquerading
as a request, that any meaning is really there. But traditional forms in
novels, plays, poems, and paintings, are not so different from experimental ones in their susceptibility to misinterpretation. The circumstance from which perhaps most comfort can be derived is that there
is always likely to be understanding at some, though often a very
general level, and that out of the population of ideas a book contains
many will be received at quite specific levels by its future readers,
however rare the event of one understanding them all.

2. CONTRASTING RICHARDS' AND THE AUTHOR'S THEORIES OF COMPREHENDING

Turning now to Richards' recommendations for improving reading
ability, his main theory, as we have seen, is that misunderstanding is
due to the Proper Meaning Superstition, which made readers always
attribute the same meanings to words and blinded them to the
variety of different meanings that words in fact take on. His chief
remedies against this were the following: instruction in a proper
theory of meaning, that is, his Context theory of meaning, which
stresses the individual circumstances of the learning of meanings; the
practice of multiple definition; and the microscopic study of the way
words are actually used, such as he demonstrated in comments and

[1] See also the evidence from reliability studies in content analysis. It is well known
that such studies are rare. But where they are made the measures are very coarse and,
not even these are always successful. Cf., for instance, Kaplan and Goldsen's study
of the reliability of coding newspaper headlines in terms of the attributing of strength
or morality to allies and enemies in the last war. (*The Language of Politics*, by
H. Lasswell, V. Leites and associates, (1949)). See also Richards' comments on how
we hide from ourselves recognition of "the inevitable ambiguity of almost all verbal
formulae" (*P.C.*, 341).

translations, with their strong stress on the varying meanings the same word might have.

On the basis both of experimental studies, somewhat similar to Richards' own, but more controlled and followed up by interviews with the subjects on their interpretations, and of "microscopic" studies of communications, such as letters in the correspondence columns of newspapers, I believe that this source of error, though it occurs occasionally, is much less important than Richards thought. In contrast with his theory which, despite his stress on the sentence as the "unit of discourse", concentrates on single words, I believe, firstly, that we bring to our reading larger scale semantic units than word-meanings and, secondly, that these do in fact determine the senses in which we take the individual words. It follows from this that we do *not* tend always to attribute the same meanings to the same word.

The larger scale semantic units are categories in terms of which we are always ready to group what we perceive. We have expectations about the arguments people will use, the attitudes they will hold and what other attitudes go with them, the intentions they will have in different communication-situations, the kinds of personality likely to be associated with different attitudes and so on. For whatever we perceive and whatever we read, we are ready with these expectations. Many of these expectations are products of social learning, fostered by mass media—films, plays, television, books (including textbooks), newspapers, advertisements, and wireless—though often in fact transmitted by individuals with whom we are intimate. As such, these expectations will be to some degree stereotyped, which one might almost say was a requirement of communication, particularly of mass communication, such as books and articles. However there will often be quite a number of different such interpretations available and, since any passage of writing is multi-faceted, those that are chosen from the different *sets* of interpretations may combine with one another so as to produce for every interpreter a unique interpretation, which will be revealed if the questions by means of which we elicit it are specific enough. Individual factors of need, personal hobby horses, will sometimes produce idiosyncratic interpretations, but I stress the degree to which many interpretations are like variations upon a *common* theme, in order to account for the paradoxical finding that we may get a great *variety* of interpretations of the same message, which are nevertheless all relatively stereotyped, so that a new idea is very difficult to communicate successfully.

To call these categories "larger scale semantic units" is not strictly correct, because the term 'semantic' in the linguist's sense should, as I understand it, be limited to the coded or codable meanings of words, morphemes, and constructions; and these categories are not coded by linguists, nor are they codable unless they can be shown to have some consistent relationship to some linguistic form. Nevertheless I call them this in order to bring out the important rôle they play in interpretation. It is not a matter, as Richards' treatment suggests, simply of piecing together the meaning out of the known meanings of individual words, so that all one has to do to improve comprehension is to break down the One and One Only Meaning Superstition and alert the reader to the fact that a word may have different meanings depending upon the 'context' and the other words in the sentence. This is indeed an atomistic approach, despite Richards' protestations that he favours that of Gestalt psychology. What happens rather is that some part plays a dominant role, determining the way in which the whole is categorised. Other parts are then interpreted in such a way as to fit in with this, the reader justifying his interpretation of them by appeals to the "general tone" of the argument, to the "whole attitude" it shows, to "its general colouring", and so on. Such justifications mean, as the reader who is questioned will often make explicit, that words are continually taken as varying in their meaning according to context. Far from finding that incorrect reading was due to taking words as fixed and definite in their meaning, therefore, my experiments suggested that it was rather the other way round, and that there was too great a tendency to make *meanings* subservient to a favoured interpretation.

This attitude is perfectly consistent with a belief in words having their "proper meanings", which Richards thought the "Usage" theory of meaning encouraged. Readers will back up their interpretations by saying that the writer was not using his words very carefully. Even one of Richards' own exercises, the distinguishing of different meanings of 'is' (see page 123), revealed this. As Richards commented of one of his protocolists, "he was not alone in feeling that if IS is used in various ways, all but one of them should somehow be wrong".[1] But even if this is an erroneous view, it obviously does not result, as Richards argued elsewhere, in readers *failing* to attribute meanings different from the so-called 'correct' one to words in their actual use.

The contrast I have drawn between my approach and Richards' refers to Richards' *theory*, not to some of the things he said about

[1] *I. in T.*, 305. This example provides an instance of my analysis. It seems that subjects such as this one *categorised* the communication-situation (Richards' purpose in asking them to "distinguish between the uses of 'IS' in [six specimen sentences], and say which, if any, of the sentences you take to be true by definition") as being one of detecting loose writing. This subject, as Richards wrote, "is one of several who took 'true by definition' not as applying to the sentences as wholes but to some supposed true or 'correct' use of IS".

causes of misinterpretation in the course of his writings. If we examine these, we find he does from time to time refer to categorisation determining particular meanings. Richards however often shows some rigidity himself in failing to incorporate detailed observations into his theories, which remain as a result comparatively crude and over-simple. In the present case, that of comprehension, there is a continuous refrain concerning the harm done by an over-rigid theory of Proper Meaning and continuous emphasis upon Multiple Definitions. Furthermore, when we examine in detail Richards' comments about categorisation, it becomes evident that he does not appreciate the pervasive role this process plays, indeed must play, in reading. Let us consider for a moment some of the things he says about it.

In *Practical Criticism* he recognised the part played by categorising in respect of "irrelevant associations", such as personal hobby-horses, "stock responses", and judgments of the poem's intention. He says with regard to the last of these, "the rapidity with which many readers leap to a conviction as to a poem's general intention, and the ease with which this assumption can distort their whole reading, is one of the most interesting features in the protocols".[1]

This is certainly a true comment. But Richards is very vague about the part played by Intention, his fourth function of language (see pages 250-252 below). As regards categorisation by stock responses and irrelevant associations, he is inclined to regard these only as an occasional odd feature of interpretation, his interest being mainly in the effect rather than in the process itself. Thus he rejected the argument of one of his subjects that "*every* poem calls up stock responses"[2] —from which it would follow that correct identification or categorisation was necessary for *successful* reading—by denying that this was in fact true of all poetry. The trouble is that phrases like "stock responses" and "stereotypes" have, in addition to their meaning, a pejorative connotation, so it is difficult to make acceptable the kind of point Richards' subject was trying to make. Of course, poetry does differ from prose in being more concerned with effect than just with communication, and more, too, with *individuality* of effect. Nevertheless, that correct categorising in prose is important may be judged from Richards' own description of the *Principles of Literary Criticism*. "Few of the separate items", he wrote, "are *original*. One does not expect *novel* cards when playing so traditional a game . . . This book might . . . be compared to a loom on which it is proposed to re-weave some ravelled parts of our civilisation."[3] Clearly correct categorising of the "items", "cards", or "ravelled parts" is necessary for proper

[1] *P.C.*, 206.
[2] *P.C.*, 252.
[3] *P.L.C.*, 1.

understanding, something which, as we shall see, by no means always happened.

Further remarks on categorising which show that Richards had not got this in its right perspective, occur in *Basic in Teaching: East and West*. There he evidently regarded the bringing to bear of a set of already learned categories in interpreting a verbal message as being a specifically *Chinese* approach. For him it was part of the conservative pragmatism of the Chinese, spoken of with rather more admiration in *Mencius on the Mind*. "Traditional Chinese scholarship", he wrote, "has spent its great resources of memory and ingenuity upon *fitting the passage into* an already accepted framework of meanings."[1] That the tendency was quite general, he indicated by, amongst other things, quoting from Chinese university students' interpretations of English novels to show how they saw them in terms of their own categories.[2] Richards was not, however, able totally to ignore the evidence he had so often seen, and we find him saying later in the book that "a tendency to accommodate a passage to a preformed view . . . [is] not unknown elsewhere".[3]

When we come to *Interpretation in Teaching*, it looks early on as though he were at last recognising the importance of categorising, for he states there at the beginning of his fourth chapter:

No writer supplies the full setting which controls the reader in his reading. He cannot. Always the major part must be left to the reader to bring in. This is perhaps the truism which in practice we most neglect.[4]

However, the means by which he believes we can best ensure that the reader brings the right categories to bear betray how he understands this point. These are, "for English-speaking people", "studies in English . . . (including) a common body of literature familiar to all". Richards adds,

That we can no longer refer with any confidence to any episode in the Bible, or to any nursery tale or any piece of mythology is a clear and well-recognised sign of the urgency of taking these things more advisedly in hand.[5]

The contrast between his approach and the one I have been recommending lies in his failure systematically to stress the importance, for comprehending any message in a given subject matter, of studying that subject matter itself. By this I mean reading and re-reading, discussing and having ones views corrected; in other words, learning

[1] *B. in T.: E. & W.*, 29.
[2] But see Bartlett's evidence as to how English university students categorised the folk tales of North American Indians. (F. C. Bartlett, *Remembering* (1932), Chap. IV, V, and VII.)
[3] *B. in T.: E. & W.*, 48.
[4] *I. in T.*, 66.
[5] *I. in T.*, 67.

the relevant categories. This is not the only requirement;[1] but it is an indispensable one. We may apply against Richards what he himself said; it is "the truism which in practice we most neglect".

We shall take then, as Richards' official view, the one we described on page 145. It was this he put most energy into and exemplified by his practice, Multiple Definition and emphasising possible alternative meanings in translation-exercises, in order to break down the effects of a theory of language, which is said to have overstressed single words and their fixed meanings. But in opposing it, though I mention the evidence I go on, I have not presented it in any detail. To do so now would be to take the reader too far from the topic of this book. However, wrestling over a number of years with Richards' meaning, and reading other writers' interpretations of him, has provided experience concerning comprehension of which some use should be made. I propose therefore to present a number of different interpretations of some of Richards' theories and to show how these interpretations can be seen as faulty categorisations derived from certain cues in Richards' writings. Such a procedure will have the incidental advantage of enabling me to say a little more concerning my interpretations before going on to the criticism of others of Richards' theories. But first let us consider the nature of our sample.

In contrast to Richards' procedure, or that of my own experiments, or indeed any likely experimental approach, we shall be concerned with the understanding not of short passages but of whole books. The disadvantage of this is that we are less likely to guess correctly where the mistakes come from. Furthermore, we cannot present the whole of that which was misunderstood so that the reader can form his own judgment. We shall have to rely instead upon the plausibility of the exposition we have so far provided, or the reader's checking of it by looking up the references to Richards' writings that I have given. Nevertheless I think there is much to be said for supplementing small-scale studies by one on a larger scale. Whether as scholars or scientists we are after all mainly dealing with larger communication-units, whether books, articles, or papers read at

---

[1] Richards' evidence derives from University students. But I would not wish to deny that some of them may have suffered from different weakness in language-use of a *general* nature, i.e. ones which should be tackled by general training in language-use. Richards' evidence, however, is not of the sort that allows such weaknesses to be detected. Furthermore these weaknesses are likely to differ from case to case, and only training based upon study of the *individual* is likely to be effective. Of this there is very little, since, except perhaps with children learning reading and arithmetic, i.e., *sine qua non* skills of our society, our educational system inevitably skimps with the individual. What is needed is more educational psychology with a clinical approach. Richards himself recommends something like this (*I. in T.*, 74), but he does not really practice it.

meetings. For social and historical sciences, this size of unit is much more likely to be appropriate. We need to take a look at these larger units in order to be able to assess how much we are likely to be able to generalise from the smaller-scale studies. We always do generalise in psychology from small, carefully constructed models to larger, laxer happenings. Such generalisations are not actually made in the dark because we have, as social beings, unprofessional experience of these areas which we believe our experiments may illuminate. But we tend to deny such experience, because it is not scientifically acquired. It needs therefore to work on us unconsciously. I think it is important that we should become more conscious of it and, by observational studies such as the one I am about to describe, make this experience much more articulate.

I have not attempted to read *all* that has been written about Richards. Book reviews, which would not have been difficult to trace, have for instance been largely neglected. Nor have I tried to read a sample designed to be representative according to one or another set of rational principles. On the other hand, I have read most that has been written (apart from book reviews) that has been influential or has been written by those who are recognised as authorities in their own field, as well of course as some that do not come in these categories. The authors I have read fall into two groups—philosophers and literary critics. I will show that most of them, who of all people one would expect to be skilled readers, show marked failures to understand Richards' meaning, so that this will perhaps be some contribution according to Richards' belief that "the only way . . . to change our attitude to language is to accumulate enough evidence as to the degree to which it can be misunderstood".[1] I will present my evidence discursively, philosophers first, then, in my next chapter literary critics, as if they were a series of case studies.

3. HOW PHILOSOPHERS HAVE UNDERSTOOD RICHARDS

We will start with Max Black, who has written two critical articles,[2] which are sometimes regarded as an authoritative philosophical critique of Richards. These articles are intended as examples of the "Linguistic Method in Philosophy", being designed to show how linguistic considerations are relevant to some philosophical problems.[3]

[1] *P.C.*, 336.

[2] "Ogden and Richards' Theory of Interpretation", *J. Phil.*, XXXIX, 1942; Questions about Emotive Meaning," *Phil. Rev.* LVII, 1948. These are reprinted in *Language and Philosophy*, which also contains comments on Richards' answers to Black's second paper, both of which were given in a symposium. Page references to Black's articles will refer to *Language and Philosophy*.

[3] *Ibid.*, ix.

It is all the more important therefore that they should be correct in their interpretation of Richards. As we shall show, however, this basic requirement is not fulfilled.

In his first article, "Ogden and Richards' Theory of Interpretation," Black adopts a familiar philosophical procedure of seeking out a basic argument upon which all the other arguments and all the pretensions of *The Meaning of Meaning* depend. This argument he takes to be Ogden and Richards' theory about what takes place in a simple act of interpretation. He writes,

. . . unless the theory to be examined can provide an acceptable account of *these* situations, its contributions to the understanding of such disputed subjects as aesthetics or the foundations of mathematics are hardly likely to be of much value.[1]

According to Black, Ogden and Richards' view is that whenever we say people are interpreting a sign—that is, when a sign causes a person to make a reference—all we are saying is that "a determinate physical structure" in the brain is causing this response to happen. This is by virtue of the co-occurrence of experiences of sign and significate in the past, which produced this "physical configuration in the brain". Similarly, Ogden and Richards are also said to believe that "*all* acts of interpretation must be accompanied by uniquely indicative bodily [in this case, neural] characteristics".[2] What Ogden and Richards are after, in Black's view, is clear-cut objective criteria, which they pretend to have discovered, thus bringing to an end all the uncertainties which have dogged philosophical and psychological discussion. Black takes the Canon of Actuality as an example of how Ogden and Richards' theory attempts "the solution of a practical difficulty". For Black the Canon means that "in case of dispute concerning interpretation (as when we wonder whether a hearer has understood our words) [we should always] . . . ask what cerebral events in the past have been *similar* to the cerebral event which occurred in the course of the act of interpretation in question".[3] And he adds that "the 'Canon of Actuality' functions as a prohibition against finding the denotation of a symbol in anything other than some specific physical event".

Such an interpretation, which makes the theory appear so very much more definite than it is and quite mistakes its purpose, is little more than a travesty. Difficult though Ogden and Richards' presentation often is, it can hardly be held responsible for *this* misreading. Ogden and Richards nowhere assert a one-to-one correspondence

[1] *Ibid.*, 190.
[2] *Ibid.*, 198.
[3] *Ibid.*, 194.

between a class of psychological events, or a class of classes of psychological events, and a class of neural events. Still less do they appeal to *neurological* study to answer philosophical problems or to clear up misunderstandings. When the Canon of Actuality is described in *The Meaning of Meaning*, in both the preceding and the following paragraphs, referents which were *"sensations"*[1] and *"images"* were specifically mentioned. So far from being intended as a "prohibition against finding the denotation of a symbol in anything other than some specific physical event", the Canon of Actuality was introduced for dealing with situations where the referent was *not* the "specific physical event" one thought it was, but rather some sensation or feeling that one had misinterpreted. Though this of course was itself likely to have been caused by some other "specific physical event", the point was that Ogden and Richards were concerned with not taking words at their face value but discovering their meaning by searching out the "sign-situation" from which they originated. Whatever criticism might be made of Ogden and Richards here, they were not trying to establish certainty by pinning things down in the brain, but to warn *against* misleading certainty that arose from pinning meaning in actual use to the dictionary.

But let us continue with Black's interpretation. Black is naturally astonished that anyone should have put forward so absurd a theory ". . . it is no more than a sweeping hypothesis based upon as good as no evidence", he says, so "how can we account for the remarkable fact that the theory is apparently used as a ground for specific answers to disputable questions concerning specific complex inter-pretations . . .?"[2] His answer is that the reasoning by which it is established is circular. This, he says, is shown "by an examination of almost any case of attempted application of the theory". He takes as an example Ogden and Richards' treatment of 'beauty':

. . . we are to reject with impatience and contumely the suggestion that beauty may be indefinable or a name for a "simple quality". Anybody who holds such a view "postulates" a quality which is a "mythological referent" and is guilty of relying upon word magic and the survival of "primitive word-superstitions". But no ground is given for all this fury at what has seemed to many thinkers a reasonable hypothesis except the suggestion that an aesthetic character *could not* be a referent, and so could not be that with which any interpretative act is concerned. And so we get the following chain of argu-ment: referents are spatiotemporal particulars, interpretation is of referents, the alleged quality of beauty is admittedly not a spatiotemporal particular,

---

[1] At one place Ogden and Richards write "feeling", but they were referring to the feeling of "burning tobacco" and so clearly meant sensation. Feelings, of course, could not be *referents* for Richards.

[2] *Ibid.*, 195-196.

therefore no statement can be interpreted as being concerned with a simple quality of beauty. The same line of thought seems to inspire the authors' obvious preference for the view that "beauty" is a word whose function is mainly the emotive, noncognitive one of expressing feelings.[1]

One of Ogden and Richards' grounds for denying that 'beauty' was "the name of a simple quality", was that the fact that the same word was used on all sorts of different occasions did not mean that there was a *single* unitary property it stood for. This was one of their major theses about language and was responsible for their emphasis upon Multiple Definition. Nevertheless this did not later prevent Professor Black from using the same kind of argument against them, attributing to them a belief that a word could be uniquely defined for all its uses and "in isolation from the context of usage".[2] This was Black's "linguistic consideration relevant to this problem", and it was this belief too that led him to attribute to Ogden and Richards the belief that "*all* acts of interpretation must be accompanied by uniquely indicative bodily characteristics". This phenomenon, the repeating against an author who has not been understood the argument he himself advances, we shall come across again in our review of misinterpretations.

The main reason why Ogden and Richards denied that an "aesthetic character could . . . be a referent" was that they believed that, if we find a thing beautiful, this means we are moved by it and that no limit could be set to the sensory characteristics that in one pattern or another, at one time or another, or in one society or another give rise to these emotions. Attempts to set such bounds had resulted in a variety of aesthetic theories, but the whole truth was with none of them.[3]

How did Black himself come by *his* astonishing misinterpretation of Ogden and Richards' theory? Partly he seems to have gone by what was written in a particular place and not to have interpreted it in the light of what had been said elsewhere in the same book. When, in multiply defining 'beauty', Ogden and Richards mention the theory of it as an "intrinsic quality", they do, it is true, dismiss it with few words. But again and again in the book, in the discussion of 'good', of 'meaning', of the entities hypostatised by the Realists, and in explaining what they meant by Word Magic, Ogden and Richards

---

[1] *Ibid.*, 196-197.

[2] Ogden and Richards' multiple definitions were of how the word being defined was used in different "contexts of usage".

[3] Cf. Richards' statement: "Whenever we have any experience which might be called 'aesthetic', that is whenever we are enjoying . . . an object, there are plainly different parts of the situation on which emphasis can be laid. As we select one or other of these so we shall develop one or other of the main aesthetic doctrines". (*M. of M.*, 6th ed., 141.) *The Foundations of Aesthetics* illustrates this thesis.

have presented their argument in more detail. But the main reason for Black's misconstruction is the fact that he *categorised* Ogden and Richards' theory as a certain type of theory that he seems to have been tilting against. For him, it was a "behavioristic theory". The very use of this word suggests the preconceptions Black was ready with, as did also his references to "the semanticist",[1] his allegations that Ogden and Richards' procedure was "characteristic not only of other behaviouristic theories of language, but of much pseudo-scientific philosophising", and his mentions of "the pitfalls of scientism".

The categorisation was carried out partly by extending the normal meaning of 'behaviourism', and partly by selecting certain phrases only and either specially interpreting or ignoring the meaning of others which on the face of it did not fit in with this categorising. Black called the theory 'behaviouristic' because the authors clearly believed that all psychological processes were at least paralleled by neurological ones. But this of course does not mean denying the phenomenon of consciousness or asserting that psychology must limit itself to the studying of behaviour. By separately mentioning "the Behaviourists", Ogden and Richards distinguished themselves from them and clearly did not regard themselves as belonging to that movement. Much of their speculative mention of events in the brain is quite conventional for psychologists. Black seized on their use of the word "engram", but this, as the authors remind us, was coined by Semon, who was no behaviourist. For Ogden and Richards it was no more than a fancy word for 'trace' which had for long been postulated as the physical vestige of an experience, thought to be required for explaining the past's influence on the future. If Black had been objecting that there was "as good as no evidence" for the general theory that neural events were a necessary condition for psychological ones, as certain literary critics seem to have thought, then we have a genuine difference of opinion and not just a misunderstanding. But then Black would have been quite wrong, because there is a great deal of *evidence* from injuries to, or diseases, of the nervous system, from drug action and from anaesthetics for such a thesis.

It is by attributing to Ogden and Richards quite specific statements as to what happens in the brain that Black makes their theory look absurd. We have seen examples of this in what he attributes to them in respect of "*all* acts of interpretation" and in respect of the Canon of Actuality. Black does not produce any quotations. He simply says

---

[1] In *Language and Philosophy* there are also critical articles on "The Semiotic of Charles Morris" and "Korzybski's General Semantics". The influence of *The Meaning of Meaning* on these writers does not imply that it shared, respectively, the behaviouristic approach of the one or the hopeful neurological speculations of the other.

that this is what Ogden and Richards mean. This then enables him to say that their "assertions are unsupported by relevant evidence", adding that this was "an excellent example of what William James had in mind when he spoke of psychology as being only the hope of a science".[1] But Ogden and Richards equally affirm the rudimentary status of psychology as a science,[2] and *that* is why, in Black's triumphant words, "the authors [do not] even hint at the existence of such evidence."

In this account of simple interpretations, upon which Black fastened, Ogden and Richards are at pains in two footnotes to deny the necessity for their theory of *any* reference to brain processes. Black refers to one of these and also to the fact that "such terms as 'thoughts', 'feelings', 'experiences', are freely used as interchangeable with locutions concerning *'reactions to stimuli'* and *'adaptations of the organism'* ", thus revealing the kinds of cues he thought indicative, or not indicative, of "behaviourism". But, despite this, "there seems no doubt from *the general progress of their argument* that a *behaviouristic* theory is being presented. This is demonstrated by such a passage as "to be directly apprehended is to cause certain happenings in the nerves . . .".[3] But we often find such a way of talking amongst some philosophers concerned with analysing perceptual statements, as, for instance, Bertrand Russell, who, though influenced by them, was not a behaviourist. Black points out that Ogden and Richards describe their statement—"to be directly apprehended is to cause certain happenings in the nerves"—as "the correct answer" to questions concerning perception, as though this were a point against them, but he omits the rest of the sentence, which is, "as to which at present neurologists go no further than to assert that they occur".[4]

Professor Black made the wrong categorisation, presumably

[1] *Ibid.*, 196.

[2] Cf. their statement that it is difficult to give "a detailed account" of complex interpretations, "because few important psychological laws have as yet been ascertained and these but vaguely" (*M. of M.*, 6th edn., 200). It should be noted that this refers to the psychological, not the much more remote *neurological* level. See also—"No Copernican revolution [in psychology] has yet occurred, although several are due if psychology is to be to be brought into line with its fellow sciences" (13).

[3] *Ibid.*, 192. I have italicised "the general progress of their argument", because I have found this a characteristic response to the presentation of evidence contrary to a given interpretation. See page 147 above.

[4] *M, of M.*, 6th edn., 81. Ogden and Richards later (page 86) suggest that further reduction can be made from nerve cells to "molecules, atoms, electrons . . ." There is a great deal of evidence for the theory implied, since the theory is so very general. The analysis, as it is expressed, is crude, and, of course, if taken literally, logically incorrect, since 'direct apprehension' is of a different logical category from "certain happenings in the nerves". But what Black is objecting to is the absence of *evidence.*

because he wanted to. He had an answer to a faulty theory, one which perhaps, like Wittgenstein and Ryle, he had once himself been entoiled in,[1] and which now in his convert-enthusiasm he saw as a universal heresy. But though something like this is fairly widespread, the meanders of history since *The Meaning of Meaning* have led the fashions of those to whom its temper was agreeable to be retrospectively attributed to this book. Like so much of the past, we see it now in the distorting light of subsequent events which it influenced but did not determine.[2]

Black, as well as making the wrong categorisation, failed to make the right one. He failed to see, for instance, that the references to "science" in *The Meaning of Meaning* were generally in connection with language, with suggesting that science limited itself to the observing of correlations, with answers in terms of the 'how' rather than with the 'what' of things, answers moreover which are expressed in terms which are the same as any we use in the natural sciences. So far from explaining "simple interpretation" in terms of a special brain configuration recurring for each recurrence of a particular interpretation, Ogden and Richards' is a more general theory:

> The current scientific account . . . which reduces causation to correlation, is awkward for the purposes of exposition . . . If we recognise, however, as the basis of this account the fact that experience has the character of recurrence, that is, comes to us in more or less uniform contexts, we have in this all that is required for the theory of signs . . .[3]

But the language in which the "theory of signs" was expressed was much less important for its authors than the lesson it was meant to convey, namely, heightening awareness of the complexity of thought *simple* wording might hide, and the variety of thoughts, because of our different learning experiences, that the *same* wording could on different occasions and for different people signify. By means of analysis, definition, and being constantly on the alert, we were to reduce the obfuscations both of our words and of those of others. Why should Ogden and Richards write *four* chapters on definitions, if they believed appeal to neurological happenings was what language differences required for their solution?

Of course Black might have been indulging in rhetorical exaggerations, and might argue that philosophy is not scholarship like literary

---

[1] See his sympathetic introduction to his translation of Carnap's *The Unity of Science* in 1934, and his account of his change of attitude to "behaviourism" in *Language and Philosophy*, page 211.

[2] Another example of this was the unwarranted belief that certain words, such as 'good' or, according to Black, 'beauty', were mainly or entirely emotive.

[3] *M. of M.*, 6th edn., 55.

criticism or history, that it is concerned with general arguments and not with who precisely did what. But I do not think he *would* argue like this, because he singled out a particular book for attack and would not be indifferent to its reputation. His very method, that of singling out a step in the reasoning upon which all subsequent reasoning depended, seems to me misguided. The book is not logically close-knit. I think Black may have been right in his suggestion that Ogden and Richards were advancing a substitution theory of learning (see footnote 4 on page 21). Certainly, I think it is highly oversimplified. But other theories, which could be empirically investigated, could be constructed, and this is all that Ogden and Richards need. Black's logical jiu-jitsu leads to an overemphasis upon language and upon how it might cause a fatal error at a particular moment of reasoning. An alternative approach, one which I adopt, aims at studying the book as a whole, divining its *purposes* and judging what is important in the light of these, an approach which also recognises how much the interpretation of any one part of the book depends upon the understanding of other parts. It lays more stress on individuality, less on general arguments that may only quite conventionally be represented in a given book. Nevertheless in both approaches we have to categorise in the light of previous experience.

Black's second article, written six years later (1948), "Questions about Emotive Meaning", is much less at fault than his first. It makes a number of valuable criticisms, pointing out the vagueness of Richards' theories, describing his later views as involving "an intrusive and pervasive dissolution of structure" and noting Richards' tendency, in spite of the *theory*, to concentrate in practice on single words rather than on sentences. The article is much more tentative in its interpretation of Richards, suggesting difficulties and asking questions with regard to his meaning. However Black still adheres to his view of Richards' theory as being a "behaviourist" one. He describes Richards as believing in "a science of criticism", which he never did,[1] and condemns him for "failing to provide criteria for practice" in judging the value of a poem. If Black meant the kind of criteria which science demands, that is, something readily and un-ambiguously applied, no part of Richards' theory ever demanded this, if only on the grounds that psychology was as yet far too elementary to enable us to do this. But in fact, although Richards did sometimes talk as though it were just a matter of another hundred years' research, I think to be consistent, he must really be taken as referring to the *theory* of aesthetics. From the point of view of *practice*, the purpose of the arts was not fulfilled by being able to judge whether a given work of art was good or not, but by experienc-

[1] See pages 36-37 above.

ing, fully and correctly, good works of art. The criticism that a correct interpretation of Richards entails is not that he didn't provide universal criteria for judging the value of a work of art, but that he worked out a theory of what the effects of good works of art were. Unlike the associationist theory of meaning presented in *The Meaning of Meaning*, this theory was specific enough to be obviously too remote from any evidence we were likely to get. But it is incorrect to say that Richards advanced his theory as a scientific certitude.

The main misunderstanding Black showed in this second article was one to which we have already referred and which was shown by many critics of Richards. It was the failure to see that, for Richards, reference played an important part in poetry. Black considers Ogden and Richards' statements that a poem "tells us, or should tell us, nothing."[1] "If to 'tell' means to *assert*," Black writes; "the doctrine has some truth." This, as we saw, was how Ogden and Richards meant it. Black however decides otherwise and takes it to deny that poetry should use references at all, confessing himself puzzled as to ". . . how a poem that 'tells nothing' can induce a fitting, or valuable, attitude".[2] So Black, as the New Critics also did, convicted Richards of "fail[ing] to do justice to the cognitive factors in aesthetic or ethical experience".[3] Later on, Black shows some qualms about his interpretation, since he notices some remarks that are inconsistent with it. Nevertheless by picking out two hard nut assertions, difficult ones, which we attempted to explain (page 57 above), about the relative independence of emotive and referential functions, Black is able to persist with his interpretation. "Similar statements", he writes, "are scattered throughout Richards' early writings." I have found hardly any, unless one is to count the many statements about feelings being aroused by means of references, and to interpret these as meaning that the relationship is "tenuous . . . external, vague, and fluctuating"[4], though they don't in fact say so.

What is interesting about Black's approach is that, though the accusation he makes is a familiar one, the reasons he adduces for it are novel. These are that Richards failed in his analysis of language to distinguish between the functions of presentation and assertion. It is as though, having made his categorisation, Black then sought for some reason in linguistic theory for it.

All referential discourse is treated as if it were *assertion*, and so necessarily either true or false. And if some use of language is patently not intended to

---

[1] See page 28 above.
[2] *Ibid.*, 207.
[3] *Ibid.*, 208. Stevenson, as we shall shortly show, held the opposite opinion about Richards' neglect of cognitive as opposed to emotive factors in *ethical* experience.
[4] *Ibid.*, 209.

have such truth claims (as is usually the case in literature), there seems no recourse but to relegate it to the realm of "emotive" or nonreferential utterance.[1]

This is the reason why Black does not interpret "tell", in "[a poem] tells us, or should tell us, nothing", as meaning to assert.

The trouble about the therapeutic method in philosophy, into which Black's merges, is that it requires much greater care than philosophers by reason of their main interests are disposed to give, in working out precisely what the writer they wish to cure was actually saying. If Ogden and Richards wrongly treated all *purely* referential statements as assertion, this was because, according to their view, they would not be purely referential unless information-giving were the purpose of the writer. This was Ogden and Richards' point about purely referential discourse being a rare and late development in the history of language, and limited to science. It does not follow from this that their theory requires that *any* use of reference in language, which was mixed or purely emotive (as to its intended effects), was for the sake of assertion. And in fact we have seen that they did distinguish between reference used for assertion and that used for the sake only of its further effects in attitudes, emotions and feelings.

Furthermore, as we have seen (pages 25-26 above), Ogden and Richards had rather a peculiar way of using 'true' and 'false', according to which the fact that one called certain symbols (words or sentences in actual use) 'true' or 'false' did not entail saying that they were used for the purpose of information. A false statement, like 'all swans are white', is by virtue of being false, not a complex symbol but a succession of simple symbols each of which is true; though you might not be meaning to give information, in speaking an object word like 'swan' or 'white' you were in effect asserting (because implying) the existence of swans and white things. Whatever we may think of this analysis, it does not make Ogden and Richards inconsistent in saying that references *can* be used in poetry for the sake of their emotional effects or Richards in saying that "the questioning verificatory way of handling [references in poetry] is irrelevant". *This* misunderstanding of Black's is one of that not uncommon class where the necessary right categorisation is not made because of its unlikelihood. It is likely to happen wherever a word or phrase with well-recognised uses—in this case, the word 'true'—is employed in some unusual manner. This is something to which Richards' practices make him rather liable, but, by definition, not something which Multiple Definition can assist us with—for it gives us only the usual definitions.

[1] *Ibid.*, 207.

The next philosopher I shall consider is Professor Stevenson. In his well known book, *Ethics and Language*, he paid frequent tribute to Richards' influence;[1] indeed the first of the two epigraphs to the book as a whole consists of quite a lengthy extract from *The Meaning of Meaning*. The book is characterised by the very close attention it gives to language, in particular to the persuasive element in what stands for referential discourse. It might without exaggeration be regarded as an example of the movement for close reading associated with literary criticism, an area in which Professor Stevenson is himself clearly interested. Yet here too we shall find misreadings of Richards.

Professor Stevenson describes Richards as having two different ethical theories. The first of them is the one we described when dealing with the *Principles of Literary Criticism*. Stevenson categorises it as "one of many which, though emphasising attitudes, virtually ignores agreement and disagreement in attitude".[2] This judgment seems odd in view of Richards' stress on the relativity of value to the level of organisation an individual has achieved, according to which what is valuable to one person cannot be to another. Similarly, it scarcely does justice to Richards' recognition of ethical relativity in such remarks as "there are evidently a great number of good systematisations and what is good for one person will not be good for another . . . With different conditions different values necessarily arise . . ."[3]

Stevenson goes on to say that "there are divergent elements in Richards' theory of value, not always brought together in a consistent fashion."[4] He then attributes to Richards quite another ethical theory which he claims to discover in *The Meaning of Meaning*. This second theory, an emotive theory of the function of ethical words, later made fashionable by the Logical Positivists, was regarded by Stevenson as anticipating his own, so that we might regard this as a hobby-horse categorisation.

The theory is derived from a short passage plus footnote in *The Meaning of Meaning*, which is given the place of honour as an epigraph to Stevenson's book, paired with, but leading, a passage from Dewey. Seeing this passage there is rather like suddenly discovering that the guest of honour at a foreign dinner party is a well-known fraud from one's home town. The trusting foreigners do not know him for what he is. For this passage, instead of being an original ethical theory Ogden and Richards brilliantly adumbrate in advance of their time, is a typical piece of debunking of the postulating

[1] On such details of interpretation as ambiguity and its virtues, multiple definition, and sleeping metaphors.
[2] *Ethics and Language* (1944), page 10.
[3] *P.L.C.*, 60.
[4] *Ethics and Language*, 9.

of *sui generis* entities. Here is Stevenson's epigraph from *The Meaning of Meaning* in full:

"Good" is alleged to stand for a unique, unanalysable concept [which] is the subject matter of ethics. This peculiar ethical use of "good" is, we suggest, a purely emotive use. When so used the word stands for nothing whatever, and has no symbolic function. Thus, when we so use it in the sentence, *"This is good,"* we merely refer to *this,* and the addition of "is good" makes no difference whatever to our reference. When on the other hand, we say, *"This is red,"* the addition of "is red" to "this" does symbolise an extension of our reference, namely, to some other red thing. But "is good" has no comparable *symbolic* function; it serves only as an emotive sign expressing our attitude to *this,* and perhaps evoking similar attitudes in other persons, or inciting them to actions of one kind or another . . . Of course, if we define "the good" as "that of which we approve of approving", or give any such definition when we say: "This is good", we shall be making an assertion. It is only the indefinable "good" which we suggest to be a purely emotive sign. The "something more" or "something else" which, it is alleged, is not covered by any definition of "good" is the emotional aura of the word.[1]

But what Ogden and Richards are doing here is attacking a theory like G. E. Moore's. They are saying that, so far from producing some high-sounding theory—the "supersensuous Idea" of good, as Richards calls it in the *Principles*—Moore has been led up the garden path by his failure to realise the emotive aspect of words. The whole panoply of *Principia Ethica,* they suggest, is arrayed in the cause of a grunt of approval. Now though purely emotive language is all right in poetry, Ogden and Richards clearly disapproved of it in controversy. In ethical discussion they thought words ought to have content, however much they might at the same time be expressing emotion. That is why the paragraph from which Stevenson picked his epigraph starts with the warning . . .

if *scientific* methods of statement are to be extended to fields such as those traditionally tended by philosophers, certain *very subtle dangers* must be provided for. Amongst these is the occurrence, in hitherto quite unsuspected numbers, of words which have been erroneously regarded without question as symbolic in function. The word 'good' may be taken as an example.[2]

and why Stevenson's passage is immediately followed by the words

The recognition that many of the most popular subjects of discussion are *infested* with symbolically blank but emotively active words of this kind is a necessary preliminary to the extension of *scientific method* to these questions.[3]

---

[1] *M. of M.,* 6th edn., 125. The last three sentences, starting with "Of course", are really a footnote, which is signalled at the end of the first sentence quoted.
[2] *M. of M.,* 6th edn. page 124—my italics.
[3] *M. of M.* 6th edn., page 125—my italics.

Possibly Stevenson started a process of distortion of Ogden and Richards' theory, which made it like theories that later became fashionable. At all events we find Toulmin and Baier in an article, "On Describing", written eight years later,[1] quoting from the same passage as Stevenson and with similar effect. They identify a theory they call "The Great Divide", according to which "there are two large classes into which sentences, and the words which figure in them can be divided"—statements, that is, 'descriptions', "which are the concern of the sciences" on the one hand, and those which are not statements and "which are the concern of, for instance, ethics, aesthetics, poetry and cognate activities", on the other. Ogden and Richards are held to have played an important part in creating this theory, a view which is backed up by a number of sentences from Stevenson's epigraph. All the sentences and phrases in the paragraph which would oppose this simplified view are omitted, and the context and purpose of the paragraph do not seem to have been noticed at all. "The authors do not say whether certain words are descriptive entirely and others emotive entirely, or whether all words are both descriptive and emotive, but in different proportions", is an accusation which is contradicted again and again in *The Meaning of Meaning*, for Ogden and Richards never held that *any* word was in itself emotive or descriptive, for this was entirely a matter of how it was *used*.

Six years later, we find a third philosopher, Professor Frankena, who mentions Toulmin and Baier's article a number of times, but now goes further, asserting that Ogden and Richards "insist that 'good' and 'beautiful' are "purely emotive" terms, apparently in spite of any ideational associations they may have", and that they "have no symbolic reference"[2]—an extraordinary assertion when we remember that a chapter is given up to discussing sixteen different types of referential definitions of 'beauty'.

We have suggested that these examples illustrate the way in which a given theory influences not only what happened later, but also what occurred before. Ogden and Richards, who may have had an influence by reason of their theory about the emotive *uses* of words, have suffered for it because they are now seen as early examples of the view, propagated by the Logical Positivists, that ethical words were nothing more than emotive. My most recent example of misreading shows this process being carried to its logical conclusion by presenting Ogden and Richards as actually contemporaries of the Logical Positivist view. Mrs. Warnock, in her book *Ethics Since 1900* (1960), actually describes *The Meaning of Meaning* as published in the same

---

[1] *Mind*, LXI, 1952.

[2] In *Language, Thought and Culture*, ed. Henle (1958), pages 151-152

year, 1936, as Ayer's *Language, Truth, and Logic*. That she was influenced by previous interpretations, probably Toulmin and Baier's *Mind* article, is however suggested by her statement that Ogden and Richards "first introduced the word 'emotive' " (which it would be difficult to know if the book had indeed been published in the same year), and by the fact that the passage she quotes to illustrate Ogden and Richards' 'theory' is, once again, Stevenson's epigraph. But a further elaboration is introduced, for this passage is quoted to demonstrate that Ogden and Richards' 'theory', "being derived from the same sources, and the outcome of the very same influences, is, even verbally, very close to [Ayer's]".[1] The "sources and influences" referred to are Russell and Wittgenstein, who are mentioned in Ayer's preface, but this acknowledgment is not, I would have thought, much more than the conventional recognition of Logical Positivism's debt to these two philosophers. It is their interest in Logic that is important. Ayer's ethical theories came mainly from Carnap, and it is highly unlikely that Ogden and Richards derived their emotive/referential distinction from either Russell or Wittgenstein. Any influence is more likely to have been the other way round.[2]

One last example, and our show-case of philosophers' exhibits will be complete. This is Manuel Bilsky's critique of "Richards' Theory of Value".[3] It is a useful example because it quotes from Richards' writings in some detail in order to back up given interpretations. Bilsky refers with approval to Stevenson's view that Richards had in fact two different theories of value, and classifies these as "analysis" and "naturalism"—Richards, for him, is "the advocate of analysing concepts and the proponent of a particular naturalistic position". In fact this does not seem to be at all what Stevenson had in mind, and it fails to realise that the purpose of Richards' *analysis* was to improve communication which would include knowing how to take the referential sense, so that the right emotional responses would be created in the reader. Bilsky seems to have been reading Richards with spectacles that split the sense prismatically into qualitatively different types of conventional ethical theory.

Of Richards' standard of value he says, "there is very little that is surprising or unconventional in the means he takes to reach it".

---

[1] I have noticed a few similarities in the kinds of words used by Ayer, and Ogden and Richards; for instance, Ayer's reference to "the *primitive superstition* that to every name a single real entity must correspond" (*Language, Truth and Logic*, 2nd edn., page 42, my italics). But of course this reference to Word Magic is more likely to indicate the direct influence of Ogden and Richards' book upon Ayer.

[2] Ramsey's 1925 review of *The Meaning of Meaning* in *Mind*, for instance, though fairly critical, awarded points to Ogden and Richards for their introduction of the distinction between emotive and referential uses of language.

[3] *Phil. Phen. Res.*, XIV, 1954.

Richards' "first step is psychological egoism", and Richards' state-ment, "anyone *will actually prefer* to satisfy a greater number of equal appetencies than a less", is quoted. But, continues Bilsky, "the egocentric position to which [Richards'] initial formulation of the standard has led him apparently troubles him". Richards "is disturbed by the charge of egoism, or selfishness [which] can be brought against a . . . morality such as this . . ." Consequently he "converts [this egoism] to utilitarianism". The problem, says Bilsky, is an "ancient" one, and all Richards is able to do to answer it is "to appeal to the authority of Jeremy Bentham". Hence "Richards' standard of value . . . appears to be a rather orthodox nineteenth century British utilitarianism". As to the question, "How does he propose to get people to live according to his standard?", "he gives us no systematic answer such as we find in Bentham or Mill, but he does, perhaps inadvertently, give us some sources of motivation: he appeals to certain consequences". These Bilsky summarises as "motivation . . . supplied by the threat of social ostracism, by the law enforcement agencies, by the individual understanding", the third from a remark of Richards that, if a person understood his own interests, "he would be a useful and charming member of his community", which Bilsky describes as a "hint at a Platonic kind of motivation". But "in developing his ethical theory, Richards, in some important respects, has made the same mistakes, and has fallen into the same traps, as many of his predecessors". In demonstrating this, Bilsky concentrates on how Richards answers the question why a person "should choose to gratify the desires of another rather than his own", i.e. how he takes the step from psychological egoism to utilitarianism. The answer, according to Bilsky, is that Richards "uses another kind of appeal to authority, namely, to those he considers to be the best qualified judges of what we ought and ought not to do". Richards is accused of doing what he condemned the usage theorists for, when they used as a standard the practice of the *best* writers. "He has, apparently without being aware of it," Bilsky writes, "brought in a qualitative element, thus abandoning the purely quantitative amount of value which he thinks he has. He has made the transition from Bentham to John Stuart Mill." Richards has fallen "into the trap which awaits any empirical theory of this sort. For ulti-mately the judge, in arguing that one experience is better than an-other, must, if he goes beyond their quantitative equality, rely on an intuition."

Now we are not concerned with the defects and virtues of Bilsky's criticism, but solely with what it tells us of what he understands Richards' theory to be. The picture that is presented is of a piece of highly incompetent theorising that is nevertheless rather conventional and commits the normal mistakes. The fact that Richards' theory has been to quite a large extent misunderstood arouses the suspicion that expectations, based upon stock categories in ethical thought, have caused words and sentences that fit in with these categories to be selected to determine the sense in which other words and sentences are taken. Furthermore, although many quotations are made from Richards' writings, these are only from the *Principles* and *Science and Poetry*. His thought does not therefore appear to have been considered as a whole—later developments often indicate what the original structure was—and, in particular, the *application* of the theory, given in detail in *Practical Criticism*, does not seem to have been considered.

As an indication of how an interpretation may be forced upon a sentence, let us look at the evidence Bilsky quotes for his belief that "the egocentric position to which his initial formulation of the standard [of value] has led him apparently troubles him". Richards, says Bilsky, is disturbed by "the charge of egoism or selfishness [which] can be brought against a . . . morality such as this . . .". This suggests a rather weak, even guilty, approach. But what Richards actually says is "the charge of egoism, or selfishness, can be brought against a naturalistic or utilitarian morality such as this only by over-looking the importance of these satisfactions in any well-balanced life".[1] "These satisfactions", as the previous sentence makes clear, are ones "which require humane, sympathetic and friendly relations between individuals". Bilsky's way of characterising Richards' approach fits in with his emphasis upon the "converting" of egoism into utilitarianism. But I think Richards' approach is much less conventional than Bilsky thinks it is. There is, for instance, no such pure theoretical split between "psychological egoism" on the one hand, and utilitarianism on the other as Bilsky believes. Though Richards recognises that social sanctions may provide part of "the motivation . . . to get people to live according to [Richards'] standard", he again and again emphasises that *these* motives are relatively unimportant. "Swindling and bullying . . . have their cost; which the best judges agree to be excessive. [But] . . . the greater part of the cost lies *not* in the consequences of being found out, in the loss of social esteem and so forth, but in actual systematic disability to attain important values."[2] Richards' approach is a phenomenological one. He finds it a fact of experience that impulses are interrelated, that a form of selfishness, for instance, may prevent us from having those experiences that may spontaneously come from the emotional generosity of love. Possibly people *might* change their behaviour if they could realise this. Something like this is an assumption of psycho-

[1] *P.L.C.*, page 53.
[2] *P.L.C.*, 53, 54.

analytical theory, but I doubt whether there is much point in describing such an insight as "a Platonic kind of motivation".

Furthermore the "appeal to the authority of Jeremy Bentham"—"about the best Richards seems able to muster"—which suggests great weakness on Richards' part, is not an appeal, but a putting of a point for the sake of clarity in Bentham's words—"the best brief statement" as Richards called it. Perhaps this error was due to Bilsky's interpreting the sentence, "To extend this individual morality to communal affairs . . .", for which the lines from Bentham were quoted, as meaning 'To convert egoism into utilitarianism . . .' But Richards had already described the individual morality as a "utilitarian" one when dealing with the charge of "selfishness" in a preceding paragraph we have already quoted. Here he is about to do something new, and it is evident from the next paragraph that "communal activities" refers to the activities of *governments*. The Bentham quotation *is* misleading here, and Richards wrote very elliptically, but Richards does very clearly intend concern for others in his "individual morality" and it is highly unlike him just to rest on the authority of another.

The crucial misunderstanding, however, was that that caused Bilsky to perceive Richards as having "made the same mistakes, and . . . fallen into the same traps, as many of his predecessors", namely, that he had, "apparently without being aware of it, brought in a qualitative element, thus abandoning the purely quantitative account of value which he thinks he has". Now we have already seen, when describing Richards' theory of value, that Richards was perfectly consistent and nowhere introduced qualitative considerations. He was able to regard some experiences as more valuable than others, not only because they satisfied more impulses, but also because they resulted in such improvements in organising capacity that greater numbers of impulses could be satisfied in the future. But hardly any commentators on Richards seem to have noticed this. Even where they show no positive misinterpretations of Richards, as for instance Professor Harding's *Scrutiny* article[1] on the *Principles*, there is a sort of negative misinterpretation in not having noticed this aspect of Richards' theory, which is fundamental for a complete understanding of the theory advanced in that book.

The particular reason why Bilsky attributed the surreptitious reintroduction of qualitative differences in pleasure to Richards was Richards' use of phrases like "the best judges", whose opinion about value he was ready to take as a standard. Phrases like this, or "universal qualified opinion", which should have warned critics against assuming that Richards believed in a "*science*" of criticism, have puzzled many of those who have written about him. But already

[1] D. W. Harding, *Scrutiny*, I, 1933.

in *The Meaning of Meaning*, which to a far greater extent than his critics have realised is of a whole theoretical piece with the *Principles* and *Practical Criticism*, Richards (and Ogden) indicated their ground for trusting to a good literary critic's judgment. "The evaluation [of the attitudes aroused by works of art] must rest ultimately," they wrote, "upon the opinions of those best qualified to be judges by the range and delicacy of their experience and their freedom from irrelevant preoccupations".[1] Given Richards' assumption about the growth of our ordering capacity as a consequence of enjoying ordered satisfactions of impulses, and given his assumptions (see *P.L.C.* pages 192-196) about our similarity to one another and the existence of a certain degree of cultural homogeneity in the population under discussion, then, since we cannot judge the value of a work of art except by experiencing it, and cannot experience it without having a certain amount of organising power achievable only by disciplined study of art, it will follow that critics will on the whole be able to tell us which works of art we would come most to value. I do not therefore think Richards was inconsistent in his particular development of utilitarianism. His theory of value is more original, more competent, and probably more wrong than Bilsky's account of it. We shall be criticising it later, but first it is well to be clear what the theory is.

[1] *M. of M.*, 6th edn., 159.

Chapter Seven

COMPREHENDING COMPREHENDING (II)—LITERARY CRITICS

NOT all the literary critics who have written about Richards and whose works I have read, show evidence of misunderstanding him, any more than all philosophers do. Only about half fall into this class, though if we were to include a *full* understanding of Richards' theory, then the proportion would dwindle considerably. As I pointed out earlier, few writers seem to have appreciated Richards' theory about the way in which experiences are valuable, because of the increased capacity for fulfilling impulses that they bring about, something which we need to understand in order to understand his later notions of growth, and self-fulfilment. If these ideas are noticed at all, they are dismissed as "mysterious" or treated as simple, rather than as the complex abstractions they are. The means to understanding them lie in Richards' speculative theory about attitudes. But his critics are generally too ignorant of psychology to follow Richards' reasoning, or so much reacting against what they conceive to be an overemphasis upon science, psychology, and neurological models that they are prevented from seeing the distinct and well articulated pattern that is presented in the *Principles* and which should act as a frame of reference for the later works.

Then again there may be some who reveal no misunderstanding of Richards because they limit themselves to reproducing extracts from his writings and do not essay much comment on them, except to indicate approval. These writers do not give us the opportunity of testing their understanding of Richards. Cleanth Brooks is an example here, and, amongst philosophers, Karl Britton.

Those who do provide clear-cut evidence of misunderstanding are no minor figures, as I hope to show by my examples. They are all apostles of the close reading of poetry, and consideration of their faults in reading prose obviously has implications for their interpretation of poetry.

I. AN EMPSON-EYE VIEW

My first example is one who is often described as a disciple of Richards as well as being a master in his own right, William Empson. I shall

169

consider what he says about Richards in the first chapter and appendix of his book, *The Structure of Complex Words*, published in 1951, and dedicated to Richards as "the source of all ideas in this book." The book, written in a casual, informal style, is very difficult to read; Empson writes his detailed ideas down very much as they come, so that in reading him one follows a zig-zag course. Returns to the main theme are liable to be made by means of somewhat elliptical sentences, whose subjects are demonstratives or pronouns where it is often rather unclear what they stand for, so that one gets an impression of someone talking to himself. Perhaps Empson's tendency to atomise Richards' theories is simply another example of his waywardness, his tendency to be intrigued by trees so that one despairs sometimes of one's path through the wood. Mr. Empson's eye is like that of an insect, thousand-faceted.

Empson's book is devoted, as his two previous ones were, to detailed analysis of the way in which individual words function in poetry. It is more systematic than its predecessors, partly in that its separate chapters are devoted to the study of single words in some literary work, but mainly by virtue of its attempt to classify different types of relations between a word and its senses, implications, moods, emotions and statements. This latter operation is introduced by a critical consideration of Richards' early views on the same matter. Empson's criticisms are continually tempered by generous acknowledgements of Richards' influence, and he recognises that he may have misunderstood Richards or that Richards may not have meant what he said, so that it was only the way he put things that may have been misleading. However what matters for our purposes is how Empson in fact understood Richards.

I believe, as I hope to show, that, perceptive and just as many of his criticisms were, Empson nevertheless misunderstood Richards to quite a degree. Though he showed some evidence of categorising, his interpretation of Richards, in contrast to those of other commentators, showed much overindividualising of Richards' meaning, a taking of Richards' meaning as more specific than it actually was. Empson's case is interesting, of course, because his closeness to Richards and his detailed care in reading should make him least likely to misunderstand his former teacher. Unfortunately it is difficult to present his misunderstandings without appearing pedantic. This is because Empson's comments on Richards do not seem to have been made in the interest of taking up any general theoretical positions. Therefore I cannot present them in that kind of way. Empson commented and indeed, in his rather wayward manner browsed over Richards' various theories, as he mentioned them, and I have to take this evidence as it comes. Possibly we have to do with a relationship between Empson's own way of thinking and the manner in which he took Richards. Empson's style reveals that he constantly sacrifices the communication of his argument to giving full rein to his sensitivity. There seems to be no suppression in the interests of logical consecutiveness. His comments on philosophy reveal a certain amateur quality that I suspect enters to a small degree even in his approach to meaning in poetry, and which I would attribute to a *reluctance* to submit himself to any other discipline than that of his own very highly developed consciousness. He should be scholarly and he should be skilled in philosophy, since he is clearly very well read in that subject, but I suspect that his concern for the *particular* prevents this properly developing,[1] as was also the case, though to a much more obvious degree, with Virginia Woolf. At all events, since Richards, in contrast to Empson, thought in terms of very *general* categories, which he had disciplined himself to understand, we might expect some difficulty in comprehension here. Empson's interpretations should therefore have an additional interest for us.

Empson starts off by attributing to Richards a twofold view. The first is that "the emotions given by words in poetry are independent of their sense",[2] so "that a writer of poetry had better not worry about the sense".[3] This is backed up by an odd misreading of some remarks made by Richards in *Mencius on the Mind* on Keats' "Ode on a Grecian Urn". We have already seen (see pages 28-29, 49-59) that this view was one Richards held only about some, certainly not about all or the bulk of poetry, so we will not say anything further about this, but go on to the second view Empson attributes to Richards. This was that "the function of poetry is to call out an attitude which is not dependent on any belief open to disproof by facts".[4]

It is never easy to smoke Empson out, not least because, as in this typically ambiguous statement, his bolt-holes have so many exits. In one sense this statement is an accurate description of a view Richards held, for, as we have seen, he pointed out the dangers of substituting "an intellectual formula" for the poetical means by which certain attitudes are aroused. Empson, however, to judge by his arguments against Richards, was meaning something more extreme by his state-

---

[1] A rather obvious example is Empson's comment on a definition of 'attitude' in Stevenson's *Ethics and Language*. This definition was: "An attitude is a complicated conjunction of dispositional properties . . . marked by stimuli and responses which relate to hindering or assisting whatever it is that is the 'object' of the attitude." Empson's comment starts off, "This sounds rather altrustic, in a vague way, . . .". (*The Structure of Complex Words*, 2nd edn., 415). Such a comment, by personalising a conventional definition, reveals an odd misreading.

[2] *The Structure of Complex Words*, 2nd edn. (1952), page 6.

[3] ibid., 14

[4] ibid., 7.

ment. He says that this view was "intimately connected" with the other, that is, the one about words in poetry acting on the emotions directly and not *via* their sense. And he believes that Richards' "crucial belief" in this matter is the one indicated by the statement in the *Principles* that

> awareness of the nature of the world and the development of attitudes which enable us to live in it finely are almost independent.

As we saw when discussing this on page 58, this statement is either in flat contradiction to one made earlier in the same book, or to be taken in rather a limited way in which "awareness of the nature of the world" is to be equated with actual *scientific* knowledge. It is not a good candidate for being "crucial". On the other hand, the view that really is crucial, the one about poetical effects not being made dependent upon intellectual formulae, is not mentioned by Empson at all.

At all events, what we find Empson doing is correcting Richards by making points that, in fact, Richards himself made. Referring to plays and poems where, in order to get the effect, you have to understand the beliefs held by the characters or persons referred to, Empson wrote,

> The solution of the 'Problem of Belief', as to how we can enjoy the literary expression of beliefs which we don't hold, is not that we separate them from their consequences but that we imagine some other person who holds them, an author or a character, and thus get a kind of experience of what their consequences (for a given sort of person) really are.[1]

But, in discussing the way in which beliefs enter into poetry, Richards himself mentioned, as *one* kind of belief, those beliefs as to "how any person of a certain character would speak or act, probably or necessarily", upon which so much drama seems to depend. He described them as "acceptances involved in the *understanding* of a play", his point being that we "accepted" them "as conditions for further effects, our attitudes and emotional responses"[2] (see also page 54 above). Indeed Empson, later in his exposition, quotes a statement to similar effect from *The Meaning of Meaning*, as though now revealing inconsistencies in Richards. "Put in this way", he writes, "the doctrine seems so reasonable that I must make a new set of admissions".[3]

Empson's "new admissions" lead him, as we shall see, into some very peculiar by-paths. He categorised the statement in *The Meaning*

---

[1] ibid., 9.
[2] *P.L.C.*, 277-278 (my italics).
[3] *The Structure of Complex Words*, 2nd edn., 11.

of Meaning about references in poetry being used "not for the sake of their truth or falsity but for the sake of the attitudes which their acceptances will evoke", as "the old line of joke that the poets tell 'excellent lies' ".[1] Now although "excellent lies" in poetry would be an example of referential statements being used for their effects on attitudes, it is very obvious that they need not be the only example. The proper way of categorising Richards' statement is as a warning that the function of poetry is not the providing of information. This, I think, is also how we should take Richards' idea of pseudo-statements. Although Richards sometimes wrote as though they were to be limited to statements expressing the "Magical View of the Universe"[2], his definition of them in *Science and Poetry* as "a form of words which is justified entirely by its effect in releasing or organising our impulses and attitudes" suggests a much wider class of statements, and the wording is the same as he used in his previous books in describing the part played by reference in poetry. Richards, in fact, was totally opposed to the use of lies in poetry. Statements expressing the Magical View of the Universe were not *lies* when used in the past, because then they were believed to be true. They were, in other words, the product of sincerity. Today we had to respond to these statements in the poetry of the past differently. The attitudes that gave rise to them could be re-aroused in ourselves, provided we did not have faulty ideas about the function of reference in poetry. But modern poets should not use these kinds of statements, except dramatically. To do so otherwise would indeed be to lie. This is what Richards criticised in Yeats and Lawrence.

Now although Empson was aware of this attitude of Richards to modern poetry, he categorised pseudo-statements as "inspiring lies told by the poets".[3] Consequently he found himself in the absurd position of trying to determine what sort of pseudo-statements, conceived as lies, we should use today. "One does not get clear from *Science and Poetry*", he complains, "what sort of pseudo-statements can still be valuable when they are recognised as such, and yet some of them must be of this sort because they are to save us from the collapse of the Magical View of Nature". He considers various candidates, interposes a reminder—"you must be able to use them as statements for emotional effect without feeling that you are cheating yourself"—and looks at some further candidates. Finally, he re-formulates his task once more: "I am looking for the pseudo-

---

[1] ibid., 426.
[2] Richards characterised this as "the belief in a world of Spirits and Powers which control events and which can be evoked, and to some extent, controlled themselves by human practices". (S. and P., 47).
[3] ibid., 426.

statements which are to be the basis for the arts of the future, which can be a reliable support for valuable attitudes".[1] Having thus prepared the ground, he whisks out of his top-hat the following rabbit:—"The Theory of Value itself is the only important candidate." A not untypical piece of Empsonian ingenuity perhaps, but won, it seems, at the cost of standing his master on his head. We have only to compare Faustus's

> See, see where Christ's blood streams in the firmament!
> One drop would save my soul . . .

with

> Anything is valuable which will satisfy an appetency without involving the frustration of some equal or more important appetency

to see how far Empson has wandered from Richards' meaning.

How did Empson come to make such an identification? That Richards' theory of value was false, or at least, though asserted as true, in fact unprovable, Empson argued on a number of grounds. In particular, he argued that it was impossible to determine the relative value of different experiences because of the difficulty of counting fulfilled impulses, and that we could not really say that the impulses were all equal. But the path by which Empson came to assert that the theory was also an *emotive* statement was a tortuous one. Let us see whether we can trace it.

What seems to have played a part in Empson's understanding of the theory of value is once again that short passage in *The Meaning of Meaning* from which Stevenson derived his epigraph. In the Appendix of his book, Empson considers Stevenson's theory of value and ends his discussion by suggesting that "Stevenson's views . . . derive eventually from *The Meaning of Meaning*". Empson then quotes that part of the epigraph of Stevenson's book that came from the footnote in *The Meaning of Meaning*. He does this in order to convict Ogden and Richards of an inconsistency. The relevant words in the footnote are: "if we define 'the good' as 'that of which we approve of approving' . . . we shall be making an assertion. It is only the undefinable[2] 'good' which we suggest to be merely an emotive sign." Empson describes the sample definition ('good' is that of which we approve of approving) as an "emotive" one, and comments, "so if this man wants his assertion to be emotive, or about emotions, this is precisely what stops it

---

[1] ibid., 423.

[2] Ogden and Richards wrote "*in*definable". Judging by Empson's interpretation of Richards' theory of value (see next page) it looks as though Empson might have taken this word as meaning 'undefined'. If this were so, the misprint might indicate a step in this process.

from being emotive."[1] This he regards as inconsistent with "the supposed close connection between the Emotive use of language and the intention of exciting Attitudes, by which any piece of language which is "predominantly" concerned to excite an Attitude is called Emotive".[2]

But clearly, and I think this is what the philosophers were doing too, he failed to distinguish between emotive language and an 'emotive' *theory* of ethics. The holding of the latter does not entail that all uses of ethical words, as, for instance, when one makes a moral judgment that a given act is good, are themselves purely emotive, or "symbolically blank", as Ogden and Richards sometimes put it. The word is not just the product of feeling, as a shiver or breathless intonation might be. It is used as the result of a cognitive judgment, relating our perception of the act to our *perception* of our feeling in relation to it. This is true, however much the statement of one's judgments might be emotive in the other sense of that word, that is, when its function is to affect our hearer's attitudes and behaviour.

Furthermore, it is not the case that the statement of "an Emotive definition", as Empson calls it, is itself emotive, simply because the definition, that is to say, the *theory*, is an emotive one. It might, of course, be argued that all definitions are emotive in the sense that they are prescriptive in intent, but this would be another matter.

When Empson comes to Richards' theory of value in the *Principles*, he applies to Richards' definition of 'valuable' the same interpretation that he showed with regard to the footnote in *The Meaning of Meaning*. Of the starting phrase of Richards' definition, "anything is valuable which . . .", he says "The word ['valuable'] may be supposed to be primarily emotive," as though Ogden and Richards meant by their footnote that only the (as yet) undefined 'good' was 'merely an emotive sign".[3] Empson then goes on to assert that the definition gives "the word ['valuable'] its new sense, [so that] it is no longer "merely emotive" (though still emotive) and can be used to make true or false assertions." Empson further argues that since the theory is emotive, the statement of it is too. That is to say, the statement has "the intention of exciting Attitudes".

But how can a statement about value consisting in the satisfaction of appetencies possibly arouse important attitudes? Empson's case is similar to Richards' own case for the special value of tragedy, namely, that it is unillusioned. For Empson, the theory of value recognises

[1] ibid., 419.
[2] ibid., 420.
[3] See footnote 2 on previous page.

"the necessity of egoism". This he finds valuable by contrast with most religious theories of the present.

> I . . . think that believing more rosy things about the universe, on the specific ground that we will otherwise feel frustrated (and this is what the arguments that are preferred nowadays by nearly all religious leaders tend to make us do), is extremely harmful . . . By comparison with that kind of thing, the glumness of the theory of Professor Richards is the most attractive feature.[1]

To summarise Empson's argument, the statement of Richards' theory of values is a pseudo-statement because it is not in practice possible to determine whether the theory applies or not; being an emotive theory, the statement of it is partly emotive too; and it is a valuable statement because it does not lead us up the garden path as much as do other pseudo-statements today. This extraordinary muddle, of which I have only described part, seems to me a consequence of that style of thinking which wishes thought to be immediately reflected in words, trusting to the word's ambiguous wealth to pay to sense any price that it requires.

2. THE NEW CRITICS

The last and fullest set of interpretations of Richards I shall consider is that of the New Critics. For this group, Richards served as a frame of reference. He was a predecessor by virtue of the fundamentalness of his approach, his concern with detail, and the appearance of being technical that his interest in language and philosophy gave; he enabled the New Critics to define themselves by contrast, rejecting his 'psychological' approach, his treatment of art in terms of the emotions, and his praise for science; and he confirmed them in this view of poetry by his apparent change of attitude, which started after the *Principles* and was virtually completed by *Coleridge on Imagination* and *The Philosophy of Rhetoric*. At least, this is how some leading New Critics interpreted him. The question is, were they right?

In answering this question, I shall not confine myself to considering their interpretations, but shall also consider to some extent the justice of their criticisms of Richards. Let us start with a look at the New Critics themselves.

The term, "The New Criticism", was first widely promulgated in 1941 by John Crowe Ransom's book of that title. He used it in two senses; one, to refer to certain important near-contemporary predecessors who nevertheless should be faulted in certain respects; two, to refer to their successors, men such as himself, who had won clear

---

[1] ibid., 426-427.

of these errors. The predecessors were Richards "(and his pupil Empson)", T. S. Eliot and Yvor Winters. They were described, respectively, as a "Psychological", an "Historical", and a "Moral" Critic, and these labels pointed at their errors, basically those of bringing non-literary considerations to bear in their judgment of literature.

The way in which Richards is regarded as predecessor is indicated at the book's beginning:

> Discussion of the new criticism must start with Mr. Richards. The new criticism very nearly began with him. It might be said also that it began with him in the right way, because he attempted to found it on a more comprehensive basis than other critics did.

and, in writing of Empson's *Seven Types of Ambiguity*,

> Writings as acute and at the same time as patient and consecutive as these have not existed in English criticism, I think, before Richards and Empson. They become frequent now; Richards and Empson have spread quickly. That is a principal reason why I think it is time to identify a powerful intellectual movement that deserves to be called a 'new criticism'.[1]

Ransom also referred to the New Critics as seeming "eclectic with respect to their predecessors". In a foreword to a collection of essays devoted to propagating the new approach,[2] Mr. Cleanth Brooks expands this remark of Ransom's. "The rise of modern criticism", he wrote, "is part of a general intensification of the study of language and symbolism. The development of semantics, symbolic logic, cultural anthropology, and the psychology of Jung and Freud may all be taken as responses to the same general situation."

These quotations hint at another aspect of the New Criticism, a considerable concern with technique. This meant a greater interest in the poem itself than in its historical or biographical significance, its relations with things outside itself. It also meant a more intellectual approach which, if we add the influence of Hulme and Eliot, encouraged a reaction against Romanticism. In many ways, the New Criticism seems a manifestation of increased specialisation, a consequence, particuarly in America, of a number of departments in universities devoted to teaching and writing about literature, whose members were ripe for self-consciousness as practitioners of a separate discipline. This would lead us to expect a more microscopic approach and a rejection of the notion that some other discipline, such as psychology, was more fundamental. In this respect, the

---

[1] *The New Criticism*, 111.
[2] *Critiques and Essays in Criticism*, 1920-1948, ed. by R. W. Stallman. This collection adds T. E. Hulme as predecessor and F. R. Leavis and his school as allies to the movement. Cf. also *The Importance of Scrutiny*, ed. by Eric Bentley (1948).

history of literary criticism is no different from that of philosophy, linguistics, or sociology. But there are different ways in which a specialism can define itself. An additional one that many New Critics adopted, scarcely new in the history of literary theory, was for art to contrast itself with science by stressing the complication, rather than the simplification, of the experience art dealt with.

We can now introduce a distinction amongst the New Critics. Some stuck to their last, concentrating on the consideration of individual poems, considering the way in which the poet realised his effects. In this group I would include critics like Cleanth Brooks, Blackmur, and Leavis. Their general theoretical position was implied rather than stated. Others concerned themselves more with constructing a theory to justify their practice. Prominent amongst these were Ransom and Allen Tate, leaders of the Southern school of critics. It is with their critique, particularly Ransom's because it is detailed and accompanied by full quotations from Richards, that I shall mainly deal. Since their criticism is necessarily related to their theory, I shall describe their theory first. In Richards' terminology, I would characterise it as a mainly emotive statement, masquerading as a referential one. It is a myth created to justify the specialist tendencies we have been describing.

The heading of the last chapter of Ransom's book is "Wanted: An Ontological Critic". It is a modest way of indicating the role he intended to fulfil himself. The characterisation betrays Mr. Ransom's rather fatal love for philosophy. The New Critics, he thought, referring now to those who have been influenced by the persons his book was about, did not "usually have enough background in philosophy". This was a particular reason why he liked Richards, though disagreeing with him.

"Ontological" criticism Ransom had already introduced in his essay "Poetry: A Note in Ontology", written in 1934. Poetry, he wrote, "may be distinguished . . . by virtue of its subject-matter and subject-matter may be differentiated with respect to its ontology, or the reality of its being." The distinctions he made were between "Physical", "Platonic", and "Metaphysical Poetry". The first tended to the extreme of the concrete, the second of the abstract, whilst the third achieved a balance between the two.[1] The second type of poetry was, according to Ransom, motivated by the same intentions as science, "the love of truth and zeal for human improvement",

---

[1] This notion of a balance is a marked feature in the theory of many New Critics. Cf. the essays by Allen Tate, Cleanth Brooks, and Robert Penn Warren that follow Ransom's essay, reprinted in Stallman's anthology. It is also, as Cleanth Brooks points out in *Modern Poetry and Tradition*, an important part of Richards' theory, though not noticed amid the dust raised by controversy.

178

characteristics which Ransom particularly attributed to Plato. But poetry of the highest order such as metaphysical poetry, that is, "*genuine*" poetry, was concerned with things for their own sake and not for the benefits they would bring us. We did not abstract in the services of some ulterior purpose; instead we regarded things as they were, contemplating and experiencing what the poem presented with personal disinterest. Poetry, therefore, was concerned with "knowledge", whilst science aimed at power or control, something which Ransom sometimes expressed by calling it "predatory". One might have expected that, in his hostility to abstraction and interest in things for their own sake, Ransom would prefer Physical poetry. His grounds for not doing so are somewhat adventitious. While "Platonic Poetry is too idealistic, . . . Physical Poetry is too realistic, and realism is tedious and does not maintain interest".[1] Something in between is required. Though it wishes to be free, "the poetic impulse is not free, yet it holds out stubbornly against science for the enjoyment of its images. It means to reconstitute the world of perceptions".[2] A compromise solution seems to be suggested.

In *The New Criticism*, Ransom distinguished between structure and texture in poems. Structure is the argument, paraphrasable in prose; it is logical, rational, and abstract, the part of poetry that is like science. Texture is the local detail irrelevant to the prose argument, which we enjoy for its own sake. Various poetic techniques, like rhyme, metre, tropes, Ransom suggests, are devices for bringing in the "local detail" for our enjoyment. An illustration he gives is that of the elaborate similes with which Homer or Virgil interrupted the course of their narratives, though I should have thought these need be regarded as no more irrelevant than cadenzas. The impression Ransom gives is one of achieving a victory over science by (*a*) incorporating it in poetry—"the intention of Metaphysical Poetry is to complement science"; (*b*) by extracting science's fangs in the claim that poetry, too, gave us *knowledge*—he refers to that "most blinding of all illusions", "the habit of regarding scientific discourse as comprehensive of the whole range of cognition"; and (*c*) by implying a higher moral status for art. This he does by means of two claims. First, that poetry tempered the shallow optimism of science, "positivism", by drawing our attention to actuality, "the world's body", which stubbornly resisted our turning everything to our purposes, thus inducing greater realism.[3] Note how once again poetry is made superior to science by including it. Second, by his suggestion that art

---

[1] Stallman, 46.

[2] ibid., 40.

[3] Cf. ". . . poetry, when it is tragic, is an exercise in negativism, over-throwing positivism". (*The New Criticism*, 94).

did not, like science, have practical, merely utilitarian functions. "Aesthetic interest", he wrote, "is not a practical interest. It does not make better scientists, for example, nor better moralists".

Tate's theory in broad outline is similar to Ransom's, though some of the emphases, such as that on the role played by society, are different. His classification is twofold, according to whether the activity is the product of the will or of the imagination. Poetry should be a product of the latter and therefore disinterested, but much poetry, including Romantic poetry, is a manifestation of the will. In his essay "Three Types of Poetry"[1] he introduces a new distinction, that of "negative Platonism", to describe the reaction of the Romantics against science. His point is that their poetry is just as much a manifestation of the will as science is,

> Because it cannot participate in the infinite series of natural conquests, the romantic spirit impresses upon nature the image of its own passions . . . The style [of romantic poetry] is inflated and emotive, without definable objective. The poet, instead of fixing his attention upon a single experience, instead of presenting objectively the plight of human weakness—the subject of his poem—flies from his situation into a rhetorical escape that gives his will the illusion of power.[2]

But, because science is an infinitely more powerful instrument of the will, the Romantics were doomed to failure. Their attitude is basically a self-destructive one. They may collapse into self-pitying disillusion; retreat into a world of make-believe, comforting themselves with lies; or write a poem which aims at saying nothing at all, "pure" poetry, that seeks "immersion in the supposedly pure sensation of experience".[3]

This last reaction, though characterised as a form of Platonism, is similar to the poetry Ransom classified as Physical. However, in a later essay, "Tension in Poetry" (1938), Tate makes use of the concrete/abstract dichotomy, using, in a way that is quite characteristic of these two critics, up-to-date philosophical terms to describe this distinction, namely, the terms 'extension' and 'intension.' The best poetry is said to combine these two extremes, which are also referred to as denotation and connotation, and the result is described, by what looks like a bad pun, as "tension". This essay is interesting because it reveals that Tate and Ransom are, without being aware of it, using the word "abstract" in at least two different senses in order to win their arguments. According to one, it is opposed to concrete, referring to universals rather than to particulars, and, as such, an

---

[1] Reprinted in *Reactionary Essays in Poetry and Ideas* (1936).
[2] ibid., 96.
[3] ibid., 108.

easy though surely superficial means of contrasting different kinds of poetry. According to the other, it refers to the abstracting, *from* what is presented, *of* that alone which is relevant to our practical purposes.[1] But this abstracting does not mean a concentration on the abstract as opposed to the concrete. Scientific activity aims at producing simpler substances, like chemical elements, not qualities like blueness. And the language of science has had extensionalist rather than intentionalist terms much recommended to it.

So much then for the frame of reference of these New Critics. Let us turn now to the interpretation of Richards upon which their criticisms of him depended. I shall concentrate mainly on Ransom's chapter in *The New Criticism*. This has the advantage of providing full documentation for his interpretation of Richards. Moreover it seems to have been influential in determining the way in which many critics have taken Richards. My thesis will be that Ransom and others have very considerably misunderstood Richards and that there are no major theoretical differences between Richards' early theories and those of Ransom and Tate. Richards' later books, on the other hand, which have been interpreted as coming much closer to the views of the New Critics, do not do so to anything like the extent believed. Whilst I shall be presenting a critique of these New Critics' position, I shall once again be illustrating the process of misunderstanding as it takes place in academic discussion. We shall find that these New Critics are more emotive in their reading than the Richards they attack in the name of literary objectivity.

3. HOW RANSOM UNDERSTOOD THE EARLY BOOKS

(a) The Meaning of Meaning

An initial idea of how Ransom reads can be got from the remarks he makes about *The Meaning of Meaning*. Ransom shows his hand from the start by categorising it as revealing two biases, those of "nominalism" and of "positivism", pet enemies of his. How he understands these can be seen from his statements that the "positivist bias" is that "through which the thinker is led to take the referential capacity of science as perfect . . . and by comparison to judge all other kinds of discourse as falling short"; and the "nominalist" one, the being "very

---

[1] One criticism that might be made is that any "thing, person or experience", that a poem or work of art presents, will also involve abstraction from the initial experience. Study of the revision and development of a work of art will show that not all of the "world's body" initially included is present at the end. The artist's purpose also leads to selection. Why should one say that here only the imagination is at work, whilst in scientific creation it is only the will?

181

alert to the possibility that a word which seems to refer to the objective world . . . really refers to a psychological context and has no objective reference". The latter bias, Ransom adds, "has governed Richards' conception of poetry . . . almost from that day to this".[1]

"The *crucial commitment* made by Richards in [*The Meaning of Meaning*]", Ransom continues, "will appear if we examine its two companion tables showing the *history* of two respective ideas . . . the meanings of Meaning and . . . the meanings of Beauty". Ransom saw these two tables of definitions (see pages 31-32 above) as proceeding "more or less serially from the cruder forms in which [the] idea has been entertained towards the more enlightened". This meant, Ransom thought, that the two ideas went in opposite directions. In the case of "beauty", the first, and therefore "cruder", definitions were those "in which the term stands for something in the objective world", whereas in the later, "more enlightened ones", "it stands for certain affective responses to objects."[2] In the case of 'meaning', the order was the other way round.

This makes a very nice simple case for the interpretation Ransom had in mind, Richards' "crucial commitment", but Ransom was hopelessly at fault. *Both* lists start with definitions in terms of unique, unanalysable qualities or relations, which represented not something early in history but the then up-to-date philosophical realism of a Moore that Ogden and Richards were in revolt against. And *both* lists end in psychological definitions. Ransom quite fails to realise that Richards favoured a psychological theory with regard to the scientific as well as the emotive use of words. Nor, apart from the fact that both lists ended in psychological definitions, were they meant to be proceeding "from the cruder to the more enlightened" forms. Indeed Ogden and Richards' last definition of 'meaning', that in terms of the word's effect on the *interpreter* as opposed to the writer (see page 260 below), so far from being, as Ransom called it, "the perfect sense", was described by Ogden and Richards as "perhaps the richest of all in opportunities of misunderstanding."[3] This misreading of Ogden and Richards is a nice illustration of the tendency to see things as being more symmetrical than they actually are, which is often a feature of perception and memory. It is something that Ransom particularly shows, not only in his perceptions or memories of Richards' meaning, but also in his own theorising.

One last example from his interpretation of *The Meaning of Meaning* will show how ready Ransom is to read his interpretation into Ogden and Richards' words. He takes their eleventh definition

[1] *The New Criticism*, 5.
[2] ibid., 6-7 (my italics).
[3] *M. of M.*, 6th edn., 208.

of 'meaning', which is "Emotion aroused by anything", and quotes their statement: "[this definition] requires little comment. It is a definite sense of meaning which except amongst men of letters is not likely to be brought in to confuse other issues." Ransom does not mention that they refer the reader to their discussion of this in their next chapter, or that they add, "a detailed examination of this sense of meaning is almost equivalent to an investigation of Values . . ."[1] Ransom's interpretation of Ogden and Richards' statement is this: "Richards confines meaning in the strict sense [sic] to valid objective reference and denies it to the *mere* emotion that words may cause. Meaning is knowledge, not affective experience; and men of letters are not very scrupulous, or at least not very reliable where knowledge is concerned".[2] Now Ogden and Richards were, it is true, unkind from time to time to "men of letters", but "men of letters" are not to be confused with poets writing poetry, and gibes against them should not be extended to the "definite sense of meaning" as "emotion aroused by anything". Ogden and Richards, in other words, were not being derogatory about the use of 'meaning' as "emotion"—it was for them a perfectly respectable use which needed "little comment" only because it was not a use likely to confuse philosophical discussion, whatever might be the case with literary topics, and they were certainly not regarding poets as unscrupulous or unreliable "where knowledge is concerned".[3] Such a view suggests the attribution to Richards of a stereotype about poets and artists which Richards, with his emphasis upon the "normality" of the artist, was very far from possessing, and shows how much a preconception can override a host of verbal cues indicating a contrary view. This particular example of misinterpretation is interesting because, not being one that has been mentioned by anyone else, it illustrates in how many different places a justification for a given categorisation may seemingly be found. Just as group prejudice will cause us to interpret a facial feature, the cut of a man's clothes, the way in which he wears them, even his posture or a facial expression that would be unremarked amongst people of our own race, as *confirmatory*, so here too the operation of a category judgment is pervasive in its influence.

(b) A Literary Critic Categorises a Psychologist

The Meaning of Meaning, Ransom held, "rather incidentally legislates a status for poetry", and so he thought it "hardly in order for me to

---

[1] *M. of M.*, 6th edn., 198-199.

[2] *The New Criticism*, 7.

[3] This view is shared by other New Critics. Tate, for instance, attributed to Richards the view that "the poets . . . were too backward in the sciences", and Stallman, that poetry was "an inferior kind of science".

review a book of that kind." This is why he is brief with it, which I think is a mistake, for much of Ransom's failure to appreciate Richards' position comes from his neglect of the epistemological position that the book outlines for Richards' later writings about poetry. When he comes to the *Principles of Literary Criticism*, it is quite another matter. He deals with this book in more detail than any other. Ransom writes in a pondering way and doesn't mind admitting to puzzlement about an author's meaning. There is no doubt however, that he found the *Principles* very difficult to understand. Though Richards' synthesis may not have been entirely successful, Ransom is very far from seeing it at all. What he does is to fragment the complex pattern and impose instead a typically simple, arbitrary one by categorising Richards as playing a number of overlapping roles. These roles are, firstly, those of a traditional psychologist and romantic critic combined, which result in a tendency to "subordinate the cognitive element in [aesthetic] experience to the emotive"; secondly, those of a "behaviouristic" and "neurological" psychologist, and "almost uncritical admirer of the sciences and their methods", which leads him to subordinate "the emotive to the conative", and produce a very mystifying theory about attitudes; and, finally, that of a romantic critic again, in that Richards is held to have lent support to the view that the effects of poetry depended "upon consoling lies". This last ascription Ransom only hinted at, but Tate replaces him here, since it was upon this, as we shall see, that he mainly based his criticism of early Richards.

The first categorisation, that of a psychologist, is, as we have already indicated, an unpopular thing to be among the New Critics. As such, it is worth examining closely. Ransom describes psychologists in the following way:

A psychologist, I should judge, is a thinker who invades our discussion by telling us that what we think is knowledge testifies less to any objective referent than to our own subjective emotions and desires.[1]

But this sounds much more like an activity of psychiatrists, that is, of one kind of psychologist only and not the kind that Richards represented. However, Ransom goes on to connect it with an "uncritical" attitude to science and to assert that "Richards is a psychologist in taking . . . [the] general position" that "the cognitions we have in the arts . . . could not stand up under the rigorous standards of science, and the the real values of art are not cognitions at all, but the affective states which art induces and expresses."[2]

This is not yet the "newer modes of psychology", that is, of

[1] ibid., 11-12.
[2] ibid., 12.

"behaviouristic" and "neurological psychology", which Ransom held responsible for the doctrine of attitudes and emphasis upon conation, so what other categories are at work? One is indicated when Ransom later suggests that this is a typically romantic position, and mentions "lay aestheticians" who have "for . . . about two psychologising and romanticising centuries [been] talking about the arts as rousing and communicating the passions".[1]

The connection between psychology and aesthetic theory was, of course, prominent in the case of Coleridge, though this example is a little confusing because Coleridge was taken by Ransom and other New Critics as very much on the side of the angels; indeed, Ransom held that the rescue of Richards, as shown by his later books, was largely due to his "assimilation" by Coleridge.[2] It does not, therefore, follow that being a romantic and being psychologically-minded have the effects Ransom asserts they have, and certainly the association between a psychological approach and romanticism was something quite independent of the *experimental* psychologists' attitude to science. The latter have, in fact, been more concerned with cognition than with feeling and emotion. They do not believe that scientists' cognitions are correct, only that for scientific advance they *ought* to be correct. One might, in fact, say that their main contribution has been to show how easily would-be scientists perceive incorrectly and how these incorrect cognitions are explained in terms of *cognitive* laws. My own analysis of misperception of meaning through the operation of previously learned categories is an example of this. Greater stress on dynamic or "functional" factors is a recent development which has taken place since the publication of Ransom's book, and even now, with regard to perception, learning, and thinking, explanations of error in cognitive terms play the larger part so far as experimental psychologists are concerned. This is not, of course, the case with psychiatrists, particularly Freudians, but *they* are not the ones who so loudly cry the praises of science, nor are they the ones with whom Richards identifies himself. We can summarise the argument, then, by saying that Ransom's categorisation was a condensation of a number of not very compatible categories. This composite categorisation was unlikely to apply to many people and was therefore a probable source of misperception.

The way in which Ransom treats these categories indicates his rather intuitive, impressionistic approach. He is constantly inferring biases from intellectual positions or professional activities. "A psychologist is one who . . .", and then follows not a description of his professional job nor of particular theories held by psychologists, but

[1] ibid., 15.
[2] ibid., 74-77.

of a kind of wrong-headedness. Such categorisation of meaning by attribution of various prejudices to the individual writer, which follow from a stereotype one holds about the class of person he is, are by no means uncommon in reading. In Ransom's case it goes with a failure ever to be very precise and *hard* with his own word-meanings, so that it is perhaps not surprising that he fails to be this with others as well. He seems to *feel* his way intuitively through Richards' writings and not to be on the same wavelength of specificity. Therefore, even if he did not have the wrong categories and had the right ones, he would probably not have taken them at a sufficient degree of specificity for getting Richards' meanings. Much the same was evident in his treatment of Ogden and Richards' nominalism in *The Meaning of Meaning*. Thus, the denial of the existence of universals was generalised as a bias which "is deeply nominalist" in the sense that "it is very alert to the possibility that a word which seems to refer to the objective world . . . really . . . has no objective referent". It is not merely that the term 'nominalism' is being impressionistically dissolved, but also that an intellectual position, one about the ubiquity of hypostatisation, is being treated simply as a sort of prejudice. I do not wish to deny the existence of underlying biases, but one has first to determine what the theories are. This seems to quite a large extent to be by-passed by Ransom. One might say that his attitude to what Richards says exemplifies what he accuses Richards of doing, for he takes what Richards says as "testifying less to any objective referent than to [his] subjective emotions and desires".

But did Richards, in fact, "subordinate the cognitive element in [aesthetic] experience to the emotive"? What this means is elaborated in a little more detail by Wimsatt and Beardsley in their article "The Affective Fallacy".[1] "In our time", they write, echoing, as they frequently do, Ransom's phrases, "the emotive form of psychologistic or affective theory has found its most impressive champion in Mr. I. A. Richards."[2] The kind of quarry they have in mind is suggested by quotations from Saintsbury and other critics, which, Wimsatt and Beardsley held, suggested that the greatness of a work of art is shown by the power of feeling it induces in the critic. "Criticism on this theory", they wrote, "has approximated the tone of the Buchmanite confession, the revival meeting." They refer also to physiological indices of value, such as Housman's inability to shave because of the bristling of his skin while thinking of some lines from *Lycidas*. They do not think Richards' theory was quite as crude as this. "Certain theorists, notably Mr. Richards", they wrote, "have anticipated some

[1] Written in 1948 and reproduced in *Critiques and Essays in Criticism, 1920-1948*, ed. R. W. Stallman. Page references will be from this volume.
[2] ibid. 402.

difficulties of affective criticism by saying that it is not intensity of emotion that characterises poetry . . . but the subtle quality of patterned emotions which play at the subdued level of disposition and attitude."[1] Nevertheless Richards is still taken as an exponent of the mistaken theory.

Wimsatt and Beardsley are careful to show that they are not against any mention of the emotions in poetic analysis. What they are opposed to is writing in an autobiographical way of the emotions and feelings aroused by the poem in the reading. It is only legitimate, they hold, to refer to emotional effects in terms of the situations and images in the poem that gave rise to them. Ransom is evidently intending a similar point when he refers to the barrenness of our affective vocabulary and suggests that for precision one has always to describe the objects that give rise to our feelings. Oddly enough, both Ransom, and Wimsatt and Beardsley, admit that Richards does in fact produce analyses in cognitive terms. But they regard it as an inconsistency. "Instead of producing [his] own school of affective criticism", Wimsatt and Beardsley write, "[Richards has] contributed much to recent schools of cognitive analysis, of paradox, ambiguity, irony and symbol." And both they and Ransom regard the practice Richards showed in *Practical Criticism* as not being consistent with the position taken up in the *Principles*. "In applied criticism", say Wimsatt and Beardsley, "there would seem to be not much room for synaesthesis or for the touchy little attitudes of which it is composed".[2] But in fact Richards was not being inconsistent, because there is no logical reason whatever why a belief that poetry works on us when we respond with affect to it should not go with careful 'cognitive' analysis of it.

There are three possible points that these New Critic enemies of the emotions might be making. First, they might be opposing something which is easy to condemn, namely, the idea that a work of art is good in proportion to the intensity of emotion it calls forth. This, as we have seen, does not apply to Richards, and in thinking so (see his remarks to the effect that "art feels not hot but cool"), Ransom is misreading Richards. This, the obvious point, gives most dynamic to these New Critics' case, as so often happens in controversy. Second, they might be denying that art *need* have any effect upon the feelings.

[1] ibid., 406.
[2] ibid., 405. Cf. also Rene Wellek's article, "The Mode of Existence of a Literary Work of Art" (1942), where he comments, "Curiously enough, Mr. Richards . . . holds to an extreme psychological theory which is in flat contradiction to his excellent critical practice". Richards' "psychological theory", however, seems to be an invention of Mr. Wellek's to judge by his description of it—"the value of poetry is in some sort of psychical therapy [which] leads [Richards] finally to the admission that this goal may be accomplished by a *bad as well as a good poem*" (my italics).

This would mean that one would remain unmoved by a work of art, observing it without any feeling at all, which seems an unlikely theory. Ransom himself recommends the following definition:

A beautiful poem is an objective discourse which we *approve*, containing objective detail which we *like*.[1]

He uses affective terms, characteristically mild ones, perhaps, though he can also talk of poetry's "constant provision of exciting detail".[2]

Third, these New Critics might be saying that the theory that the function of the arts is to arouse feeling puts the matter in the wrong perspective. I think they do mean this, and that in certain ways of taking this theory they are right. These ways are those which seem to subordinate art to some psychological need, which we do not naturally regard as commensurate in value to works of art we most like. But Ransom goes too far when he says that "art is among the highly reflective or cognitive activities, not recognisable when cited for its effectiveness as a mode of *passion*".[3] This combines for persuasive effect the first and the third points that we have described in the argument. What is missing here is Coleridge's emphasis on the dependence of 'knowledge' upon feeling, which differentiates it from mere intellectual knowledge.[4] I think it is phenomenologically well attested that we can have *degrees* of awareness; that we can be merely aware of something or deeply aware of it; that we can read and know what a poem is about and yet feel empty about it one day though not another, without this being due to over-Romantic expectations about what poetry should do for us.

In their objections to Richards' theory on the grounds of misplaced emphasis, many New Critics seem to regard feeling as though it were in some way frivolous, subjective, private, not related to the actual world we live in. This is why they like to use in contrast such words as 'perception', 'knowledge', 'objective', 'logical', and the like. But was this the view that Richards really held about emotion and feeling? The answer is that it was not. Richards made it clear in his theory of attitudes that emotions and feeling were closely related to the world we live in, because they represented the effects in consciousness of our needs or of incipient adjustive action, namely, the attitudes, which arose in response to perceptions of the outside world. As Richards put it, they "are primarily signs of attitudes and owe their

[1] Ransom, 54 (my italics).
[2] ibid., 42.
[3] ibid., 16 (my italics).
[4] Ransom himself is capable of recognising this. Cf. his remark in "Poetry: A Note in Ontology" (1934), to the effect that metaphysical poetry "leaves us looking. marvelling and revelling in the thick *dinglich* substance that has just received its strange representation" (Stallman, page 46).

great prominence in the theory of art to this".[1] But Ransom missed this because his understanding of Richards' theory of attitudes was defective. Let us now examine the way in which he understood it.

(c) The "Mysterious" Theory of Attitudes

Ransom's second categorisation of Richards was as a "behaviouristic" or "neurological psychologist". According to Ransom, this "leads" Richards, after having "subordinated the cognitive element . . . to the emotive", to subordinate the emotive element in its turn to the "conative" one. This gives a very mechanical and simple picture of Richards' thinking, or even, since this was presumably what Ransom had in mind, of Richards' "biases". It is true that Richards must bear some blame for this conception of Ransom's. His initial exposition is extremely confused. Moreover, it is manifestly self-contradictory (see, for instance, the passage quoted on page 311 below) and later parts of the book clearly need to be consulted.

The trouble seems to be that, as with his conception of psychologists, Ransom is not in possession of the right categories. I infer this from the fact that he does not mention them and that he frequently refers to Richards' theory of attitudes as "mysterious". Richards, it will be remembered, said of his book, "few of the separate items are original" and "what is most important about [the book is] the interconnection of its several points of view". These "items" and "points of view", which I call 'categories', include psychological functionalism, an effect of Darwinism prominent among such American psychologists as James, Dewey, and Angell, which looked for the functions that psychological processes fulfilled. We have already seen an example of this in Richards' treatment of emotion and feeling. In regarding them as the effects in consciousness of adjustive processes within us, he was further showing the same point of view as that of the James-Lange theory of emotions and Cannon's physiological studies. His theory of attitudes, however wrong it might be, would certainly not be a mystery to anyone familiar with the introspective studies of thinking of the Würzburg psychologists, Lipps' theory of empathy, or the motor theory of consciousness favoured by some American functionalists, to say nothing of Henry Head's studies on posture, which had much influence on contemporary Cambridge psychology. Of Richards' great ingenuity in applying such ideas to utilitarianism so as to give to art the highest value, there is no mention in Ransom. He writes like one who is unaware of the ideas that are being used. To use a favourite image of Richards, he is a carver who cuts across bones instead of at the joints. He simply characterises Richards as

[1] P.L.C., 132.

an "anti-intellectualist aesthetician" and produces an astonishingly naïve version of Richards' theory of attitudes. We might be tempted to regard this in its literalness as the product of no categorisation at all, did we not remember Ransom's frequent allusions to mystification. We have thus to recognise a category of *mysteriousness*, which is the opposite of conventionalisation. It is one which frequently occurs in controversy. For that reason it is worth looking at this example in more detail.

In the *Principles*, Richards tried a pictorial way of presenting his theory of attitudes:

> Those to whom visual images are of service in considering complex matters may find it convenient at this point to imagine a circle or sphere constantly bombarded by minute particles (stimuli). Within the sphere may be pictured complex mechanisms continually changing for reasons having nothing to do with the external stimuli. These mechanisms by opening little gateways select which of the stimuli shall be allowed to come in and take effect. So far as the subsequent convulsions are due to *the nature of the impacts* and to lingering effects of impacts which have accompanied similar impacts in the past, the convulsions are *referential*. So far as they are due to the independent motions of the internal mechanisms themselves, reference fails.[1]

This passage expresses the writer's background of experience and depends upon a similar one in the reader. With this background one can interpret it. The "sphere" is, of course, the body. The "complex mechanisms continually changing for reasons having nothing to do with the external stimuli" are chemical and internal neural changes in the body which are occasioned by our needs and their satisfaction, of which we have evidence in the case of needs, such as hunger or sex. The "little gateways" are a fairly conventional way of describing the way in which needs and desires affect selective attention. When Richards talks of "convulsions" we don't take this particular term too seriously, but we know that here he is referring to attitudes. Now lacking this background, I suppose the passage might seem odd, but surely not as odd as that which results when Ransom actually draws Richards' "circle" and says what goes on in and outside it.[2] He draws an arrow in it with its point touching the circumference. This "represents an attitude . . . which looks outward, as if to invade the external world at the periphery and make use of it . . . It is extremely mobile, hung loosely, so to speak, and capable of altering its shape and

[1] *P.L.C.*, 263 (my italics).

[2] Though Ransom is ostensibly discussing the *Principles*, it is possible that the diagram he draws refers to another pictorial way of presenting the theory of attitudes, which is developed at some length in *Science and Poetry*. This is more obscure than the presentation in the *Principles*. Nevertheless this too, I think, should be categorised in the light of current psychological thinking. And Ransom was certainly referring to the theory of attitudes developed in the *Principles*.

position. Such alterations constitute its activity and its life. But it is stimulated into activity by events both within and without the circle". Ransom then goes on to argue, despite the words in the extract from Richards we have italicised, that there is very little relationship between an attitude and such "events . . . without the circle" that "stimulated [it] into activity".[1] ". . . the cognition which comes from the object in the external world", he writes, "appears to be stopped at the boundary, where we will assume that it stays just long enough to pass its stimulus over the barrier; whereupon the attitude which has been stimulated starts upon business of its own, and moves about within the periphery till finally it takes up [another] position, where it poises ready for stimulus from some other object".[2] This mystification of Richards' theory Ransom summed up later in these words. "The feelings [in Richards' theory] . . . flourish like plants on mysterious food-particles which they appropriate from their cognitive element and metabolise by secret processes".[3]

The language Richards used Ransom claimed confirmed his interpretation. ". . . Now we can see", he says in connection with his diagram, "why Richards has always liked to refer to . . . a "stimulus" or a "cause" rather than [to] a "cognition" or an "image". An activity is not at all analogous to its stimulus, nor an effect to its efficient cause."[4] Ransom gives as examples of a stimulus, the taking of a liver pill, and of a cause, the cleaning of sparking plugs, neither of which are "like" their effects, "the secretion of bile" or "the fast running of the car". He doesn't appreciate that 'stimulus' is a technical word in psychology, convenient because it is used with a high degree of abstraction, and standing generally for the objects that we perceive and not for our perceptions or "cognitions" of them.[5] Furthermore, both this word and 'cause' are used in Richards' analysis of reference in scientific statements as well. References, scientific descriptions, are completely determined by the external stimuli that "*cause*" them. So

---

[1] ibid., 27.

[2] ibid., 29.

[3] ibid., 46-47.

[4] ibid., 28. Cf. also "when you think of a thing as the cause of something else, you waive interest in it for itself."

[5] It is convenient to have a general word to stand for *objects* in order to differentiate them from both our perceptions of them and other objects also in the field of perception, which are not perceived—which are not "stimuli". The usefulness of distinguishing between an object and our perception of it lies particularly in the fact that the same stimulus may give rise to many different perceptions, something which Richards was very conscious of in the case of poetry, but which, so far as I can see, very few of his critics were, which is another reason for their failure to understand him. 'Stimulus' had originally a behaviourist connotation, it is true, but this does not justify the implications Ransom drew, and now it is a general word in psychology used instinctively without the attendant ideology.

it is clear that Ransom is quite wrong in the implications he draws. These are once again due to his own "anti-intellectualist" tendency to infer biases from theoretical positions.

Ransom, however, claimed that his reading "could be documented rather copiously". The documentation he produces is generally of passages where Richards is warning against projecting into objects qualities that derive from our own reaction to these objects. This standpoint of Richards, so far from being a freakish off-shoot of "neurological psychology" is a well-known position in philosophical psychology. It consists in saying of an object that we call 'exciting', that being exciting is not a quality of the object, as being round and blue would be, since this description refers rather to a complex reaction within ourselves (i.e. the state of excitement) that this object causes. It is all right, of course, indeed inevitable, to call objects exciting or beautiful, as a convenient linguistic shorthand, but in doing so we are constantly liable to hypostatise these qualities, and to forget the complexity of judgments involving them, the extent to which these qualities depend upon the condition of the perceiver, and the great variety of features in the object which may bring about such responses in us. As we saw in his treatment of 'beauty', for instance, Richards believed that different theories were due to the picking out of particular qualities of the art objects in question. Only a definition of 'beauty' "so vague and general that it ceases to be useful"[1] would apply to all cases. Now with all this we may well disagree, but that is quite another thing from taking it as a theory that the referential or representational aspects of art play no further part than to serve as triggers to explosions of feeling.

In addition to this 'evidence' Ransom also quotes some of the remarks Richards made at the beginning of the last chapter of the *Principles*. These we have already attempted to explain (see pages 56-57 above), and do not need to repeat now. Finally, Ransom refers to Richards' "objectless beliefs", states of mind characterised by a sense of certainty, as though we were having some truth revealed to us, which Richards held, reasonably enough, were not necessarily self-legitimising. Ransom compounded this with the other type of belief Richards thought entered into our poetic responses, namely, "provisional acceptances . . . made for the sake of the imaginative experience which they make possible". By giving to the latter the name of the former, Ransom was able to suggest that *references* to objects in poetry played a very small part in Richards' theory.

We have now dealt with two of Ransom's three categorisations, which we described some pages back. Each justified, for Ransom, his belief that Richards considered the cognitive analysis of poetry

[1] *P.C.*, 359.

unimportant. If Richards did, in fact, carry out some cognitive analysis, this showed a healthy inconsistency between his theory and practice. But Richards, as we know, certainly did in his theory also recognise that reference often played an important role in poetry. Some slight recognition of this led Ransom to consider the possibility that his analysis of Richards' theory of attitudes might be at fault. But he had a third category ready at hand to meet the situation. This was that of the Romantic critic in another aspect. "If Richards really regards valid references as indispensable . . . then he would be representing the attitudes as grounding their activities not on fictions but on lies, and I do not see how he would escape the stigma that attaches to the romantic view." This view, as we saw, was described as negative Platonism. It made poetry into "a conscious retreat from reality and a morbid indulgence; or at best a heroic but childish affirmation in defiance of the most conscientious revelations of science". "I would question", Ransom adds, "whether there can be any important effects in emotion and attitude flowing from what the subject knows to be nonsense or falsehood."[1] Ransom himself doubts whether Richards really did hold such a view, but criticises it just in case.

4. RICHARDS, THE "NEGATIVE PLATONIST"

Allen Tate, on the other hand, is much more positive about the matter. In the essay we have already referred to, he categorises Richards fairly and squarely as a negative Platonist. This is how he describes Richards' theory:

The "certified scientific statements" about the world make the metaphors, the images, the symbols, all the varieties of "pseudo-statements"—similes like the dome of many-coloured glass—look extremely foolish, because in the exacter light of science, they are patently untrue. . . . One part of the theory, I believe, may be dismissed at once. How can poetry, a tissue of lies, equip the public with "relevant responses" to an environment?[2]

Tate did not confine himself to the view that Richards thought statements in poetry were lies. Noticing Richards' attitude to Eliot, and presumably Hardy and the early Yeats, he interpreted Richards as also recommending that poets "in order to avoid saying wrong things . . . *must say nothing*".[3] Tate interpreted this as supporting the notion of "pure poetry", and this, as we have already seen (page 180), he describes as another form of negative Platonism.

As for Richards' theory about the value of art, Tate, like Ransom,

[1] Ransom, 40-41.
[2] *Reactionary Essays*, 104.
[3] ibid., 107-108 (my italics).

characterised it in terms of mystification. He is scarcely able to refer to it without using the word "mysterious". Nevertheless, he interprets it as meaning that Richards justified poetry in terms of practical utilitarian purposes. He categorised it as a type of theory that is "covertly or avowedly concocted in the interests of social schemes", as manifesting the impulse "to abstract for use [from poetry] those features that are available for immediate action, and to repudiate the rest".[1] Once again, then, Richards is convicted of negative Platonism.

Yet, despite all this, as we read what Tate's own theories are, again and again we come across phrases which remind us of Richards' own doctrines. Taking this into account, together with Tate (and Ransom's) misunderstandings of Richards and, we might add, their misunderstandings of themselves as shown by the contradictions between their theory and what they say it is, it becomes more and more doubtful whether more than *minor* differences exist between these critics and Richards. Of these minor differences there may well be a number, but not the grand emphatic differences that energise their writing. But before I argue this, let us glance at a different interpretation of Richards that provides a nice contrast with Tate's belief that Richards thought of poetry as lies.

This interpretation comes in a book by Professor D. G. James called *Scepticism and Poetry* (1937), in the course of which he criticises "the literary aesthetic" of Richards, which he considers "will not bear more than the most cursory inspection".[2] This book has been commended for the way in which it disposes of Richards by Owen Barfield[3] and by Stallman, who includes a long extract from it in his anthology. The critique makes, I think, some valid points. Nevertheless it also betrays a lot of misunderstanding. It would, however, overburden this chapter to consider these properly, so I shall confine myself to raiding Professor James' book for an occasional example of miscomprehension.

The example I wish to consider now is interesting not only because it gives a contrast to Tate's interpretation, but because it is one of the few I have come across where misunderstanding is due to simple verbal ambiguity, which is normally so much stressed as the cause of faulty communication. This is the interpretation. "Mr. Richards apparently believes that Othello, Tintern Abbey, or any other poem we wish to mention, is either true or false, does or does not reveal reality."[4] This contrasts of course not only with the "lies" and the

---

[1] ibid., 110.

[2] *Scepticism and Poetry*, 7.

[3] See Preface to the second edition (1951) of *Poetic Diction*. Barfield also thought Richards believed that the "figurative language of poetry has no referent".

[4] *Scepticism and Poetry*, 63.

'poetry has no referents' interpretations of Richards, but also with Richards' own insistence that the purpose of poetry is not to tell us of the nature of the world we live in. Professor James shows some realisation of this in a footnote, saying that "in view of Mr. Richards' view of what he calls 'revelation theories' of poetry, it is surprising that he should think it worth while to discuss whether or not a poem is 'true' or 'reveals' reality." Professor James does not, however, seem to doubt his own interpretation, and lectures Richards that "it is not the business of the critic to make pronouncements upon the "truth" or otherwise of poems and plays."[1] How did he arrive at so odd an interpretation? The answer comes from Richards' statement in the *Principles* that "for the understanding of poetic, musical and other experiences a theory of knowledge is needed . . . at . . . the point at which we wish to decide whether a poem, for example, is true or reveals reality, and if so, in what sense".[2] James seems to have taken this as meaning that the critic needed the theory of knowledge to judge in *particular* cases whether this or that poem was true or revealed reality. This is certainly a meaning that the passage will bear. On the other hand, the evidence of the whole book is against it and in favour of another possible meaning, namely, that we need a theory of knowledge to tell us whether *any* poem[3] is in fact true or reveals reality. As we know, for Richards the answer was that poems were only true in the emotive sense, not one which implied any referential knowledge.

5. ALLEN TATE, NEGATIVE PLATONIST?

The phenomenon we have just noticed, Professor James' preaching to Richards Richards' own lessons, is something we come across frequently with Ransom and Tate, particularly the latter. It gives the impression that they are running in parallel with Richards rather than in lines that will cross.

Thus we find Tate doing what Richards was continually doing, namely, attacking the idea that poetry should provide "information".[4] For instance, Tate criticises "the crudely practical reader who abstracts" the moral ideas in certain literature, such as *The Divine Comedy*, "and contents himself with the illusion that they are the total meaning of the work".[5] Or he attacks "the kind of criticism that

---

[1] ibid., 64.

[2] *P.L.C.* 91, quoted on pages 56-57 of *Scepticism and Poetry*.

[3] When Richards wrote "a poem, for example . . .", he did not mean a *particular* poem, but a poem as contrasted with a painting, a piece of music or a sculpture.

[4] "Three Types of Poetry" (*Reactionary Essays*, page 87).

[5] ibid., 89-90.

dominates our intellectual life [today which] is that of the French mathematician who, after reading a tragedy by Racine, asked "Qu'est-ce que cela prouve?" "[1]

In an essay on Ezra Pound he goes further and, despite his condemnation of the view he attributed to Richards that poets "must say nothing", writes of Pound's cantos that they are "not about anything. But they are distinguished verse".[2] And, "It is doubtless easier for us . . . when . . . poems are about God, Freedom and Immortality, but there is no reason why poetry should not be so perplexingly simple as Mr. Pound's, and be about nothing at all."[3]

As regards pseudo-statements, Tate thought he was correcting Richards when he wrote that for "a genuine poet . . . they were neither true nor false, but . . . a quality of the total created object: the poem."[4] Of some images in *Macbeth*,

> Life's but a walking shadow; a poor player
> That struts and frets his hour upon the stage,
> And then is heard no more . . .

he wrote, "the lines . . . are certainly not "true": we know that life is not a shadow, it is a vast realm of biological phenomena; nor is it a player. Neither are the lines false: they represent a stage in the dynamic unfolding of Macbeth's character . . . None of the pseudo-statements in the play . . . is either approved or disapproved by the poet . . .".[5] Similarly, in an essay on Hart Crane, Tate wrote about how "it was a sound impulse on Crane's part to look for an American myth" in his poem *The Bridge*, and added:

> The soundness of [Crane's] purpose is witnessed . . . by the kind of history in the poems: it is inaccurate, and it will not at all satisfy the sticklers for historical fact . . . [His purpose] is sound, for it ignores the scientific ideal of historical truth-in-itself, and looks for a cultural truth which might win the spontaneous allegiance of the people. It is on such simple integers of truth, not truth of fact but of religious necessity, that men unite."[6]

What all this amounts to is that when Richards is making his distinctions about pseudo-statements, about the dramatic nature of much poetry, or about provisional acceptance of fictional situations for the sake of their further effects upon our feelings and emotions, Tate accuses him of asserting that poems consist of "lies" and "nonsense". But when Tate himself is making similar points, then the

[1] ibid., 112.
[2] ibid., 45.
[3] ibid., 46.
[4] ibid., 112.
[5] ibid., 106-107.
[6] ibid., 34.

196

statements in poetry are not so much not true, as not "true". The inverted commas save him from saying they are false or lies. In fact being not "true" is a virtue, because they are not *mere* "truths of fact" that only pedants or "sticklers" want. Tate, in other words, denies to Richards an interpretation he claims for himself. Of course, he does claim that poems have some kind of truth, as, for instance, that of "religious necessity" which he contrasted with "truth of fact". But how much, one wonders, does this differ from "truth" in the emotional sense which Richards recognised poems had, only concerning himself with warning critics against attributing referential implications to this usage? Certainly the force of Tate's attack on Richards' pseudo-statements, which were introduced to account for the effect on our feelings of religious statements, would lead us to expect that Tate himself did consider religious statements to be true. But what, in that case, would be the point of distinguishing them from "truths of fact"?

An answer to this question is suggested by a book of Ransom's called *God Without Thunder*, published in 1931, which Stanley Edgar Hyman describes in *The Armed Vision* as "a book in defence of orthodox religion". This would lead one to expect that Ransom believed one religion was true and others false, that this religion would very likely be the Christian religion, and that the book would contain defences of such doctrines as those of Original Sin, the Incarnation, Redemption, and Atonement. Certainly it starts off in orthodox style by criticising various attempts by scientists to emasculate religion, to rob God of His thunder. Yet already in the Preface there are signs that his defence may be more destructive than otherwise; for he describes "how roundly the world has of late been disabused of the most and best of its *myths*—and as a consequence been stricken with an unheard-of poverty of mind and unhappiness of life" and talks of "how sorry a reputation the true priests, the *devout keepers of the myths*, enjoy now in the Western World". The purpose of his book, is to help reverse this bad state of affairs by elucidating the "function of myths in human civilisation".[1] And, in effect, we find that, when he has finished describing the attempts of scientists to arrive at an acceptable religion, he presents an interpretation of the Bible that takes its statements as myth. Ransom claims that in this he is reverting to an earlier tradition of Biblical exegesis, though I should have thought such a view, except with regard to certain parts of the Bible such as the account of the Creation and the Fall, or the Book of Revelation, unlikely to be one that would commend itself to the framers of the Creeds.

The Bible is for Ransom a huge and motley poem, whose value is

[1] *God Without Thunder*, xii (my italics).

justified on the same grounds as poetry's value is, namely, that it makes us more intensely aware of the actuality of things, in their own right and independently of our purpose with them. Just as poets use devices like rhyme, metre, and trope to achieve this, so "myth resorts to the supernatural in order to represent the fullness of the natural."[1] For instance, the myth of God serves the purpose of "stinging us into awareness" of the "indefiniteness in extent of time and of space" of the universe and of its "inexhaustible fullness or particularity".[2] As for "the myth of Christ", this is contrasted with that of Satan. Both are "Demigods". But whereas Satan represents the arrogant positivist spirit, "the role of Christ . . . the Man-God, who represents the highest human development," is that of "the Demigod who refused to set up as the God "[3]. He represents "the Logos as partial and subordinate to God."[4] This statement should be taken in conjunction with Ransom's remark about the amount of myth that accumulated round Christ, for "the age in which he lived was fertile in myth-making". "One of the most important functions of the ecclesiastical authorities", Ransom adds, "was to make a modest selection from it all which would be enough to go on, and to throw away the rest".[5]

As for Tate, who never spells things out like Ransom does, I have found no explicit statements of this kind in his two books of essays. Nevertheless, remarks he makes about religion suggest that his views are similar. For instance, in his essay on Hart Crane, "it is still a nice problem among higher critics, whether the authors of the Gospels were deliberate myth-makers or whether their minds were simply constructed that way."[6] And in *Religion and the Old South*, he contrasts religion, as he did poetry, with science and its instrument, the human will. But his treatment of religion is markedly relativist, manifesting almost a pragmatic, functional point of view. He refers, for instance, to the South's failure "to create its appropriate religion," one that is "fitting [to its] social structure"; to the old Southerners having "had a religious life . . . [which] was not enough organised with a right mythology"; and to the South's failure to have "sufficient faith in her own kind of God."

How is one to judge what makes one religion or another more fitting

---

[1] ibid., 67. Cf. also, "Poetry: A Note in Ontology", "it is the poet and nobody else who gives to the God a nature, a form, faculties and a history . . . Religions are periodically produced by poets and destroyed by naturalists . . . the medieval Schoolmen . . . recognised myth . . . as a device of expression; its sanctity as a consequence of its public or social importance." (Stallman, 45).

[2] ibid., 69.

[3] ibid., 144.

[4] ibid., 167.

[5] ibid., 141.

[6] *Reactionary Essays*, 35.

to a given society? Ransom in *God Without Thunder* (pages 89-93) suggests a number of criteria for judging myths. The relevant one here is that it should "suit us racially or culturally". Under this he would include, when it is poetry that is being judged, that it should not in its assertions too grossly conflict with views of things that science has led us to take for granted, else it will be likely to fail of its effect. This is again similar to Richards' approach in *Science and Poetry*. Ransom, however, and I think rightly, is less struck than Richards is by the collapse of the "Magical View of Nature". He suggests for instance, that modern poets might in their poetry use "even gods, demons and spheres again, if it should not prove that these formulations, by reason of *specific historical condemnation*, were *strategically out*".[1] Here also then we only get differences of degree, differences of opinion as to what is the right tactic at the present time, rather than differences of principle.

One possible difference between Richards and these New Critics remains, however, to be considered. This is shown in their attack on Richards for denying the uniqueness of aesthetic activity and aesthetic value. If this difference really exists, it would certainly be a fundamental one. But does it?

In order to answer this question, we should have to get as clear as possible what it means, something which is not easy owing to the vagueness of its formulation. I think, however, we can take as crucial the New Critics' claim that what you observe in poetry and other forms of art you observe *for its own sake* and not, as in science, for the sake of certain practical benefits. This is what Tate was stressing when denying that "genuine poetry" was, like Platonic poetry or science, a product of the will. Artistic activity then was *disinterested* activity, something which would be expressed by using a word like 'contemplation', instead of 'observation'. But in so far as this was its differentiating attribute, this would not make aesthetic activity unique; it would merely make it a member of the class of disinterested activities or states of mind. However, Ransom's and Tate's justification of *religion* in the same terms as they justified genuine poetry, suggests that the phrase, "aesthetic activity", could be conveniently extended to get over any difficulties of this kind. You maintain something is *sui generis* by extending its *genus*.

Richards, because he claimed that successful aesthetic communication had beneficial effects upon us which could be manifested in other spheres of life, was taken to be in opposition to this general view. Tate, as we saw, attacked Richards' theory as one "concocted in the interests of social schemes". It is not, however, easy to maintain that something is *very* valuable and yet only enjoyed for its own sake.

[1] *The New Criticism*, 43 (my italics).

199

When Ransom, for instance, defines "a beautiful poem" as "an objective discourse which we approve, containing objective detail which we like", that is consistent with his claim that the experience is enjoyed for its own sake, but does not suggest the very high value that other remarks of his and of Tate's claim. Using the word 'knowledge' is a device by which they try to deal with this difficulty. The poem presents for contemplation a person, state of mind, or thing, either directly (Tate) or in the poetical texture irrelevant to the argument (Ransom) and we are said by reading it to have *knowledge* of this person, state of mind, or thing. 'Knowledge' of course, is famous for its connotation of a very special kind of value. But it is so by virtue of a suggestion that the possession of it benefits us beyond the occasion which gave it to us, and, in fact, we find that Ransom and Tate do not confine themselves to assertions that the knowledge we gain is limited to the objects of the poem we read.

Ransom, for instance, believes that poetry—and, of course, religion—will make us more aware, independently of our purposes, of the world we live in. It presents "the world's body", the aim of poetry being to "reconstitute the world of perception". Its "intention" is "to complement science" whose "discourse . . . starves the sensibility".[1] This suggests that the effects of aesthetic experience will be to vivify our perceptions in "local situations which might engage our liking . . . during the day's work".[2] And Tate, in his turn, generalises this knowledge to "knowledge . . . of the poetic order", something which again suggests an extension in the meaning of words like 'poetic' and 'aesthetic'. Elsewhere, in the preface to *Reactionary Essays*, he makes a different generalisation, one which hints at the particular value of this knowledge. It is, he says, "knowledge of ourselves".[3] Evidently the value of this lies in its effects upon our personality.

When Tate answers the question asked by the French mathematician about Racine's tragedy, "Qu'est-ce que ce prouve?", with "It proves nothing", he elaborates this by saying: ". . . poetry finds its true usefulness in its perfect inutility, a focus of repose for the will-driven intellect that constantly shakes the equilibrium of persons and societies with its unrelieved imposition of partial formulas upon the world".[4] What we have here, it seems, is a secular version of a religious theory. Grace will come to us as a gift and not through our willing; it is something that only the truly disinterested are likely to attain. The practical impulse, that Ransom describes as "always sciencing

---

[1] Stallman, 46.
[2] *The New Criticism*, 56.
[3] *Reactionary Essays*, xii.
[4] ibid., 112.

and devouring", and Tate as "predatory", will ultimately destroy us. In the Romantic poet it leads to self-destruction, as in the case of Hart Crane, whose suicide was "the sole act of will left to him short of a profound alteration of his character".[1] The prevalence of its operation in our society today will bring about "the coming of the slave state" for, with "a society made up of persons who have surrendered their humanity to the predatory impulses, the quickest way to improve matters is to call in a dictator".[2]

"The function of criticism" should be to oppose this, "to maintain and to demonstrate the special, unique and complete knowledge which the great forms of literature afford us", so that we may recover "the independence of judgment, the belief in intelligence, the confidence in literature, that informed the human tradition".[3] In *Religion and the Old South*, Tate attributes the weaknesses of the South to its failure "to create its appropriate religion", which I take to mean that it failed "to institutionalise successfully the having of 'genuine' " artistic experiences. This had for Tate two particular consequences— "the South separated from the North too late, and so lost her cause" and "the South began grievously to break down, two generations after the Civil War".[4] From all this, then, it seems that genuine poetry is after all valuable because of the effects it has on us in situations which would not normally be called "aesthetic".

But, it might be said, Ransom's and Tate's point was that poetry has no *practical* or *utilitarian* purpose. Did not Tate say, for instance, that the "function [of poetry] is ... not explanation for the purpose of external control by the will"?[5] This is true, but the quotation might equally well have come from Richards. For Richards, too, believed that the valuable effects were those on the personality, and that it was quite wrong to read poetry for the sake of what one could get out of it. Ransom and Tate, it is true, did not like Richard's psychological theory, but they offered no alternative, simply postulating unique agencies to preserve the uniqueness they claimed for art. So it was the imagination that produced all art that was not produced by the will; or a "perceptual impulse" was postulated as that which art aimed at gratifying.[6]

---

[1] ibid., 29.
[2] *Reason in Madness*, 7-8.
[3] ibid., 9.
[4] *Reactionary Essays*, 182.
[5] ibid., 88.
[6] Richards' psychological theory is perhaps not so different from Ransom's as may appear at first sight. As I pointed out, when Richards talks of art satisfying 'impulses', he is using two senses of 'impulse' and in effect arguing that works of art have the greatest degree of perceptual complexity. His neurological model involves the idea that every perception has a motor effect, but this does not mean

As for all Richards' promises of the good that art could do us, it is true that he was more rapturous about the condition we could attain than either Tate or Ransom. He advances throughout his books with his eyes fixed on the horizon star of human perfectibility. Tate by contrast is much more in the camp of Hulme and Eliot. Nevertheless Tate and, to a lesser extent, Ransom do argue the reader into valuing poetry on the ground of its effects on us, and these effects are not limited to the appreciation of art or states of mind valuable independently of any behaviour that may result from them. As for abstraction, the will, and negative Platonism, Tate could certainly argue that Richards abstracts well beyond his experience. For instance, in claiming as a result of certain feelings that follow successful reading of poetry that there is a permanent increased harmonising power within us, Richards' will is wresting what it wants from his experience so as to obtain a kind of dreampower. But Tate is very much such an 'abstractionist' too. This is shown by his considering it sufficient to analyse much poetry in terms of concepts as vague and general as those of 'extension' (denotation) and 'intension' (connotation)[1] and by his simple generalisations concerning hundreds of years of the history of Western society, which he utilises in support of his aesthetic programmes and philosophy.

How does it come about then, if they agree so much on fundamentals, that so many New Critics saw themselves in opposition to Richards? We have examined a number of misinterpretations, which show how their categorisations lead them to ignore or distort whatever contradicted or at least qualified their interpretations, but the question remains—Why did they categorise in this, rather than in the opposite direction?

6. WHAT DETERMINED THE DIRECTION OF CATEGORISATION

The evidence available to us for answering this question is naturally limited. Nevertheless, I think that a plausible case can be made out that the language Richards used played an important part. The New Critics we are considering were much more impressionistic in their use of language than Richards. This not only prevented them from properly understanding his theory. It also caused them to respond impressionistically to the kinds of words he used.

Though Richards himself, as I have often shown, was rather slapdash in his use of language, we know that he had, for instance, worked out an epistemological theory. His elliptical sentences on questions

---

[1] Cf. "Tension in Poetry," printed in *Reason in Madness*. See also page 180 above.

that these effects have 'utilitarian' functions any more than the movements in dancing need have. Action does not entail the will (in Tate's sense).

of reference and the like, which contain words used in different senses and with different logical categories, can generally be expanded and given definite meanings in terms of his basic theory, though it may be a laborious business working out how the words should be taken. On the other hand, one can have little such confidence in the case of the writings of the New Critics. I have already mentioned the vagueness of Ransom's abstract language. It is particularly something he manifests when using philosophical terms. They degenerate into slogans, biases, or words used mainly for their suggestive power. Key epistomological terms, like 'cognitive', 'true', 'objective', are, as far as their logical categories allow, used as virtual synonyms, with the same connotation of value. Here are some examples of the way in which he uses words, relevant to his differences with Richards:

> The poem . . . [whips] itself into a discourse having *objective truth* for its end, and *logical syntax* for its method.

> The idea [behind Richards' objectless beliefs] is . . . that there must be just enough *object*, just enough categorical or referential statement, to deceive our *cognitive sense* . . .

> If Richards really regards *valid references* as indispensable and the attitudes as not quite managing to escape from their original *cognitions* . . . he would be representing the attitudes as grounding their activities not on *fictions but on lies*.

> Poetical discourse does not deny its logical structure as a whole, but it continually takes little departures from it by virtue of the *logical impurity* of its terms.[1]

Two things should be noticed about these quotations. Ransom is using the word "logical" in a different sense from that in which Richards used it when writing about poetry. Richards was using it in its more rigorous sense as referring to the formal relations between sentences by virtue of which deductions could or could not be made. The phrase, 'logical syntax', is generally used in contrast to the 'syntax of ordinary language', which is not considered at all logical. The ideal of logical syntax is an explicitness that would be a denial of poetry. Ransom, on the other hand, clearly means by 'logical' something like 'rational'. Since he does not see that Richards is using it in a different sense, he is bound to misunderstand him, and he is exploiting technical-sounding phrases like 'logical syntax' and 'logical structure' for the sake of their effect.

Secondly, in many of Ransom's phrases, like "objective truth", "valid references", and "cognitive sense", there is an element of

[1] *The New Criticism*, pages 33, 34, 40 and 42 (my italics).

redundancy, the adjective being used as an intensifier, though I think the effect is often to weaken rather than to emphasise. Indeed, "valid references" or "objective references", used *á propos* Richards' analysis of the role played by words in poetry, are pleonasms, for Richards' 'references', when he was discussing poetry, were by definition always 'objective' and 'valid'. Tate, too, does not understand Richards' use of "references", for he attributes to Richards the belief that "poems may designate but they do not denote, because you can designate something that does not exist, like a purple cow". Therefore, he concluded, Richards' view was that "the words of a poem [are not] referents".[1] Apart from the fact that Richards never held the words to be the referents, 'purple' and 'cow' in the hypothetical poem *did* refer to referents, namely, purple things and cows.

Much of the language of the New Critics we have been considering is hard to interpret precisely, which has made the assessment of their criticisms of Richards often rather difficult. They use words and phrases to suggest that poetry is of very high value indeed. One feels that if they could, they would use coloured instead of plain black print, and fancy lettering too. The obscurity of their utterances seems itself a device to this end, a hint of the ineffable in what poetry does. Thus Ransom describes his approach as one which "differentiates" the "subject matter [of poetry] with respect to its ontology or the reality of its being".[2] Likewise we find Tate distinguishing the best poetry as resulting from an "attitude [that] is nameless because it is perfect, because it is complete and whole",[3] that is a manifestation of "the creative spirit" which "occupies an aloof middle ground" between positive and negative Platonism, "its function [being] the quality of experience, the total revelation".[4] Characterisations of this thesis by others are not much more helpful. "For Tate", Stallman writes in his essay, "The New Critics", "art aims at nothing outside itself." "This formalist creed", he adds, is similar to the "principle of art for art's sake [but] must be interpreted very differently from the aestheticism of the Nineties. Rightly understood, the principle has tremendous implications."[5] Stallman quotes by way of elucidation a remark of Middleton Murry, another precursor of the New Criticism:

Art is autonomous, and to be pursued for its own sake, precisely because it comprehends the whole of human life; because it has reference to a more perfect human morality than any other activity of man.

[1] "The Present Function of Criticism." Printed in *Reason in Madness*, page 12.
[2] "Poetry: A Note in Ontology" in Stallman, page 30.
[3] *Reactionary Essays*, 83.
[4] ibid., 88.
[5] Stallman, 495.

Richards wished to avoid this kind of writing, which he described, in the Preface to the *Principles*, as writing which aimed at "exciting in the mind emotions appropriate to the august subject matter [of poetry]". He regarded as "debilitated", speculation which "requires a flavouring of . . . the literary spices, mystery and profundity". It is indeed interesting to see how much more Romantic in the spirit of their writing some New Critics are than the Richards they attack in the name of the New Classicism. "I have used, I believe, few words which I could not define in the actual use which I have made of them, and necessarily, such words have little or no emotive power."[1] In fact, in one sense, these words *did* have a lot of emotive power, for they were technical psychological words, which Richards himself described as "repellent", "uncouth", "turgid". He was forced to use them, though, because of his "desire to link even the commonplaces of criticism to a systematic exposition of psychology".

In spite of Richards' explanations, the language he used led to his being categorised in two similar ways. One was as an uncritical science-worshipper, the other as a materialist, not just in the sense of a philosophical theory, but in the sense of a particular *attitude* to art.

Richards was categorised as a science-worshipper because, though he held that the great advances in science had resulted in an all-round decrease of value from which our civilisation was suffering (a theme of *Science and Poetry*), he did not show the specific hostility to it as such that was so militant in Tate and early Ransom. Indeed, he praised science and, as we have seen, used its language. Tate and Ransom, on the other hand, in their psychological reasoning, seem to be so hostile to psychological science as never to have considered whether its concepts and distinctions might not have helped in developing their theory, which did not after all need to be orthodox from the point of view of present-day psychological theory. Further, they resented Richards' use of scientific psychological language. We have already noted the effect on Ransom, for instance, of Richards' use of words like 'stimulus' and 'cause'. Tate even seems to have gone so far as to regard scientific language as a shibboleth. When arguing

---

[1] Black (*Language and Philosophy*, 212) has commented that the *Principles* is "full of emotive meaning". I do not think Richards could in consistency deny this. After all, he held that all writing, except rigorous language used in the physical sciences, would be mixed in function and in genesis. He overstates his case in the Preface to the *Principles*. Nevertheless his language is distinctly more prosaic and more capable of being spelled out in explicit detail than that of the critics he was contrasting himself with. Further, though technical or scientific jargon *can* be exploited, I do not think Richards did exploit it much. Ransom and Tate, in using words like 'ontology', 'extension' and 'intension', 'logical structure', etc., seem to me to exploit it much more. They plunder philosophy and do not, like Richards, try to use it.

that Richards was a positivist, he described positivism as "more than a strict scientific method. It is a general attitude towards experience"; and added "If it is not, why should Mr. Richards have attempted in his early criticism to represent the total poetic experience and even the structure of poetry in one of the positivist languages—experimental psychology?"[1]

But this is not the only way in which Richards' language seems to have determined the direction in which he was to be categorised as a whole. There is also the fact that he used *prosaic* language whilst the others, as we have seen, used more 'poetic' language in their theorising. Possibly we should, when writing about poetry, take present manners of writing into account. In my own case I know that in writing in this chapter about poetry, when using language which is as neutral, as plain statement, as possible, I have again and again felt that I was cue-ing adherence to a way of thought which simplifies, flattens, and makes shallow artistic experience, even though I do not in fact subscribe to such an attitude. For my purposes relatively non-commital language was required, but a *tradition* of plain statement needs to be developed before this kind of language no longer misleads.[2] In Richards' case this language led indeed to a very materialistic interpretation of his theory. Thus Ransom described Richards' theory as requiring poetry to give the attitudes "their daily work-out", and compared Richards' interests in them to the abiding concern of a Henry James character with the state of his liver.[3] Mr. D. G. James attributed to Richards the belief that "the literary masterpieces of the world, the *Iliad*, the *Aeneid*, the *Inferno* . . . were stimulated into existence by things like a good meal or a comfortable chair".[4] T. S. Eliot described Richards' conception of value as "Efficiency, a perfectly-working mental Roneo Steel Cabinet System".[5] And Sir Herbert Read conceived it, in Richards' words, as "that kind of deliberate planning and arrangement which the controllers of a good railway or large shop must carry out".[6]

---

[1] *Reason in Madness*, 54.

[2] At present we may have a vicious circle because, in order to avoid the wrong inference being drawn, many may find it necessary to use emotive language in making plain statements.

[3] *The New Criticism*, 26.

[4] *Scepticism and Poetry*, 65.

[5] Review of *Science and Poetry* in *The Dial*, 1927, Vol. 82.

[6] Richards is referring to Sir Herbert Read's review of the *Principles* in *Criterion*, 1925, III. Both this and Eliot's *Dial* review are referred to by Richards in *Practical Criticism* (footnote to page 285) as instances of "certain large misunderstandings that I had hoped to have guarded myself against."

7. THE LATER BOOKS. RICHARDS, A REFORMED CHARACTER

After *Science and Poetry*, one widely held opinion[1] is that Richards gradually came to renounce the position for which both Empson and the New Critics criticised him. Ransom saw a beneficial modifying of his views already in *Practical Criticism*. Thereafter, he thought, under Coleridge's influence, Richards got better and better, a process which culminated in the *Philosophy of Rhetoric* and *Interpretation in Teaching* and was represented by a "conviction [on Richards' part] that the only profitable topic of literary criticism is the objective literature itself".[2] Tate, in his turn, uses Richards as a stick to beat present positivists with. "From 1926, the year of *Science and Poetry*, he has come a long way. It is perhaps not an extravagant claim to make for Mr. Richards' intellectual history, that it will probably turn out to be the most instructive among critics of our age." Tate went on to quote a passage from the *Philosophy of Rhetoric*, and urged that "These words should be read and re-read with the greatest care by critics who still cite the early Richards as the continuing head of a positivist tradition in criticism."[3]

As we saw, however, in our exposition of Richards' books, his views did not change anything like as much as these statements suggest. He certainly dropped his belief that the emotional effect of words in poetry was independent of the senses in which the words were taken. But since, as we saw, he never regarded this as a *general* feature of poetry but only as an occasional one, this change is not as important as Ransom, or even Empson, made out. It is true he changed his view about poetry giving knowledge. But this did not mean that he laid *less* emphasis upon emotion and feeling. It was a development, not an abandonment, of his early views, and was intimately tied up with his theory about increasing ordering of impulses as a result of artistic experience, a doctrine which as we saw, Tate and Ransom rejected as "mysterious" (in the pejorative sense), "morbid", or a "social scheme concocted in the interests of the will".

[1] Not shared by James or Stallman. See also the hostile assessment of *Coleridge and Imagination* by Leavis (*Scrutiny*, 1937, VI).

[2] *The New Criticism*, 75.

[3] From "Literature as Knowledge" (*Reason in Madness*, 55-56). Ironically enough, the passage quoted is part of an attack on Hulme's statement that the language of poetry "always endeavours to arrest you, and make you continuously see a physical thing, to prevent you gliding through an abstract process." On the contrary, says Richards, "the language of the greatest poetry is frequently abstract in the extreme." In the passage Tate quotes, Richards argues that the great value of language is that it is abstract (see pages 99-100 above).

Richards does not in his books consider in much detail his earlier views in order to indicate to the reader his present position with regard to them. This shows indeed how little systematic his *presentation* is and how fluid his thought. But references he makes in *The Philosophy of Rhetoric*, and, particularly, in the footnotes of *How to Read a Page* to *The Meaning of Meaning* and the *Principles* suggest that he is still satisfied with much in those books. The same applies to his comments in the symposium on *Emotive Meaning* on Max Black's criticisms of his 'early' views:

> ... in re-reading *Principles* ... I am more impressed by its anticipations of my later views than by the occurrence of anything to retract. I changed my vocabulary and my metaphors somewhat ... to present much the same views again.[1]

But what is most revealing is a comparison of the first and second editions of *Science and Poetry*. The second edition came out in 1935, a year after *Coleridge on Imagination*. In view of all that has been said about Richards' rejection of his early 'positivist' views, one would expect considerable changes. In fact, however, the changes are slight, and instead we get some additions to deal with *misunderstandings* of the first edition. There is an explanation of what he meant by his statement, which "seems to have puzzled Mr. Eliot and some other readers," about Eliot's having effected a "complete severance between his poetry and all beliefs"[2]; a footnote further clarifying the concept of pseudo-statements; and an appendix presenting multiple definitions of the words 'belief' and 'nature', because "they seem likely occasions of misunderstanding ... and they have in fact misled some readers." Apart from these additions, indicating not that he had changed his views but that they had been misunderstood in the first place, the only major alteration is one in which, following what he said in *Coleridge on Imagination*, he describes the scientific world-view as a myth, in the same way as religious and metaphysical systems. But even this is not such a big change from his early views as might appear, for he is referring to the metaphysical elements of comprehensive scientific theories rather than to the data of scientific experiment.

[1] *Speculative Instruments*, 53.

[2] As an indication of how a given categorisation, in this case that Richards had changed his earlier views, can affect perception of meaning, the comments of Mr. Hyman on the 2nd edition of *Science and Poetry* are instructive. Richards' explanation of what he meant by his statement about Eliot's "complete severance of his poetry from all beliefs" is described as a "*cancelling out*" of this statement. And his defence of his critical remarks about Yeats' poetry, namely, that, when he wrote *Science and Poetry* the later poetry had not yet been published, is described as an "apology" for his "vast underrating of Yeats". (*The Armed Vision*, 283).

Of course, as we pointed out, the big differences that his critics saw between his theories and theirs did not really exist, so the fact that Richards did not renounce his earlier views, however much he developed them, is not so important. On the other hand, since his critics now agreed with Richards' later views so much more, they had to believe that he had changed unless they recognised that they had misunderstood him in the first place. What then was responsible for this change in attitude? Why did they accept these writings, when they were so hostile to the very similar earlier ones?

8. FURTHER ERRORS

(a) Change of Language

If an important reason for the hostile categorisation of his early writings lay in the language he used, we would not expect this categorisation to be reversed unless the language were also changed. This indeed we find to be the case. Organic images, as we pointed out earlier, become more and more common after *Practical Criticism*. Instead of talking so much of our increased capacity for the satisfaction of impulses, Richards talked of *"growth"*, or *"self-completion"* or even *"self-fulfilment"*. Though he was expressing the same ideas (see pages 86-88 above), the language he used no longer sounded so "positivist". His reference to science as "myth", indeed his later use of this word instead of 'fiction' to describe religion, which conformed with Tate's and Ransom's practice, was taken as another sign that he was now on their side. But in fact his admiration and respect for science had abated not at all. In *Coleridge on Imagination* he gave, to use his own words, a "materialist" analysis of Coleridge's Idealism.[1] Having done this, Richards himself, in contrast with his earlier writings, constantly used strongly emotive language, fortified by quotations from Plato and Coleridge. We have given a number of instances of this in *The Philosophy of Rhetoric* and *How to Read a Page*. But it should always be remembered that he had already given what he called a Materialist interpretation of these statements. Having worked out his basic theories about self-development and the part poetry and philosophy contributed to it, Richards felt free to give full rein to the expression of his *feelings* on these matters.

Though the change in Richards' language removed an important

---

[1] Mr. James in *Scepticism and Poetry*, unlike Tate and Ransom, shows no alteration in his attitude to Richards. Richards' appeal to "modern psychology" on the constructive nature of perception in connection with Coleridge's similar analysis is interpreted by James as suggesting that Coleridge "was stating a *trivial* commonplace and what any associationist would accept". (*Scepticism and Poetry*, 60, my italics).

cause of his theories being categorised as giving to poetry an inferior position *vis-à-vis* science, examination of what Ransom says about his agreements with Richards suggests the operation of two other factors as well. These are a failure to understand correctly the relations of Richards' books to one another and the reading into Richards' works of favoured hobby-horse theories of his own. I will conclude my analysis of the comprehension of literary critics with a description of each of them.

(b) The Relation of Richards' Books to One Another

As I see it, nearly all Richards' books were concerned primarily with heightening the reader's awareness about the nature of language so as to improve his reading and thinking and thus to bring about development in his personality. Two possible exceptions to this are his first two books, *The Foundations of Aesthetics* and *The Meaning of Meaning*, and all that was missed out in *The Meaning of Meaning* was the development of personality, first tackled in the *Principles*. Many of these books had specific purposes within this wider framework, as indeed the prefaces to the successive editions of *The Meaning of Meaning* ought to have made clear. *The Meaning of Meaning* itself was concerned with the relationship between words, things and references or emotions, in order to remove many errors that were due to faulty theories of language and which bedevilled abstract thinking as well as prose communication. *Principles of Literary Criticism* applied the approach of *The Meaning of Meaning* to confusions in literary theory. In doing so, it used the analysis of that book but extended it to include a theory of value, according to which value would result from *correct* communication. *Science and Poetry* was a topical popularisation of this; *Practical Criticism*, a practical application. Thereafter, with the exception of *Coleridge on Imagination*, Richards' purposes were more with prose, philosophy taking over from poetry as the material which it was most valuable to communicate. But pointing out that the difference between prose and poetry was not so great as normally believed was part of the purposes of *Mencius on the Mind*, otherwise concerned with applying the approach to the problem of translation, and of *The Philosophy of Rhetoric*. *Interpretation in Teaching* was the companion-piece to *Practical Criticism* in the case of prose communication; *Basic Rules of Reason* was a popularisation of one of the messages of *The Meaning of Meaning*, namely, that of Multiple Definition—and so on.

All these books made use of the same general theory, which altered only partially in the course of time. What happened much more frequently was that particular parts of it were developed as the need arose. These later developments can often be discerned in embryonic form in earlier books, as we shall show later. Similarly, *after* they have been developed, they often go underground, being referred to much more elliptically, or concealed by a change in a semi-technical word. Nevertheless they continue to be used.

We have already come across some examples of critics' failure to identify Richards' purposes. Failure to recognise Richards' abiding concern with heightening his readers' *awareness* led to such absurd consequences as Max Black's interpretation of the Canon of Actuality in neurological terms. It also allowed the faulty idea that Richards wanted a science of criticism to occur, as Mr. Blackmur for one believed.[1] Connected with this is the failure to recognise what I can only call the experimental pragmatism of Richards' approach. In a sense all his books were *exercises* for the purposes of alerting his readers, making their minds grow. Therefore I think it is not true to say of *Mencius on the Mind*, for example, as Mr. Blackmur does, that its *"real point . . .* is the impossibility of understanding, short of a lifetime's analysis and compensation [sic] the mechanism of meaning in even a small body of work".[2]

Again, only blindness to Richards' predominant concern with communication from the reader's point of view could allow Professor James to describe the *Principles* as "for the most part . . . an attempt to describe the psychological and physiological conditions . . . necessary for the writing of great poetry",[3] a mistaking of purpose that affected other interpretations he made, such as, for instance, this odd inversion of Richards' theory:

> the labour of imaginative synthesis is a *product* of a rather mysterious and fortunate adjustment of impulses; and [the] literary masterpieces of the world . . . were stimulated into existence 'by something'—possibly a good meal or a comfortable chair.[4]

More generally, failure to recognise that Richards' concern was with communication rather than with literary criticism prevented his critics from appreciating why he so much stressed the differences in interpretations of poems, which affected the way he defined 'poems', and why he so much concentrated on the *effects* of poems on readers. Even if, unlike the situation in *Practical Criticism*, we read what the best critics have to say about a poem, how else can we, if qualified,

---

[1] "A Critic's Job of Work" in *Language as Gesture*. Blackmur wrote "literary criticism is not a science—though it may be the object of one; and to try to make it one is to turn it upside down" (page 390). Richards himself would have agreed with this.

[2] ibid., 389 (my italics).

[3] *Scepticism and Poetry*, 52.

[4] ibid., 65 (my italics).

judge for ourselves about a poem, except in terms of its effects upon us?[1] The New Critics' remarks about poems they value are shot through with expressions of feeling.

These examples of confusing Richards' purposes were all ones which led to his work being categorised as faulty in one way or another. But Ransom's confusions, as we have already pointed out, had the opposite effect. It is time we returned to him and the more detailed evidence he is able to provide. We shall find that he, too, failed to take into account the different purposes of Richards' books and their intimate relationship with one another as regards Richards' general theory. He presents a picture of them as though they were all concerned with literary criticism and were simply advancing along a straight line.

Ransom's neglect of Richards' purposes comes out straightaway when he turns to *Practical Criticism*. "The views", he wrote, "are a little soberer, just as the style of writing is less epigrammatic . . . Mr. Richards has mellowed and toned down, with some loss of native tang,"[2] a comment which once more suggests that Richards' language was a factor in determining how his meaning was taken. In fact, one would expect *Practical Criticism*, because of its purpose alone, to be quieter in tone than a book with the more ambitious purposes of *Principles of Literary Criticism*, and it is certainly not true that any increased sobriety of tone can be taken as evidence of a fundamental change of attitude in Richards. There are more intoxicated statements in *The Philosophy of Rhetoric* and *How to Read a Page* than any we find in the *Principles*.

Ransom continues:

> The attitudes almost drop out of Richards' critical vocabulary. They are lumped with the feelings which give their title to the whole emotive-conative aspect of poetry. There are now for Richards four separate 'meanings' which a critic must disentangle in his discussion of the poem: its Sense . . ., its Feelings, its Tone and its Intention. The last two come to our attention for the first time; the first two we have seen before, but not exactly in the same light.

Two comments can be made about these remarks. Firstly, it is not true that Tone and Intention "come to our attention for the first time", for they were already described in *The Meaning of Meaning*[3] (see page

---

[1] It will be remembered that, for the communication to be fully effective, Richards believed the reader should eventually make a judgment about a poem. Therefore one of his concerns in *Practical Criticism* is to help the reader in this task.

[2] *The New Criticism* 45-46.

[3] Max Eastman made a similar mistake, leading him to a faulty judgment concerning the purpose of *Practical Criticism*. "[Its] essential theme and reason-for-being", he wrote, "was to distinguish four different ways in which words are normally used",

29 above). Secondly, it is not true that Richards "almost" dropped his concept of attitudes. Two of his four kinds of meaning, 'Feeling' and 'Tone', are defined in terms of them[1] and these two, plus Intention, belonged to the rubric of the emotive use of speech,[2] so that Ransom was mistaken in thinking the emotive use of speech had now shrunk to merely one (Feeling) out of four of the uses of language.

These misunderstandings, which led Ransom to believe Richards was paying less attention to the emotions, were due to his mistaking the purposes of Richards' books in the following way. The *Principles* was concerned with what is common to the emotive use of language, and, with the theory of attitudes, tried to work out a rationale for the high value we attribute to poetry in terms of a general theory of value. That was one of its functions. The term, "attitude", was not used later because the different forms in which attitude entered in our use of language would now be more briefly and neatly expressed by terms like 'feeling', 'tone', and 'intention'. Furthermore, attitudes were never strictly part of Richards' "*critical* vocabulary", for the reason that we could only tell about them through the emotions and feelings. It is with these latter that the reader who has to judge a poem is obviously concerned. This example indicates what I mean by the close interrelationship between Richards' books from the point of view of theory. Neglect of *The Meaning of Meaning,* which seems to have contributed quite a bit to the New Critics' failure to understand Richards and which enters into this example, is further evidence of their failure to appreciate this interrelationship. Stevenson's attribution to Richards of two different ethical theories in successive books, and Empson's attribution to him of different views about the relation of reference and emotion in the same two books (see pages 161 and 173 above), are further examples of this tendency to treat books as independent entities, insulated from one another by their covers. Though, in contrast to Ransom, they each rather oddly attribute the better theory to the earlier book.

Practical Criticism in Ransom's view represented a first step in Richards' progress to the truth. The three books that show the final

---

[1] *P.C.* 181-182.
[2] See Richards' remark in the Appendix:—"Originally language may have been almost purely *emotive*; that is to say a means of expressing feelings about situations . . ., a means of expressing interpersonal attitudes . . ., and a means of bringing about concerted action." (*P.C.*, 353).

---

which seems very much to be confusing the ends with one of the means. This judgment also led him to interpret Richards' distinction between sense and emotive metaphors, which was implied in both *The Meaning of Meaning* and the *Principles,* as "a weak effort" to overcome difficulties in the intention attributed to *Practical Criticism.* Actually the distinction between "sense" and "emotive" metaphors was already made in *The Meaning of Meaning* (6th edn., 111).

exorcising of Richards' Romantic, psychologistic, and pseudo-scientific heresies in Ransom's opinion were *Coleridge on Imagination*, *The Philosophy of Rhetoric*, and *Interpretation in Teaching*. In the first, though,

> Richards is still trying to saddle poetry with the responsibility for stimulation, . . . he is finally acknowledging, with Coleridge, its cognitive office. But . . . in the *Rhetoric* Richards' earlier doctrine finally disappears. He seems perfectly content now to go . . . with the literary community . . . in the conviction that the only profitable topic of literary criticism is the objective literature itself. How fixed he is in this conviction is probably indicated by a still later book, *Interpretation in Teaching*. It is an important work . . ., in which he proposes the revival . . . of the old university disciplines of Rhetoric, Grammar and Logic. These three studies have maximum intimacy with our ways of thinking, but none with our ways of feeling, except to the extent that our feelings are strictly correlative with our thoughts."[1]

But Ransom fails to appreciate that in *The Philosophy of Rhetoric* Richards is no longer dealing with aesthetic theory. The reason why Richards "seems no longer trying by constant reiteration to enforce his subjectivist aesthetic upon us" and why "his discussion of metaphor lapses into the language of ordinary usage"[2] is, to put it into Richards' own words, "My subject is Rhetoric rather than Poetics and I want to keep to prose which is not too far from the strict scientific or 'rigid' end of this scale."[3] and *Interpretation in Teaching* was, of course, *entirely* concerned with prose.

(c) Hobby Horse Interpretations

The second factor operating in Ransom's change of categorisation that he applied to Richards' later works, was the reading into Richards of many of his own ideas. We have already come across this process in Stevenson and others reading into *The Meaning of Meaning* an emotive theory of ethics. Psychologically, it is probably the same process as the reading in of pet heresies, which we have abundantly illustrated. Both processes we call *hobby horse* interpretations. They are common sources of error. Other people's work is generally much obliquer to our own than we like to believe.

Ransom, as we have pointed out, held a theory that poetic, in contrast to scientific, discourse held much that was irrelevant to the argument of the poem. This was its texture that fed our perceptual needs, making us constantly aware of the body of the world to be

---

[1] ibid., 74-75.

[2] ibid., 67. Ransom's comments illustrate well his *own* impressionistic way of reading.

[3] *P.R.*, 49.

savoured in its own right, independent of our purposes. It sounds very much like an attempt to provide a philosophical justification for a Decorative theory of art, and it would be difficult to imagine an approach, with its emphasis upon "irrelevance" and "diffusion of interest", more unlike Richards' own. For Ransom, reading a poem seems like going for a country walk with constant stops to admire the dog-roses or a view from a stile;[1] for Richards it is like climbing, where, locked to the rock face, all one's energies are concentrated, achieving their final release only in the exhilaration of the climb completed. How strange then it is to read Ransom writing of Richards that "irrelevance in poetry is a very important discovery, and I do not know anybody who seems better entitled to the honours of being its discoverer".[2]

The passage that evokes this tribute comes, of all places, from *Principles of Literary Criticism*. Ransom is referring to some remarks of Richards on the subject of metaphor. Two points that Richards is making seem to be responsible for Ransom's interpretation. The first, a point he was frequently to make, was that "metaphor and simile . . . have a great variety of functions in speech", and that the function of illustration, which is common in prose, is rare in poetry. Rather, "some attitude of the speaker to his subject or to his audience is using the metaphor as a means of expression".[3] Whatever we may think of Richards' theory, this denial of what Ransom calls "the logical relevance" of metaphor does not mean an assertion of "irrelevance". It is rather one further example of Richards' general attack on the taking of poetry as *literal* statement, which aims at informing. Richards' second point was expressed in his statement that metaphor is "the supreme agent by which disparate and hitherto unconnected things are brought together in poetry for the sake of their effects upon attitude and impulse which spring from their collocation and from the *combinations which the mind then establishes between them* . . . [It] is

---

[1] There is a sort of obstinate prosaicness about Ransom. For instance, those lines from Bishop King's *Exequy*, addressed to his dead wife:

But heark! My Pulse, like a soft Drum
Beats my approach, tells Thee I come

which for Eliot have "an effect of terror", are for Ransom suggestive of the Bishop's watch "ticking away the moments which separated" him from his wife. And he opposes Richards' rhapsody about the lines from *Venus and Adonis*, that show the working of the Imagination, with the comment that the theme is "bawdy". Though the difference in theory between Richards and Ransom is no very fundamental one, their difference in temperament is tremendous. In this respect, Tate is much closer to Richards.

[2] *The New Criticism*, 10.

[3] Richards quoted by way of illustration Gibbon's "The freedom of my writings has indeed provoked an implacable tribe but as I was safe from the stings I was soon accustomed to the buzzing of the hornets."

215

a semi-surreptitious method by which a greater variety of elements can be wrought into the fabric of the experience . . . [for] what is needed for the *wholeness* of our experience is not always naturally present . . ."[1] Ransom's reading of this passage seems to be too much influenced by phrases like "disparate", "unconnected", and "greater variety of elements", and too little by the phrases in the passage that I have italicised. His hobby horse has led him to read selectively and in defiance of what was probable, as judged by the rest of the book.

When Ransom came to *Practical Criticism*, failing to recognise Feeling, Tone and Intention for what they were, and identifying the first, instead of all three, with "the whole emotive-conative aspect of poetry", he was left with Tone and Intention to explain. Ignoring Richards' definition of Tone as expressing the attitude of the writer to his audience, he noted, like someone solving a jig-saw puzzle, that there was "connection . . . between tone and style, between tone and manner, and between tone and the person addressed", and suggested that "all these connections are realised more explicitly under another term . . . Dramatic Situation". So, he added, the poem "becomes the speech of a "character" in a "situation" and its idiom becomes a feature of poetic "texture",[2] i.e. a means of introducing irrelevance. Intention, on the other hand, though he admits that he does "not always feel sure [that he] understands precisely what Richards has in mind", Ransom identifies with "the poet's logical thesis, or argument: the structural principle proper".[3] This is a hobby horse assimilation of Richards' meaning, for Richards made it quite plain that, by "the speaker's intention", he meant "the effect he is endeavouring to promote", which was an *affective* effect, however much it depended upon taking the sense of the poem in the right way.

Finally, when Ransom comes across Richards' technical terms, *vehicle* and *tenor*, which described, respectively, the metaphor and what the metaphor is of, he again sees it in terms of his own theory. As Empson did with Richards' technical term, "Mesopotamian",[4]

[1] *P.L.C.*, 240.
[2] *The New Criticism*, 61-62.
[3] ibid., 63-64.
[4] 'Mesopotamian' was a word Richards coined for "the use of a word prior to fixing any specific sense for it" (see page 116 above). The reader has to wait until he has read further before he knows the sense in which the writer will be using it. Empson took the term as referring not only to this but also to "the opposite extreme . . . [that is] the word used as a compacted doctrine". How he arrived at this typical complication of Richards' meaning is difficult to tell, because the passage in which Richards introduces his term is quite clear. What seems the most likely explanation is that Empson took the derivation of 'Mesopotamian', which is 'between two rivers', to mean, for Richards, "between two meanings". Empson reasoned further that the old woman, "who got great comfort from that blessed word 'Mesopotamia' ", got great comfort from a word which for her was "merely emotive because the senses

Ransom extracts further implications from Richards' own metaphor.

> I feel morally certain that [Richards] is aware of the quite different meta-phorical implication of his terms *tenor* and *vehicle*. Tenor is metaphorical for the prose argument, and vehicle for the poetic amplification of it . . . Tenor means tendency, or the steady direction of a progress, but there echoes in us the "noiseless tenor" of the rude forefathers' way: we think of a course that is pedestrian and downright plodding. If suddenly we exchange our plodding for a vehicle, we are pedestrians who have caught a ride. But the reservation to make against this happiness is that the vehicle is not going our way . . . and . . . we shall have to ask to be put back presently upon the highway some-where near the point where we left it.[1]

Having read into what Richards said about metaphor in the *Principles* his own idea of textural irrelevance, Ransom sees further confirmation in the technical terms Richards invented to deal with the ambiguity of 'metaphor'. It is true Ransom says this "is not Richards' *official* presentation of metaphor", adding "perhaps I go too *fast*, representing his view more as I should like it to be than as he *allows us to believe it actually is*", but the odd phrasing (which I have italicised) together with Ransom's assertion of "moral" certitude, suggest obliquely a higher knowledge of what Richards meant than Richards himself possessed.

9. THEORY OF COMPREHENSION RESTATED

Our study of the misreadings of Richards has shown how extensive they are. It has also shown how they may be analysed largely in terms of the categories his readers brought to bear on him.

Two features of this categorisation may be noted. Firstly, con-ventionalisation. Perhaps the best example of this is Bilsky's assimila-tion of Richards' theory of value to utilitarianism. We noted there the simplification of Richards' argument and the neglect of its original features. Secondly, there is hobby horse assimilation. This may operate in one of two ways. The reader may see a pet theory of his in what he reads. We saw this with Stevenson, and we have just considered further examples from Ransom. Or the reader may see a pet heresy, as we saw with Max Black's interpretation of *The Meaning of Meaning*. Hobby horse and convention often combine in their action. This was shown particularly in the New Critics' categorisation of Richards' early writings as a combination of positivism and Romanticism. The tendency to read the present into the past, which we saw in the

[1] ibid., 73.

---

of it were wholly confused", (*The Structure of Complex Words*, 313)—at least, this was the reasoning he attributed to Richards, but as we have seen before he was over-particularising.

attribution to Ogden and Richards of an emotive theory of value that became popular some ten to twenty years later, is another example of this.

The categorisation is based upon certain parts of what is read. It may be based on certain words, as was shown, for instance, in Ransom's reading of Richards' description of metaphor in the *Principles* or in his interpretation of Richards' terms 'tenor' and 'vehicle'; or certain types of words, for instance, technical terms of scientific psychology; or the *failure* to use certain words, such as emotive words, or the right kind of emotive words, in discussing literary theory. Sometimes a newly coined phrase may cause trouble. This we saw particularly with the phrase 'pseudo-statement', where trouble was caused by the way in which 'pseudo' was taken. Once the categorisation is made on the basis of these cues, other parts incompatible with the categorisation are either not noticed, or reinterpreted, or dismissed as inconsistencies.

The categorisation may well proceed on a hierarchical basis, reflecting the arrangement of the categories in the reader's mind. For instance, Ransom categorised Richards as a positivist on the basis of such cues as his use of technical psychological terms. This in turn determined how he later categorised Richards' use of 'cause' in the analysis of the relation of experience to poetry, neglecting the fact that Richards had also used it in his analysis of scientific language.

Often, in justification of a particular interpretation, the *general impression* made by the work as a whole is appealed to. We should treat such explanations with caution, however, since we know from many psychological experiments that early cues may determine the categorisation,[1] so that everything read subsequently is seen in this light, or not noticed because incompatible with it. The 'general impression' in this case would be determined by certain words and phrases one read at the beginning.

This process of judging a person's meaning as a result of the cueing of certain *stock* categories or personal hobby horses, so that the rest of what is read is all seen in this light, did not account for all the cases of misreading we came across. It did not account, for instance, for Ransom's reading of Richards' theory of attitudes, though, as I suggested, we might regard Ransom's complete failure to find any categories into which to place Richards' theory as another kind of categorisation, namely, that of mystification. It is not at all uncommon as perhaps an unconscious technique in controversy, and, as a mass reaction, it has characterised popular responses to modern art. Similarly, Empson's misreading of Richards is difficult to account

---

[1] Cf. for instance, the experiments of Asch, summarised in Chapter VIII of his book *Social Psychology*.

for in terms of categorisation. He over-individualised Richards' meaning, but what he saw in Richards was no particular hobby horse of his own. Nevertheless, *some* categorisation took place. His detailed search for a much more specific meaning than 'pseudo-statements' were ever meant to bear, was due in the first place to his categorising of Richards' theory as "the old line of joke that the poets 'tell excellent lies' ".

Categorisation is not merely a cause of faulty reading. It is also a requirement of correct reading. Ransom's mystification of Richards' theory of attitudes seems to have been due to his ignorance of the categories Richards was employing. Another example was Empson's failure to understand Stevenson's definition of attitude (see footnote page 171). Further, Empson's treatment of Richards showed in general a failure to understand the extent to which Richards was thinking in terms of rather broad categories. Category-writing, we might say, is the complement of category-reading. The principle of economy of effort which, on the whole, shortens the words we speak most frequently and reduces in size movements we make habitually, results in our writing more elliptically than we know. Similarly, the selective, interpretative approach we instinctively apply when reading others applies when we monitor our own writing as well.

New information may be resisted in one of two ways, by mystification or by conventionalisation. How the former operates to this effect we have already described. As for the latter, it will take the form of categorising the new information as something we already knew anyway; in other words, as something which is not new at all. This is a problem teachers often find themselves confronted with; so also do those who attempt to apply scientific method or elaborate procedures in the social sciences or psychology. Sometimes, of course, the reader is in the right. Writing which makes qualifications, as I have just done, is that which is particularly liable to be reacted to in this way. This may be a reason for the simplification we so often find in early theories, as well as for the dichotomisation into either-or categories that characterises much controversy. We need, both to interest ourselves and to interest others, to exaggerate our pictures. The psychology of perception requires it.

Will the reader make the correct categorisation of the theory I am at present advancing, or will he conventionalise it into understanding is correct categorising, misunderstanding is faulty categorising, and not understanding is not categorising at all? My approach is a phenomenological one and is intended to bring out two things. First, that there are important semantic units of a larger order than word meanings. These units are the categories I have been describing. They exert considerable control over how we take word, phrase, and sentence meanings, and communication depends upon our guessing them correctly. Owing to the way in which meaning has been coded by lexicographers, we tend to look upon reading as a process of building up meanings by the combinations of the meanings of separate words, morphemes, and constructions. Faulty reading is generally regarded as due to a failure to pay proper attention so that not every semantic element is given its due weight. This is a purely negative explanation, which is only occasionally valid. It leads to over emphasis on the doing of linguistic exercises as a means to improving reading ability. Though this basic skill is important, it is not by itself enough. I would lay greater stress on learning the background of knowledge and ideas that the writer is using and, in general, on being much more aware of what happens when we read (or misread). This implies more detailed study of the processes of reading and writing.

The second point my approach is intended to bring out is the extent to which the categories we bring to bear are shared ones, the products of social learning. Though I distinguished hobby horse categorising from conventionalisation, I pointed out that the former often involved fairly conventional categories too. I made the distinction to draw attention to the element of personal involvement that sometimes comes in, but in my experience the hobby horses generally come from a public stable. As a social psychologist, I am opposing the over-abstract individualist treatment to which this aspect of social perception has been subjected.

It would be wrong, however, to give the impression that merely having the right categories causes right reading to follow. We have to determine which of the many categories we possess are the ones to apply. To do this successfully is no easy task. It is here, I think, that the emphasis upon close attention and hard study that right reading requires is justified. It is appropriate to say something about this because of the unanswered question that has doubtless stirred in the reader's mind, namely—How do I know that my interpretation of Richards' meaning is in fact the right one?

The first thing to say is that of course I am not uniformly sure that my interpretations are correct. Also there are a number of problems regarding Richards' meaning which I have not solved. Nevertheless, the reason why I believe my interpretations are more likely to be correct than those I have been criticising is this. In so far as I possess the right categories, I believe that, by virtue of my particular interests, I have worked harder and spent more time on trying to understand Richards' books than, with the possible exception of Empson, they have.

Some people in the face of disputed interpretations give up the problem of determining meaning by saying that it is impossible to solve. Richards himself sometimes writes as though he favours this answer. My experience, on the other hand, is that much that was obscure becomes clear if one re-reads sufficiently often, with sufficiently long intervals between each set of re-readings, and includes the whole of Richards' writings. It may be said that there are very few writers who are worth this degree of effort. This may well be true. Nevertheless, most writing with high potential to value is in the same position as Richards' writing. I shall therefore dwell a little on my own experience in getting to understand Richards because, if at all representative, it has important implications for our attitude to communication.

I have found that in order to understand Richards I have had to read his main books[1] at least three times over, and many parts of these books far more frequently than that.

Quite fundamental changes in my understanding have sometimes come about after an eighth or ninth reading. They often depend upon the reading of other passages—sometimes in other books—than the one that finally triggers off the altered perception. They also seemed often to depend upon a long interval having elapsed since the last set of re-readings. Though these changes in understanding were frequently the consequences of special efforts, powered by a sense of an unsolved problem, this was not always so. Books, one might say, are full of puzzle pictures—that is, mutually incompatible ways of seeing what is there. One can read some passages many times over without suspecting that there is another way of understanding them. So the more frequently one reads a book, provided one has given oneself a chance of forgetting the precise way one saw it on the previous occasion, the more chance there is of suddenly seeing it in a different way. Therefore, to understand properly the *whole* of a writer's work, one may need to spread out one's task over a number of years. Few writers may expect this treatment, particularly in their lifetime. If, as was the case with those whose readings I have been criticising, the readers' main concerns were with points of literary theory or philosophical error, they are very unlikely to have gone to the extremes that a full understanding of Richards requires. This is peculiarly a danger with the History of Ideas approach.

Let us now illustrate this in more detail, mainly by drawing on my own experience in trying to understand Richards. I would roughly distinguish four sources of difficulty. These are those due to inadequate signalling by the writer, that is to say, bad writing; those due to failure to perceive connections between different parts of the writing,

---

[1] *The Meaning of Meaning, Principles of Literary Criticism, Science and Poetry, Practical Criticism, Mencius on the Mind, Coleridge on Imagination, Philosophy of Rhetoric, Interpretation in Teaching, How to Read a Page.*

which may be called bad reading; those due to unusual theories; and those due to the writer's individual use of language.

There were many passages in Richards the meaning of which I for long found obscure simply because they seemed to be badly written. I have, in the course of writing, already given a number of examples of statements by Richards which, if taken alone, are extremely difficult, if not impossible, to understand, and shall doubtless give further ones later. It would be tedious to give detailed examples here, but to illustrate my general point, we could take the case of Ogden and Richards' failing to make explicit that, when they talk of the emotive use of language, they have one or other of two senses in mind, according to whether they are referring to the genesis or the function of the words that are used. They do, of course, in different places describe these two different ways in which speech can be emotive, but they never state explicitly that there are *two* different senses, and they use indifferently many of the same words and phrases for either. It is therefore very easy to miss this point, and Richards' theory will be difficult to understand and appear inconsistent until it is understood. Once it is understood a lot becomes clear and falls into place, but it certainly took a number of readings of *The Meaning of Meaning* before I noted that there were two different definitions of emotive writing, so that in fact two different processes were being distinguished.[1]

I call this 'bad writing' partly because this is a convenient label, though it may seem paradoxical to characterise in this way a writer of Richards' eminence, who is also an authority on the teaching of English in our schools. It may seem especially paradoxical if we also characterise in this way many other eminent literary writers, who are also highly regarded poets, like Empson and Tate, on the grounds that their writing is no better than Richards' in this respect. This paradox comes from the fact that to call something bad suggests some current social norm that one is applying, and this cannot be the case here as far as our present literary establishment is concerned. On the other hand, if one contrasts these writers with professional philosophers, then I don't think there can be any doubt that their standard is poor by comparison—at least, that is, when they are writing on matters which the philosophers have made their professional concern. The other part of my purpose in calling some of Richards' writing bad is to oppose current trends, which Richards, particularly in *Interpretation in Teaching*, fosters. These trends manifest a state of mind which is hostile to any kind of grammatical prescriptions or stress in writing on the virtues of logical sequencing. Influences at work

---

[1] Morris is the only commentator I have come across who seems to have noticed this (*Signs, Language and Behaviour*, page 70).

222

appear to have been the much greater freedom in poetry that has grown during the last forty years; linguists' hostility to standard languages and to any (not only absurd) pedagogic attempts to control how languages should be used; the cult of free associating which applications of psycho-analysis and its popularisation have spread beyond its pale; and, in recent years, the growth in the use of tape recorders and the consequent invasion of the realm of written languages by styles of the spoken, without the spoken languages' other sources of information, such as stress and pause, or the safe-guard of audience feed-back, which allow speech to be so much more elliptical than writing. The consequence of all this is that though some writing may be able to express subtler thoughts than could be spoken since the 17th century, a good deal more can be said to decline in value, since it is more difficult to understand, whilst its matter has undergone no commensurate improvement.

Having affirmed this, I would prefer not to go on using the phrase, 'bad writing', because it does suggest something more than 'difficult to understand to a degree greater than is compensated for by the value of what is trying to be expressed'. Furthermore, 'bad writing' suggests a rather too ready moralistic attitude with regard to a process that is difficult enough to carry out. Its effect has been inhibiting. What is needed is more understanding of how writing may succeed or fail in communicating.

The second source of problems, those that might be considered to manifest bad reading, are ones whose solution involves the perception of connections. One cannot say all one has to say in a sentence. One has to connect the sentences with one another, and these are not necessarily consecutive sentences. They may come from other chapters or even from other books. Just as with the problems posed by 'bad' writing, so also I found connection-forming was something which went on taking place over a period of years and after many re-readings. It is astonishing how easy it is to miss connections even between successive sentences. On most occasions, this missing of connections seemed to be due to preconception. I categorised without noticing what did not quite fit in with the category.[1] If I give examples here from others rather than from my own misreadings, it is because they are rather central to the particular interpretation of Richards I have been dealing with in this chapter. One of these is Professor Frankena's not noticing the relevance to "The best test of whether our use of words is essentially symbolic or emotive is the question—'Is

---

[1] Sometimes this may have been a memory rather than a perception effect. One remembers sometimes having noticed the connection at the time, but this seems to have been suppressed when one summarised to oneself the points the writer had made, a process which often takes place very rapidly as the reading continues.

this true or false in the ordinary strict scientific sense?' ",[1] of the next sentence, "If this question is relevant then the use is symbolic, if it is clearly irrelevant then we have an emotive utterance". Professor Ransom similarly missed a connection *within* the same sentence when he quoted Richards' sentence—"This fact makes most verbal analysis of poetry irrelevant"—without its first two words, "Neglect of", which make a significant difference to the sense of the sentence (see footnote to page 56 above).

Often the connections that have to be noted are much further apart than are successive sentences. I was very puzzled, for instance, as to why Professor James attributed to Richards the view that "any . . . poem . . . is either true or false, does or does not reveal reality" (see pp. 194-195 above). It was only on the third set of re-readings, separated by some months from the second set, as the second was from the first, that I discovered that this was due to a quotation from the *Principles* that he gives and comments on six pages earlier. Two other such connections between remarks separated by a few pages, which clarified points previously obscure, were noted on this third set of re-readings of the twenty odd consecutive pages devoted to a critique of Richards. It is interesting that these connections were only noticed when there was a time lapse greater than the few days devoted to a single set of readings. It is as though one had a 'set', which blinded one to these connections but which slowly evaporated with time. Perhaps this should also be taken as an example of our first source of difficulty, since I think the writer bears some responsibility for signalling the connections here.

Sometimes making these connections will result in our giving a more precise, literal weighting to a word that we had not particularly attended to at first. This I have found, for instance, with Ogden and Richards' use of 'actual' in *The Meaning of Meaning*. When, at last, after many wrestles with it, I extracted from the Canon of Actuality its rather ordinary meaning, I came to realise that when Ogden and Richards used the words 'actual' and 'actually' (see examples on page 25 above), they were not using them, as we do often so, simply as verbal habits indulged in for stress and euphony. Similarly, the more one comes to understand Ransom's theory, the more, on successive re-readings, one pays attention to words, like 'particularly' or 'particularisation', which one had not especially noticed before.

Finally, there are the connections between different books, which we often only notice as a result of re-reading them. In Richards' case, I have often found earlier statements of themes which were later

---

[1] *M. of M.*, 6th edn., 150, quoted by Professor Frankena in *Language, Thought and Culture* (ed. P. Henle) page 150.

elaborated and which I had not taken in any particular way on earlier readings. A very simple example of this, perhaps, is Richards' statement at the beginning and end of the *Principles* that a book is "a machine to think with". It was only some time later that he came to develop his concept of "speculative instruments" and of the beneficial effects of exercising ourselves with theories. *Mencius on the Mind* was perhaps the first occasion on which he put his precept into practice, and *Coleridge on Imagination* where he gave it theoretical treatment. Another example is his mention in *Practical Criticism* of the "systematic ambiguity" of words, that is, that groups of related words had the same ambiguities. The idea is merely mentioned there. It is not clearly demonstrated till *Coleridge on Imagination*, nor does he give it a full theoretical treatment till *How To Read a Page*. But use of the word suggests the idea was already in Richards' mind, which is relevant to my thesis that Richards' later books develop points that are present in embryonic form in earlier ones.

An example, that we can consider in more detail, is that of Richards' theory of metaphor. This concept is not dealt with extensively by Richards until *The Philosophy of Rhetoric*. One of the distinctions he makes there, in opposition to what he considers a common fallacy, is that between metaphors that "work through some direct resemblance between the . . . tenor and vehicle, and those which work through some common attitude which we may (often through accidental and extraneous reasons) take up towards them both"[1]. But, until one has read this,[2] one is, I think, unlikely to note that the distinction is also made in a single sentence in *The Meaning of Meaning* and in a few sentences in the *Principles*. The latter sentences we have already quoted (pages 215-216), when showing how Ransom derived from them an early statement of his own theory of the necessity of irrelevance in poetry. Ransom contrasted Richards' position in the *Principles* with that he held in *The Meaning of Meaning*. In that book, however, there also occurs the sentence that metaphor is used in poetry "*not*, as in *strict symbolising*, to bring out or stress a structural feature in a reference, but rather to provide, often *under cover of a pretence of this elucidation*, new sudden and striking collocations of references for the sake of the compound effects of contrast, conflict, harmony, interanimation and equilibrium which may be so attained, or used more simply to *modify and adjust emotional tone*".[3] I think this makes the same points as were made in more detail in the *Principles*, though Max Eastman, in calling them "stock remarks of the scholiasts

[1] *P.R.*, 118.
[2] The distinction is also treated more fully in *Practical Criticism* (pages 221-223), but it is not given the theoretical prominence that it is given in the later book.
[3] *Meaning of Meaning*, 6th edn., 240 (my italics).

[which] are happily forgotten[1] [in the *Principles*]", evidently misses this.

Seeing connections between different books is not of course limited to understanding brief statements in earlier books in the light of more detailed treatment in later ones. As we have seen in the case of Richards' theory of attitudes, this works in the opposite direction also. Statements in later books are often rather cryptic condensations of doctrines elaborated in earlier books. These earlier books provide the key for unlocking these later remarks. The belief that Richards fundamentally *altered* his earlier theories separates the earlier from the later books and obstructs their proper interpretation.

The last two types of problem in reading can be dealt with very briefly. That due to the putting forward of an unusual theory, in which we might include using a word in an unusual sense, is fairly obvious. Correct categorisation is unlikely because of the rarity of the category in question. A good example of this was provided by Ogden and Richards' theory of truth which was designed to make unnecessary the postulation of negative facts (on page 26 above). This, as we have shown, led Professor Black astray in the second of his two articles. The theory also led Ogden and Richards to use the word 'symbol' of any sentence that, when it was used, was true. (If the sentence was false, then it was not a single complex symbol but a string of simple symbols and symbolic accessories, which latter were logical words, words for universals and so on). This odd use of 'symbol' certainly took me some time to notice, although in fact it is made quite clear by the authors.

Lastly, there is the question of getting Richards' proper measure. I have pointed out from time to time the connection between Richards' theory of language and his writing practice, the way in which he uses words in different senses and in different categories and his reliance upon our using the whole in determining the meaning of the parts; his tendency to produce disjunctive theories (pages 57-58 above); and his free association way of thinking, which we illustrated both with regard his arguments for the independence of the two functions of language in the *Principles* (section V, chapter III above) and with his grounds for emphasising the importance of metaphor in *The Philosophy of Rhetoric* (pages 101-105 above). Obviously, one has to know a writer pretty well to recognise these individal features of his writing, and failure to recognise those of Richards often led his critics astray. If one realises, for instance, that Richards free-associates arguments for a theory, one will not labour to discover hidden logical connections between them, and one can discard some of his arguments without feeling his whole case must be discredited. One will not be so

[1] *The Literary Mind*, 305.

impressed by the few extreme remarks that many of his critics quoted when arguing that he would neglect altogether the senses of words in analysis of poetry. Similarly, one will not just take as evidence of self-contradiction or loose thinking, as Bilsky does, the fact that Richards used the same word in different senses. At times this may be a case of bad writing, but I do not think this is always so. One frequently finds writers, enamoured of scientific jargon, who themselves use it very loosely and commit bad definitions, rejecting out of hand informal writing, where the different senses in which the same word is used are perfectly well signalled by the context. This type of categorisation, which one must admit can work the other way too with equal lack of justice, is one of the most insidious barriers to communication between "the two cultures".

The general picture presented here of the difficulties involved in reading and the time and labour needed to overcome them, is an appalling one, not easily acceptable to common sense. Though we might be able to improve the general level of reading and writing, our resources, given our present knowledge of these processes, are limited, and anyhow there are other causes of difficulty than these, such as our ignorance of the right categories. Further, however much we improve reading ability, it will always take a long time to take in and see, in the correct perspective, the large amount of information that any book provides.

One solution, championed by the 'philosophy-is-the-philosophy-of-science' school of thought, is that of linguistic reform. They wish to further certain trends of scientists' language, such as more precisely defined technical terms and the use of mathematics, by getting scientists to adopt a number of inventions in logic, or even, on occasion, to logically formalise complete theories. This attitude with regard to language is similar to a certain interpretation of scientific method amongst psychologists and social scientists, that would restrict the data, which scientists use in their attempts to construct laws, to those which all observers, with very little training, would agree on. This is a very different kind of approach from the one that has been adopted here. The implication of my approach, one which it shares with clinical approaches and the attitudes of literary critics and art critics, is that a lot of training will result in increased agreement between observers, and, further, that such observations will help us in developing theories which could not otherwise be achieved. Where my approach may differ from these may lie in the further assumption that deductions will ultimately be made from these theories, which can be more easily (more rigorously) tested. The danger is that in our efforts to demonstrate scientific maturity we shall attempt this step too soon.

227

As regards the suggestion of linguistic reform, we have no right to deny that it might improve communication. What is in question is to what extent present proposals are likely to bring this about. Here we are immediately confronted with the dilemma that, if everything is stated and made explicit, the communication will be extremely prolix. It will be tedious to read and difficult to take in and, of course, very dull to write. Further, as my analysis of the misunderstanding of Richards was designed to show, non-linguistic factors, that is, the categories we naturally and unthinkingly operate with, play an important part. Scientific communication, though technical and more precise-sounding, is always liable to such category-interpretations as regards, for instance, the writer's basic theoretical alignment. The difficulty of understanding new theories is also well known. Philosophers have suggested that partial linguistic reform might remove certain dangerously misleading types of expression,[1] but I have never found the evidence for these beliefs clearly formulated or critically considered. It seems, as I shall argue in Chapter Ten, to have been very much taken for granted. Proposed linguistic reforms, with the purpose of improving communication, seem to have been based on general ideas. The moral of this and the previous chapter is that detailed observations are also needed.

---

[1] Cf. Carnap's recommendation that "pseudo object sentences" should be expressed in the "formal mode of speech" (*Logical Syntax of Language*, Part III (1934)), and Neurath's tabooing of certain words in the social sciences (*International Encyclopedia of Unified Science*, Vol. II, No. 1).

Chapter Eight

MAN, NATURE AND SOCIETY

WE have now presented the whole of Richards' theory as it developed from book to book. In doing this, we have made a number of criticisms. It is time we attempted a general evaluation of the theory. I do not however wish to carry out detailed criticism of the nailing-down variety. Indeed, Richards' theory does not lend itself to detailed analysis. The reasons for this will be clear from our description of it. One of these is that his audience is never limited to technicians. He writes for students or teachers, and for the intelligent man with general interests. I do not think his concern is ever that of *only* making a theoretical contribution. He wants to make his readers better people; to advance, in practical ways, the good of mankind. For this reason, too, he never attempts a foolproof presentation of a theory—or, to use other words, a presentation that conforms with current practice in the discipline concerned as to the degree of detail, precision, and ellipsis that should be employed. His theories are sketches, not Academy pictures. The important thing for him is to get his reader's minds to grips with fundamental problems. Detail and technical language must be sacrificed to scope and audience size. Indeed, as we have seen in our discussion of his attitude to syntax, he believes his mission more likely to be accomplished if comprehension *is* difficult.[1] It may be, too, that apart from his views about what is good for his audience, Richards himself fears the stillness of solid form, requiring instead the continuous flickering of alternative vistas in the scenes he sketches. A preacher may after all judge what is good for his audience by what he felt was good for him. What is important with Richards is to *reveal* his thinking, and this not just two-dimensionally. It is of course worth doing this with any thinker, but, in Richards' case, the temptation to treat the theory as independent of its maker, as something other than a complex whole the exposition of which was

[1] One should perhaps make the proviso that for Richards' purposes the difficulty should come from *looseness* rather than closeness of weave. Philosophy is more often difficult because syntax bears a heavier burden of the meaning than is customary in ordinary uses of language—that is to say, because the language is *more* precise, requiring greater concentration than usual. This is in contrast with Richards, where one might say what is required is a greater than customary *dispersion*.

necessary for the understanding of its parts (words, sentences, paragraphs . . .), should, for the reasons I have given, be less than usual, though in point of fact it has resulted only in a neglect that reassures itself by saying that Richards was at all events a *good* man (doing useful practical work). Ideally, the exposing of a theory should be done as, according to some critics, a novel should be written—with such skill that comment would not only be unnecessary but would spoil the effect.[1] But that of course would be to confine ourselves only to a certain type of novel. Evaluation after all *can* be made into a kind of description. But the ideal mentioned illustrates the kind of thing we are after.

It is however necessary to consider certain general aspects of Richards' theory. In this chapter, we will examine his theory of transfer of value from poetry and philosophy to our behaviour as a whole, his ethical theory and the relative role he assigns to the individual and to the social in his explanations. In the next chapter, we will consider Richards' theory of language, and in the last two, what we may call the aetiology of his ideas.

1. TRANSFER AND GROWTH

The evaluation of Richards' theory of transfer of value is of critical importance, not only because it concerns the very ambitious claims he made for the reading of poetry and the carrying out of his exercises with language, but also because he regarded his own writings as themselves an exercise of this sort. Therefore he believed that, even if his philosophical theories were wrong, consideration of them would be growth-provoking because of the centrality of the issue with which they dealt. It is this theory that enables him to claim to be doing important, urgent work, in opposition, say, to the narrow specialisations of modern scholarship.

From the start we can grant one claim of his, at least as regards poetry. His emphasis upon close and detailed reading (providing the matter is worth it), upon personal involvement and committal to the experience, upon unremitting effort, and upon testing theories by experiencing their concrete applications and understanding them in terms of these, seems, from the evidence we have, to be good and necessary advice for the cultivation of a skill. It is also reasonable to describe such a skill in terms of better organisation, though in the case of poetry it would seem to be a perceptual rather than a motor

---

[1] Such an attitude would be consistent with one of Richards' reasons for his separation of functions in poetry. If poetry were understood as having an informative function, the poet would be tempted to substitute a formula, words that simply say instead of words that *work* on the reader. Cf. *P.L.C.*, 274-277.

organisation, unless of course one were considering the skill of reading poetry aloud—but that would be something different. The skilled behaviour might show itself in a looking for, and a greater sensitivity to, variations of rhythm and their relation to the sense of the poem and an appreciation of the relevance of the choice of one word rather than another. All this would take place relatively speedily and at a comparatively low level of consciousness, making it possible for the reader to cogitate on and test with his experience aspects of the total resulting effect. An unskilled reader, on the other hand, would notice far less, would be less likely to see interrelations between what he did notice—that is, his perception would be more fragment- and and less unitary—and he would give undue weight to features that would be little regarded by the more skilled reader. Skills also frequently show increases in the intervals between their cultivation, suggesting some sort of silent, internal reorganisation, which would fairly naturally, though not helpfully, be described as growth.

The admissions that I am making might be disputed, particularly on grounds of vagueness of formulation, but my target is large implausibilities rather than adjustments within probabilities. For when Richards writes of order or organisation, he is not referring to the kind of organisation I have been describing but to an organisation of the *attitudes*. Skilled poetry-reading, he maintained, would result in a reproduction within the reader of the organisation of attitudes that occasioned the poem. It is important to distinguish between skill in attitudes and skill in poetry-reading. To have the emotional attitudinal pattern reproduced in one's own experience as a result of reading a poem properly is to enjoy, as it were, a finished product. It is not the same as following step by step the poet's process in writing the poem, with its re-readings, its judgings, and its revisings, its con-comitant development of "attitudinal" organisation. Then again one might imagine that different readers could read the same poem with the right emphases and perceptions, having freed themselves from misleading ideas, and yet have emotional experiences of different power and consequently greater or less satisfaction of impulses. Some readers after all are more inhibited in their capacity to feel than others, and this capacity might also be regarded as a skill, independent of that of poetry-reading. Acting or the recital of poetry aloud might, it is true, be means of increasing this capacity to feel; but so, for that matter, might psycho-analysis.

Even if we were to grant that the having of a highly ordered emotional experience, as a gift from an expert, would improve our own ordering, would this generalise to poems of a different structure, and, above all, would it generalise to emotional responses to situations other than poetry-reading ones? Richards thought that it would,

231

because he believed in the efficacy of formal transfer of training. This belief, though it has energised his life's activities, is a most criticisable part of his thought. Let us consider again its formulation.

We first come across it in *Principles of Literary Criticism*, where Richards talked of the way in which our having an ordered experience, through having another person's experience, generalised to an increased capacity for ordered experience in *any* situation (see pages 46-48 above).

Finer adjustment, clearer and more delicate accommodation or reconciliation of impulses in any one field tends to promote it in others. A step in mathematical accomplishment, other things being equal, facilitates the acquisition of a new turn in ski-ing.[1]

and elsewhere he says "Neither the subject nor the closeness of correspondence between the experience and the reader's own situation has any bearing upon these effects [of reading poetry] . . . The effects . . . depend only upon the kind and degree of organisation which is given to the experiences".[2] By "kind and degree", he appears to mean only the degree relative to the reader's present stage of development.

According to the theory, then, there must be a unitary factor, that of capacity to organise an experience, which can vary in amount and can manifest itself indifferently in motor, intellectual, aesthetic, and social skills. The undergoing of any experience will raise or lower this capacity according to whether the experience demands less or more of this capacity, *provided* that the experience is accepted and enjoyed. Such elevating and depressing effects Richards believes are generally restricted to experience whose degree of organisation is near to that of their enjoyer's present level. Enjoyment and complete acceptance is unlikely if the experience is very much more or very much less complex than what is at present within his grasp. As for evidence, Richards makes passing mention of the theory of a general factor in intelligence and its relation to emotional stability, but, as we pointed out before, such a theory is only likely to be affirmed if this general factor is considered to be inherited and not influenced by learning. One might of course say that Richards had allowed himself an escape clause, the familiar "other things being equal" that occurred in the quotation from the *Principles* in our last paragraph. Indeed Richards followed his remark there by saying that "other things" were in fact rarely equal. However Richards is not theory-building but urgently advancing an educational programme. And he is asserting not a faith, but an experience. "Everybody knows", he writes,

the feeling of freedom, of relief, of increased competence and sanity, that

[1] *P.L.C.*, 234.
[2] *P.L.C.*, 236.

follows any reading in which more than usual order and coherence has been given to our responses. We seem to feel that our command of life, our insight into it and our discrimination of its possibilities, is enhanced, even for the situations having little or nothing to do with the subject of the reading.[1]

And it will be remembered that in *Practical Criticism*, Richards talked of how "behind our rejection or acceptance (even of a minor poem) we feel the sanction and authority of the self-completing spirit". But the experience is not self-validating, and though it is important to trust personal experience as a source of evidence, I should have thought personal experience ill-adapted to give evidence on such a very general hypothesis, relating to events which stretch over a long period of time and may be very dissimilar. In other words, the inequality of other things is so great as to defy even the huge natural generalising capacity of the best of brains.

Another type of evidence Richards refers to is that of the effects of mediocre art. Here he is very much concerned with popular art of the best-selling variety. That he should be concerned with this rather than with, say, the meretricious, follows perhaps from his concern as an educator. Over and above this, I think such partiality follows from his basic postulates. The effect of such art is to implant more deeply the stock responses it purveys. Some order and stability is thus achieved, but at the cost of further experiencing by which alone we can learn,[2] because everything new is perceived in terms of the stock categories. It is easy to see that such responses are often of greater generality than those expressed in valuable works of art. We may however wonder whether artistic instruction is the best way of combating this general rigidity or indeed whether it would ever hold the attention and reach the understanding of those who had adopted such defences, which may anyhow be determined by group identifications. In so far as they were so determined, exercises in increasing sensitivity might be dealing with symptoms rather than with cause.[3]

We have already pointed out how after the *Principles* Richards continued to use the idea of formal transfer, and that it was implied in his use of phrases like "growth", "self-completion", or "self-development". Therefore our criticism applies to much more than the theory advanced in a single book. It suggests that *many* of Richards' most ambitious claims for the value of his teaching were

---

[1] *P.L.C.*, 235.

[2] This is a basic theme of Richards, which is also shown in his desire to combat wrong conceptions, for these prevent us from seeing things properly and thus having fructifying new experience.

[3] Cf., for instance, the evidence of association between stereotyping and relying strongly on groups for one's standards. G. W. Allport in his book, *The Nature of Prejudice* (1954) (Chapters 10, 17 and 25), gives a brief account of some of this.

unjustified. I write "many" rather than "all" because there is also Richards' theory of material transfer which he used alongside his other theory, and which, as was noted earlier, tended to be used more frequently in his later books. But with regard to this also he was over-optimistic.

The material transfer theory has two forms—implausible and plausible. According to the implausible, which was relied on particularly in *How to Read a Page* (see pages 135-136 above), we construct, by dint of learning about words and their parallel sense-shifts, an order within ourselves which is isomorphic with that of Nature, and are able to make use of this in satisfying our needs. I will not present arguments against this since it shares a feature with the plausible form of the theory. In criticising this feature, I shall be criticising both forms.

As for the plausible form of the theory—let us call it the Miniature Models theory—we have already come across instances if it. For example, in *Coleridge on Imagination*, there was the suggestion that study of poetry, that is of "minor myths", will help us to manage the major myths of religion or politics. Again, in *The Philosophy of Rhetoric*, Richards argued that study of metaphor may help us to deal with our infantile fixations.

> . . . as the small and local errors in our everyday misunderstandings with language are models in miniature of the greater errors which disturb the development of our personalities, their study may also show us more about how these large scale disasters may be avoided.[1]

Interpretation in Teaching frequently appealed to the Miniature Models theory, the main argument being that the opposition between Richards and the Usage theory was like that between the democracies and the dictatorships, so that

> the world crisis, 'Shall we accept others' views (good or bad) or learn to see?' is reproduced inside every genuine experiment in interpretation, . . . What we need is to induce the struggle between the rival forces repeatedly on a small controllable scale so that the different outcomes of the choices shall become apparent.[2]

Similar claims are made in *How to Read a Page* with the additional claim that the centrality of the words there defined—"the very hinges of all thought"—made the transfer much more potent.

I do not, however, think the material transfer Richards claims does in fact follow. As is so often the case with Richards, his argument lacks any satisfactory *concrete* specification. The examples he gives,

[1] *P.R.*, 136-137. See also pages 105-106 above.
[2] *I. in T.*, 170.

such as the Freudian one about metaphor and fixation, are absurdly general. But even if he were right and there were common principles, into which we had had no insight, "modern psychology" does not support the implied view that, simply by discovering these insights in the one situation, we would then apply them in others. We have to *notice* their applicability. This is by no means always easy. Literary critics seem no more likely to transfer their learned capacity for discrimination, as regards the interrelations between sense and feeling, to political questions or, indeed, to personal ones, such as their attitudes in bringing up their children, than natural scientists are likely to transfer their scientific attitudes to questions of the social sciences. To make material transfer likely, what has to be written about is not only the miniature model but that with regard to which it is meant to help us. If, for instance, the improvement of our under-standing of the working of language is meant to transfer to politics, then it must be shown *how* this would follow by considering particular political problems. There is no short cut, such as this typical myth of the educationalists seems to promise. In making his grandiose claims, Richards is himself manifesting a belief in word magic, though there probably lurks in the back of his mind the simplified psychology of the "substitution" theory of learning.[1] As regards the reliance on material transfer to solve personality problems, of a kind that would entitle us to talk of "self-development" and "self-realisation", the objections apply, but with more force, because of powerful emotional forces opposed to our perceiving the necessary connections. Of all people Coleridge, whether we apply Richards' theory of formal or material transfer, should have realised Richards' ideal, yet, as Richards himself recognised, this was not so.

2. RICHARDS' ETHICS

We come now to the consideration of Richards' ethical theory, particuarly with regard to that component of ethical behaviour, our obligations towards others. Doing this will also lead to a consideration of Richards' attitude to society. We shall be concerned more with Richards than with the issues with which he deals, and will therefore not only go by what he says but by the attitudes his words and thoughts evidence. Taking what he says as sign as well as symbol calls for a content-analysis approach. But this can only come out of experience that gradually articulates as it grows. My approach must be tentative and discursive. It will be haunted by the question whether Richards is an over-individualist.

One of the puzzles that Richards' theory sets the reader is to work

[1] See pages 21-22 above.

out exactly how the increased harmonisation of impulses gained by art will actually be applied in valuable behaviour in daily life. In order to solve this we search Richards' pages for examples of what a good man does. It is after all the best way of discovering how a theory of value, which is described in abstract terms, should be taken. The first result of such a search in Richards' writings is one of disappointment. He subscribes in rather a general way to conventional notions of what is good. He claims his theory of value will do justice to altruism, even to the conventional martyr's case, he values religion, though rejecting of course its transcendental claims—Christianity is rated highest by the criteria used in judging art for its "answer is the most central, rejects least and unites the most conflicting components"[1] —and our social interdependence, the impossibility of achieving the highest value except in society, is from time to time mentioned. But when we look for any individual characterisation, all we can find is that the man Richards appears to value most is the one who has the richest emotional and intellectual life, the man, that is, who comes nearest to fulfilling himself. But the experiences by means of which he does this are those not of life but of literature.

The experiences which the arts offer are not obtainable, or rarely, elsewhere. Would that they were! They are not incomplete; they might better be described as ordinary experiences completed. They are not such that the most adequately equipped person can dispense with them and suffer no loss, and this loss is not momentary, but recurrent and permanent; the best equipped are precisely the people who most value these experiences.[2]

In ordinary life a thousand considerations prohibit for most of us any complete working out of our response; . . . We have to jump to some rough and ready solution. But in the 'imaginative experience' these obstacles are removed. . . . As a chemist's balance to a grocer's scales, so is the mind in the imaginative moment to the mind engaged in ordinary intercourse or practical affairs.[3]

Therefore, though Richards seemed to be claiming that, by his ethical theory and theory of formal transfer, artistic experience heightened our capacity to live valuable lives, when we search for instances of this we cannot find any other than the having of further artistic experiences. Indeed, logically, it would seem that the comparatively disorderly experiences of ordinary life would lower their author's organising capacity, so that the Ivory Tower should in fact be his fortress, but perhaps Richards would save himself these conse-

[1] *H.T.R.P.*, 172.
[2] *P.L.C.*, 233.
[3] *P.L.C.*, 237-238.

quences by pointing out that it depends on one's attitudes of awareness to the quality of the experience.[1]

It is also noteworthy that Richards is never other than vague about
the kind of experience of life we need to have before we can properly
appreciate novels and poems that are themselves products of a
maturer experience. Richards' contrasts are in terms of "cruder" and
"finer" organisations, and such preliminaries that he mentions as
being of help sound of a more intellectual kind. Indeed, the experiences he seems most to favour are those of greatest generality and
simplicity. I think this is shown in the examples he chooses in *Practical
Criticism* by means of which we can test our sincerity. These are the
feelings aroused by "Man's loneliness"; "the facts of birth, and of
death, in their inexplicable oddity"; "the inconceivable immensity of
the Universe"; "Man's place in the perspective of time" and "the
enormity of his ignorance"—all, except perhaps the second, rather
philosophical and impersonal criteria[2] by which to measure authentic
experience. It is interesting to notice also how much Richards' treatment of the poet's mind in his chapters, "The Availability of the Poet's
Experience" and "The Normality of the Artist", seemed to be in
terms of unusual sensory collocations rather than in emotional range.
One might expect some recognition of the dependence of understanding of words upon experiences, but though Richards does
mention this occasionally, any implications it has for the ability to
appreciate works of poetry or prose are not developed. Richards does
of course enormously emphasise the importance of experiencing for
understanding, but this is always a literary matter, preparatory
reading and study of a work and noticing one's reactions to it,
something, in other words, that can all be done in the classroom.

But though the search for what, according to Richards, a good man
does leads to disappointment, it is possible to extract from his writings
what a good man *is*. He is, one might say, above all things an
Individual; one who is secure in himself, possessing an internal
standard by which he may judge and therefore not easily diverted by
winds of fashion or vagaries of public opinion. He is an adventurous
experiencer, always ready to experiment. He is constantly, ever-
lastingly aware, and through tragedy, through poetry like *The Waste
Land*, he is able to see things in truth, recognising them for what they
are. Unillusioned, he is strong. He is a person, too, with a quality of
naturalness, acting with skill and ease, nowhere laboured, not forcing,

[1] Thus, in the *Principles*, Richards says that mediocre art can be experienced by
those of more developed discrimination, provided they regard it with due irony.
P.L.C., 230.
[2] Richards describes them "as the most incomprehensible and inexhaustible
objects for meditation". *P.C.*, 291.

straining, or repressing. If he finds a weakness, he will set to work to remove it. Through his concentration and internal order, because of the balance within him of his desires, he is detached, impersonal, and capable of justice.

This picture is one of a recognisable ethical ideal—non-attachment, achieved paradoxically, not by renunciation, but by fulfilment. This is made easier by Richards' theory because, since artistic experiences are relatively cheap, everyone has the means of satisfying the greatest number of his desires without competing with anyone else. In conformity with the emphasis laid on impersonality and disinterestedness, Richards' tone is rather cool. He says little about any active involvement in the troubles or achievements of others producing its direct pains or pleasures. The talk is of "humane, sympathetic, and friendly relations"; of the impulses "upon which communication and the ability to cooperate depend".

We have to recognise the different ethical evaluations that different temperaments lead to. But Richards claimed universal validity for his account. Characteristically, he appealed to the meaning of the word, 'good'. "When we say that anything is good we mean that it satisfies . . .[1]." If ever there was a case for carrying out a Multiple Definition, it was surely here. There is, after all, the meaning of 'good' we use when we call a person a 'good man', or talk about the quality of 'goodness' in people, or refer to 'good deeds', a 'good life', and so on. The reality of this concept is further indicated by the fact that one can use it ironically, but when one does so this would be indicated by special intonation, suggesting inverted commas, for example, ' "good" works', or 'a "good" woman' (with a sigh). The non-ironical use of 'good' need not imply Pelagianism, for it may be a device due to an implicit recognition that Utilitarianism doesn't work. This *function* of the word we might perhaps express by inverting Richards' definition thus:—"When we say that an act is good we mean it does *not* satisfy."[2]

Richards' practice also, to some extent, belies his theory. Though stressing so much self-fulfilment by the active reading of poetry and philosophy, he obviously considers *valuable* the activity of telling people that this is so. Further, he is constantly concerned with the state of our civilisation, never more so than in his last books, where he constantly remembers the menace from Fascist autocracies. He is

---

[1] *P.L.C.*, 58.

[2] In *How to Read a Page*, Richards distinguishes two meanings of 'love', one of which he identifies with $\alpha\gamma\alpha\pi\eta$, which he regards as "pure giving " But nowhere does this enter into his statements about ethics, which are devoid of references to 'duty' or 'ought', and, as we have seen, he continues with his conception of 'self-completion' first expounded in terms of impulse-satisfaction.

also critical of those who are not actively concerned with such questions, as is indicated by his occasional rather scornful references to scholars and specialists. They are at one with all those who set reality at a distance, living in a fantasy world populated with Abstractions from Word Magic, or viewing the real world through coarse spectacles and endeavouring to impose their stereotyped vision on others. The virtue of scientists was, I suspect, that, however specialised *their* activities, they had proved them ultimately of material benefit to humanity.

3. SOCIETY AND THE INDIVIDUAL

Richards' attitude to society, as shown particularly in *Science and Poetry* and *Coleridge on Imagination*, seems to be the following. In the past, when different societies were much more homogeneous, communication between their members was much easier and they could build up an order within themselves like the order that existed in society. Since then however the growing heterogeneity of Western societies is such that we have become more and more disordered. Salvation depends now on individuals. Firstly, the poets, upon whom we must rely for building up a new order; secondly, ourselves, who need to study so as to be able to be communicated to, either by poets or by philosophers.

But despite this emphasis upon individualism, Richards on occasion still mentions social factors as being important. As we saw, when outlining the ethical theory he advanced in the *Principles*, he laid a good deal of stress on the impulses involved in the co-operative nature of society. He also stressed ethical relativity both within and between societies. References to our mutual interdependence occur from time to time in later books, culminating in *How to Read a Page*, a book written with the war that was going on very much in the author's mind. In that book, remarks like "only as a member of society which does [its "right work" for him] can a man become fully himself"[1], and the closing words of the book,

> The greatest evil *is* injustice, things out of place and therefore against one another—in a mind, in a nation, and in the World State. Only in a state ruled by Reason can we be certain that freedom for Thought, in the only sense that matters, will not be withheld or destroyed. For Reason is what gives us that freedom, and that is why it must rule,[2]

suggest that Richards may after all be recognising a higher order than that of the individual man, an order moreover of which he is part.

[1] *H.T.R.P.*, 231.
[2] *H.T.R.P.*, 242.

When however we look for detailed specification, working out in terms of his theory how this mutual interdependence works, we are just as disappointed as we were when trying to find out how his ethical transfer theory worked in practice. In comparison with Coleridge, or contemporary critics like Eliot, Leavis, and Allen Tate, Richards' treatment of society is "macroscopic", giving rise to the suspicion that his statements about it are little more than background shading, safety clauses, or peroration points.

Richards' real concern is indeed with the individual, and this frequently shows itself, in contrast to remarks of the kind we have been quoting, in hostility or suspicion concerning society. Thus, despite the remarks we have quoted, in the main Richards shows a negative attitude to society in *How to Read a Page*. Concerned with unjust totalitarian regimes, he repeatedly warns against the danger of "forgetting what man's work and society's work are, and making a man only the servant of a state", and talks of "a society's right work for its members". When he does admit a right to the state, it is done grudgingly with a conventional example:—"A state, since a man's life is dependent on it, can, in wartime for example, require him to give up even his life to protect it. But *otherwise* it exists for him, not he for it" (my italics)[1], and throughout his books he is constantly tilting against social norms, whether literary, lexical, syntactical, or moral. With his eyes fixed always at a point high up above the average, he regards them as so many potential regressions to the mean:

Any public code of behaviour must . . . represent a cruder and more costly systematisation than those attained by many of the individuals who live under the code . . . None of the afflictions of humanity are worse than its obsolete moral principles.

The element of sacrifice exacted by any stable system explains to a large extent the tenacity with which custom is clung to, the intolerance directed against innovations, the fanaticism of converts, the hypocrisy of teachers, and many other lamentable phenomena of the moral attitudes. However much an individual may privately find his personality varying from hour to hour, he is compelled to join in maintaining a public facade of some rigidity and buttress-ed with every contrivance which can be invented. The Wills of Gods, the Conscience, the Catechism, Taboos, Immediate Intuitions, Penal Laws, Public Opinion, Good Form, are all more or less ingenious and efficient devices with the same aim—to secure the uniformity which social life requires.[2]

What Richards seems to be doing is identifying society with the state, and setting society up, too, as an abstraction over against the

[1] *H.T.R.P.*, 231.
[2] *P.L.C.*, 56-57.

individual. He then concentrates only on some bad aspects of social influences, neglecting, both here and in such remarks as:

All societies hitherto achieved . . . involve waste and misery of appalling extent,[1]

the enormous degree to which our potentialities are developed by our social inheritances. The optative mood is one which is pervasive throughout society; it cannot simply be frowned away. When Richards talks about "a tendency towards increased order"[2] which results in our becoming "more appropriately responsive to the outer world", he forgets that our environment is largely a social one. Perhaps we might apply to Richards the words from *Lord Jim* that he himself quotes concerning what should be our attitude to feeling— ". . . to the destructive element submit yourself, and with the exertions of your hands and feet in the water make the deep, deep sea keep you up". In "trying to climb out into the air", Richards is of course in part representing the tradition of individualism. Nevertheless I believe he goes beyond this and that his attitude requires explanation in terms of his individual psychology. This I shall deal with in my last chapter; at the moment I shall only be concerned with illustrating the ways in which Richards seems to be neglecting the social dimension.

The first way in which Richards does this is in his psychological theorising. In this respect, he is no different from any other psychologist of his time or indeed from many of today, since the widening of our awareness that social psychology brings is only slowly developing. Broadly speaking, the conception of perception and learning that individual psychology operates with is oversimplified and unduly atomistic, as far as its application to social processes is concerned. It fails to take into account the social setting in which these activities take place, as well as the pressures to conformity that are acting because of the social nature of the process, of which the learner is himself aware. Furthermore, in studying processes like perception and learning, no account is taken of the *average* characteristics of what is perceived or learned, and the corresponding social pressures, with a view to determining the part they play in the so-called laws of learning, or in perceptual tendencies such as those of making more symmetrical, conventionalising, and levelling or simplifying. Just as the eye-movements we make in reading are determined in part by conventions of printing, so the degree to which we simplify in our comprehension of what we read is likely to be affected by the relation

[1] *P.L.C.*, 56.
[2] *P.C.*, 285.

between what we read and the average degree of complexity of the class of reading-matter concerned.

The point of view I am putting forward is, very largely, point of view rather than experimental fact (which, once we have it, could of course be differently interpreted). General, as opposed to social, psychology works on a different set of assumptions. It is not very conscious of these, nor has it critically considered the other assumptions I am suggesting. However, the analysis of comprehension that was put forward in Chapters Six and Seven may be taken as one example of a different approach to perception that social psychology suggests. It is an approach which presents the perceiver as bringing to what he perceives a social map ('grid' would be too geometrically abstract), which has been learned through his different group memberships, such as being a university lecturer in literature, and belonging to a certain school of thought which has particular attitudes to the past, to science, and to society. What is read is then given a position on this map and evaluated in terms of this position. In fact, as we have seen, the resultant social stereotyping produces a good deal of faulty reading. Of course, this effect of expectation on perception has long been recognised by individual psychologists. But this has been treated atomistically, rather than in terms of a structure of categories that have been learned as the words of a dictonary have been learned[1]. Furthermore, the tendency to treat expectation in terms of recent learning experience made it seem unduly arbitrary as though it was the result of what just happened to occur. The viewpoint is one of atomistic individuality rather than of the social web or harmonic system.

These considerations particularly apply to Richards' match-scrape/flame-expectation model of language learning. This is oversimplified not only in presenting speech as though it were an automatic rather than a willed and purposeful activity, but also in the way it presents the sign-situation as something one just happened to stumble across. But in fact it seems likely that in language-learning, in learning the meanings of words and constructions, children have an overall theory of what language is (which would of course not necessarily be the same as what they would, if they could, say it is). This would mean that in learning a word, they would already have an idea of the class of thing a word was; they would have a particular learning-set. The trouble about psychological theories of language-learning is that they concern themselves with how we learn words rather than with how we learn the kinds of things words are and what these kinds of things

[1] See *Interviewing in Social Research* (1954), by H. H. Hyman and others, Chapters 1-III, for an interesting account of the effects of three systems of expectations on interviewers' perceptions of what their respondents say.

are. The theories about language that a child has are not of course only worked out from observing the uses to which people put language. To a very large extent, they are taught him, either directly or implicitly, by others. This has implications for our attitude to the norms governing language behaviour that we shall discuss in our next chapter.

The second way in which Richards neglects social factors lies in his underrating of the strength of our social needs. Though he does not justify "due sensitiveness to the reciprocal claims of human intercourse" on grounds of simple expedience but on the grounds of the other functions this comes to fulfil (see pages 37-38 above), it remains in its origins an instrumental motive. Such a view contrasts with biological theories concerning the satisfactions which the stimuli provided by social intercourse in pair-relationships or groups can give us. Richards' underestimation of the role played by social satisfaction is I think particularly evident in his theory concerning the taking over of the functions of religion by art. This theory quite neglects the dramatic and especially social nature of religious ceremonies. As a substitute for these, Richards' recommendation of individual artistic experience seems thin gruel indeed. Though he may be right in criticising the mythologies of Yeats and D. H. Lawrence, he does not seem to appreciate the motives lying behind a book like, for instance, *The Plumed Serpent*.

Richards also neglects the importance of the need for social acceptance and recognition of achievement and the kind of motive that used to be called *honour*. He forgets, what is complementary to these, the influence of the groups we belong to on our opinions. He argues as though it were simply a matter of each person's relying on his own judgment, so that his efforts are directed to improving that judgment by carrying out his various exercises. It is surprising that one familiar with such periodicals as *The Criterion* and *Scrutiny* should not show more awareness of the massive influence of group affiliation, which, amongst other things, determines the very way in which what one says is interpreted. Indeed Richards' individualism shows itself in the way in which he has himself neglected to form a coterie, found a journal, or otherwise attempt to give institutional impetus to his attempts to reform people's minds.

The third and last way in which Richards neglects the social dimension lies in his very lofty ambitions for the *individual*. This is shown in the difficult tasks he sets his readers, wishing them to be able to respond properly to the best modern poetry—which on the whole is difficult poetry—and to understand and think intensely on the most fundamental philosophical problems. He sets his sights similarly high when it comes to improving reading; we have seen what demands he puts on his own readers by his own style. In effect, all this means that he is concentrating on the few. I think this is also indicated by his attitude to norms. He seems to consider only those whose potentiality is above the norms. But there are many for whom social norms, of taste, of style in the interests of clarity, of morals, act as an aid. To destroy them is to threaten anarchy, or less trained, more dogmatic local standards. Every suburban builder his own architect in the recent past and every man his own decorator today show the kinds of results that may follow. Is the price worth paying for the few who do succeed?

The question this raises is that of quantity *versus* quality—how should society allocate its resources? Should we in the interests of more mass literacy set our sights as low as present comprehension tests imply and impose the discipline of the Readability Index? Should we in research in the social sciences or psychology limit our theories to data which require little special training to observe, or should we cultivate more elaborate observational skills, requiring the institution-alisation of 'apprenticeship' systems, as in psycho-analysis, to pass the skill from one person to the next? How much of our economic resources should be allocated to the needs of backward countries? Are modern art and poetry getting altogether too esoteric?

This last question may not seem on a par with the others, yet it is relevant if we maintain, as both Richards and his New Critic critics did, that art has some kind of social value. The sum, or perhaps I should say, the product of good may be greater with the best poets writing more simply so that they fire a wider public than the highly developed few. It is surprising how intemperate attitudes on this question tend on the whole to be. Merely to raise it is to invite a simple categorisation in terms of Folk Art *versus* Mandarin Art. Either we must be two nations, the rich and the poor, or there must be complete equality, producing, by virtue of some social equivalent of the second law of thermodynamics, a static society. Probably the reason for such a reaction is the suspicion that poets may be dictated to. But to raise the question is not to advocate such a solution. The kinds of proposals that might be made would be ones directed at the conditions that affect art. If, to take a simple example, there were a considerable intensification of art education, including its techniques, on the creative rather than, as with Richards, on its receptive side, it is more likely that the resulting art would become more universal in its appeal. But, above all, the carrying out and teaching of art needs to be done with greater awareness of our actual social interrelationships, some-thing that may be expected to follow as studies in the social sciences develop.

Chapter Nine

RICHARDS' THEORY OF LANGUAGE

RICHARDS' theory of language needs to be considered, not only for its own sake, but also because of Richards' identification of thinking with the use of language. If we supplant bad theories with good, he thought, the result would be better thinking too.

In this chapter, we shall first of all consider the main features of Richards' theory of language, and then his identification of thinking with language-use. This will put us in a position to consider the specific ways in which Richards thought language could mislead us— the topic of the chapter that follows this.

I. DISTINCTION BETWEEN EMOTIVE AND REFERENTIAL MEANING

The distinction between emotive discourse on the one hand and referential, scientific or "strictly symbolic" on the other can, as we saw when considering *The Meaning of Meaning*, refer either to the purpose of the discourse or to its psychological causes. The distinction in its former sense, though perhaps not in its latter sense, is present throughout Richards' writings. We will consider each of them in turn.

The purely referential use of language Richards held to be "a very special limited use of language, comparatively a late development"[1], which he connected with science, or, at least with the "tamer, more settled parts of the sciences".[2] He called it "pure exposition" or "neutral exposition" and suggested it was also a feature of things like railway time tables. He contrasted the function of exposition with that of persuasion. Persuasion, he wrote, "poaches on the other [aims of discourse]—especially on that of *exposition*, which is concerned to state a view, not to persuade people to agree or to do anything more than examine it".[3]

Of this view I would make two criticisms straightaway—it is either too narrow or too broad. It is too narrow because there is at least one other use of language where neutral exposition exists, which is not a scientific use of language but which has as much right to be

[1] *P.R.*, 40.
[2] *P.R.*, 41.
[3] *P.R.*, 24.

245

called "neutral exposition". This is the language of instructions, telling people how to proceed if they wish to bring about a certain end. This is not persuasive or, as Professor Morris calls it, "incitive"[1], any more than a motoring map is. Anyhow much expository scientific prose describes the evidence upon which theories are based with the explicit purpose of making it possible for the observations to be repeated.

But the view may also be seen as too broad. The trouble about talking of the "expository" or "informative" *function* of language is that it suggests that information or 'truth' is sought for its own sake, as though language-users as a class were psychological structuralists and not functionalists (in the sense in which these terms have been used to differentiate psychological theories). They must believe that people may read *solely* for information and not for the information's use, whether it is for passing examinations, teaching, mastering a particular statistical tool, disproving a theory, or satisfying a metaphysical need. Of course it might be said that *among* the audience a writer has in mind may be some who are interested in knowledge for its own sake —scientists, for instance, who are solely concerned with finding out how that aspect of nature that is their particular province is constituted— that is to say, *pure* researchers. The trouble is that such a distinction to any one who has much experience of such activities is too blanketing. It seems indeed an example of what Richards himself describes unfavourably as the macroscopic approach. Closer concern with its details would, one might suppose, result in a description along phenomenological lines of the different things scientific writers were trying to do, such as posing problems, playing with and exploring the possibilities of models, demonstrating methods or types of theory, using shock tactics against entrenched theories, and so on. It is necessary, because of its influence on budding social sciences, to *humanise* our conception of science, and the broad "scientific" or "referential" use of language category stiffens further the rigid view given us by the 'logic and scientific method' approach to the activities of scientists.

It might however be argued that the distinction serves a negative function. We wish to draw attention to the use of language to influence people or to express our feelings, but we need to say that language is not always used like that. What is misleading is to express the distinction in positive terms so that we talk of the "expository" or "informative" use of language. This is misleading because for exposition one may want more than an account that accurately portrays the writer's understanding of the matter. An exposition has, after all, to be got across. One wants one's readers to understand,

[1] *Signs, Language and Behavior*, pages 102-104.

and not only to understand, but to be interested and to feel that what one writes is worth the effort of continued reading. This may result not only in a certain sacrifice of detail so as not to clutter up and confuse the reader's mind, but also in a careful organising of one's matter, with introduction, statement of what one wants to do, summary of the main conclusions, and so on. This is often institutionally recognised in science by custom and editorial pressure. Scientific writing is sometimes bad in that it fails to take these considerations into account except in a ritualistic way. One may also raise the question of the circumstances under which one applies the classification, 'expository'. A new idea is often refused understanding. To expound it, exaggeration, metaphor, and paradox may be needed. If our views are not surface features—as though a writer has only to put a transfer on our brains—, if they have roots down into us, in order to change them or get new ones perceived, a reader may need to be dazzled, bludgeoned, and enticed to see what is before his nose, true in the referential sense. I do not necessarily mean that scientists in the natural sciences nowadays do this, except for popular audiences.[1] Only that if they did, this might still be "pure exposition", at least as regards the function of the writing. Pure exposition, in short, is not the simple notion Richards treats it as being.[2]

Let us examine now the other way in which Richards distinguished between referential and emotive use of language, in terms of its psychological causes. We have seen that, in so far as words are caused by emotions only, they are signs, but not symbols, of those emotions. For them to be symbols, references are involved, whether or not they are themselves caused by, or in turn give rise to emotions. This is why Richards employed 'symbolic' as an alternative locution for 'scientific' or 'referential'. Fairly early on he pretty well gave up his idea of words acting as signs only. In his treatment of metre in *Coleridge on Imagination*, he recognised that the sense of words in poetry was always relevant and controlled the emotional associations. Though I would like to think Richards' change here was a result of paying more careful attention to his experience, it may have been connected with

[1] I think however there might be as much individuality and personal air of authority in their technical writings as in the writings, not so much of Wittgenstein, Wisdom, and Ryle, examples which would be loaded in my favour, as of Moore, Russell, Quine, or Max Black.

[2] In *Practical Criticism*, page 184, Richards does in fact recognise that scientific writings and, particularly, the popularisation of science may involve the use of more of the functions of language than the referential one, but, typically, this individual insight is impotent against his despotic Abstractions. He is confused too by the ambiguity of his non-referential function, Intention or Purpose, which we shall turn to in the next section.

his growing tendency to insist upon the interanimation of everything. Certainly this influenced his attitude to the complementary question, namely, whether *references* could work alone in causing our words in response to situations.

Richards started off in *The Meaning of Meaning* with the view that references, thoughts, perceptions of things as they actually were, could be alone sufficient in determining the words we used, and he continued in this way in the *Principles*. Such determination of our words was contrasted with that in which emotions, needs, and desires were also amongst the causes. These latter, in Richards' view, distorted our thoughts and perceptions, and resulted in words which no longer corresponded with things as they actually were. Writing (or speaking) that was thus determined was, at least in part, emotive. Richards seems to be using here the well-known dichotomy of Reason *versus* Emotion, although one can see, if one pays close attention to his psychological theory, that he is really using the dichotomy of Thought *versus* Action, emotions being for him "primarily signs of attitudes". This dichotomy is paralleled by Richards' use of a centralist theory (see footnote to page 47 above), which has thoughts for its units, for *referential* language, and of a peripheralist theory, with movements as its units, for *emotive* language.

But at the same time as Richards is employing this dichotomy in the *Principles,* he is also saying such things as "Stimuli are *only* received if they serve some need of the organism and the form which the response to them takes depends *only in part* upon the nature of the stimulus, and much more upon what the organism 'wants' "[1], and "*every* mental event has an origin in stimulation, a character, and consequences in action or adjustment for action".[2] This means that no reference, thought, or perception can occur without its attempting to satisfy some need and without its resulting in some action. It follows that there can be *no* purely referential, non-emotive causes of language.

It is evident that Richards is indulging in a favourite pastime, the enjoyment of incompatibles. He is universalising something, in this case the concept of purpose as applied to perception, thought, and behaviour, and at the same time contrasting it with behaviour which is not of this kind, rather in the way he operated with the concept of metaphor in *The Philosophy of Rhetoric*. Here he has hidden what he is doing by using on occasion words like 'need', and 'desire', with their stronger suggestion of feeling and emotion. But since, as we have seen, he uses psychological for logical categories, 'purpose' has meaning in his system only as it is contrasted with 'reference' and 'thought'.

[1] *P.L.C.*, 87, my italics.
[2] *P.L.C.*, 85, my italics.

Richards, we might say, is oscillating between a functionalist and a non-functionalist theory.

In his later books, starting with *Mencius upon the Mind*, where he flirted with the notion, attributed to Chinese pragmatism, of there being no such thing as pure cognition, he emphasised more and more strongly the purposive nature of perception and thought. Thus, in *The Philosophy of Rhetoric*, we find him saying, "Pure exposition has its guardian passions no doubt—though I do not know their names"; though he added: "they are not often as strong as the poachers[1] and are easily beguiled by them".[2] But in *How to Read a Page*, he does name them when, in asserting that "no thinking can be *motiveless*", that we never "in practice leave off desiring, feeling . . . wanting", he suggests that "in mathematics only a very general motive—an interest in order and consistency of thought—is needed, and other motives may be irrelevant"[3]. This is something of a giveaway, for the motives he mentions would hardly be accepted as a satisfactory account of what the mathematician was trying to do. In so far as the mathematician's thought was purposive, in so far as he was trying to do something such as prove a given theorem, there is no reason why *he* should be picked out as a special case. So what Richards still seems to be doing is deriving from the belief that all thinking is motivated the belief that all thought has a feeling-component, which is important for his special theory of knowledge as a form of becoming.

2. THE FUNCTIONS OF LANGUAGE

Apart from the "symbolising" function of language, or "sense", as Richards also called it, three other functions were frequently distinguished in his books. These are the expression of the writer's attitude to the reader, which Richards called "Tone"; the expression of his attitude to what he is writing about, or "Feeling"; and the expression of his purpose, or "Intention". Richards' concern with the reader, that is, with interpretation rather than with the *use* of language by the writer, is evident here. As a classification of the functions of language it is very one-sided. There is no mention of functions from the writer's (or speaker's) point of view, such as the complementary ones of *arousing* an attitude in his audience to himself or to his subject matter.

This very broad and general classification of language functions was used by Richards throughout, whether he was dealing with trans-

---

[1] "The *other* language functions [that poach] on the preserve of pure exposition", (my italics).

[2] *P.R.*, 41.

[3] *H.T.R.P.*, 99, (my italics).

lation, the correct reading of intricate poems, philosophical analysis, or writing. It gives the lie to his insistence, repeated in book after book, that the way in which one categorised or conceptualised depended upon one's purpose, and that different purposes demanded different classifications. One misses very much the illumination that the distinguishing of varied uses by linguistic philosophers has given to language. Richards' 'uses' are a few old flags set above a mass of percipience. Perhaps it is once again his need to render all logical distinctions into psychological terms that is responsible for the poverty of his classification.[1] This may be the truth behind Professor Ransom's criticism concerning the poverty of the language of feelings for the analysis of poetry.

Richards' poor sense of form is indicated also by the ambiguity concerning the principle of division underlying his classification. We have already indicated this in criticising his distinction between referential and emotive writing. As for his first two emotive functions, Tone and Feeling, since both are concerned with the expression of feeling or emotion, they can be regarded as complementary to the referential function of Sense. But it is difficult to see how his third function, Intention, fits in with this principle of classification. Intention would seem to be concerned with action rather than with feeling. This criticism is not however easy to bring home since, as we have seen, feeling and emotion are for Richards aspects of attitudes, and attitude is a form of action.

The confusion is probably to be explained by an ambiguity in Richards' notion of Intention. On the one hand, he referred to "the speaker's intention, his aim, conscious or unconscious, and the effect he is endeavouring to promote"[2], and said of the analysis of political speeches that here "Function 4, the furtherance of intention (of all grades of worthiness) is unmistakably predominant"[3]. On the other hand, he said that "ordinarily [a speaker] speaks for a purpose . . . the understanding of [which] is part of the whole business of apprehending his meaning . . . Sometimes, of course, he will purpose no more than to state his thoughts . . .". In similar vein he stressed the importance, for correct understanding of a poem, of understanding "the

---

[1] In a later essay, "Towards a Theory of Comprehending" (in *Studies in Chinese Thought*, ed. A. F. Wright, 1953, and reprinted in *Speculative Instruments*), Richards, under the influence of communication theory, produced a somewhat larger list of what language does, the analysis now being in functional terms. That it is still limited to seven functions and gives the impression of would-be comprehensiveness may perhaps be due to the fortifying influence, to which a footnote refers, of Professor Charles Morris' *Signs, Language and Behavior*, that monument of latter-day scholasticism.

[2] *P.C.*, 182.

[3] *P.C.*, 185.

aim of the poem"[1] or "the general intention of the passage"[2], and in an Appendix, where he confessed to some uneasiness about having "intention as a fourth additional function",[3] he justified it by saying that it is often impossible to value correctly the interrelationship of the other three functions unless we are clear what the poet's intention is, which we may judge from other cues than those informing us of his sense, tone, and feeling.

We might bring out the confusion by saying that for Richards this category stands for both use and meaning. It stands for use, because it refers to the purpose or function of the communication, apart, that is, from Richards' other three functions. It is indeed used as a hold-all for all other functions, as Richards from time to time admitted. As for the sense in which this category stands for meaning, we need to recognise what we may call a meaning-hierarchy. There is the meaning of morphemes, of constructions, phrases, sentences, paragraphs, and whole communication-units: sensemes, episemes, macrosemes, and linguisemes, to use Greenberg's terminology,[4] though we must remember again that with Richards we are dealing not with words, sentences, and so on, so much as individual cases of these as actually used. It is to the larger units in this hierarchy, the meanings of sentences, paragraphs, and similar communication units, that Richards is sometimes referring when he talks of Intention. It is the sort of thing a writer or speaker means when, in reply to a suspected misunderstanding, he prefaces a reformulation by saying, "My point is . . ." Perhaps a better way of putting the difference in Richards' two meanings of 'intention' would be this. The second is relevant to attempts to answer the question 'What is he trying to say?', and the first, the question, 'Why is he saying it? What is he up to?'

Let us conclude this section with an example that illustrates in a nutshell the main confusions in Richards' thinking about purpose and reference with which we have been concerned in this and the preceding section. In *How to Read a Page*, Richards uses a passage from Whitehead (see page 131 above) to illustrate the difference of "proper" from *actual* meaning. Whitehead is interpreted as distinguishing 'Nature' in the scientist's sense from nature as we actually experience it, by saying that in the former sense it is conceived as independent of our emotions and wishes—"Nature is devoid of impulse". This Richards takes as an *abstraction*, all right so long as it is relevant to our purpose in making it and not confused with actuality. Richards then, as he was fond of doing in his last books, draws an analogy

---

[1] *P.C.*, 204.
[2] *P.C.*, 205.
[3] *P.C.*, 355.
[4] See *Language in Culture*, ed. H. Hoijer (1954).

between our perception of Nature and our perception of the meaning of words. Nature, in the scientist's sense, is like the "Proper Meaning" of a passage—"a kind of scholastic ghost", Richards calls it. The implication is that the actual meaning of any passage we read differs from the "Proper Meaning" because we take the writer's purposes into account.

How this works can be seen from an example. Richards takes a sentence from Whitehead, "The whole of science is based upon neglected modes of relevance", and says

[it] should mean 'based upon modes of relevance which we neglect', but what he is saying (unless I mistake) is that in science we carefully keep out certain modes of experience and that only through our doing so does science become possible. Science is based not on the neglected modes but on the neglect of these modes. If we read Whitehead here in accordance with Proper rather than actual Meaning we would be distorting his view.[1]

If Richards' interpretation is correct, I would say of this example that it was bad grammar on Whitehead's part, anathema though such a formulation may be to Richards. But the point, if we are to take his analogy seriously, is that Richards believes that, if we are to understand Whitehead properly, we have to take his "purpose or intention" into account. 'Purpose' here is very evidently being equated with 'meaning of the passage as a whole', and *that* does not imply feeling at all.

That this kind of error can occur, Richards himself suggested already in *The Meaning of Meaning*. The seventh of the meanings of 'meaning' that Ogden and Richards described was

"(a) An event intended. (b) A Volition."

Here, they said, was "a dangerous source of confusion", "[due] to the practice of disputants who compound the sense of reference with the sense of intention in the phrase "what I *meant* was" (="what I intended to refer to was")"[2]. Dangerous indeed, and one evidently that Multiple Definition does not cure.

---

[1] *H.T.R.P.*, 95.
[2] *M. of M.*, 6th edn., 192. The confusion in the example, viz., one between 'intending to refer to X' and 'actually referring to X', is not quite the same as the confusion that Richards committed with regard to the function of Intention. There, the confusion was between 'actually referring to X', when one is talking of the whole linguistic unit, and one's purpose in 'actually referring to X'. But the point is that distinguishing the different meanings of 'meaning' has not saved Richards from a major confusion.

3. THE CONTEXT THEORY OF MEANING

Richards constantly stressed the purposes for which theories were devised. If we bore these purposes in mind we would, he thought, avoid the dangers of 'abstractionism', that is, taking our theories as absolutes, as constituting the only one possible picture of reality. Let us see what purposes his Context Theory of Meaning, which we described in Chapter Two (21-28), served for him. In *The Philosophy of Rhetoric*, Richards described three misconceptions from which the theory was designed to protect us. These were, first, "our habit of behaving as though, if a passage means one thing it cannot at the same time mean another and an incompatible thing . . . [the theory] regards all discourse—outside the technicalities of science—as over-determined, as having multiplicity of meaning."[1] Secondly, it would prevent us taking words as the units out of which utterances are built. "The theorem recommends us rather to turn the problem round and ask what happens when, out of the integral utterance which is the sentence, we try to isolate the discrete meanings of the words of which it is composed."[2] And, thirdly, it would prevent us from expecting that each word has only one meaning, rather it would "make us expect ambiguity to the widest extent and of the subtlest kind nearly everywhere".[3] I shall, for ease of reference, describe the views that Richards advances, in opposition to the three misconceptions, as Richards' three *preconceptions* about language.

The evidence for his first preconception is twofold. To start with there is the fact that different people have found different meanings in a given passage, or that the same person does so on different occasions. "Different minds have found such different things in them that we would be very rash if we assumed that some one way of reading them which commends itself to us is the right one"[4]. The trouble here is how to tell that the ways of reading that differ from one's own are not in fact wrong readings. Richards elsewhere does not hesitate to fault other readings than his own, not just, as we have seen, those of his students, but also those of literary critics of comparable standing to his own. We referred to this when dealing with *Coleridge on Imagination*; indeed Richards brought the charge against Coleridge himself. I do not wish to deny the possibility of what Richards is asserting; only to point out that he does not indicate how the two cases are to be differentiated. On his theory of language, I should have thought

[1] *P.R.*, 38-39.
[2] *P.R.*, 39.
[3] *P.R.*, 40.
[4] *H.T.R.P.*, 11.

it a difficult question to decide, and astonishing that he should have stressed and bemoaned so much the prevalence of bad reading, and continued to have devoted such efforts to improving it.

The second source of evidence for Richards' first preconception is provided by examples of given passages. These are convincing in the case of poetry, but not, I think, in prose. Of course there will be an occasional multiple meaning, but Richards' demonstrations of translation and comment on passages from philosophers such as Aristotle and Whitehead do not reveal anything commensurate to the few examples he takes from Shakespeare. The only evidence of multiple meaning he gives for the prose passages is shown by his willingness to say on occasion that he cannot decide which is the right interpretation, and to offer to his readers different alternatives. This is shown most markedly with Mencius. But Chinese prose is not English prose, and we are separated from Mencius not only by 23 centuries but also by a very different culture, so it is a very risky business to attribute the ambiguities in his writings to his language as such.

It is true that Richards' own writing provides some evidence of double meanings, and that this is not necessarily a consequence of his theory, however much it might subsequently have been encouraged by that theory. Examples of this are Ogden and Richards' treatment of the Canons of Symbolism, sometimes as prescriptive, and sometimes only as descriptive (see page 27 above), and the two different versions of " 'Nature' (Sense I)" as cause of our perceptions and as a reality that we seek to divine—Kant's things-in-themselves or Plato's Ideas. These examples suggest, however, that what may be a virtue in poetry is merely a confusion in expository prose. Indeed, as we have already seen in the case of the meanings of 'impulse' and as we shall see in other instances too, it is at times a direct source of error.

The third of Richards' preconceptions about language, that words have many different meanings, was entailed by the first, so in criticising it we shall be further criticising the first as well. This preconception came largely, I believe, as a result of his treating words as *signs*[1] (see pages 289-291 below). Utterances, which consist of sentences, take place in different situations, and in many of these the same words occur. Therefore these words become associated with many different experiences for us. As Richards pointed out in *The Meaning of Meaning*, it is "extremely unlikely" that any symbol will be used by references that are "strictly similar" as between one person and another, since these people all have different histories. For the same

---

[1] "To describe words as signs is a way of reminding ourselves of the mode by which they acquire and maintain their meanings and a useful warning against simple-mindedness". (*I. in T.*, ix).

reason it would follow—though Richards does not mention it—that any use of a symbol by a *particular* user would have behind it a series of contexts, none of which was "strictly similar". The *reductio ad absurdum* to which this argument is leading was avoided by Richards by his statement that it was a matter of degree. But evidently his "degree" was small in comparison with those he was trying to instruct, and I cannot help feeling that his treatment of language-learning solely on the model of the match-strike/flame sign-situation was extremely convenient for his particular bias.

In fact, only some of the situations in which we learn language are ones where we learn as a result of overhearing particular words being associated with particular situations or objects. In many others, we learn by asking the meaning of words, being praised when young for mastering particular words, and subjected to ridicule when mis-employing them. Language learning is socialised learning and norms play a pervasive role in it; it is, as we have seen, very characteristic of Richards to neglect this. Furthermore we learn language, not as a result of casual observation of concomitances, but in a purposeful way and in the belief that words *have* meanings which we can discover by asking people or consulting authorities. This is very different from sign learning in the match-scrape/flame sense.

Now it may be said that this imposition of norms was just what Richards was attacking. This is true, but he cannot justify his attack by contrasting these theories with the way in which people actually learn language, because the way in which they actually learn language is itself influenced by theories. This would be so even if no attempt was made to educate, because the language behaviour, which the child would copy, *shows* these theories all the time—just as Richards' own language use shows his theories (plus of course the theories of his language community).[1] Richards attributed the prevalence of the normative attitude to language largely to teachers, because of their influence over the young. But even if teachers taught differently, we should probably still have the ontogenetic recapitulation of the 18th century's attitude to language in everybody's life history. According to Piaget and others, children go through an absolutist stage in their attitude to rules and will do so no matter what their teachers say. And even after that stage, it is not the teachers and special interest groups

[1] This fallacy of appealing to *what is* in order to attack what *oughtn't to be*, when 'what oughtn't to be' partly determines what is, often characterises linguists' attacks on schoolmasters, and may be due to comparing one sub-language, *spoken* by a certain class of users, with the theories that characterise a *different* sub-language, spoken or written by a different class of users. The latter, 'standard English' for example, attempts to impose its theories on the other, which may be a dialect. But I do not think evidence is hard to come by that the speech-community of the dialect may also try to control its members or others from speaking in ways foreign to it.

who are plotting against common sense; they merely formulate something that is implicit in social life. We cannot avoid having values, preferred ways of doing things, which are to a large extent shared; nor will we avoid mutual influence in our social commerce one with another.

This neglect of the actual social conditions of language learning seems also to be responsible for the second of Richards' preconceptions, according to which he stresses much more the sentence and much less the word.

The sentence, of course, as Aristotle taught, is the unit of discourse. We can hardly give too much importance here to the influence of our modern way of separating words in writing. In conversation we do not ordinarily separate them so—unless we are asking questions about words. With languages which have not been used in writing and thus subjected to a special kind of grammatical analysis . . . there is often very great uncertainty as to where one word ends and another begins. The written form gives words far more independence than they possess as units of sound in speech and we derive thence a habit of supposing that they have far more independence as regards their meanings than they usually have in either written or spoken discourse.[1]

However much this may be true of language, historically considered, English, which is the language Richards is considering, has long been codified and the codification is largely of words (we do not have dictionaries of constructions or forms of rhetoric). Therefore, in language learning, great stress is laid upon individual words, however much it may be true that subsequently some learning in context is necessary before many of the words can be used idiomatically.

As for the sentence's being "the unit of discourse", it is only one of the units, since single words or phrases are often used in communication on their own. They are used, for instance, in commands, warnings, answers to questions, as labels, titles, indicators, and instructions, as advertisements, as headlines. They have the same right to be considered independent as "the sentence" and, of course, the sentence as often used is not much more independent than the words of which it is composed. Take, for instance, this sentence from the paragraph in *The Philosophy of Rhetoric* that follows the quotation we have just given—"That is the ideal limit towards which we aim in exposition".[2] Here some larger linguistic unit is necessary for the

---

[1] *P.R.*, 47-48.

[2] We may of course define a sentence formally, in terms of a range of intonation patterns and juncture pauses, but no satisfactory solution of this problem seems yet to have been achieved, and it would obviously not make the sentence *the* unit of discourse. Anyhow Richards was not meaning 'unit' simply in a structural sense.

communication to be effective. Indeed any communication-unit functions within a non-linguistic context. Just to speak a sentence, like Sapir's "The farmer killed a duckling", would not be considered communication but folly, or done to annoy; we communicate for a purpose, and there are non-linguistic cues upon which we rely for the communicating of this purpose to us. I would rather say that the unit of discourse is the 'communication-situation'.

In my treatment of Richards' second and third preconceptions, I have been critical because I have had in mind certain views which others besides Richards have held; in particular I have had in mind a phenomenological approach which is pure surface and fails to take into account structure and genesis. Phenomenology is indeed valuable as a method, but only to suggest theory, and not as a substitute for it. I have also wished to illustrate once again, this time in connection with language, how Richards neglects social facts in his individualistic simplifications. If I have expressed myself too sweepingly, I should add as a guide to how my statements should be taken that, viewed in one way, Richards' theory is both right and important, because there are certain features of the use of language which receive scarcely any reflection in theories about it or in prescriptions about how it should be used. I do not think one can study the use of language microscopically, as Richards did, without becoming aware of the inadequacies of theory. The important point, however, is to recognise the theory of good usage as an actuality rather than to deny it, to see it as an over-simple account rather than one which is completely false, and just as one can see that, as a result of the Good Usage theory, some people might be unduly narrow in their use of language, limiting its expressive possibilities, so also one has to recognise the possibility of other weaknesses as a result of *accepting* Richards' theory. As an example of this, we can mention the way in which Richards in his multiple definitions always seems to find rather a large number of different meanings, which are treated without consideration of differences in degree or of frequency. A striking example of this is provided by his treatment of the word 'living' in *How to Read a Page*.

In order to show how various, how multiply ambiguous, a word can be, Richards recites the thirty different meanings of the word 'living' that had been distinguished by Ogden.[1] The first thing we may note is that he gives no indication of the relative frequency of occurrence of these different meanings. By neglecting to consider this, he maximises the impression of variety, for we are inclined to take each meaning as being as common as any other. Secondly, he includes many specialisations of the word, where it occurs in restricted phrase-

[1] *H.T.R.P.*, 128-129.

settings, such as 'living images', 'living coal', 'living language', 'living room'. These are almost compound words, and are not therefore likely to present problems of interpretation. Thirdly, many of his distinctions are questionable, as, for instance, the use of the word in the following phrases, which Richards believes to be different in each case—'the greatest living authority', 'he was a living skeleton', 'living tissue', 'living statuary'. Nor is it easy to see the difference between 'living at an address', 'living in a house', 'living in a room', and 'living in a suburb'. Richards gives as synonyms, 'sleeping', 'inhabiting', 'dwelling', and 'residing' respectively, but a *lived-in* house is a *dwelling* place, and towns and suburbs may also be *inhabited*. Finally, the meaning attributed to the *word* sometimes belongs rather to the *phrase*; as, for instance, where 'living', in 'a life worth living', is equated with 'enjoying', or, in 'living on the fat of the land', with 'luxuriating'.

Likewise, in his Multiple Definitions of the more general words which are Richards' chief interest, we find again an enhancement of the sense of variety of meaning, this time because of his inclusion of theories with his definitions. We have already pointed this out with such words as 'truth', 'beauty', 'meaning', 'knowledge', 'idea', 'sincerity', and 'reason'. That you do get theories, which owe what plausibility they have to unconscious tamperings with the meanings of the words for what the theory is about, is, I think, undeniably true. We can see this, for example, in psychological theories of emotion. Some theories evidently limit the term's application to powerful feelings only, others extend it to include any, however mild,[1] and yet others include unconscious feelings as well. There are theories that emotion is essentially disruptive,[2] and others that it is integrative in function.[3] And finally, there are the theories that regard emotion as the *cause* of certain kinds of behaviour as opposed to other theories, such as the James-Lange theory, which regard it as the *effect* of the same kinds of behaviour. But even here we cannot be certain in the case of all these theories that they entail different uses of the word 'emotion'. It is necessary to distinguish between a definition and a wrong theory, a distinction which some philosophers ignore when they say of a given theory that in fact it is a proposal that a given word should be used in a new way. The criterion as to whether we are dealing with a definition or a wrong theory is whether the theorist, on an exception to his theory being pointed out to him,

---

[1] This is true, for instance, of any theory that considers emotion to be the affective accompaniment of all purposive behaviour, as in the well-known theory of William McDougall.

[2] e.g., those of P. T. Young, N. L. Munn, F. Dockeray.

[3] e.g., R. W. Leeper, *Psych. Rev.*, 1948, 55.

agrees that his theory is faulty or denies that the exception *is* an exception. In our example, if he denies that certain feelings, which don't fit in with his theory, are in fact emotive, although a substantial proportion of language-users with certain characteristics that we can stipulate as qualifications hold they are, then, at least for this class of language-users, he can be regarded as in effect, though not actually of course, proposing a redefinition. The trouble with Richards is that he seems to think that every theory involves a new definition and never considers the possibility that the differences may be limited to the theories alone. Furthermore, as a consequence of his preference for actuality, he does not distinguish between what we may call the lexicographer's and the psychologist's meanings. The former, after all, is not interested in meanings unless they are widely accepted. Many of Richards' meanings which are based upon theories will be limited to small groups of users, who themselves may only use the words in the theory's sense when dealing with that particular theory. When dealing with other theories or prosecuting other philosophical or, as the case may be, psychological researches, they may be using the word in one of its ordinary lexical senses[1]. In other words, their special meaning, which fits in with their theory, is a cheat, and is of as much relevance to a general theory of language as are cases of bad writing, such as the sentences from Whitehead we discussed on page 252.

Many of the deficiencies of which we have written show themselves when Richards, together with Ogden, in *The Meaning of Meaning*, considered 'meaning' itself. A number of different theories of meaning, such as the Pragmatist theory, Mill's theory of meaning in terms of the relation of connotation, complications of this according to the ontological status of that which is connoted, Mentalistic theories of meaning as associated image or other mental event,[2] are briefly mentioned, but no attempt is made to show whether they do in fact involve different uses of 'meaning'.

The list reveals, as does so much of his writing, Richards' poor sense of structure, though perhaps he would account this a virtue because of the potentialities of ambiguity thereby released. This is shown not only in his and Ogden's failure to relate the different theories of meaning to one another, to show what their authors were trying to do, but also in an odd confusion between *theories* of meaning

---

[1] It seems to me *prima facie* unlikely, for instance, that William James ever used the word 'emotion' in the sense implied by responding to a question like 'Why was X angry with Y?' with an answer like 'Because X hit Y', except of course in his examples in *The Principles of Psychology*.

[2] The verification theory of meaning of early Logical Positivism is of course not included, its development being subsequent to *The Meaning of Meaning*.

and *actual disagreement* as to what the meaning is in any particular case.

The last four meanings of meaning are:

XIII That to which the User of a Symbol actually refers.
XIV That to which the user of a symbol Ought to be referring.
XV That to which the user of a symbol Believes himself to be referring.
XVI That to which the Interpreter of a symbol
    (a) Refers
    (b) Believes himself to be referring
    (c) Believes the User to be referring.[1]

Definition XIII is the Canon of Actuality. Ogden and Richards describe it as "the most important sense in which words have meaning". The last one, XVI (c), is described as the definition which "is perhaps the richest of all in opportunities of misunderstanding."[2] But I don't think Definitions XV and XVI are held by anyone. Certainly they are not treated as official theories, and no one's name is mentioned in connection with them. What Ogden and Richards are referring to here is interpretation—what the user or interpreter takes the meaning to be in any actual instance of interpretation, and not what they take 'meaning' to mean. To think otherwise would be to hold that there is an official theory that what a word means is what any reader or listener may take it to mean, from which it would follow that there is no such thing as misinterpretation. In defining 'meaning', therefore, Ogden and Richards are doing more than one thing at once under the guise of doing the same thing.

Again, Ogden and Richards seem to treat as different meanings of 'meaning', 'meaning' in a situation where one asks (i) for the meaning of a word,[3] (ii) for the meaning of a word in a particular sentence,[4] and (iii) for the meaning of a word in a particular sentence as its speaker used it.[5] The answer in the last case may, of course, be the same as that in the second, but need not be, because the speaker may be using the word wrongly, i.e. what *he* means by it may be different from what the word means. But I see no reason why these instances, or the first one, should be treated as involving three *different* meanings of 'meaning'.

It is also evident that, though Ogden and Richards regard 'meaning' as involving a complex relationship and prefer to break it down by substituting their terms 'referent' and 'reference', they are in their

[1] *M. of M.* 6th ed., page 187.
[2] ibid., 208.
[3] *M. of M.* 6th edn., 186. Definition III: "the other words annexed to a word in the Dictionary".
[4] Definition XIV: "That to which the user of a symbol ought to be referring".
[5] Definition XIII: "That to which the user of a symbol actually refers".

last four definitions identifying 'meaning' with 'referent', which is their equivalent for 'denotatum'. When they do this, as opposed to when they use 'reference' for 'meaning', they lay themselves open to all the charges linguistic philosophers make against such an analysis. Furthermore, by taking as common denominator for all meanings the relation of referring and not further complicating it, they neglect differences of logical type or category. Consequently, theirs is an over-simple, two-dimensional theory, for which defect their distinguishing of other functions of language is scarcely an adequate remedy.[1]

On the other hand, Richards' approach to meaning is, as the example of the meanings of 'living' also showed, within the limits of his general theory, markedly a polymorphous one. He conceives a word as having many different fairly specific meanings, rather than a few general ones arrived at by abstraction from collections of specific meanings. Thus in writing of Definition III, he and Ogden emphasise the number of "substitute symbols" that the Dictionary provides. This approach of Richards is partly determined by practical con-siderations. He believes it is necessary constantly to stress variety in meaning because of the faults in communication and in thinking that he believes are due to unawareness of this. But, as we have seen, he backs this up by theoretical considerations; in particular, the implicit appeal to the fact that every event, and therefore every *context*, is different from every other event and *context*. His attitude expresses his distrust of social norms and complementary concern with the development of the *individual*, as well as his fear of abstrac-tions. But I think meaning *has* to be taken at a fairly abstract level if we are to preserve his cherished virtue of the elasticity of language. We may attribute a fairly general meaning to a word and allow the other words which occur in the same sentence to take over the functions that attributing more rather specific meanings would other-wise have performed. The more this is in fact true of a language, the more flexible is the language in question. If the Dictionary seems not to recognise this, this is because one of the Dictionary's functions is ready reference. From the philosophical point of view it is an *ad hoc* compilation.

The emphasis on the polymorphous nature of many concepts is

---

[1] There is a tendency on the part of Linguistic philosophers, such as Ryle, for instance, ("The Theory of Meaning" in *British Philosophy in the Mid-Century*, ed. by C. A. Mace (1957), pages 254-256) to refer to different logical categories as different 'uses'. But this meaning of 'use' seems to be different from that applying to different uses of language, such as praying, telling a story, giving orders, describing a scene, and so on. One can use the same sentence for many different purposes, but any given word tends to be limited to one or two different logical categories. Ogden and Richards' other functions of language were, of course, purposes and not logical categories.

something that characterises linguistic philosophy. Although their stress upon variety served a purpose similar to Richards', namely a therapeutic one, this particular emphasis was justified on other grounds. Let us take the well-known example of the meaning of 'game' which Wittgenstein used in *Philosophical Investigations* to illustrate the great variety of things one can do with languages. He suggested it was a mistake to look for what was common to all these different employments of language ("language-games") by suggesting there was nothing common to all the different activities we called games, such as "board-games, card-games, ball-games, Olympic games and so on."[1] What was common was "a complicated network of similarities overlapping and crisscrossing" which he described in a well-known phrase as "family resemblances". This conception he made more plausible by appealing to how we learned words. We should ask, "How did we *learn* the meaning of this word . . . From what sort of examples? In what language-games?" If we do this "then it will be easier . . . to see that the word must have a family of meanings."[2] In making such an appeal, Wittgenstein is doing the same kind of thing as Ogden and Richards did in *The Meaning of Meaning*, and particularly Malinowski in his supplement to that book.

But more is relevant than the specific situation in which we first learn that a particular word applies. If we have a theory of meaning according to which we regard it as something rather general, then we shall generalise from these particular situations. Wittgenstein asks his reader to look at the things we call games. But we should also look at how people use the word. If we do, we shall see that they often find *new* uses of it for themselves, as in metaphor, of a kind which suggests that the disposition manifested in their correct uses of the word can be described in quite general terms. The theory about meaning which manifests itself thus may be 'wrong', but if it affects use to a significant extent, then the phenomenologist must accept it.

There is a danger of Wittgenstein's phenomenological technique merging into phenomenological realism. Obviously, *something* common to all the uses of the word 'game' that are not specialisations can be found. What is the peculiar virtue of that particular level of specificity which Wittgenstein and those acknowledging his influence themselves employ when distinguishing uses? Somebody else could accuse them in their turn of failing to admit enough distinctions, of labelling at too general a level.

The same reasoning as Wittgenstein applies to 'game' could be

---

[1] *Philosophical Investigations* (1953) section 66. "Olympic games" is the translator's improvisation for "Kampfspiele". I think this is cheating, because Olympic games is more or less a proper name.

[2] ibid., section 77.

applied to 'boat'. Many different kinds of things are called boats, many different features are common to different types of boat but not to all boats, yet I think it would be far less plausible to say there is nothing common to all boats that is relevant to our use of the word 'boat'. I suspect that Wittgenstein, in combating his earlier notions, is still too much influenced by them. He is still identifying meaning with denotation, but now draws from it the conclusion that the meaning of any word is very various. But he should in consistency say that 'game' means many things that have only a single application. These would be features that differentiate any game from all others.

Advancing this kind of argument does not entail accepting an essentialist conception of definitions.[1] It may be that one should recognise two basic dimensions for 'game', that associated with 'play', as when a dog may be said to be having a game with his ball with no question of rules arising, and that where it is played with a set of recognised rules. Here one would accept that there were some applications of 'game' that used only one or the other dimension. There is, of course, also the difficulty of stating how one distinguishes between sports and games. Our difficulty in formulating this, or the falsity of a formulation that we make, does not mean that there is not a unitary disposition operating in our use of the word, nor does the fact of vague boundaries to a concept mean this either—not, that is, in any way relevant to our argument. We cannot read from pheno-types straight to genotypes. As far as possible we should aim at accounting for variety as a result of the interplay of a relatively small number of highly general dispositions, however much we may also have to recognise a number of very specific habits, so as to allow for specialisations in language (such as 'game' in 'play the game' or as a unit of score in bridge and tennis).

The point I am making can be put in this way. There are uses of words that require that their meaning can be taken as very general. An example of this is Wittgenstein's own use of 'game' in his metaphor 'language-game'. Though his development of the metaphor showed that he wished to emphasise the variousness of the different things we can do with language, the metaphor has no point unless one regards these games as all having rules. Otherwise Wittgenstein might just as well have referred to 'language activities'. Nor, if we are not to treat as relevant what is common to all language, would we be able to make such remarks as "a calculus is not a language" significantly. For

---

[1] Wittgenstein's deluded reader is represented as seeking for the "essence of language". Hence all the play with 'game'. The English translation may be a little tendentious here, since the German refers to "das Wesentliche", i.e. 'that which is essential'.

obviously calculation is a language-game, and calculi have more than one use.

In developing his argument, Wittgenstein makes much play with the variety of uses the *same* word can be put to. If these uses had been those of different logical categories, this would be very relevant to the question we are considering. Examples he gives include the words 'blue' and 'yellow ochre'.[1] Acceptance of the value of the points he makes with these examples does not require denial that there is something common to the different uses of either word, which we would have to point out to anybody who asked what *the* "meaning" of one or the other word was.

4. LANGUAGE AS RACIAL EXPERIENCE

Occasionally Richards offsets his individualistic bias in dealing with language by appealing to factors that are common to all of us. These he suggests help to make communication easier. Though we have lost the homogeneous tradition that operated in the past, we can, he thinks, still rely on "the all-in-each of all men". But though he makes assertions of this kind continually from the *Principles* on, I should have thought that on his own evidence, to say nothing of his critics' interpretation of him, this is not something that has repaid his trust.

A further factor to which Richards appeals is the distinctions which are preserved in the language which we all speak. Since this view is quite fashionable today, we will examine Richards' version of it in some detail.

Richards has an eloquent statement of this view in *Practical Criticism*. How, he asks, do we, "in spite of our feebleness in introspection and our ignorance of the general nature of our feelings, . . . manage to discuss [them] sometimes with remarkable facility and success"?[2] He adds that "psychologists have never . . . resolutely faced this question of how we know so much about ourselves that does not find any way at present into our text-books". The answer "seems to be that this knowledge is lying dormant in the dictionary. Language has become its repository, a record, a reflection, as it were, of human nature". The following passage is characteristic.

No one who uses a dictionary—for other than orthographic purposes— can have escaped the shock of discovering how very far ahead of us our words often are. How subtly they already record distinctions towards which we are still groping. And many young philologists and grammarians must have indulged dreams of bringing some of this wisdom into the ordered system of

---

[1] ibid., sections 33 and 72.
[2] *P.C.*, 218. The positions of two clauses have been transposed.

science. If we could read this reflection of our minds aright, we might learn nearly as much about ourselves as we shall ever wish to know; we should certainly increase enormously our power of handling our knowledge. Many of the distinctions words convey have been arrived at and recorded by methods no single mind could apply, complex methods that are, as yet, not well understood. But our understanding of them is improving—psychology has notably helped here—and our power of interpreting the psychological records embodied in words is increasing and capable of immense increase in the future. Among the means to this end a combination or co-operation of psychology and literary analysis, or criticism, seems the most hopeful. Neither alone can do much, both together may go far. There is a possibility that something parallel to the recent advances in physics might be achieved if we could combine them. As geology, in the early stages of inquiry into radio-activity, came in to supply evidence that experiments could not elicit, so the records, hidden not in rocks but in words, and accessible only to literary penetration, may combine with groping psychological analysis to produce results as yet unprofitable to conjecture.[1]

But when we come back from "these high speculations", as Richards calls them, "nearer to the problem of sense and feeling", we are once more disappointed by the contrast between Richards' promises and his performances. Perhaps he has chosen a bad example, for earlier he had spoken of the *poverty* of our linguistic resources for dealing with the feelings—"a few clumsy descriptive names for emotions, some scores of aesthetic adjectives . . ."[2]—and the example he gives with these latter, also described as "projectile" adjectives because through them we "project rather than describe our feelings",[3] is very much of a mouse:

. . . we use this notation in a very unsystematic fashion, though a very curious and interesting order may be sometimes glimpsed behind it. Some of these words, for example, may be used together, while others bar one another out. A thing may be both grand and sublime, it can be glorious and beautiful, or gorgeous and ugly; but it can hardly be both pretty and beautiful, it can certainly not be pretty and sublime. These accordances and incompatibilities reflect the organisation of our feelings, the relations that hold between them.[4]

As far as the description of feeling is concerned, this is the only evidence I have been able to find that Richards quotes for his theory about the wisdom that reposes in the dictionary. But does he support it by means of any other considerations?

Two further ideas of Richards may be relevant. The first is the

[1] *P.C.*, 218-219.
[2] *P.C.*, 217.
[3] "We express our feeling by describing the object which excites it as splendid, glorious, ugly, horrid, lovely, pretty . . . words which really indicate not so much the nature of the object as the character of our feeling towards it". (*P.C.*, 220).
[4] *P.C.*, 220.

notion of words as "compacted doctrines", the second, the idea that metaphors never die.

Many of the meanings of words that Richards listed in his multiple definitions were theories of which he was very critical, at least in his earlier works whilst he was still relatively unrelativist. Clearly, language was not being wise in preserving these. Presumably the treasure lay in the favoured, "most important", meanings that Richards specially developed. Such would be the Context theory of 'meaning'; the Confucian sense of 'sincerity'; Richards' definitions of 'word,' 'poem', 'nature' and 'language', so as to include the "whole of the meaning we give to them"; his theory of metaphor; and the Platonic conceptions of Reason and Knowledge. But Richards' argument is circular. He regards different theories as always entailing different meanings of the words for what the theory is about. For instance, different theories of meaning meant different meanings of 'meaning'. Therefore every theory entails a lexical innovation. Therefore, he argues, we can learn the truth about certain things by examining language. This may seem a caricature, but why else should Richards present his theories as one of a number of *definitions* of a word? I do not mean that Richards all the time believes in this view, only that his tolerance of ambiguity enables him sometimes to act as though his theories were what language, as best used, asserts. The clearest example of this is his theory of sincerity, where he elucidates what critics mean when demanding 'sincerity' in the artist, by the theory he fathers on Confucius. Such a procedure suggests the critic as the mouthpiece of language. But his case for language as "repository ... of human nature" lay in the *distinctiveness* of words. If we can make discoveries in English from ancient Chinese or Greek, and if every word has so many different meanings, and any meaning can use different words—as, for instance, when 'good sense' and 'sanity' were later used as synonyms for 'sincerity'—, then this distinctiveness disappears, and language becomes Babel.

The second idea, relevant to Richards' thesis about language's wisdom, was shown in his belief in the continued efficacy of so-called dead metaphors. For him they are never dead, but only sleeping and may be woken or may sleep-walk within us. This belief of his is indicated by his frequent reference to the etymologies of words to justify (or explain?) a theory he is putting forward. But when we look more closely at these references, of which we have already made mention,[1] we find his view to be by no means self-evident. Take, for instance, the case of 'concrete'. Richards, it will be remembered (pages 97-101 above) was in effect denying what we normally understand by this word, emphasising instead "the primordial generality and

[1] See page 102 above.

abstractness of meaning". "When we mean the simplest-seeming concrete object", he added, "its concreteness comes to it from the way in which we are bringing it simultaneously into a number of sorts. The sorts grow together in it to form that meaning. Theory here, *as so often*, can merely exploit the etymological hint given in the word 'concrete' ".[1] The theory, in other words, is built into the language—it does no more than "exploit" it. But similarity does not prove causal relationship. Yet this is the only evidence Richards mentions. He is being here quite false to his methodological recommendations with regard, for instance, to inferring a direct connection between sense and sound from the mere existence of the so-called expressive morphemes.[2]

One source of evidence, not perfect of course, is the *Oxford English Dictionary*. According to this, the word to which Richards refers was invented to *distinguish* 'concrete' from 'abstract' qualities. Since Richards wishes to deny this as an absolute distinction, the intention of the word seems to be opposed to his theory. Further, selection of this particular word is explained thus—"applied to a quality viewed *concreted* or adherent to a substance".[3] The example given is of 'white' as opposed to 'whiteness'. This is a different notion from Richards', which was one of different qualities growing together. The "etymological hint", therefore, is against the theory rather than for it. An earlier use of 'concrete' is also distinguished in the Dictionary. But the "general" use is not derived from this, and the way in which this one is described, "Formed by union or cohesion of *particles* into a mass" (my italics), contains an antecedent notion of particularity, which is just what Richards thought the etymology denied. His treatment of 'realise' is similar. In writing of what it means for man "to realise his own nature", Richards claims that 'realise' "here . . . unites the two senses: 'to see clearly' and 'to become actually' ", and adds, "This is one of the innumerable suggestions in language that BEING and KNOWING are somehow one".[4] Presumably what this means is that these two meanings of 'realise', in this use of it, indicate linguistic support for Richards' theory according to which in the act of knowledge we are conscious of the act of knowledge, so that we ourselves are involved and thus benefit from this intense mental activity. The phrase, 'self-realisation', therefore is one packed with fruitful ambiguity, and the theory is a gift from language, not from experience.

---

[1] *P.R.*, pages 35-36 (my italics].
[2] See page 98 above.
[3] This is taken from the *Shorter Oxford Dictionary*, which does not however differ from the statement of the case in the full edition.
[4] *H.T.R.P.*, page 179.

It is possible however that a less complex meaning of the phrase was intended by Richards, for the statement we have quoted is followed by a reference to the etymologies of 'conception' ("that best of metaphors by which we describe the formation in us of an IDEA") and of 'know', 'cognition', 'apprehend', and 'grasp'. This suggests that the metaphorical extension of words for physical processes to psychical ones was due, not simply to analogy, but to the fact that those who introduced and accepted the new usage were conscious or unconscious Idealists. Or even that the truth worked within them and was revealed in their language though they knew it not. The Aladdin's cave of language can be entered, Richards suggests, if we know the formula, something which the new white magic of science can determine. The trouble with this theory with its belief that language is always right is that, since we have to use language in countering it or considering it, it is difficult to see how it could be disproved. Richards' position here is rather similar to that suggested sometimes in *Coleridge on Imagination*. The Canons of Actuality and Expansion ["a symbol refers to what it is actually used to refer to", and "The referent of a contracted symbol is the referent of that symbol expanded"] together mean that no statement can be untrue. It is simply a matter of right interpretation. This of course was not Richards' considered view; nevertheless it provided him with an attitude which enabled him at times to talk as though *everything* were true, if seen in the light of the All. The sign-situations that statements of theories could be reduced to were "facts of the mind". Seen thus, different theories did not really disagree. One of the greatest deficiencies of Richards' theory lay in his failure to make clear what he meant when he talked of the falsity of abstractions.

I do not wish to deny that etymology may on occasion work, though in general I find that prefixes in Latin or German, together with certain common roots, are so protean in their manifestations that knowledge of them separately, the prefix and the root, is hardly ever sufficient to tell one the meaning or meanings of the whole, and the occurrence of 'false etymology', frequent enough to have received a name, is evidence against the universal operation of etymology. We may guess that a belief in this is due to the same restricted and selected data that caused the belief in a natural connection between sound and sense, when this was based on expressive morphemes, the exceptions not being noticed. The important point about theses to the effect that language is a repository of wisdom is that they are often—certainly in this case—insufficiently analysed from the point of view of meaning, nor are counter-arguments, involving the opposed experience of others, considered. It is as though certain discoveries are generalised so that an attitude of deep respect is held with regard to language as a whole, without opposite thoughts having been tried. An example of this is provided by a recent paper, which we may consider since it brings in another argument and because the leading position its author enjoyed in contemporary British philosophy suggests that Richards' thesis may be of widespread acceptance. The paper is Austin's "A Plea for Excuses", his Presidential Address to the Aristotelian Society.[1] The thesis of the address is that a phenomenological study of language, as it is used "in all ordinary and reasonably practical matters", is the best corrective to the oversimplified distinctions and classifications that philosophers have made in their analyses in the past. It is a consequence of the linguogenetic view and, to the corrective of inventing an Ideal language where syntax and logic are one, it opposes that of making our distinctions fit actuality by studying ordinary language in all its oddness and apparent arbitrariness, free from intellectualist preconception. Austin illustrated his theme by showing the distinctions, in words used for actions, that the excuses we make imply. The work is subtle and very suggestive. Unfortunately, despite its claim to be linguistic phenomenology, it betrays an ideology as separate from experience as a mirage from the desert sands. It is this ideology that unites Austin with Richards. "Our common stock of words", Austin writes, "embodies all the distinctions men have found worth drawing, and the connections they have found worth making, in the lifetimes of many generations". These represent, he adds, "the survival of the fittest, and [are] more subtle at least in all ordinary and reasonably practical matters, than any that you or I are likely to think up in our armchairs . . .".[2] A number of wise qualifications are then made, but none of these, I think, are consistent with the kind of language we have just quoted. It is as though a questioning of the mirage has led him to confess that the spacious lakes are actually smaller than they appear and the trees bordering them not quite so green. We find similarity to Richards' attitude again in Austin's writing that "experience has convinced me . . . that a word never—well, hardly ever—shakes off its etymology and its formation".[3] We find it also in his reply to an objection to his thesis, based upon the existence of "loose usage", which states that, since words often do not exactly fit the thought, it is dangerous to infer the latter from the former. His reply is, "when we come down to cases, it transpires in the very great majority that what we had thought was our wanting to say different things of and in the *same* situation was really not so—we had simply

[1] *Proc. Arist Soc.*, N.S. LVII, 1956-1957.
[2] ibid., page 8.
[3] ibid., page 27.

imagined the situation slightly differently . . .".[1] Evidence of looseness of fit, different words applicable "of and in the same situation", is disputed then by the experience of the microscopic approach. It is the Canon of Actuality in a lounge suit. As with the point about etymology, we must rest content with assertion. Are these not also armchair decrees on the empire of language?

One support of this general attitude, evidenced by our quotation from Austin, is the notion of evolution by natural selection.[2] From different languages having different distinctions, we might reasonably deduce different cultural ecologies. And the individual should go carefully in criticising his language, just as he should with our social and political institutions in so far as they are the products of adaptation and compromise. But "survival of the fittest" refers to an environment, and if environments, as they have during the last few centuries, change quickly and natural selection is slow, they will not select the fittest and our understanding of the situation may be needed to assist or even to counter its operation. We do not spend our lives in armchairs, but in armchair moments we may distil our detailed experiences, and, though many may be wrong, it is conceivable that some may to a valuable degree be right. After all we may use many, many times over all the distinctions our language possesses, so that the individual experience need not be all that feeble in comparison with the racial. Indeed, the strongest reason I can think of *against* our attempts to control language is our failure to live up to the precisions that our inventing of terms in careful situations requires, as well as the blunting that poor reading constantly occasions. Many fine distinctions that have received verbal embodiment only survive in a crude form, which is even evident in *special* groups of language-users, as can be seen in psychology from the fate of words like 'conditioned reflex', 'homeostasis', 'response', and, to take an example quoted by Austin, 'displacement'. Language, we might say, is a record of the poor, because averaged, distinguishing-power of an educated elite which contrasts with that of any of its individual members on particular occasions. On the other hand, the strongest reason for *maintaining* initiative revision *vis-à-vis* our cultural inheritances like language is that, however misconceived our first ventures may be, we are only

---

[1] ibid., pages 9-10.

[2] Not so long ago some wireless talks, announced as "The Revolution in Philosophy" and later, 1956, published under that name, broadcast similar views. Thus Mr. Strawson—"common speech is subjected to the severest of all tests for efficiency as a medium for the expression and communication of our thoughts—the test of common use" (page 103); and Mr. Warnock—"For after all, except in certain exceptional areas, there is nothing artificial about language, and it is most unlikely that it should have taken on the shapes that it has if there were not very good reasons why it should have taken on those shapes" (page 119).

likely to attain fruitful experiences *by* making such attempts; in the process we create the institutions upon which advance depends, altering the language and preserving what is valuable by educational means, *should* we discover this to be profitable.

It is true that philosophers have sometimes legislated as if to ban words like 'know' which had a contextually limited useful function, through not understanding the function they fulfilled. But there is an equal danger of forgetting contextual limitations in attempting a *general thesis* in opposition to this, a thesis which is assisted by the belief that philosophical theories are unconscious outgrowths of theories about language so that a better understanding of language must therefore be considered necessary to correct them. But this belief owes little to any scrupulous public setting forth and considering of evidence. It is based largely on philosophic gossip. This does not mean it is untrue, though a consideration of the evidence suggests it may be exaggerated, as I hope later to show. If I am right in this, what Austin is doing, however valuable and stimulating, is something different from what the philosophers he is opposing were doing. And what he is doing is only acceptable in so far as the ideological element that I believe can be discerned in his writing is disavowed.

A further point in Austin's article is that, in analysing the distinctions of thought, language, studied phenomenologically, should have "the first word"—language, not behaviour; language, not explanations of our actions or motives; language, and no other instrument. Again, this is reminiscent of Richards' position, though language for Richards also has the *last* and certainly the most profound word. The reason why Richards held this view was his belief that language was to a very large degree the medium in which thinking took place. But it is time we had a new heading.

5. LANGUAGE IS WHAT WE THINK IN

Richards accepts "an identification of Thought with an activity of the nervous system", but holds this "hypothesis . . . [to be] too large to have interesting applications"[1], for we know too little about the nervous system to be able to study thought very fruitfully by physiological means. "At present it is still Thought which is most accessible to study and accessible largely through Language". This I think is one of those ambiguous, overdetermined statements Richards is proud of. It seems to suggest that there is no other alternative to physiological research on the brain than introspection. This is so obviously false that it is probable that we should interpret it in terms of Richards' theory that we can only learn as a result of *personal*

[1] *P.R.*, 13.

experience. Taken this way, it could be consistent with believing that we can learn about thought by watching behaviour. However this is not something that Richards ever suggests, nor indeed do philosophers like Austin appear to consider it.

Words are often nowadays described as tools. But one difference between a word and a tool is similar to that between conventional and natural signs. Given some knowledge of man as a tool-making animal, it is possible to infer from the shape of a tool—the markings resulting from wear and so on—the use to which it is put. But with language this is hardly ever possible. To learn about words one would have to observe them being used, what happens as a result of their use, and so on. But thought is not limited to speaking. The way in which we categorise objects, our expectations about the relations between events, can be inferred from any intelligent, purposeful activity such, for instance, as watching somebody trying to solve a wire puzzle.[1] Many intelligent activities, by which we satisfy complex desires, are ones in which, if the agent were to speak his thoughts aloud, a very poor vocabulary would be revealed, largely confined to demonstratives. We would get phrases, like 'try pushing *that there*,' 'I think *this* might have something to do with it', which do no sort of justice to the complexity of the task being tackled. There are, too, many areas, very poorly served by language, where we show considerable skill. Painting would be an example; and it is an artistic activity that Richards, by his theory of value, must prize highly. One can indeed get a measure of Richards' *bias* when he denies the evidence from factorial studies of intelligence that there is such a thing as non-verbal intelligence.[2] That is to say, he denies the implications of the evidence that some of us are better at problem-solving when the medium is language than when some other medium is employed.

It may of course be that Richards would uphold language as easily the most *important* means by which we can study thought, on the ground of its higher generality. We have seen how he concentrates on very general words on the ground that improvements of the *widest* application could be expected by means of them. In combating Hulme's emphases on the concrete in poetry,[3] he pointed out the regional and temporal limitations of the concrete. "Words are the meeting points at which regions of experience which *can never combine* in sensation or intuition come together";[4] or "our world and our life have grown and taken what order they have for us through

[1] Cf. for instance, Ruger's classic study, *Arch. Psychol.*, 1910, Vol. 15.
[2] *I. in T.*, ix.
[3] Cf. pp. 99-100 above.
[4] *P.R.*, 131 (my italics).

separated meanings which we *can only hold together or keep apart through words*".[1] Indeed a large part of his case for language comes both from his emphasis upon perceiving always being a classifying activity, involving, in Bartlett's phrase, "an effort after meaning",[2] and his view that meanings are above all the province of language. Our last quotation reveals this, as does also the remark we quoted earlier that "the way I propose to treat meanings has its analogies with Mr. Whitehead's treatment of things . . . No one to whom Berkeley has mattered will be very confident as to which is which", or his statement that "the formation and transformation of meanings . . . we *must* study with and through words".[3]

But if we are communicating with ourselves in designing, say, the decoration and furnishing of a room or in planning or executing a painting, a visual image may act as a symbol, standing in consciousness for more than we are conscious of, just as thought in words is notably shorthand in nature. Learning something from someone else is not done through language alone. We can learn a lot by watching him perform. Often words in such a situation play the part of marks of expression in music. They may be a sort of commentary, giving small flicks to our attention. But a conductor of an orchestra does much without words. Similarly, in painting and in designing, there may be a constant interaction between what we are on our own performing and brief visualisations of what we want. Again an idea may be given us for the solution of a problem through our seeing some formally similar event in a different context. Examples of this are familiar to those who have studied the psychology of invention. There are also problems we may solve which deal with material which is scarcely verbalised. I may solve a simple mechanical problem of the kind set, for example, in Cox's Mechanical Models Test,[4] but yet be dissatisfied by my solution as not the best. Further thoughts of a visual nature, imaging the model working and so on, may end with the discovery that too much friction is involved by the direction in

---

[1] *C. on I.* 230 (my italics).

[2] *Remembering*, 1932, page 20 and *passim*.

[3] *P.R.*, 18 (my italics). Perhaps the strongest statement of Richards' belief comes in *Basic in Teaching: East and West*, p. 62:—"All our intellectual and most of our emotional discriminations keep their order and clarity through words. The whole abstract world of moral values is held for us by a framework of words. Still more important, our skill in sorting and manipulating these values in imagination is chiefly a skill with words. Our forms of thinking are verbal. Our modes of purpose and feeling, if they are not verbal, can at least only be examined and compared by means of words. A decline in our sensitiveness and discrimination with words must be followed soon by a decline in the quality of our living also. In this situation, any technique . . . which offers any hope of improvement in our training in the use of *words* deserves attention."

[4] J. W. Cox, *Mechanical Aptitude*, 1928.

which the induced force operates.[1] The solution, in other words, though correct, was relatively inefficient. There is of course some verbalisation taking place here, notably after discovering the solution to the felt dissatisfaction, which is verbalised as "undue friction". But this is a verbalisation of the solution, like writing it down on paper, a sort of recording and not the process itself, which could have taken place without knowledge of any word like 'friction'. Of course the mechanical problem could also have been solved by a process of mathematical deduction, some would say more quickly. But again evidence from the thought of scientists and inventors suggests considerable variations between individuals in the kind of imagery they employ.

In addition to this, there is also thought that does not seem to take place in any imagery at all, visual, auditory, kinaesthetic, whether verbal or other—the so-called 'imageless thought'—that the first introspective studies of thinking revealed to the surprise of the eminent philosopher-psychologists, such as Külpe, who were the subjects.[2] Ryle in a recent British Academy Lecture[3] has raised the question why thinking should be '*in*' anything particular at all. He does not mention imageless thought, but presumably, since he does not see the need for thinking to take place in words or images, regarding these when they occur as *accompaniments* to thinking but not the thinking itself, he would regard imageless thought as a face-saver, a consolation for having failed to find images and words as invariable accompaniments. If he were to think this, it would be high-handed, since the matter has been many times carefully investigated. But he would have a motive to hand, namely, an explanation as to why psychologists should ask this question which, once understood, should, so the theory goes, banish their need to have it answered. Since this is relevant to the whole question we are at present considering it is worth examining such an objection.

Ryle's explanation of the psychologists' question is that we mistake the kind of word 'thinking' is. We regard it as describing a concrete activity. "No singing without noises, no testimonial-writing without ink marks, no thinking without . . ., but we can nominate no proprietary things or sets of things to fill this gap. Indeed, we have, I hope, become suspicious of the very attempt to assimilate in this way thinking with these other special activities, which do possess their own proprietary implements or materials".[4] But Ryle has given

---

[1] I am describing an actual experience, but the function of the example is like that of an architect's model, an illustration of a possible *alternative* building.

[2] See G. Humphrey, *Thinking*, 1951, Chapters 2 and 4, for a clear account of this.

[3] *A Puzzling Element in the Notion of Thinking* (1958). *Proc. Brit. Acad.*, Vol. XLIV.

[4] ibid., 137. Ryle has argued that the concept of thinking is polymorphous. But there can be few concepts that are so polymorphous as to be unclassifiable. Anyhow

specific examples of thinking, such as "... and then the idea occurred
to me that, since it was Sunday, I might not be able to get petrol at
the next village". How does one know such a thought occurred without becoming conscious of it? A basic concern of introspective
psychologists who investigated such questions is to know in what
modality this consciousness was. To see anything, we must experience
a colour. To be conscious of anything stands in a supraordinate
relationship to seeing and, just as seeing with colour, so does it entail
a sense modality or modalities, whether vision, taste, touch, pain,
pressure, hearing ... The notion of imageless thought seems to deny
this and, negatively formulated as it is, is in that respect unsatisfactory.
We need a theory to link it with other conscious experiences. But that
the experiences to which it refers are socially recognised we might
ourselves use the device of appealing to language to demonstrate. 'It
is difficult to put into words', 'a barely formulated notion', 'to
verbalise', 'he has difficulties in expressing his ideas' are counters we
all know how to use, nor are we blank when others employ them.

I do not want to deny that thinking often takes place in speech—
that is to say, that one may considerably advance in one's thought
on a problem as a consequence of talking or lecturing or even writing
about it, and this does not mean that one's speech or writing is
preceded in any *one-to-one* way by thoughts that one then makes
public. Indeed it sometimes strikes one more the other way round,
so that one may be surprised and interested by the things one finds
oneself saying. Nevertheless the ideas that come to one as one speaks
need to be confirmed, and one often confirms them by memories, as
well as by new experiences, as they occur. Similar considerations
apply to one's reception of the ideas of others that are communicated by lecture or by book. Such ideas in fact often are accepted without being confirmed by one's personal experience. But when they are,
this is like learning to talk in a certain kind of way. Certain philosophers learn, for instance, that whenever they come across an error they
search for analogies in the use of language where the same procedure
as that imputed to the author of the error would in fact be correct, and
then assert that he had been led astray by the analogy. This proceeding
can never fail because, since they deny that they are concerned

---

psychologists who investigated thinking did not necessarily believe that all the
processes described by the word 'thinking' were of the same psychological kind.
What the Würzburg psychologists were investigating was *problem-solving* thinking.
In regarding this process as, from the psychological point of view, potentially
homogeneous, they were not showing themselves to be the dupes of language, else
they would have examined other processes to which the word applies. Of course,
Ryle thought that even problem-solving thinking was a polymorphous concept, but
his analysis could be wrong. He is altogether too definite in vetoing psychologists'
problems.

with empirical questions, they are unencumbered by any elaborate scruples as to the checking of whatever evidence there may be.

Furthermore, their theory leads them to have a derogatory attitude to the view they are against and a rather sceptical attitude, at least in the present case, to the very evidence one might first quote in opposing theirs. The first of these arises because, having 'explained' how the offending theory arose, though they quote no evidence for their diagnosis, the fact that they have made it relieves them from feeling any need to search out evidence upon which the theory *might* in fact have been based. And as for the evidence we might quote against them, though the Behavioural Dispositionalists do not deny the occurrence of 'private'[1] mental events, and may on occasion recognise their usefulness in aiding us in theory-building and problem-solving, they still seem to underrate them. Ryle, for instance, in *The Concept of Mind*, denying that when we are trying to recall something, details of what we are trying to remember must come back "in imagery", describes the following hypothetical example:

If a concert-goer wishes to recollect just how the violinist misplayed a certain piece, he may whistle the bungled tune, or play it on his own fiddle just as the artist had done it; and, if he repeats the mistake faithfully, he is certainly recollecting the artist's error. This might be his only way of recalling how the artist had gone wrong, since he may be poor at going over tunes in his head.[2]

This of course is true enough, but I don't think it tells the whole story. What is missing in this example is not so much any mention of a confirmatory reaction but mention of marginal awareness that no *dis*confirming reaction has taken place. And this is just as relevant when recall consists in the conjuring up of images. A disconfirming reaction, fallible guide thought it may be, is that upon which we ourselves must rely for keeping our thoughts in line with reality. Just this is the tiny but vital bit of machinery I find missing in accounts such as Ryle's of how the mind works. He presents a mystery as though it were as clear as daylight.

---

[1] By " 'private' mental events" I mean ones which cannot at present, by any manipulation of the stimulus that is effective cause and which might be some previous mental event, be brought about in more than one person's consciousness. Organic sensations, as opposed to visual or auditory ones, are an obvious example. Of course, because of spatio-temporal uniqueness, no stimulus can ever be exactly the same for any two people, so in that sense all will be private. The distinction we are making is one of degree. We are forced into considering it because of the over-simplifications of philosophers of science in psychology. The practical inaccessibility of many data in psychology to more than one person, except under very loosely defined conditions, constitutes a potent reason for relaxing on occasion some methodological stringencies.

[2] *The Concept of Mind* (1949), page 275.

Of course it might be said that all this is irrelevant to what is after all Ryle's main objection, a logical rather than an empirical one, namely, that to describe the conscious processes accompanying thinking is trivial, like being a chronicler rather than a historian, because it does not and cannot take account of the *significance* of these processes. What is important is not so much a description of events, but what these events mean. But Linguistic Philosophers lay so much stress on language as the means of investigating our concepts and thinking, that their position is tantamount to Richards' of believing that all important thought takes place in language.[1] They are constantly writing, for instance, of the *use* we make of words, and describing them as *tools*. What activities are they tools for? If we answer "Speech" or "Argument", this would suggest no more than that they were means for communicating with one another or, possibly, confusing or overwhelming one another. The reason for all the concern with language is the belief that if we understand better how words operate, we shall not make mistakes in theory. Despite the belief of, for instance, Ayer (when he was talking like a linguistic philosopher) that "thinking . . . [is] not the sort of thing that [is] done with any instrument at all"[2], I think the assumption is being made that, *because we use words in thought*, we have to be careful we are not misled by them. One of the first statements of the modern philosophical concern with language, Russell's lectures on Logical Atomism,[3] made this point. He said, "unless you are fairly self-conscious about symbols . . . you will find yourself attributing to the thing properties which only belong to the symbol . . . there are different kinds of symbols, different kinds of relation between symbol and what is symbolised, and very important fallacies arise from not realising this..."[4]. Russell was critical of ordinary language—"as long as you keep to ordinary language you find it very difficult to get away from the bias which is imposed upon you by language"[5]—and the Linguistic Philosophers, of course, were not. Nevertheless I do not think, as far as the point at issue is concerned, that Russell's attitude differs so very much[6]

---

[1] Ryle indeed showed a marked tendency in *The Concept of Mind* (see particularly pages 309-314) to treat any kind of private event of a purposive kind as giving orders to, or talking to *oneself*, albeit "with some skill, industry, or care". Similarly, Ayer, "following Professor Ryle", was "inclined to say that the process of thought cannot be validly distinguished from the expression of it" (*Thinking and Meaning*, (1947) page 7).

[2] *Thinking and Meaning*, 5.

[3] 'The Philosophy of Logical Atomism,' *Monist*, 1918 and 1919. Reprinted in *Logic and Knowledge*, ed. R. C. Marsh (1956).

[4] *Logic and Knowledge*, 185-186.

[5] ibid., 234.

[6] Early Russell differs still less. From *The Principles of Mathematics* (1903) to *Problems of Philosophy* (1912), Russell in fact appealed to ordinary language to

from, for instance, Austin's, when Austin wrote, "Ordinary language *blinkers* the already feeble imagination",[1] or, "Words are our tools, and, as a minimum, we should use clean tools: we should know what we mean and what we do not, and we must forearm ourselves against the traps that language sets us."[2]

What Russell, early Wittgenstein, and the Logical Positivists shared with many Linguistic Philosophers was the belief that philosophical mistakes are to an enormous extent due to language. This led the former group of philosophers to concentrate on reforming their symbols. The latter, however, believed that the fault lay in poor observation of language. If it were more closely studied, these errors would be obviated. Whatever the remedy, I think the theory greatly exaggerated the influence of language on philosophical error. What plausibility it has comes from two features of philosophical activity. First, the fact that many philosophical theories may be backed up by some juggling with language. An example would be the ontological argument for the existence of God. Or, if we accept Moore's and Russell's explanations, confusion of the dual meanings of words like 'sensation' and 'idea' in Berkeley's Idealism. But, *pace* Max Müller, I do not think belief in gods arises from language, and many must have experienced at an early age the realisation that there was no way of proving that our life was not wholly a dream. In my own experience, solipsism as a possible belief came by analogy from the experience of dreaming and telling others about it. Unless one holds *a priori* that all thinking is a process of deduction in conventional symbols, one would not consider it obvious that such beliefs were due to bad grammar or misunderstandings about language, which would be exorcised by getting a true view of language.

The second reason for the plausibility of the theory is that some philosophical work is concerned with language, particularly of course that which is due to the belief that language was an important source of error. Theories about language are naturally partly determined by language, and on the whole an earlier theory will contrast with a later theory within the same tradition by being based upon poorer observation. It will be more oversimplified and will neglect distinctions which later thinkers notice. The increase in distinctions of logical types or categories from Mill to Russell to Ryle is a common enough feature in the history of any science, where the same thinkers are working in roughly the same tradition. I say "roughly the same"

[1] "The Meaning of a Word", (1940), published in *Philosophical Papers*.
[2] "A Plea for Excuses," *Proc. Arist. Soc.*, N.S. LVII, 1956-1957.

---

correct certain features of classical logic. Cf. his remark in the former book, "grammar seems to me to bring us much nearer to a correct logic than the current opinion of philosophers" (*The Principles of Mathematics*, section 46).

because from one time to another there are likely to be alterations in purpose, methodological preference, and conceptual model. This is certainly the case if one compares Russell with his great need for economy and structure, which found a natural outlet in logic and science, on the one hand, with the later Wittgenstein, Wisdom, Ryle, and Austin, on the other.

The exaggerated role that all these philosophers ascribed to language was not, however, limited to explaining *philosophical* error. Mistaken theories in physics, biology, psychology, and the social sciences have, both by Logical Positivists in the past and Linguistic Philosophers today, been liberally attributed to mistakes about language. But they are liable to confuse the often misguided aim of some scientists to produce rather fundamental, comprehensive theories with a consequent economising of terms, with the similar approach of logicians concerned with mathematical logic. What the scientists try to do is a consequence mainly of a certain conception of science, shared with the logicians, and not of mistaken conceptions about certain words, however much their semi-technicalised words may have to be distorted in order to act up to this conception. The effort is premature and may, I think, often be criticised on the basis of their inadequate observing. In such circumstances, stress on phenomenology is often to be welcomed, but this is not linguistic phenomenology, except where language is itself the subject of pre-mature, over-ambitious theorising.[1]

Let us end this chapter, as we began it, with Austin—a last word on his "first word" theory. The trouble about his theory is that he seems to take English as the only ordinary language there is. But anybody who is concerned with translation, or with explaining to the speakers of other languages the limitations to the range of any given dictionary synonym, must have experienced how difficult it is to match any two languages at the level of subtlety at which Austin is operating. Austin distinguishes, for example, between "by accident", or "by mistake". He could also have distinguished between "by accident" and "by chance". But to which of these would *par hasard*

---

[1] Though Austin is careful not to seem critical of experimental psychology, this cannot be said of all those who use his approach. Professor Peters, for instance, who is far better informed about experimental psychology, has in a recent book explicitly argued that psychologists should pay attention to ordinary language. In criticising psychologists' use of words like "drive", "motive", "need", he states, "common sense, which is incorporated in the concepts of ordinary language, has creamed off most of the vital distinctions. Psychology has the task of systematising what is already known and adding bits of special theory to supplement common sense", (*The Concept of Motivation*, by R. S. Peters (1958), page 155). This does not hold in high regard, seems indeed totally to ignore, the contributions of phenomenologists like Rubin, Katz, and the Gestalt psychologists to psychology.

279

correspond, and where are these distinctions in German? *Zufällig* is quite a bit different. What becomes then of his claim, "Our common stock of words embodies all the distinctions men have found worth making, in the lifetime of many generations"? It looks very much as though we are back in the illusion of an Ideal Language. If different languages make different distinctions—we are still working at his level of subtlety—then each language must ignore distinctions, which brings us back to the first position, that language is misleading. But in fact what Austin seems to be neglecting is the significance of words with fairly general meaning having more *specific* meanings through the restrictions of context. In other words—admittedly loose rather unpopular words—we build meanings up out of single words. There is not one word for each concept. Concepts can be drawn with a number of lines, and the same concepts can be portrayed by different arrangements of lines. The reader or hearer *categorises*, in the way we showed in our chapters on comprehension. Most words are not single concept-holders, but, in conjunction with others, *cues* to concepts. And this, to quite an extent, is how, in speaking or writing, we use them.

Of course, if we say, as Austin, to judge by his paper, "The Meaning of a Word," was inclined to, that each word has many different meanings, then we cannot make our point quite in the way we have just done. However, in this case it is clear that words *don't* make distinctions, but hide them. And if we agree, but claim that examination of the different uses of a word shows us the many different distinctions that ordinary language makes, this would obviously be circular. Indeed, I suspect that the thesis about language's wisdom put forward today is in part itself due to a confusion of language, namely, that which has been described as the confusion between an assertion and a definition. We shall return to this in Section 2 of the next chapter.

6. LANGUAGE-THEORY AND THINKING-SKILLS

What are for Richards the practical applications of his theory that all important thinking takes place in words? One is that the practice of Multiple Definition will make us less likely to be misled by the fact that the same word will have different meanings. In Chapter Six we criticised him for his over-great reliance on Multiple Definition as a means of improving communication. And in our next chapter, we shall see that his devotion to this procedure does not in fact prevent him from using the same words in different ways so as to ease certain theories he holds.

Another practical application of Richards' doctrine was his

exposure of 'faulty' theories of language on the grounds that they reduced our skill in language-use and therefore in thinking. This was part of his general thesis that faulty theories interfere with skill in the area to which the theories refer. He introduced it and documented it first in *Practical Criticism*, where he tried to show how all sorts of preconceptions about poetry interfered with appreciation of it. His case there was persuasive; in the parallel book, *Interpretation in Teaching*, much less so. The reason for this, I think, lies in the fact that in the first his subjects *revealed* their preconceptions by the things they said about the poems, whereas, in the second, he often asked them in effect to say what their theories were and judged their theories by the subjects' formulation of them. But it is very difficult to put into words what one's theories are if one has not thought about them much beforehand.

From *Coleridge on Imagination* on, Richards is very insistent about the extent to which all our activities imply theories. But it is naïve of him to identify these theories with what people say their theories are. Their descriptions of them are often the product of social learning and, as such, necessarily stereotyped and not necessarily standing in any close relationship to what people *actually* do. Here probably lies the explanation of that ambivalent attitude Richards constantly displayed in *Interpretation in Teaching*, where he oscillated between praise of our skills in using language and being shocked at the crudity of his subjects' theories. Perhaps just to the extent that a given thinker equates thinking with using language, he will expect the theory that guides a given use of language to be easily stateable in words.

Let us examine in more detail, as an example of Richards' theory about the effects of theory, the views he puts forward about the harm done by wrong ideas and teaching about metaphor. His statements about this illustrate the pendulum swings occasioned by the ambivalence we have just referred to. In *Interpretation in Teaching* (page 212), after summarising the faulty notions about metaphor that his students' protocols revealed, he described these as "deplorable and disastrous" and as "hinder[ing] its victims in acquiring control of an immense range of the most important uses of language and *modes of thought*" (my italics). In an earlier book, *The Philosophy of Rhetoric*, on the other hand, we get a more moderate statement. After referring to all *thinking* as "radically metaphoric", Richards describes "our skill with metaphor, with thought . . . [as] prodigious and inexplicable", and the purpose of better theory as being "to protect our natural skill from the interference of unnecessarily crude views about it; and, above all, to assist the imparting of that skill—that command of metaphor—from mind to mind".[1] Apart from the obvious effect upon

[1] *P.R.*, 116.

281

Richards of reading what his students actually wrote about metaphor, yet another reason for the difference in attitude between these two statements may lie in the meaning of 'metaphor' he had in mind whilst making his statement. In the second case (*Interpretation in Teaching*) he was dealing with 'metaphor' in its conventional sense; in the first (*Philosophy of Rhetoric*) in his greatly extended sense of the word, which he controls, in the passage we quoted, by pairing it with "thought". In considering his views, we shall in this section take 'metaphor' only in the more limited sense. This should be all right because it is the sense that Richards' exercises with metaphor imply.[1]

But what does the typically vague phrase, "immense range of . . . modes of thought", refer to? Probably what would be more naturally described as 'modes of feeling'. If we break down the tabus about metaphor, such as the notion that it is limited to decoration or that, because it is considered incompatible with scientific writing, it "is not a serious way of thinking", with the result that freer use is once again made of metaphor, then, it is argued, we shall be made to *feel* more or become more *aware* of our feelings, and we shall have these feelings in greater variety, articulation and precision. We shall not separate our feelings off from our objective referrings; we shall respond in a more integrated manner; in short, there will be a *re*-association of sensibility.

The theory, as we are taking it, seems so implausible as to be scarcely worth considering, but let us briefly make the following points. Though the thesis that all important thinking takes place in words may have a certain initial plausibility, this can scarcely be said of the thesis that all *feeling* takes place in language. Yet this is what is entailed by the view that our skill in feeling will be increased by correcting wrong theories of metaphor. How did it come about? Presumably it arose from the emphasis in *Coleridge on Imagination* on the need for feeling in imagination and creative thought, as opposed to what Coleridge described as "abstract knowledge, or the science of mere understanding". But the effect of such a theory seems to me to weaken the case for saying that all important thinking takes place in words.

---

[1] The following exercises "in the interpretation and judgment of argumentative metaphor", reported in the Appendix of *Interpretation in Teaching*, may be given as an example.
    "Please frame parallel sentences to the following, indicating whether your parallel supports, or does not support, the argument that the author in your view intended to urge . . .
    The teaching of a foreign language can as little replace the teaching of the mother tongue as a finger can replace the use of the hand.
    Meaning is an arrow which reaches its mark when least encumbered with feathers."

'Metaphor' is a word we use of *language*. We say of a given expression that it is a metaphor. But the perception, which is expressed in language, is not itself a metaphor. Richards seems to have identified the two and, because there is a literary theory about metaphor, to have thought that changing the theory would result in our observing likenesses we were previously blind to. Similar identifications, as we have seen (pages 271-273), enabled him to make all sorts of claims about how instruction in language would generalise to other skills. Observations of likeness can however be expressed in other media. Musicians may make use of it in programme music. Wagner in particular was a master of it, as, to take a rather obvious example, the music suggesting sea and storm of *The Flying Dutchman* shows. A recent example would be the synaesthetic suggestiveness and ominousness of Britten's *Turn of the Screw* theme. In the plastic arts, Picasso's construction of a monkey's face out of the bonnets of two toy cars, one inverted, is a nice case. But less obviously, there are Henry Moore's perceptions of the human body in forms of stone and wood, Bosch's juxta-positions of magnified and diminished scale, and, in general, painters' compositional perceptions of their subjects as approximations to simpler forms, pyramid, interlocking triangles, receding cone. Can *this* "command of metaphor" be said to have been "imparted to us from others, with and through the language we learn, language which is utterly unable to aid us except through the command of metaphor which it gives"[1], in such a way as to imply that our better understanding of the literary theory of metaphor will considerably enhance it? Indeed, even when we are properly talking of metaphor as a 'figure of *speech*', we can distinguish between the skill and elegance with which it is used on the one hand, and the originality and impact of the observation that is described in language on the other. A person may have great power in this and yet be crude and untutored in his language.

[1] *P.R.*, 90.

Chapter Ten

GENESIS AND REVELATION (I)

IN the last chapter we touched on Richards' views about features of language and wrong theories of language causing errors in theorising. Similar views have been prominent in modern philosophy from the time of Russell's lectures on *The Philosophy of Logical Atomism* on. They have led to recommendations either for developing with logic's aid a technical language for philosophy, free from ordinary language's defects, by means of such procedures as making the syntax of the language a logical one, or for simply alerting the language-user to the *true* nature of ordinary language. The former recommendation is generally associated with an uncomplimentary opinion of ordinary language of a kind often observed amongst scientists, who are the exemplars for proponents of a technical language for philosophy. Views about ordinary language such as that of Austin, which we criticised in the previous chapter, are reactions against the former approach and naturally express themselves in the counsel that the language-user should be instructed in the misunderstood subtleties of his tongue. The ingenuities shown in these recommendations are however quite lacking in any consideration of the evidence upon which they are said to be based. So it is with this that we shall concern ourselves in this chapter, making use of our detailed study of Richards' thought as a check upon this particular aspect of it.

I. AMBIGUITY

One of the sources of error in language most commonly appealed to is the possession by the same word of more than one meaning. In *The Meaning of Meaning*, as we saw, Ogden and Richards distinguished two forms of this error, the "Utraquistic" and the "Phonetic". Nothing more was heard of these distinctions in later books, but certainly one reason for all the emphasis upon Multiple Definition was to warn thinkers of such dangers for reasoning as the fallacy of *quaternio terminorum*, that came from multi-meaning.

Many other writers have stressed this type of error. It has been held, for instance, that there are two different senses of the word 'law', with and without normative implications, as in the *laws* of a society and scientific *laws* respectively, and that failure to realise this has led to such diverse results as faulty ethical theories[1] and mistakes about linguistic change on the part of the neogrammarians.[2] Similarly, errors have been attributed to failing to distinguish between different meanings of 'is'. Aristotle has been considered guilty of this, and he in his turn accused Parmenides of making this mistake. Failure to distinguish between the psychological and logical senses of the word 'idea' was held by Russell to have trapped Berkeley into his variety of Idealism,[3] whilst Bradley accused it of misleading the Empiricists in their theory of the mind.[4]

Although this kind of error has often been mentioned in support of the general thesis that language misleads its users, hardly any evidence has ever been given to substantiate it. In the case of the effects of confusing different meanings of 'is' on Aristotelian logic, for instance, the proponents of the view do not bother to consider it in ancient Greek, the language that Aristotle used. Even when they consider it in English, they do not take into account that the form of the proposition—subject-predicate, class-membership, identity, and so on—may be signalled by the word-class following 'is', whether, that is to say, it is an adjective, an article ('the' or 'a'), or a noun (as in 'Truth is Beauty'), so that, the form of the proposition being otherwise signalled, 'is' could be taken as much emptier, being limited more to such functions as occasional indication of tense or number. Even the best-known case of the kind of error we are considering, J. S. Mill's apparently equivocal use of the word 'desirable', where he seems to condemn himself by his own words,[5] has recently been questioned,[6] making us aware that it is as easy to deny as to assert linguogenetic explanations. Richards himself did consider two examples of possible ambiguity in some detail—that of a dual meaning of 'metaphor' having misled Hulme[7], and that of a surreptitious introduction of a different meaning of 'grammar' by Campbell giving a tautological underpinning to his theory of what it was,[8]—but even here the detail consists much more in explaining *how* the error might have happened than in providing evidence that it did.

[1] Cf. for instance, K. R. Popper, *The Open Society and its Enemies*, 2nd ed. (1952), Vol. 1, Chap. 5.

[2] Cf. J. Vendryès, *Language*, 1925.

[3] *The Problems of Philosophy* (1912), pages 65-66.

[4] F. H. Bradley, *Principles of Logic*, pages 6-8.

[5] "The only proof capable of being given that an object is visible, is that people actually see it. The only proof that a sound is audible, is that people hear it: and so of the other sources of our experience. In like manner, I apprehend, the sole evidence it is possible to produce that anything is desirable, is that people do actually desire it." *Utilitarianism*, Chapter IV.

[6] N. Kretzmann, *Phil. Quarterly*, July 1958, Vol. 8.

[7] *I. in T.*, 131-139.

[8] ibid., Chap. XV.

However, I do not wish to deny that ambiguity *may* be a source of error in thinking, but only to warn that we should preserve our critical faculties in considering it. Bearing this in mind, can we account for any of Richards' errors by means of this explanation?

We have already come across one example of this in the *Principles of Literary Criticism* (pages 43-45 and 48-49 above) where analysis of the language used, such as the kinds of synonyms Richards employed on different occasions and indications as to category for the word 'impulse', suggested that, without being aware of it, he was using this word in two different senses. The temptation was to explain his theory that artistic experiences are the most valuable ones, as being due to this equivocation. But, as we saw, there is no real reason why this should be so, and we can at most hold the mistake responsible for affecting the particular *quality* of his theory, his emphasis, because he was thinking of *nervous impulses*, on their concreteness, their microscopic nature, their all being of equal value, and their having to be organised. Even here, though this ambiguity certainly seems to have been operating, it is unlikely that it alone *caused* these features of his theory. After all, the idea of pleasure being unidimensional long preceded Richards' view about the equality of impulses. The confusion of the two different meanings of 'impulse' may only have strengthened Richards' belief in this, and there are other reasons why a thinker may value harmonisation of impulses than the conception of organisation of impulses in the nervous system. We should perhaps look for a population of influences in any one theory, a notion which suggests an eventual statistical treatment. In the last section of this chapter (pages 310-314), we shall examine Richards' use of 'impulse' in more detail and suggest another reason why he confused its meanings.

With this example we were perhaps lucky in the relatively clear-cut nature of the evidence. It is not easy to find anything as obvious elsewhere. But perhaps another candidate would be his theory about what 'good' meant. We have already criticised this theory (see page 238) and suggested that his statement, "When we say that anything is good, we mean that it satisfies",[1] neglects another meaning of 'good', which is one we may apply to a person or to conduct. Richards' meaning is one which we apply to objects, when we say of something that it is a good house, or a good watch, or is good soil, meaning thereby that it ministers comparatively well to our purposes. In such a case one may talk of efficiency, as when Richards writes that "Keats, by universal qualified opinion, is a more efficient poet than Wilcox, and that is the same thing as saying that his works are more valuable".[2]

[1] *P.L.C.*, 58.
[2] *P.L.C.*, 206.

But I do not think 'good' has this meaning when we say of a person that he is good, or that he is doing good. This second use is in part at least prescriptive, which implies that it is necessary to influence people, and that the behaviour you recommend is not sufficiently pleasing of its own accord to go on happening. Richards' theory may, of course, be correct in an ultimate analysis, but this is not the same thing as saying this is what the word in the cases we are considering *means*.

Assuming, then, that there are these two different meanings, is there any evidence from Richards' language that he was only considering examples of the one? The answer I think is that he was, but the evidence is rather complex.

In the six chapters[1] where he presents his ethical theory, Richards never uses the word 'good' of people or of conduct. He also never refers to the notion of 'ought' or to the concept of duty or uses the words 'right' and 'wrong'. 'Good' he uses quite frequently but very largely when he is discussing ethical theory, which is in fact when he is arguing against Moore. He uses it to refer to "things" or as a noun, or in sample sentences like " 'This is good' ". Various forms of the morpheme, 'moral–', occur, but all similarly abstract, as a noun or as in "moral aspects", "moral questions", "moral preoccupations". About a third of the uses of 'good', 'moral', 'ethical', and their morphological relations are special uses, pejorative in intention, indicated by inverted commas, as in "some 'moral ideal' ", or by capital letters, as in "the Good", or in referring to some theory Richards disapproves of, as when he talks of "absolute goods".

To sum up, only certain of the terms customarily used in ethics are mentioned by Richards. The ones omitted are the ones most obviously associated with the prescriptive view. Those he does mention are mentioned either in the instrumental sense, that is, the first of the two meanings distinguished earlier, or as labels of an area of philosophy or of a theory within that area. Apart from that, the way he does use them suggests not that he is proposing a theory about what they mean, so much as opposing a theory implicit in their use. This would lead us to expect him to favour other words, and this we find to be so when he comes, in the last three of the chapters we are considering, to deal with art. The word he favours is 'value'. In these chapters, this word in its different forms occurs nearly six times[2] as frequently as non-pejorative uses of the conventional ethical terms we have been talking about, whereas in the first two chapters, when the problem

---

[1] *P.L.C.*, Chapters V–X.

[2] In the counting, from which these ratios were derived, no more than one occurrence per sentence was allowed. Some complex sentences, to make a single point unambiguously, need to use the same word two or three times.

of 'what is good' was introduced and the main opponent routed, the relationship was reversed, the latter terms being nearly three times as frequent. Appropriately enough, the third chapter, where Richards presented his own theory before going on to apply it to art, is transitional, his own term being used more than half the time[1].

Against the case we have been putting forward, it might be said that Richards probably worked out his theory before writing it, that he probably went over it in his own mind, discussed it with colleagues, taught it, and so on, so that the evidence of his final presentation is not the evidence we should be using; indeed that all it would show would be the rhetorical tricks one uses to win the reader over.

Objections such as these *may* be valid, and would be relevant as regards all the evidence upon which the linguogenetic thesis is likely to be based. On the other hand, what is written may be largely a repetition of what had been thought or said many times before. As for the charge of using rhetorical devices, Richards' writing, as we have seen, is not very consciously controlled. He himself described how thinking, for him, took place largely in the very process of writing. Putting forward a point of view as *persuasively* as possible is something that is not easy to avoid, but it could be regarded as a requirement of communication, getting the reader to *see* something which the writer has satisfied himself is in fact correct. Richards clearly is no cynical manipulator. If he misleads by a one-sided presentation, if he renders his argument plausible by means of tricks, then it seems likely he is himself just as much a victim as those he leads astray.

A more potent argument against the kind of linguogenetic explanation we are considering at the moment is that the parts out of which Richards' complex theory is compounded pre-existed it. Obviously one part was inherited from Bentham. And there are some similarities to Richards' theory in the last chapter of *Principia Ethica*, which suggest that, if Moore was *not* an influence, they were both buying from the same wholesaler. At all events, given what seems certain, the influence of previous writers' theories, then these theories may have acted as frames of reference determining unconsciously what kinds of ethical words occurred to the theorist in thinking and writing his theory.

There is one other candidate, if not for equivocality, at least for

---

[1] The proportions given in this analysis are not due to a change in what Richards was writing about. 'Good' can be applied to art as readily as 'valuable' can; indeed, unless it is to have its moral connotation, more readily, which is perhaps why Richards, *having given it this connotation*, favours 'valuable' instead. The most striking change between the first and the second three chapters is in the use of 'valuable', instead of 'good', in referring to experiences or states of mind.

theoretical distortion because of inappropriate meaning, that we should consider. This occurs in connection with Richards' theory of language. We have pointed out how Richards concentrated on the reader rather than on the writer, how his classification of the emotive functions of language was from the reader's point of view only,[1] and how he treated language-learning as though it were simple associative learning,[2] where, through regular co-occurrences, we learned on perceiving one thing (such as hearing a word) to expect another (such as a thing the word referred to), with a consequent stress on the individuality of word-meaning for each different experiencer. Might not these features of Richards' approach to language be due to his conceiving words as *signs*? We interpret signs as we interpret what a person says, so in this sense words are like signs. On the other hand, there many features of signs which are not features of words, and these may have contaminated Richards' treatment of words in the manner suggested.

It is amusing to notice how Ogden and Richards in *The Meaning of Meaning* first introduce their classification. The first example of a sign they give is the words, "To Grantchester", on a sign post! (They call it "a post"). There follow the examples of a doctor's use of symptoms in diagnosing a disease, the use of litmus paper, a cloud meaning rain, culminating in

Lessing scrutinises the Laocoön, and concludes that the features of Laocoön *pere* are in repose. A New Zealand school-girl looks at certain letters on a page in her *Historical Manual for the use of Lower Grades* and knows that Queen Anne is dead.[3]

Such cunning follows only three pages after they had been telling the reader about "the process of 'lubrication', the art of greasing the descent from the premises to the conclusion". We have to remember hard the explanation suggested above that the purposes of such devices may be to get the reader to *see* the connection. But the trouble is that too much of their treatment of language suggests words as hieroglyphics from a somewhat remote culture.

As we have already seen, Richards distinguishes two types of sign that words may function as; emotive signs and referential signs. The latter, "signs which men use to communicate one with another and as instruments of thought", he calls symbols. They are generated by references and, we can infer, are intentionally produced. The other type is generated by emotions, feelings, and moods, and as such, I think, obviously not intentionally produced (otherwise a reference

---

[1] See page 245 above.
[2] See pages 254-256 above.
[3] *M. of M.*, 6th edn., 21.

would intervene), so that they act as give-aways, revelatory in effect. We read these signs—those of intonation, rhythm, word order or synonym-choice where the synonym we use makes little difference to the sense—as a doctor reads the signs of his patient's condition.

On our theory, to describe people talking to one another as people making signs to one another or communicating by signs would be a use of language which would show up the inappropriateness of this identification. In fact, we find Ogden and Richards hardly ever use 'sign' in this way; they use 'symbol' instead. 'Sign', we might say, puts on a disguise so as not to be found out.[1] On the other hand, for linguistic features that are emotively caused, use of the word 'sign' for describing the relation between them and the emotions or attitudes which caused them seems quite appropriate. So it is interesting to see that Ogden and Richards do not have a special technical term to distinguish them from 'symbols', but continue to use the word 'sign'. In other words, they are using 'sign' at two different levels, one in contrast with 'symbol', and the other as the word for the class to which both 'symbol' and 'sign' belong.

One argument that could be made against the case we are advancing is that it is untrue that the word 'sign' is used only of things and events which we *interpret*, because we do use such phrases as 'making signs to someone'. Therefore, it may be argued, it is legitimate to classify speech and writing as sign-making processes. Now we must admit that 'sign' has many uses. Nevertheless the phrase 'to make signs to someone' is fairly specialised, referring only to signs like gestures and mimetic expressions. One would not say of a person who was scowling, for instance, that he was "making signs", even if it was only a bluff aiming at intimidation. Therefore we cannot, in phrases like 'he was making signs . . .', mean here by 'signs' anything we *could* mean by this word, when using other phrases in which the word occurs, such, for example, as 'he was showing signs of anger'. Furthermore, this use of 'signs' is certainly not that of Ogden and Richards' paradigm, the match scrape, which was a sign of flame because it led to expectation of flame. Actually, one would not use 'sign' in this situation either, which shows up Ogden and Richards' neglect of the *function* of words, of the uses they serve. But the descriptive sense of 'sign' in the paradigmatic case is the same as the one we use when we talk of a sudden wind breaking the stillness of a darkened summer evening as the *sign* of the storm to come.

[1] The following plainly untrue statement is one example of 'sign' being used of words in the referential sense—". . . the symbol is usually taken as a sign of what it stands for, namely that to which the reference which it symbolises refers" (*M. of M.*, 6th edn., 205). It would cause a great strain to use the word 'sign' thus nakedly very often.

Another argument against the case we are advancing might be that the sign-theory of language was not novel to Ogden and Richards. Many other writers from Hobbes on, if not earlier, had referred to words as 'signs.' However I do not think the theory caught on to such an extent that we would be justified in regarding this as another meaning of 'sign' in ordinary language, viz., a word for the class which contains both words and what in ordinary language are referred to as signs. To regard it as a meaning of 'sign' because of philosophical theories would be just the kind of error we referred to in our criticism of Richards for multiplying meaning in his multiple definitions (see page 259). For this reason we should not really regard the example of 'sign' as one of being misled by *ambiguity*, as in the case of 'impulse' or 'good'. Perhaps we should regard it as an example of the danger of technicalising a word that has distinct uses in ordinary speech, though even here we may question the extent to which it really was technicalised. Hobbes and Locke, after all, classified words as signs because they considered them signs of ideas. In their case, and in Richards' too, we would really have to say that they were misled by an analogy.

Then again, we must admit that there was another reason for Richards' concentration on reading rather than on writing—that is, on the passive rather than on the active side of language-use,—and on the *individuality* of meaning, namely, his interest as an educationalist in getting people to understand and read properly poetry and philosophy. Further, Richards' neglect, in his treatment of language-learning, of its normative-social aspects is a feature of a more general aspect of his approach, namely, his hostility to norms, which we have many times referred to, and which is also manifested in his treatment of ethics, with its neglect of the concepts suggested by words like 'duty' and 'ought'.

We have considered in some detail this question of ambiguity as a possible cause of errors in thinking in order to counteract over-simple, too easily accepted views about the role words may play in misleading us. Perhaps we can sum up our position by saying that, whilst there is evidence of a relationship between the kind of theory put forward and the kind of language used in devising it, which may on occasion be a causal relationship, this is not the only factor causing the error, nor does it seem likely that the error will be altogether avoided by any kind of linguistic reform or warnings about the varieties of meaning words have. Generalising from the cases we have studied, it does not seem likely that philosophers' and logicians' recommendations and warnings about language will be anything like as effective, with regard to this particular kind of error, as the amount of energy that is expended would imply.

2. CONFUSING DEFINITIONS WITH ASSERTIONS

An error which Richards believed was frequently made was the mistaking of a definition for an assertion. This, as we have seen, is a reason why he included in his multiple definitions of a word many theories about that which the word stood for. He dealt with this source of error in detail in *Interpretation in Teaching*, claiming that Campbell, in criticising Swift's statements about grammar, was in fact using the word 'grammar' in a new and different sense. This meant that Campbell's denials of Swift's assertions, as well as his own assertions about grammar, were in fact analytic. They were tautologous re-phrasings of his definition of 'grammar', masquerading as statements of fact because they were put in that linguistic form. Richards put it crudely by saying that what Campbell was doing was comparable to asserting: "It is not the business of circles, as geometric figures, to quarrel with one another",[1] on which Richards' comment was, "True, but irrelevant to the question whether literary circles don't fall out as part of their trade."

This error is obviously similar to the one we considered in the last section. The only difference is that instead of dealing with a confusion between two *accepted* meanings, we are dealing with one between an accepted meaning and a newly devised one. We cannot therefore say that we are being misled by *language* in the way we could with some of the errors mentioned in the previous section. This is because we mean by 'language' something which is a common object for its users.

Richards however attributed the error we are considering to language by means of another route, a syntactical one. The same form of sentence, he thought, could be used to state a definition as to assert a fact. We could therefore be misled into thinking that we were making a factual assertion when we were only proposing a definition, a potential source of error similar to one that many philosophers have pointed to. When Campbell asserted that grammar was "no other than a collection of general observations methodically digested . . .", Richards suggested that Campbell was probably "telling us how he and we will be using the word henceforward". Richards continued:

> Of the two forms, '——is . . .'
> and   'By "——" I mean . . .'
> the first may always be only a shortened and less pedantic-looking form of the second.[2]

A further example of this 'error', showing reasoning very similar

[1] *I. in T.*, 252.
[2] *I. in T.*, 255.

to Richards', indeed using his technical terms, is given by Professor Glanville Williams in his article "The Controversy concerning the Word 'Law' "[1]. He deals with the controversy about law between Austin, who considered that only "municipal (i.e. state or positive) law" could truly be called law, on the one hand, and those who believed it was correct to speak of "early customary law" and "international law" as well, on the other. Glanville Williams, describes this hundred-year-old controversy as "purely a verbal one although few of the parties to the controversy seem to have realised it". Austin's opponents, he suggests, should "have challenged him on the simple and unassailable ground that he was assuming a power no man possessed: the power of dictating to others the meanings in which they should use words". Clearly, this question is linked up with that of the 'Proper Meaning Superstition'. Professor Glanville Williams asserts that "there is no such thing as an intrinsically 'proper' . . . meaning of a word" and echoes Richards in claiming 'freedom of definition'. Possibly he, like Richards, has a conception of meaning such that, when asked for the meaning of a word (not the meaning of the word in a particular context), he would give a longish list of fairly specific meanings rather than a brief list of highly general ones.

This attitude, which leads to the dismissing of many controversies as purely verbal, fails to recognise an important distinction. Though sentences of the form, "By ' . . .' I mean '. . .' ", or "Let us define '. . .' as '. . .' ", are statements of intention, or proposals, those which are of forms like ". . . is . . .", are generally in part factual assertions. Thus, if we answer in this way a question as to what a given word means—if we say, for example, 'a guffaw is a kind of laugh'—we are making not a proposal but an assertion as to how the word is in fact used, and this of course means that we believe it to have 'proper' meanings. Or again, we may, for instance, say, 'To be disinterested is to be impartial, not to be bored', because we want to resist a change in the use of a word which would lose us a valuable distinction. The element of assertion here is as to how the word was used earlier by those who knew how to use it. A mistake, it is claimed, has been made as to the meaning of the word, and the speaker hopes, though it may in fact be too late, to stop it from spreading. Here it is not so much that "freedom of definition" is denied, as that a particular false conception of a word's meaning should become a feature of the language.

Sometimes, as in 'A whale is not a fish but a mammal', the assertion may be one about scientists' terminology. A feature of this when applied to ordinary words is that, as in the example just quoted, it suggests more easily identified and more self-consistent grounds for

[1] In *Philosophy, Politics and Society*, ed. Peter Laslett, (1956).

the application of the word in question, which may, in the case of concrete nouns, result in its denotation forming a slightly different class. This may in turn be used as a criticism of the way we ordinarily use words. Similarly, philosophers may slightly alter language on the grounds of internal consistency. This may even happen when they are in fact making assertions about ordinary language. That it should happen is because, like the scientists, philosophers, even linguistic philosophers, have a vested interest in a greater degree of consistency than language actually has. An example of this might be the category-analysis of psychological terms by Behavioural Dispositionalists such as Ryle or Ayer. There is the phenomenon, which many psychologists have experienced, of its being claimed that a particular psychological 'discovery' is not a discovery because it was already well known. Yet the people who assert this often do not, in fact, manifest such knowledge in their behaviour, and, *pace* Ryle, it is quite idiomatic to answer them by pointing out that though they may have known (believed) this, they did not act on their knowledge (belief). But if this type of answer were to be discouraged, because of acceptance of the Behavioural Dispositionalists' analysis and the belief that the speaker is not so much using ordinary language as distorting it because of a theory he holds, then we should in fact have a change in the use of language on the grounds of theoretical consistency.

Returning now to our question about the status of 'definitions' put in an 'is' form, we would claim that they are not proposals but assertions about language-use which often, because they are this, contain in addition criticisms of particular language-uses. They imply an élite of language-users, who are norm-determining and whom the makers of these definitions are claiming to interpret. They imply that language, which is continually changing though it may not be changing in the right way or fast enough for changing circumstances, is *criticisable*; that users may be mis-users through carelessness or ignorance, so that there is a coarsening, averaging agency at work that needs to be withstood. Underlying the phenotypes, it is implied, are *genotypes* of language; describing people's actual use of language does not give us the whole story. There are circumstances in which a speaker would recant a given piece of verbal behaviour as a result of learning more about the situation which gave rise to his verbal behaviour. An example would be the description of a given act of behaviour, such as giving money to a beggar, as "charitable", and its being later discovered that this was done in order to impress, say, a rich woman whom the donor, otherwise mean, hoped to marry. Insofar as the descriptive element in the meaning of words involves some interpretation, and it does so of course to an enormous degree, then potentially, if not actually, we are constantly in this position.

There is, therefore, great scope for such remarks as 'The true (or real) meaning of X is . . .'[1]

One of the best known examples of this is the Utilitarians' interpretation of the true meaning of ethical terms. They assume that differences about ethical theory are due much more to intellectual confusion than to basic differences in attitude. Granted that we can have different theories about the dispositions that our use of ethical terms manifests, they would claim that theirs is the most economical theory. It does not of course cover *all* uses of these terms, but they would presumably argue that such dispositions as would not be subsumed under their major one would be so narrow as to be negligible or narrow enough to be accepted by the speakers as inconsistent with their normal use and so rejected, when the major disposition is revealed to them.

Richards himself, in including among his multiple definitions of words one which he himself favours, calling it the 'most important meaning', provides examples of this procedure also. The most clear-cut example of this is in *Practical Criticism*, where he fathers on Confucius, as in the *Principles* he fathered in Tolstoy, a special meaning of 'sincerity', which makes *best* sense of the use made of it in criticism 'but not often with any precise definition of its meaning'.[2] Richards writes, after giving a number of extracts from the *Chung Yung*:

Meditating upon this chain of pronouncements we can perhaps construct (*or discover*) another sense of sincerity. One important enough to justify the

---

[1] Professor Stevenson argues that sentences starting like this are generally 'persuasive definitions' (*Ethics and Language*, Chap. 9). These he takes *inter alia* as attempts to change meanings. Examples he gives in his book and in his articles in *Mind* (1938, Vol. 47), such as 'culture', 'poet', and 'meaning', are ones in which he suggests a contrast between the normal meaning and some special meaning, tied to a particular theory, which would restrict the range of application of the word in question. But it could be argued that the propounders of persuasive definitions are not just seeking to redirect attitudes by capturing meliorative words, but rather that they are raising the issue of implication. The contrast is not between 'culture' as referring to the forms of behaviour and 'culture' as referring to state of mind, but between two theories as to what the correct application of the word implies about the person to whom it is applied. The contrast may, for instance, be between what we may roughly describe as classical or romantic conceptions of man. If the argument were of the form Stevenson for illustrative purposes imagines, this would be likely to be a misunderstanding. To deny Pope the title of poet, for instance, does not mean that those who say this are proposing the radical changes in usage that a literal interpretation of their statements would imply. Their concern is with Pope, not 'poet'. As for what has been dubbed 'the verification theory of meaning', the absurdity of describing this as a '*definition*' by the Logical Positivists of a word they held in high regard is sufficiently revealed by the fact that for them 'meaning' was a *tabu* word.

[2] *P.C.*, 280.

295

stress so often laid upon this quality by critics, yet not compelling us to require an impossible perfection or inviting us to sentimental . . . . . indiscriminate over-admiration of the ebullitions of infants. And it may be possible, by apprehending this sense more clearly, to see what general conditions will encourage sincerity . . .[1]

I have been arguing for recognition of the extent to which certain statements are factual ones. This is not the same as arguing that they are right. The probability is that they are all wrong, though those that enjoy a good deal of success are probably illuminating, if only by reminding us of points forgotten in the rush of a new fashion. But it is misleading to call them all definitions, or to say that they are all verbal though with a different point from the point of linguists' or translators' statements. It is misleading because these statements are assertions not only in declaring how certain words are in fact used but also in presenting theories about, or descriptions at a high level of generality concerning, the dispositions that their use manifests. They are only linguistic in the sense that statements of theories that attempt to explain changes of meaning would be linguistic. They are not linguistic in the sense assumed by the kind of refutation of utilitarianism that consists in pointing out that to deny utilitarianism is not to commit a logical contradiction.

It is time we returned to Richards. What I have been resisting is the theory that *language* confuses, or is systematically misleading, in being such that the same form of words may be used for definition as for factual assertion. I do not however wish to deny that in putting forward a theory about something like grammar, we may be surreptitiously altering the meaning of the word 'grammar' with the result that the theory becomes more plausible to ourselves as well as to others. I do not think that Campbell himself was doing that, but rather that he was pointing out the logical absurdity of Swift's conception of it. But even if he was being misled in this way, such a confusion could not be laid at the door of *language*. It is a feature of the individual, being much more like a misunderstanding of language. I have already suggested an example of this kind of confusion in psychological theories of emotion (see page 258). I will conclude this section by illustrating how this error misled Richards himself in a very important part of his theory, namely, where he argues that improvements in our understanding of language inevitably result in improvements in our ability to think successfully.

My thesis is that Richards' assertions are often analytic, i.e. that he defined language in such a way that removing misconceptions and learning correct theories about language was the same thing as

[1] *P.C.*, 285 (my italics).

thinking better. The analytic nature of the theory is one cause of Richards' conviction that it is right, and his ignorance of its analytic nature is a cause of his belief that his theory is a factual one—is in fact a theory at all. The kind of evidence I am going on—and much more detailed evidence could be looked for—I will present summarily, but I think it makes a *prima facie* case.

When, in *The Philosophy of Rhetoric*, Richards explicitly considered the relationship between language and thought in connection with Behaviourist theories, he denied that they were one and the same. However, it will be remembered that, in *Coleridge on Imagination*, Richards carried out a multiple definition of 'word', distinguishing senses ranging from "the least comprehensive", when it simply stood for the physical object, such as a print-mark on paper, to the "most comprehensive", where words were regarded as "containing in themselves a part or whole of the meaning we give to them".[1] This multiple definition, Richards indicated, was a paradigm for similar words as, for instance, *'language'*. So, although when he refuted Watson's view about thinking, he did not say what sense he was giving 'language', it seems evident that he must have been using one at the "least comprehensive" end of the scale. As for the "most comprehensive" end of the scale, particularly when the word is conceived as containing the *"whole"* of its meaning, I do not see how Richards could maintain there the continued separateness of language and thought. This is particularly obvious when we consider that for Ogden and Richards one way of regarding a word's meaning was in terms of its *reference*, for which the word 'thought' was sometimes used as a synonym. The state of mind Richards most wished to bring about in his readers was one having the characteristics of the Imagination, for under these conditions the mind would grow. As we saw, when considering *Coleridge on Imagination*, this state of mind was achieved when there was least separation between, amongst other things, words and their meanings. "Most poetry", Richards wrote, "which is markedly imaginative will naturally be read as though its meanings were inherent in the words."[2] For him, "the organisation of language into metre" in such poetry is "part or aspect of the self-organisation of the mind that is uttering itself in poetic composition", and he quoted Coleridge's words, "Are not words the parts and germinations of the plant? And what is the law of their growth? In something of this sort I would endeavour to destroy the old antithesis of words and things, elevating, as it were, words into things and living things, too."[3]

[1] *C. on I.*, 106.
[2] *C. on I.*, 110.
[3] *C. on I.*, 118-119.

This "most comprehensive" sense of 'language' that Richards used obviously has its dangers for him. The temptation it presents to him, of easing his theories about how understanding language better improves our ability to think, is made greater by two other factors. The first of these is his taking as *meanings* of words various philosophical theories. Instruction in language, in this case carrying out multiple definitions of words like 'free', 'knowledge', and 'meaning', is the same as learning the major philosophical doctrines. Secondly, by learning theories Richards meant practising them. Therefore, learning correct theory of metaphor, for instance, meant *using* metaphor. Now, supposing we were to argue against this view that, though a writer might in this way be made very skilful in his metaphors, though his writing ability might as a whole increase, he might nevertheless remain a derivative, uncreative thinker in comparison with a much clumsier, more awkward writer. The kind of answer we would be likely to get to this would be one denying the possibility of distinguishing *what* is said from the *way* in which it is said; in other words, an assertion that it is impossible to separate the words from the thoughts and feelings they embody. Seen in this light, the theory that understanding metaphor results in feeling more deeply, which we considered in the previous chapter, and which seemed so implausible, can be made to appear less odd.

This confusion of Richards, that once again paradoxically illustrates a source of error he himself identified, though he wrongly described it, is important because of the centrality to his book of the thesis it partly determined. Similar dangers exist for philosophers advancing comparable theses. We have already mentioned (page 280) the danger of circularity that exists when we appeal to a study of ordinary language to make us more aware of the variety of concepts that exist in any one area (such as that of excuses). What is being referred to is not just language, but our *use* of it. As Wittgenstein pointed out, any one word can be used in a great variety of ways, and there is no limit to the number of new uses to which it may be put. In the past, this would have been looked upon as a source of confusion—similarity of linguistic form concealing diversity of logical form. Insofar as this attitude has been reversed, and insofar as a *general* statement about the value of studying our use of language is made, then this may be no more than a statement to the effect that we learn about our concepts by learning about our concepts.

Similarly, with the Logical Positivists and their followers. The perils of intensionalist formulations, confusions of logical types, and the suggestion of a double-language for physical and psychological statements, often led them to refer in their statements to the words[1] rather than to what the words stood for. This can be seen in Carnap's recommendations about translating "pseudo-object" statements into the "formal mode of speech", and Neurath's of the "terminological" way of speaking as being a guard against ontological errors. The trouble arises when we find Professor Woodger recommending complete logical formalisation of scientific theories[2] on such grounds as that it is necessary for the "complete understanding" of our theories. A theory, he says, is "a system of statements ordered by the consequence relation"[3], and statements, for him, are "units of language".[4] But it seems evident from the way in which Woodger, like Carnap, treats understanding that "complete understanding" in fact consists in ability to use the calculus which is part of what the theory, according to him, is. It follows that there cannot be complete understanding without logical formalisation of the theory. I am not providing detailed evidence here, but I suspect that this type of confusion, occasionally occurring, is responsible for some of the conviction with which Woodger advances his thesis about logical formalisation or, at least, advises the use of logical symbols as preparation for eventual axiomatisation of theories.

But it is important not to exaggerate the influence of this type of linguogenetic confusion. Returning to our case study, the theories of Professor Richards, we should point out that his occasional inclusion of thought in his conception of language cannot account for his belief that no important thinking could take place without the use of language. Furthermore, not all his statements that improving our understanding of language will result in improvement in our ability to think need to be analytic ones. Apart from what empirical grounds he may have had for them, they are, in part, also due to his faith in formal transfer of training. It is inelegant to have such a complex of causes, but then it is not in nature to shave. Or, to reapply the metaphor, Occam's razor is only appropriate to highly cultured theory. It is harmful to good theory in the early stages of thought.

3. WORD MAGIC AND ABSTRACTIONISM

Word Magic was, in *The Meaning of Meaning*, the fundamental linguogenetic error. Ogden and Richards described it as "the super-

---

[1] For an early example of this, see Russell's "Personal Statement" in *Contemporary British Philosophers* (1st series), ed. J. H. Muirhead (1924).

[2] Cf. J. H. Woodger, *The Axiomatic Method in Biology* (1937), and "The Technique of Theory Construction," *International Encyclopedia of Unified Science, Vol. II, No. 5*.

[3] *Biology and Language* (1952), page 71.

[4] ibid., 5.

stition that words are in some way parts of things or always imply things corresponding to them".[1] We described its various manifestations in our second chapter, when we were considering *The Meaning of Meaning*. Mainly, of course, it was considered responsible for hypostatisation. This, Ogden and Richards thought, led to a belief in universals, symbolised by abstract nouns, and to a failure to realise that words were often used in an abbreviated way. Thus, according to Richards, 'the Good', 'Beauty', and "the aesthetic mode" were taken to refer to unique, unanalysable entities or properties of things, instead of being seen as words which had been invented in order ultimately to refer compendiously to a whole variety of feeling and attitude conditions, which had in common only some very general properties.[2]

The superstition of Word Magic Richards considered to be instinctive, in the sense of being genetically determined. Presumably this was on the grounds that its manifestations were universal and difficult to eradicate. It would have been better if he had limited himself to saying this. To call it "instinctive" seems to be an example of a fake explanation.

Attempts to explain hypostatisation in terms of learning instead of instinct have been made by a number of philosophers. Russell, for instance, argued that abstract words are treated according to the model of concrete words. "Thus the influence of vocabulary", he wrote "is towards a kind of platonic pluralism of things and ideas".[3] Carnap, in writing about the bad effects of the "pseudo-object" mode of speech (*The Logical Syntax of Language*, Part III), suggested a similar explanation.

The trouble about this explanation is that it does not account for its main object, namely Plato's theory of Universals, since, if the model of concrete words did have this effect, we would not expect the theory to claim that there was only a *single* entity which accounted for our capacity to use such concrete words as, to take a stock example, 'bed'. Indeed the theory seems to fly in the face of semantic habits.

Another theory, free from this particular objection, is that it is proper names that are responsible for these errors. Russell, on the

---

[1] *M. of M.*, 6th edn., 14.

[2] Cf. *P.C.*, 359. ". . . beautiful things . . . need have nothing *in common* . . . beyond this purely abstract property of being such as to arouse, under suitable conditions, tendencies to self-completion, in the mind". Richards went on to say that "no *general* account [of beauty] will be possible", which obviously does not follow from the preceding sentence. What he meant was that we can never lay down a general rule as to the objective qualities of works of art. There was an infinity of ways of achieving "self-completion".

[3] *Contemporary British Philosophers* (1st Series, 1924), ed. J. H. Muirhead, page 368.

same page of the article we have just quoted from, held proper names responsible for the concept of 'essence'.

It is natural . . . to suppose that a proper name which can be used significantly stands for a single entity; we suppose that there is a certain more or less persistent being called "Socrates" because the same name is applied to a series of occurrences which we are led to regard as appearances of this one being.

It is perhaps natural that Russell, with his naïve 'sense-data' theory of perception, which so much neglects the effects of past experience on what is actually sensorily given, should neglect psychological explanations of recognition, but clearly if those occurrences we call 'Socrates' are a class of differing appearances, so is the word 'Socrates'.

Ryle,[1] in his turn, accused Russell himself of being misled by the model of proper names. There is something paradoxical about such an ascription in view of the frequency with which Russell made remarks to the effect that "proper names are usually really descriptions",[2] i.e. not proper names. It would seem to follow from this that for Russell no words in a natural language were, in fact, proper names. It is at least a plausible alternative hypothesis that Russell's attitude to proper names, expressed in his concept of logical proper names, was a consequence of his acceptance of a sense-datum analysis of perception, even though he did not publish or elaborate his own views on this until after the development of his theory of meaning.

As for Ryle's more general thesis, that our familiarity with proper names was responsible for the denotation aspect of Mill's theory of meaning being picked out as our dominant model for meaning, his treatment suggests that he himself has mistakenly assimilated 'name' to 'proper name'.

This . . . theory derives partly, presumably, from the comfortable fact that proper names are visible or audible things and are ordinarily attached in an indirect but familiar way to visible, audible and tangible things like dogs, rivers, babies, battles and constellations. This is then adopted as the model after which to describe the significance of expressions which are not proper names . . . . "What that expression means" is then construed as the description of some extra-linguistic correlate to the expression, like the dog that answers to the name "Fido". (Similar reasoning might coax people into believing that since "he took a stick" asserts a relation between him and the stick, so "he took a walk," "a nap," "a job," "a liking," "the opportunity" or "time" asserts a relation between him and a funny entity.)[3]

[1] In his review of Carnap's *Meaning and Necessity*, *Philosophy*, xxiv, 1949.
[2] "Knowledge by Acquaintance and Knowledge by Description," *Proc. Arist. Soc.* 1910-11.
[3] ibid., pages 69-70.

But it is perfectly idiomatic to use the word 'name' on occasion for some nouns which are descriptive words, as in 'What is the name of this plant?', 'Could you name the objects in this room for me, please?', 'What is the name of that part of the engine which is just to the left of the what-do-you-call-it?', 'What is the name of that colour?' If the questioner had asked for *proper* names, that there was a difference which it is the function of 'proper' to indicate would have become very clear.[1] 'Name' and 'meaning' are related but not strictly complementary to one another. We ask for the *names* of objects (activities like dances, colours etc.) and for the *meanings* of words. It is sometimes relevant in answering requests for the meaning of a word to say what it names. However it is not always idiomatic to use the word 'name'. I do not think one would be easily understood if one used 'name' in trying to find out what the object we call a 'fence' was called or that which we call a 'cloud'. 'Name' seems more appropriate where the function of the word is to differentiate a number of similar objects from one another, as with plants, parts of a machine, or in a sentence like 'What is the name of *that* kind of cloud?'. But it begins to become evident that we need to use more systematic survey methods to determine such questions.

If ever there was an area where language or theory of language might be expected to influence theory, it would be that of theories about language. After all, language should provide the data from which theories of language are constructed. Some of the complained-of hypostatisation we have been referring to arises in constructing theories of language or of meaning, and one is not really saying much in showing how language or theories of language have led to subsequent theoretical distortions, if one is not indeed being altogether circular. It is quite a different matter from explaining through theories of language, implicitly held, the defects of our psychological theories, or faults in physics. Whatever we are studying, our first theories, as the history of the sciences or, for that matter, the present state of the very theory I am criticising in this chapter, show, are crude oversimplifications derived from only a small part of the relevant data. What is selected is prominent, perhaps perceptually prominent, but not necessarily of much significance. Therefore in so far as theories of universals are theories of meaning describing the relation between words and what we use words for, it is to be expected that our theory

---

[1] Since the review to which we have been referring, Ryle has written again, recognising that one can talk about certain nouns, which are not proper names, as being names. However he continues to use proper names as examples, and describes the theory of meaning he is attacking as being the view that "all significant expressions are proper names". But this presumably is *his* interpretation; he does not claim that anybody actually *said* this. ("The Theory of Meaning", in *British Philosophy in the Mid-Century*, ed. C. A. Mace [1956]).

302

will be overdetermined by simplified models derived from a narrowly restricted group of words. But in so far as it is not just this but is, say, a mystical theory, then we need to consider the matter a little further. I have often got the impression from the Logical Positivists that they were at a loss to explain how metaphysics *could* have arisen, since the only source of experience was our senses, and for this reason fastened on the fact that, because its rules were not logically watertight, language could be used grammatically to produce 'nonsense'. But psychology has many resources to explain illusion, ranging from our capacity to make perceptual mistakes so that we see something which is not actually there, to the projections uncovered by psychoanalysis. The role that these may play in mystical theories seems to have been very much neglected, possibly because of the oversimplified psychological theories that the Logical Positivists were working with. When we examine the views which are said to be determined by language, what is striking about them are features whose connection with language it is difficult to see. Plato's theory of Ideas is an obvious example suggesting, amongst other things, our conceptions of parenthood, of change and decay, of the idealised past, of perceptual error and our capacity to correct it, suggesting maybe—for how can we deny to the author of the ninth book of the *Republic* the privilege of a Freudian interpretation?—a regression-yearning, impossible to achieve and fear-driven, because it was at the same time the phantasy of rising from the shadow tomb of dependence to possess the Father's Sun. And though other later philosophers were more abstract than Plato, one can still see signs that they also were doing more than producing theories of language. In deriving Leibniz's monadism largely from his acceptance of a substance-predicate logic, for instance, Russell does not explain why the monads should have been conceived as conscious. Though it might have been attempted in Max Müller's time, I do not think anybody today would wish to explain such animism through language. It may well be of course that language influences the kinds of ghosts we choose, but the hope, particularly of the Logical Positivists and, by implication, all those who have explained metaphysical theories in linguogenetic terms, that this way of thinking could be vanquished by linguistic reform and education, seems to be merely chopping off hydra heads. How much more sensible was Bentham in suggesting that his hostility to fiction derived from his fear of ghosts.

Richards, as we pointed out when considering *Coleridge on Imagination*, paid very much less attention to Word Magic in his later books. But, as we pointed out there, "the disease of abstractionism", which is often referred to in the later books, is the same thing in more modest guise. We have seen other examples of Richards' changes of names for what he is talking about. Yet we may perhaps be warned that, with these changes of names, we do get some changes of emphasis. I think this is the case with the change from "Word Magic" to "abstractionism".

What mainly motivated Richards in his early books was the kind of theory that used capital letters and referred to 'absolutes' and denied reducibility. This, as we saw, he looked upon as due to Word Magic, and his conception of science, and why he referred so frequently to it, was that he saw it as denying 'absolutes' and always involving analysis, which was expressed in terms ultimately of a physicalist language. But his attitude to the things he was initially against gradually changed till, in *Coleridge on Imagination*, he was ready to admit the value of Platonism and Coleridge's Revelation theory of the Imagination. Though he still wished to translate such theories into his "Materialist" one, the fact that he now saw value in them prevented him from any longer using such simple explanations as that of Word Magic. Different theories were now explained as originating from different "facts of mind"; all were relative, all were metaphysical, including the world views of Science. The important thing was to realise this relativity, to be aware that one was abstracting and not to mistake one's abstractions for absolute features of the world we live in. And to prevent his own theories from being taken as absolute in their turn, Richards constantly emphasised relativity and recommended the reader to experience for himself the "facts of mind" from which they came.

Was Richards any more successful here than he was in his other efforts to avoid a source of error? When we attempt to answer this question, we find the notion of abstractionist thinking a difficult one to pin down. Sometimes Richards seemed to mean by this, theorising on the basis of rather crude, "macroscopic" observations, and being content with this, instead of trying to improve the theory by further and better observing. I cannot feel that Richards is far from this deficiency himself. His oversimplified model of language-learning that he used throughout is one example of this; his theory of formal transfer and growth, another. Often Richards seems to be trying to avoid the stigma of overgeneral theories too rigidly applied by at the same time allowing truth to contrary theories, or by accompanying the repeated assertion of the theory by mentioning observations which are never integrated into the theory. This we have noted in the case of his theory concerning failures of comprehension (see pages 147-150 above). But I do not think these devices save him; rather they incur suspicion of his wanting both to have his cake and eat it.

The more specific meaning that Richards gave to "abstractionist" thinking was that it was thinking that ignored the fact that concepts were constructed for particular purposes. This would be a similar charge to that of linguistic philosophers accusing thinkers of forgetting the particular uses different words had. The thesis in its linguistic form, where concepts are identified with uses of words, can certainly count Richards himself amongst its offenders. He offended against it in those cases where he attributed completely general meanings to certain words; for example, 'metaphor' in his assertion that *all* thinking[1] and therefore all language is metaphoric, and 'projection' in his statements that all perception involves projection.[2] But in so far as the thesis implies that one should recognise a validity for any concept, advocating for them the principle of tolerance, Richards seems to want to show his openmindedness by his constant changes of language, as, for instance, in his changes of 'sincerity' to 'Good Sense', 'Sanity' and 'Reason'. However, as we pointed out, these changes do not generally mean that there are any very significant changes in the concepts referred to.

One effect of recognising the context-bound nature of concepts that one generally expects is theories of much modester and more limited scope. Richards certainly does not show this. Indeed, his concept of the self as unity and capable of higher and higher degrees of organisation until it "realises" itself and is "complete", thereby achieving "freedom", together with the associated notion of a single order of "Nature" to which the self has perfectly adjusted itself so that it can realise all its desires in due proportion, exemplify to an extravagant degree a case of a thinker mistaking his abstractions for features of the world we live in.

4. THEORY, PRACTICE, BIAS

In this chapter, in reviewing various explanations by Richards as to why we made errors in thought, we have made a paradoxical discovery. This is that although himself alert to these sources of confusion and although he was constantly carrying out and recommending his readers to carry out exercises to make us aware of them, Richards in his own practice seemed to be one of the worst offenders. To what can we attribute this?

(a) Practising the Theory

One answer might be that Richards' errors were due to his practising his own theories; in this case, his theories of the Imagination and of

---

[1] *P.R.*, 94; *I. in T.*, 49.
[2] *C. on I.*, 164; *P.R.*, 108.

Language. These two theories are interrelated, and their effect is to make Richards ride his words with a very loose rein. Thus the theory of the Imagination states that it will work more effectively if linguistic norms are not allowed to override the requirements of self-expression. We described Richards' attitude to syntax in connection with the Imagination when dealing with *Coleridge on Imagination* (see Chapter Four, Section 5 above). It is not simply that because "the standard ... resides in us, as the active principle of communication",[1] it is inconsistent with the Imagination that ready-made norms should govern creative expression. The Imagination is also believed to be more likely to operate if we are not too conscious and explicit in what we are doing. We should act in accordance with Richards' belief that "most thought forms itself in and through experiments with the language that is to utter it".[2]

As for Richards' theory of language, this, as we have seen, held that every word had a number of meanings so that we must "expect ambiguity to the widest extent and of the subtlest kinds nearly everywhere", something which was not to be condemned, because it was "an inevitable consequence of the powers of language and . . . the indispensable means of most of our most important utterances".[3] And Richards also regarded "all discourse . . . as over-determined, as having multiplicity of meaning", i.e. as meaning more than one different, even "incompatible thing"[4], at the same time. This also, as we saw from his treatment of Coleridge, could be a sign of the very highest value, necessarily characterising the "completest" statements.

We have already come across some examples of the reflections in Richards' practice of his theories of the Imagination and language. These examples include the ambiguous status of his and Ogden's Canons of Symbolism, at once prescriptive and descriptive (see pages 27-28 above); Richards' oscillations between relativist and absolutist positions; and his free-associational way of thinking that we illustrated with his not always mutually compatible arguments against granting informational function to poetry (Chapter Three, Section 5), and for asserting the importance of metaphor (pp. 101-104). However misguided in these, Richards was not just being careless. Nevertheless I believe Richards' attitude to his writing was responsible for many of the confusions he made. These came through his highly cavalier attitudes to distinctions of logical category.

The reader will probably already have noticed how easy-going Richards is with regard to the different logical categories he used his

[1] *I. in T.*, 278.
[2] ibid., 277.
[3] *P.R.*, 40.
[4] ibid., 38-39.

words in. But to bring the point home, let us glance at the different ways in which Ogden and Richards used their key technical term, "reference", in *The Meaning of Meaning*. Listing these will also show with what difficulties the reader has to grapple in understanding the book. That the term is sometimes used for the *process* of referring and sometimes for the *object* of the process is suggested by the fact that "references" and "acts of reference" were frequently treated as equivalent, and that "beliefs", "ideas", "concepts", "conceptions", "thoughts" and "thinkings of" were all on occasion treated as synonyms of "references".[1] Sometimes also these were treated as *instances* of "references" as though "reference" were the word for the class of which these were members. "Propositions", understood as "the relational characters of acts of referring", were also identified with "references".[2] "To refer" to something was taken as equivalent to "to be adapted to", or "to be directed to", something; yet it was also taken as equivalent to "to be similar to what has been caused by" something. The relation of "reference" to "context" was also made difficult to understand because references were defined as "a set of external and psychological contexts linking a mental process to a referent",[3] and yet elsewhere it was said that "on different occasions quite different contexts may be determinative in respect of similar references",[4] and mentions were made of "the context upon which a reference depends".[5] Finally, whilst it was said that "two symbols have the same connotation when they symbolise the same reference",[6] it appears that references can also connote, for "the connotation of a reference [is] those characters of its reference in virtue of which this is what is referred to".[7]

It might of course be said that Richards was not alone responsible for this apparent indifference to category distinctions, and that his co-author should share some blame. Richards' later writings, however, are no different in this respect, as we shall show by further examples later on, whereas those of Ogden, the translator of Wittgenstein and inventor of Basic English, show nothing like this amount of looseness.

Now it does not follow that this looseness of phrasing, however irritating to the reader, means that in every case it is impossible to determine what Richards means, or that he is always up to some trickery. But when we find him making various errors, such as that

[1] *M. of M.*, 158-160.
[2] ibid., 168.
[3] ibid., 189.
[4] ibid., 345.
[5] ibid., 370.
[6] ibid., 201.
[7] ibid., 311.

arising from the different meanings of 'impulse'; or in his producing a number of apparently different meanings of 'meaning' because he is unconsciously assuming different contexts in which it is occurring (see pages 259-261 above); or in his confusing, when trying to distinguish the function of language, of intention with purpose (see pages 250-252 above); or the whole crop of errors we noted in his treatment of Coleridge's "coalescence of subject with object in the act of knowledge" (see Chapter Four, Section 6), then it does look as though in Richards' case a theory of language was responsible for errors in thought.

But this of course would only be the pragmatic effect of holding the theory. The relationship is not the same kind of relationship that Richards and many Linguistic Philosophers considered responsible for faulty theories and mistakes in reasoning. Furthermore, though the theory may have affected Richards' practice, his practice may itself be a *cause* of the theory. The theory, after all, is first properly developed in *Coleridge on Imagination* and *The Philosophy of Rhetoric*, whereas many of the examples we gave of its use, of Richards' carelessness in expressing category differences and of the mistakes which seemed to be due to this, came from earlier books. It does not seem likely that Richards held the theory earlier but did not publish it, otherwise he would surely have made some reference to it, if only in a rudimentary form, when writing about language and the Imagination in the earlier books. Though Richards' looser use of language in the later books is probably the effect of his holding the theory, which, as it were, intensified already existing trends, all we can say about the earlier books is that Richards' writing *in accordance with* his later theories seems to have been a potent cause of error.

(b) Richards' Bias against Distinctiveness

There is however another feature of Richards' thinking, which would be expected to have similar effects to his loose use of language in leading to neglect of logical distinctions, namely, a bias towards identifying different things with one another or *merging* them into one another. We have already come across numerous examples of these. Let me remind the reader of some of them.

Notably, there is the merging of the self in its experiences, which lead to the talk of "being and knowing [as] somehow one".[1] This makes possible belief in the act of knowledge, concerning which Richards wrote that it was "that activity of the mind in which knowing and doing and making and being are least to be distinguished".[2]

[1] *H.T.R.P.*, 179.
[2] *C. on I.*, 47.

308

Then again, in his multiple definition of 'word', he talked of one sense of 'word' according to which the word's sound and meaning were not separately distinguished. This was "the most comprehensive meaning", corresponding to "the most comprehensive" meaning of Nature, one in which our feelings were merged with our sensations and projected into the outside world. There is also the virtual equating of use of language with thinking, and the implied identifying of Nature and language as shown by his description of the "Realist" conception of Nature, according to which Nature is a *symbol*, and in his suggestion that the relations between the meanings of words were the same as Plato's Ideas. This, as we have seen, enabled Richards to make such claims as, "*In* the things the mind knows . . . and *in* the mind itself . . . is a structure", and when we learn this by observation of self, "what we . . . learn is not the ways of our minds (except incidentally); it is what truly is: the order of the *IDEAS*."[1]

Richards' emphasis upon merging or fusing was, as we have seen, a feature of his view of the Imagination, and the cases of it we have just mentioned all occur in or after *Coleridge on Imagination*. But in themselves they cannot be explained simply in terms of his theory of the Imagination. If Richards were right in his views about freedom from syntactic restraint and concentration of all our resources as being necessary for the operation of the Imagination, this would not entail the kinds of mergings we have just described. The actual connection is the following. The mergings are all expressions, in objective or would-be objective terms, of *experiences* of the Imagination, ones characterised by a high degree of concentration. Thus the idea of the self's being merged in its experience comes from paying attention to the effects of a poem upon our feelings *as a whole* in order to judge it, rather than standing outside it and applying some kind of mechanical formula; the coalescence of subject and object is explained in terms of the constructive nature of perception and our awareness of it at the time; the "most comprehensive sense" of 'word' is explained in terms of a certain "*attitude*" to words, in which we do not separately experience the word's sound and its sense; and so on. Therefore, if to merge or fuse different things with one another is likely to require neglect of the differences between the things in question, it is in Richards' treatment of psychological concepts that we are most likely to find this.

(i) *Merging Psychological Terms*. Turning now to Richards' early books, we find this indeed to be the case from the beginning. It is shown, for instance, in *The Meaning of Meaning*, in Ogden and Richards' use of a substitution theory of learning, according to which

[1] *H.T.R.P.*, 201.

one stimulus could substitute for another in bringing forth a response, a point of view which regarded a conditioned reflex, say, as a mere reinstatement of an unconditioned reflex, instead of a different type of response (see pages 21-22 above). So also we saw him equating perceptions with expectations, recognitions, inferences and interpretations, which in its turn made it easier for the authors to use without differentiation the notion of *cause*. The great achievements claimed for the theory in *The Meaning of Meaning* were largely due to this flattening out of differences between different psychological terms and a parallel oversimplification of logical problems.

When we come to *Principles of Literary Criticism*, we find other ambitious claims to be based on further equatings and mergings of one thing with another; in this case, of mental with neural events, and of cognition with feelings and action. Consideration of these will throw further light on what Richards did with the word 'impulse', so let us once again consider his uses of that word.

It will be remembered that Richards first introduced the term 'impulse' when putting forward his theory of value. There it was paired with words like 'desire' and 'preference', so we will call this the 'desire' sense. In a later chapter, after a paragraph which we described as a "key quotation" (see page 43 above), we found that it was used in collocations like "sensory impulse" or "motor impulse". This we will call the 'neural' sense of impulse. Now that this was not simply a confusion of two meanings of 'impulse' is suggested by a number of assertions that Richards made in paragraphs *immediately preceding*[1] our "key quotation". In these he dealt with "the Mind-Body problem" by stating that "mental events are . . . identical with certain neural events", that "we are . . . our nervous systems, more especially still the higher . . . co-ordinating parts of it" and that "the mind is a system of impulses".

By means of this identification of the mental and the neural, Richards removed one of the distinctions between the two different senses of 'impulse'. Considerable difference however still remains. With this Richards dealt by introducing what is in effect a third sense of 'impulse', a private one of his own. This was first described in our "key quotation" in these words,

The process in the course of which a mental event may occur, a process apparently beginning in a stimulus and ending in an act, is what we have called an impulse,[2]

to which he added later,

[1] *P.L.C.*, 83-85.
[2] *P.L.C.*, 86.

Sensation, imagery, feeling, emotion, together with pleasure . . . and pain are names for the conscious characteristics of impulses.[1]

It is clear that the difference between the two senses of 'impulse', has been much further reduced, and this by a sort of compromise. 'Nervous impulse' has been extended to refer not just to a single impulse passing up a single nerve, say a sensory nerve, but to the impulse this sets up in another nerve in the central nervous system, and then the impulse set up in a motor nerve, as though this were all one single impulse. Thus when Richards talked of reflexes being "bundles of . . . impulses", he had presumably the reflex *arc* concept in mind. As for the 'desire' sense of 'impulse', this too was extended. It was extended so as to be equivalent to "mental event", mental event being itself extended so as always to involve an impulse to action. This latter extension was carried out, in the same chapter as the other equations, in the process of a translation into physicalist language of Stout's tripartite division of mental events into cognition, affect, and conation.

To be cognizant of anything, to know it, is to be influenced by it; to desire, to seek, to will anything is to act towards it. In between these two are the conscious accompaniments, if any, of the whole process. These last . . . include evidently both sensation and feelings . . . The advantage of substituting the causation, the character, and the consequences of a mental event as its fundamental aspects in place of its knowing, feeling, and willing aspects is that instead of a trio of incomprehensible ultimates we have a set of aspects which not only mental events but all events share.[2]

We see, therefore, that just as 'language', 'Nature', 'Knowledge', and 'word' had for Richards very pregnant senses, due to the merging of a number of different concepts in them, so was this the case with 'impulse'. One might apply to Richards the remark of Coleridge that he quotes,[3] "Few men, I will be bold to say, put more meaning into their words than I". But having compounded, by ignoring category distinctions, his special sense of 'impulse', Richards does not use only this; he continues to employ the ordinary uses of 'impulse' in such a way as to win plausibility for his ingenious argument about art having most value because it satisfies most impulses.

One or two quotations must suffice to show how Richards alternated between his very general private meaning and the more specific public ones. One of these we have already given, namely, Richards' key quotation itself (page 43). In this short paragraph, he uses 'impulse' in his private sense, in the 'neural' sense, and in the 'desire' sense.

[1] *P.L.C.*, 92.
[2] *P.L.C.*, 88-89.
[3] *C. on I.*, 107.

Another example is the following paragraph which is going to lead to the argument, a fundamental one for Richards' theory in the *Principles*, that a poet can "admit" far more impulses without suppression than "the ordinary man":

> How far an experience is revivable would seem to depend in the first place upon the interests, the impulses, active in the experience. Unless similar interests recur its revival would seem to be difficult. The original experience is built upon a number of impulses; it came about only through these impulses. We may even say that it is those impulses. The first condition for its revival is the occurrence of impulses similar to some of these.[1]

A third example occurs in the chapter where Richards introduces his special sense of 'attitude'. The passage starts off with a very typical prosaic example which raises the suspicion in my mind that, underlying these usages, Richards may have had the 'poetic impulse' or 'creative impulse' sense of 'impulse' at the back of his mind and was advancing his theory that the aesthetic realm was not unique, by equating this sense with the 'desire' sense. But here is the passage.

> The adjustment to one another of varied *impulses*—to go forward carefully, to lie down and grasp something with the hands, to go back, and so forth— and their co-ordination into useful behaviour alters the whole character of his experience. Most behaviour is a reconciliation between the various acts which would satisfy the different *impulses* which combine to produce it; and the richness and interest of the feel of it in consciousness depends upon the variety of the *impulses* engaged. Any familiar activity, when set in different conditions so that the *impulses* which make it up have to adjust themselves to fresh streams of *impulses* due to the new conditions, is likely to take on increased richness and fullness in consciousness.
>
> This general fact is of great importance for the arts, particularly for poetry, painting and sculpture, the representative or mimetic arts. For in these a totally new setting for what may be familiar elements is essentially involved. Instead of seeing a tree we see something in a picture which may have similar effects upon us but is not a tree. The tree *impulses* which are aroused have to adjust themselves to their new setting of other *impulses* due to our awareness that it is a picture which we are looking at. Thus an opportunity arises for those *impulses* to define themselves in a way in which they ordinarily do not.[2]

We have here not only 'impulse to act', but also "streams of impulses". And mention of "tree impulses" suggests the 'mental event' sense of 'impulse', since presumably the mental events occasioned by seeing a tree are what Richards has in mind. The same also applies to the impulses aroused by seeing a picture.

[1] *P.L.C.*, 182.
[2] *P.L.C.*, 109-110 (my italics).

We have now considered the evidence from Richards' early books of his frequent neglecting of distinctions between different psychological concepts and his merging of them into one another. To this we might add his use of the word 'experience', which is very much a technical term in the *Principles*. He defined poems in terms of these and talked very largely, not of valuable poems, but of "valuable experiences", these being conceived in terms of the organisation of impulses in them. But it is very much of a simplification (neglect of differences) to regard experiences as capable of being thus ranged along a single dimension. Similar considerations apply to the conception of personality that his formal transfer theory implies. It is evident, too, in his material transfer theory. Remarks such as

it seems that the simplest scrap or *pulse* of learning and the grandest flight of speculation share a common pattern much as the inside of an atom seems to be built on somewhat the same plan as the solar system, and that again to have its analogies with the disposal of the galaxies[1]

suggest how much these psychological simplications may have to do with Richards' peculiar Chinese box outlook and the magical solutions whereby study of the atoms ("impulses", "pulses of learning") within us can win us mastery of the world.

But though neglect of distinctiveness amongst *psychological* concepts was the most marked feature of Richards' early books, there was some evidence, too, of vagueness concerning the boundaries between the psychological (or neurological) on the one hand, and the physical on the other. These, we will see, involve confusing cause and effect.

(*ii*) *Merging Cause and Effect.* A good example of two kinds of confusion is given in the passage we quoted on page 311. These are a confusion between a desire to act and action itself, and a confusion between an experience and its object.

The first of these is shown in Richards' remark that "to desire, to seek, to will anything is to act towards it." This means that impulse in the 'desire' sense is equated with an attitude, the incipient movements that follow it. What this implies is that the "*consequences*" of a mental event are regarded as actually part of the mental event. This is indeed stated in the passage quoted on page 311. And elsewhere in defining "experience", Richards equated it with "mental state, or process" and adds that "many of the 'experiences' here referred to would ordinarily be called 'actions' "[2]. We see here, before his

[1] *H.T.R.P.*, 106 (my italics).
[2] *P.L.C.*, 38 (footnote).

development of his theory of Imagination, an anticipation of his later equation of "Knowing" with "Doing".

But Richards also regarded as an "*aspect*" of mental events its' "causation"—"to be cognizant of anything, to know it, is to be influenced by it." The stimulus of a mental event is therefore part of a mental event; "knowing" is separate from the mental event's "conscious accompaniments", the latter being included in what Stout called "affect", and not in "cognition". Of course, Richards *is* being confused here and is writing carelessly. But this sort of carelessness was so common with Richards that I think it is a function of his theory. It is implicit in his use of what is essentially a logical concept, namely, reference, in his psychological theory of meaning (see page 307), as well as in his occasional mentions of sensations as referents, although referents, according to his triangle of meaning, are meant to be *things* only. It also makes easier, and is perhaps itself a consequence of, his desire to define many things in psychological terms.

Well might Richards say, "No one to whom Berkeley has mattered will be very confident as to"[1] the difference between "meanings" (i.e. "references" or "thoughts") and "things", though he conceived this as a commendation rather than as a warning. Nevertheless it has been our contention that neither the influence of Berkeley, which was clearly not operating in the early books, nor the Utraquistic Fallacy *tout court* that Russell and Moore held responsible for Berkeleian Idealism, made Richards finally believe in the coincidence of the subject and the object in the act of knowledge. It is rather one of the forms taken by a pervasive and general tendency to neglect distinctiveness and merge things with one another. Russell sought in logic an explanation of "monistic or monadistic" philosophies like those of Spinoza, Leibniz, and Hegel. He thought they were due to our acceptance of the reduction in traditional logic of relational to subject–predicate forms of proposition, *via* the concept of substance that this favoured. Richards' case raises the question why relational propositions in the first place should be robbed of their distinctiveness.

[1] *P.R.*, 12.

Chapter Eleven

GENESIS AND REVELATION (II)

IN considering Richards' various theories of the causes of error in thinking, and seeing how they apply to errors in his own thinking, we found that these causes were never sufficient to account entirely for Richards' views. For one thing, many of his views were not of his own invention. He learned them elsewhere, and may have tricked himself into believing them by false analogy or by confusing different meanings of the same word. Then again, some of his theories, for instance his views about the relation between language, thinking, and 'Nature', were supported by a number of different errors; they were, in fact, overdetermined. It is also paradoxical that he should have given so much evidence in his own practice of the very errors he was so continually warning others against. His theory about cultivating awareness by continuous practice seems to be of little use to him. Of course, as we pointed out at the end of the previous chapter, Richards' way of handling language, which reflects his theory of language, made these errors much more likely to occur. But this still leaves Richards' way of handling language to be explained.

Two other main types of explanation of the theories we make are psychological and sociological. The most thoroughgoing of the former is the psycho-analytical, the best known of the latter, the Marxist. Some philosophers, like Professor Wisdom,[1] or Professor Lazerowitz,[2] have looked to psychoanalytical theory for assistance in going further than the linguistic interpretations of philosophy, though only Dr. J. O. Wisdom, amongst modern philosophers, has made any serious attempt to develop a full psycho-analytic explanation of a philosophical theory.[3] I do not know of any attempts on the part of Linguistic Philosophers to make use of sociological theories in their aetiological approach to philosophy, though these have been applied against them by Professor Gellner.[4]

In this chapter I shall be attempting a psychological analysis of Professor Richards' theories. I shall concentrate on the central theories, with which this book as a whole has been mainly concerned,

---

[1] J. Wisdom, *Philosophy and Psychoanalysis* (1953).
[2] M. Lazerowitz, *The Structure of Metaphysics* (1955).
[3] *The Unconscious Origin of Berkeley's Philosophy* (1953).
[4] *Words and Things*, Chap. IX.

and I shall also make use of the evidence provided by his practice, that is the way in which his books are written, the relationships to the reader that are implied, and so on. No other evidence is available to me than Richards' books. The reason why I think a psychological analysis is worth while is this. In so far as what Richards says and does in his books betrays certain more general dispositions, which have to be taken as a whole, then any other type of explanation, such as a sociological one, will have to work through this. To use theorising language, if we want to get the maximum benefit from a sociological explanation of a given individual's thought, then we need to understand the intervening variable between the sociological data and the individual's behaviour. But this intervening variable is not just *one* variable, nor is it a set of variables that are independent of one another. It is a system; in other words, something that is on the surface complex, but possessing a less complex key. To the extent that we understand this, to that extent will the power of detailed sociological explanations be increased. This is not of course to deny that sociological factors may be important in the initial determination of the system or that many correlations between sociological and behavioural data on a macroscopic scale may not be usefully determined without this knowledge. But in so far as a person's responses depend not only upon his memory and his reasoning power but upon his whole psychological make-up, it is important to determine what this is.

Richards himself recognised that personality factors were important in determining the way in which we think, and quoted with approval John Stuart Mill's reference to "some natural want or requirement of human nature [which different theories are] fitted to satisfy", in terms of which, he argued in *Coleridge on Imagination*, different myths were to be explained. Richards also in the same book confessed that the "diagnostic attitude" he had "inevitably" to adopt "must seem, equally . . . inevitably, discourteous and even insulting"[1] to those whose views he was discussing. How much more discourteous one might think would be a personality diagnosis, influenced by psychoanalytical thinking. And yet now that psycho-analytical categories are so much a recognised part of the equipment of thought, and are used to explain all manner of things, should we not be freer to use them openly among ourselves? The aim is to understand a system of thought as such, as part of the study of the history of ideas. We are not concerned with the individual. It is not a matter of pathology. There has of course been a tendency in social psychology to limit psychoanalytical-type explanations to such fields as race prejudice and delinquency. Admittedly, great artists have also been subjected

[1] *C. on I.*, 173.

to it. This might be interpreted as originating from the belief that great artists are abnormal. But I do not think that the psycho-analytical way of thinking can be so limited. It is not so much that we are all abnormal as that our conception of human nature is much too stereotyped.

Two methodological comments must be made about my approach. Firstly, I shall concentrate very much more on description than on interpretation. This method is partly dictated by the fact that Richards' books constitute my only evidence, and that anyhow I am not a trained analyst. But I also believe it to be a weakness of much applied psycho-analysis that there is too close a connection between the data and the interpretation of the data. This is indeed a general failing, one that is certainly evident amongst philosophers when they make statements about the influence of language on thought. It gives a propagandistic flavour to the writing, as though the writer were paid by some pressure group of ideas to demonstrate how they operate in different areas. What then I shall attempt in this chapter will be something more like an exercise in Freudian phenomenology. Of course, the data we notice are inevitably influenced by our theories. Nevertheless we can vary in the extent to which we hold back inter-preting activities to allow more observing, uncommitted by our interpretations, to take place. When what is observed is ranged out in front of the thinker, there is a chance for a more articulated pattern to emerge, and it also enables the data to be considered separately by others who may interpret them differently, not even necessarily along psycho-analytical lines. Further data would of course be required to justify a different interpretation. But at least the data upon which an interpretation is based are fully set out and will need to be taken into account in any new interpretation. There should then be less chance of the cross-purposed controversy that so often results from the fact that the parties to the controversy are each reporting on a very different selection of the data.

Secondly, as my earlier remarks imply, not only the faults but also the merits of a theory may be susceptible to psycho-analytical inter-pretation. This of course is recognised by orthodox Freudian theory in the existence of such mechanisms as sublimation, though applica-tions of this, except to artists, poets, and musicians, are comparatively rare. Despite recognition of this fact, I have found it difficult to apply in the case of Richards. This is in part perhaps due to the too great strength of past habits of thought. It takes some practice to learn to write in an appropriate way. But it is also because I am indeed very critical of Richards' *general* theory and way of writing, as opposed to his particular and specific achievements, which are obviously con-siderable. It is in fact part of my thesis that the very qualities that so much assisted his great success, the considerable pretensions of his theory and his style of writing, were those that prevented him from realising his qualities as an observer in the development of well-turned theory.

I. A MATERIALIST FORMULATION OF RELIGION

In the nature of the case, it is difficult to present a logically consecutive account of the irrational logic of the Unconscious, for every one of its limited stock of symbols is multiply ambiguous. What we need is some scaffolding. Let us start with the idea that Richards was advancing a view that many religions advance.

What Richards values most and wishes us to have more of is an experience like a *mystical* experience. His conception of this is shown in Coleridge's description of the working of the Imagination which Richards quotes (see page 42 above), saying that "it is hard to add anything to what [Coleridge] has said," though in fact, as we shall see, he succeeds in doing this. The experience gives a strong sense of unity underlying apparent diversity, and is characterised by a sense of effortlessness. Later on, as we saw, Richards came over to Coleridge's side by regarding the experience as giving us a deeper insight into Nature, since in the experience we were at one with Nature and had simultaneously self-awareness. But the whole emphasis of Richards' teaching is that this experience is to be attained through some intermediary, a poet or a philosopher. To achieve the experience we had to be in *communion* with the intermediary, something that was only attainable as a result of rigorous exercises continuously undergone, which have a strongly ritualist character. When we are in the right condition, the taking of the poet's or philosopher's words into ourselves (eating, we might say, the Word made flesh) would give us this experience. It was not something that could be won by an effort of the will, however much the will might be used in preparing ourselves; both being in the condition for grace and being granted it come as a gift from outside ourselves. "Growth" is a reward that may be granted our works; we cannot command it.

Together with these beliefs goes a certain attitude to time, past, present, and future. In the past we did not have to labour for communication; it came naturally. There was a unitary social order; we were at one with each other, sharing a common tradition, not separate or isolated. Nor then was Nature hostile or indifferent to us; we could hold with sincerity the Magical View of Nature, according to which we could control her.

318

Out of this Eden we have been driven by eating the fruit of the Tree of Knowledge. Science has made for ever impossible continued belief in the Magical View of Nature. To try to hold onto it, or to return to it, is regressive, to be bought only at the cost of forfeiting maturity. We must give up all illusion and realise that we are alone in a cold, indifferent world. But not only are we estranged from Nature, but from one another too. For with the development of science, of conscious knowledge, has come also the break-up of the unitary order of societies. We can no longer communicate, there is a Babel-like confusion of tongues. We are forced each one of us on to our own individual resources. Every man must work out his own salvation, which he may attain by means of the intermediaries. In marked contrast with the ease and effortlessness of the past, great stress is laid on the effort needed to achieve the state of communion. Continuous exercises, unremitting aspiration, and unceasing watchfulness are required.

If we do this, then, turning to the future, Richards promises us pretty well the Kingdom of Heaven. Harmony will be restored to human society, wars will cease, we shall complete and fulfil ourselves. Science that has taken away can also give. We stand on the threshold of a Copernican revolution, of which Coleridge, that Galileo of the mind,[1] is the prophet. This revolution will be brought about in every heart, and unsatisfactory though our present condition is, the future holds a brighter promise than the past.

Now this likeness of Richards' theory to certain aspects of our religion is probably due in part to direct causes. Not only do we learn it in the course of the religious instruction that is part of our upbringing, but also parts of such a view are present in a great deal of the literature that Richards concerned himself with. These views are on offer; but they are not the only ones. We need therefore an additional explanation as to why they should be bought, or to put the matter in another way—since many people buy unthinkingly or according to the fashion of their group—why there should be special emotional investment in them.

One answer is that they reflect certain universal experiences. One such is mystical experience or, at least, certain types of aesthetic experience. We can readily understand that such experiences should be highly valued, though they are rarely justified simply for their own sake but in terms of some theory which acts like a myth, serving to hide the fact that they *are* sought for their own sake.[2] And where

---

[1] *C. on I.*, 232.
[2] This is the element of truth in the New Critics' criticism of early Richards. They recognised that Romanticism consisted in the search for certain kinds of emotional experience for their own sake, followed by an attempt to justify them on practical

does the *interpretation* of the experience come from? Where, for instance, does the idea come from that in the past there was much more union between people than in the present? Presumably it comes from historical evidence that on the whole we, who do this theorising, live in societies which earlier had more of a community, less of an associational, character. But how can we explain why this is for some people so strongly felt as a nostalgia, since relatively few people today are likely to have experienced marked changes in social structure of this kind?

One answer may be sought in the fact that we have all, in our personal pasts, first of all experienced membership of a group that had in most pronounced form the characteristics of a community, namely, the family. Dependence, not full responsibility, in infancy and early childhood, with its attendant pleasures, is a universal experience. If we hypothesise that memory tends to be unitary from the point of view of hedonic tone, then memories of a period that is predominantly pleasant for most of those of the class and society that produce these theories, will tend in retrospect to appear pleasanter, as experiences inconsistent with this general picture are forgotten. This will be greater the more distant the personal past, particularly in so far as it contrasts with a present that falls short of expectation. Further contrasts of a more immediate kind, provided by inevitable separation experiences,[1] and in adolescence, by the coming of intrusive problems of sexual management, are likely to add to this.

The theory we have been advancing, which amounts to the assertion that this view of the past is literally due to nostalgia, works at a comparatively superficial level in comparison with Freudian explanations of the "oceanic" feeling. But in accordance with the archaeological picture of the mind that Freud used, the two kinds of explanation are not incompatible. Indeed, in one of those quotations from Coleridge that Richards likes to use to restate in more elevated language a theory he has been advancing, we find a suggestive instance of this. The quotation, a fairly lengthy one, is from *The Statesman's Manual.* Richards gives it in *The Philosophy of Rhetoric,*[2] as a "symbolical" statement of his theory of metaphor. Coleridge is telling of the

---

[1] A poignant description of the sense of loss of the naturalness of childhood with the induction into a mechanical society is given in Kipling's *Kim.* There is implicit here too a contrast of Indian and Anglo Saxon ways of life, which suggests a more valid source of experience for views about the difference in terms of *Gemeinschaft* and *Gesellschaft* between different periods of time. However not many people have been in the position to have this experience of two different societies.

[2] *P.R.,* 110-111.

---

grounds. However, their failure to criticise Richards' later books from this point of view shows how, in seeking for some extraneous justification for art in abstract terms, they were not really very different themselves.

awe he feels when contemplating Nature; "I feel it alike," he writes,

> whether I contemplate a single tree or flower, or meditate on vegetation throughout the world, as one of the great organs of the life of nature. Lo!— with the rising sun it commences its outward life and enters into open communion with all the elements at once assimilating them to itself and to each other. At the same moment it strikes its roots and unfolds its leaves, absorbs and respires, steams forth its cooling vapour and finer fragrance, and breathes a repairing spirit, at once the food and tone of the atmosphere, into the atmosphere that feeds *it*. Lo!—at the touch of light how it returns an air akin to light, and yet with the same pulse effectuates its own secret growth, still contracting to fix what expanding it had refined. Lo!—how upholding the ceaseless plastic motion of the parts in the profoundest rest of the whole, it becomes the visible *organismus* of the whole silent or elementary life of nature and therefore, in incorporating the one extreme becomes the symbol of the other; the natural symbol of that higher life of reason.

Here Nature is suggesting to Coleridge "correspondences and symbols of the spiritual world." But when we read what preceded this quotation, symbols of a different order suggest themselves. Coleridge's point of departure was an actual experience.

> I have at this moment before me, in the flowery meadow, on which my eye is now reposing, one of its most soothing chapters, in which there is no lamenting word, no one character of guilt or anguish. For never can I look and meditate on the vegetable creation, without a feeling similar to that with which we gaze at a beautiful infant that has fed itself asleep at its mother's bosom, and smiles in its strange dream of obscure yet happy sensations. The same tender and genial pleasure takes possession of me, and this pleasure is checked and drawn inward by the like aching melancholy, by the same whispered remonstrance, and made restless by a similar impulse of aspiration. It seems as if the soul said to herself: From this state hast *thou* fallen! Such shouldst thou still become, thy Self all permeable to a holier power! . . . But what the plant is, by an act not its own and unconsciously—that must thou make thyself to become! must by prayer and by a watchful and unresisting spirit, join at least with the preventive and assisting grace to make thyself.

It is interesting to compare this quotation from Coleridge with the quotation from the *Timaeus* with which Richards ends the same book.

> . . . Harmony, having her courses kin unto the revolutions in our Soul, hath been given by the Muses to be a helper to the man who, with understanding, shall use their art . . . for the ordering of the circuit of our Soul which hath fallen out of Harmony, and the bringing thereof into concord with itself . . . Now unto the Divine Part in us the motions that are kin are the Thoughts and Circuits of the All. These must every man follow, that he may regulate the Revolutions in his Head which were disturbed when the Soul was born in the Flesh and by thoroughly learning the Harmonies and

Circuits of the All may make that which understandeth like unto that which is understood, even as it was in the beginning; and, having made it like, may attain unto the perfection of that Best Life which is offered unto men by the Gods, for the present time and for the time hereafter.[1]

What is striking about these two quotations, which form weighty codas to Richards' last two lectures in *The Philosophy of Rhetoric*, is this. They do not only come from and illustrate the themes with which this of all Richards' books is most concerned, that is, the interanimation and merging of things with one another; they also conceive this as a return to an earlier and *perfect* condition.

But now the question arises—Is Richards' conception of the past itself strongly emotionally charged? Certainly he gives much less expression to it than Coleridge in his yearning does. His tone is much more virile and progressive. But Coleridge was writing in the early days of Romanticism, and since then there have come Victorian Puritanism, the conception of the British Empire, the educational ideal of the Public School system, and a special kind of concern with "character" that may be found in writers as diverse as Kipling, Conrad, and Shaw. We have lost too our pre-Freudian innocence; we are more likely today to have a Nabokov than a Kilvert. But though it is no longer easy to write in the way Coleridge did, this does not mean that the appropriate feelings may not be latent. Richards indeed is very adept in using the words of others for his own purposes. Nevertheless, there is a discrepancy between Richards' thought and the religious picture we have just presented. It concerns the valuation of the self. We will examine this in our next section.

2. THE FREEDOM OF THE SELF IN THEORY

It is a well-known characteristic of many religious systems that they involve some kind of self-diminution, which may take the form of renunciation of certain desires, submission to some transcendental higher authority, losing the sense of the individual self by becoming one with some Higher Self, and so on. Mystical states of mind are commonly interpreted as ones in which the sense of self is lost. It is true that we come up here against the different meanings that can be given to the word 'self', and that, according to one of them, we might say that the effect of religion or mystical experience could be to *strengthen* the self. Submission to an all-powerful supernatural figure, for instance, can be a source of great strength in so far as a person may identify with this figure in his relations with others. Or the self he wins freedom from may be defensive in essence. Casting off its fetters of petty selfishness and anxiety-laden habit by plunging into an

[1] *P.R.*, 137-138.

identification with something conceived as bigger than this personal self may be an expanding, fear-resolving experience, enabling a person to break away from his social niche. God, one might say, was the joker in the mediaeval pack of cards.

But whether one interprets the self in such a way as to say that religion might enhance or diminish it, it nearly always requires explicit recognition of something that is considered immensely more important than itself. Here is where Richards' outlook contrasts with religious ones. The self is his highest value, and he distrusts any rival to it. This attitude suggests now a political rather than a religious category, one of *laissez-faire* individualism, which believes that the stability and health of a society depends on the stability and mental health of its individual constituents. Social norms, as we have seen, are distrusted and great faith is placed in education of a highly general, philosophical nature. There is here, as well as the contrast with the religious view we have been considering, a contrast with the Conservatism implicit in the desire to return to the past.

This political attitude of Richards' is shown throughout his books. I have given evidence of it particularly in considering his attitude to society (Section 3, Chapter Eight), and we have also seen how prominent it is in *Interpretation in Teaching* and *How to Read a Page,*[1] being justified in those books by references to Hitler and Mussolini. None of this needs to be repeated. What I wish to do now is to examine certain features of Richards' attitude to the self in order to determine its exact form.

Richards' individualism showed itself not only in regard to people but also in regard to things, including sensations, feelings, and words. His descriptions of his highly valued experience of the Imagination include references to our seeing into "the heart of things" and to our "feeling strangely alive and aware of the *actuality* of existence". This of course is a frequently reported ingredient of mystical experiences. Nevertheless use of the word "actuality" reminds us that Richards showed the same attitude with regard to the problem of meaning. We remember how much in *The Meaning of Meaning* he and Ogden treated meaning in terms of individual occurrences, which contrasted their approach so much with the normative one of logicians and philosophers. The same individualist attitude was shown with regard to the structure of poems and, as we saw in *Interpretation in Teaching*

---

[1] A further example is Richards' definition of 'have' (*How to Read a Page*, pages 156-159). This is treated entirely in terms of private property and the political merits of that institution for the training of the individual. "It enlarges the sphere of . . . personal responsibility, . . . it trains a man in foresight and accountability and in balancing values . . [and it provides] an easy way of teaching a man to respect his own claims and rights and those of others".

323

through the operation of his "jelly" model, even with regard to individual bits of prose.

It was on these grounds of favouring individuality that Richards, with one exception we shall come to later, showed himself so very difficult to please with regard to other people's theories, and so suspicious of abstractions of any kind. A frequent characteristic of his books was a general attack on all previous theories, whatever the theme—linguistics, theory of meaning, aesthetics, rhetoric—that he was dealing with, though, characteristically, he also recognised the individuality of these theories, giving them independent status as so many different meanings of words, which we have to bear in mind when reading and discussing in the areas concerned. The grounds on which he attacked past theories always included the suggestion that they were superficial, not based upon sufficiently close observation, that they were over-abstract or artificial. In effect, what this amounted to was dissatisfaction with any theory that was not a perfect description of everything to which it referred. Such a theory was of course an impossibility.

A striking feature of Richards' outlook was how often it was expressed in a negative way. He seemed concerned not just with accuracy of vision but also with warding off restriction or confinement. This led him to write nearly always in a critical way about the norms, whether logical, syntactical, or literary, that would control words. Similarly, Richards laid much stress on self-determination not only for poetry but also for ordinary prose-writing. The impression this often made was, as we have pointed out, that nothing might be criticised. In fact, of course, Richards did criticise a lot, so that he was not consistent, though if we examine this criticism we see that much of it is carried out in the interests of individuality itself. Thus in the Principles bad art is considered bad because it is obvious, suggesting stereotypes; other reasons for calling art bad, such as that it is meretricious, that it is empty virtuosity, are scarcely considered. Similarly, prose may be faulted because it shows stereotyped thought or because the writing suggests subservience to the Proper Meaning Superstition.

Richards' concern for individualism sometimes seemed to lead him to the extreme of wishing to deny concreteness and materiality altogether. This at least is one way—not the only one—in which we can interpret his abiding distrust of solid objects—"fixities and definities", in Coleridge's words. We may regard as early manifestations of this distrust of solid objects Richards' and Ogden's extreme Nominalism, their almost paranoid fear of Word Magic—"words as parts of things"—and Richards' own tendency to dissolve things, particularly aesthetic 'objects', into experiences. This dissolution reached its extreme in the flux of The Philosophy of Rhetoric. Idealism

324

in that book, we may say, carried out more satisfactorily what Nominalism had first been used for. Admittedly, the way had been prepared by Coleridge's theory of the Imagination, but given Richards' basic tendency, his fear of things being fixed and rigid with the resultant loss in their *possibilities*, this theory would have been extremely congenial to him. But of course the consequence of all this was that things became so amorphous that one could scarcely apply the concept of individuality to them at all.

Now we may interpret Richards' concern for the individuality of things as due to his seeing them as products, parts, or projections of individual selves. These latter are his most important individuals and to them other individuals may be made subservient and their autonomy interfered with. Thus the only theories about art that are not criticised, the "exception" we mentioned earlier, are ones that can be interpreted as judging works of art in terms of the benefit they bring to the individual self perceiving them. Possibly the paradox that we have just noted, whereby definiteness and articulation were lost by being dissolved into fluctuating experience, could also be explained by this priority of the individual self over other individuals. In Richards' words, "It is no exaggeration to say that the fabrics of our various worlds are the fabrics of our meanings"[1] and he quoted Yeats on Berkeley

... this preposterous pragmatical pig of a world, its farrow that so solid seem,
Must vanish on the instant did the mind but change its theme.

On the other hand, there is no individual—such as a social group—to which the good of the individual self should in its turn be sacrificed (except on rare occasions—"in wartime for example")[2], and morality is not seen in terms of the individual's obligations to others; indeed words like 'duty', 'ought', 'right', and 'wrong' play no part in Richards' vocabulary.

As with words, feelings, and poems, so with the individual self, Richards is concerned with warding off encroachment or attempts at control. This showed itself in the concept of freedom that plays such an important part in his system. We come across it early on in his descriptions of the Imagination. It was indeed something that he added to Coleridge's description despite his statement that this could not be bettered. It is true that freedom plays a part in many descriptions of mystical experience, but the things from which freedom is won, the limited personal self, the bondage of the senses, our desires, are not the things from which Richards wants freedom. Indeed, *one*

[1] *P.R.*, 19.
[2] Cf. Chap. Eight, Section 3.

sense in which he refers to it is in the freeing of our impulses from "suppression", from being "stifled".

It is not however pleasure that Richards wants. Again and again in his books, he denies this. "It is not", he writes in the *Principles*, "its thrill, its pleasure or its poignancy, which gives [the conscious experience its] value". What gives it its value is instead "the organisation of its impulses for *freedom* and fullness of life".[1] We may indeed suggest that the "sense of *release* (that is) given by Tragedy"[2] and the peculiarly high standing accorded to it, came from the extreme of freedom it represented in that *opposite* impulses could be simultaneously satisfied in it. In this respect, it represents in the emotional sphere the same extreme of freedom that freedom from the Law of Contradiction, by which a passage can at one and the same time mean "incompatible things", represents in the intellectual—or, for that matter, Richards' view that contrary philosophical theories were often both at once true.

The positive thing that Richards wanted and that gave him a sense of freedom seems to have been *activity* that requires no effort. Thus he referred to that "peculiar sense . . . of *free*, unimpeded activity"[3] that experiences of the Imagination gave, and later described 'sincerity' in Confucius' words, as that which "enables us, *without effort*, to hit what is right, and, without the exercise of thought, to apprehend";[4] thus, too, he distinguished Imagination from Fancy, referring in the passage from *Venus and Adonis* (see pp. 70-71 above), to how "Shakespeare is . . . making the reader realise, *not by any intensity of effort*, but by the fullness and ⸢self-completing growth of the response . . ."[5] Indeed, when we think of it, it was movement itself that gave value, for the attitudes were movements that satisfied the impulses. And in his later books, Richards frequently referred to the reader's own activity in reading poetry. This was specially the virtue of ambiguous syntax—"for poetry, . . . our *freedom* to fill in . . . is a main source of its powers"[6]—and Richards wrote of "movements of exploration and resultant ponderings" and how "these very *movements* . . . are the very life of the poem".[7]

In *Interpretation in Teaching*, as we indicated when describing the book, a great deal of stress is laid on freedom again, whether in Richards' emphasis upon finding out things for ourselves—for learning that is not a result of discoveries "of our own making . . . feels

[1] *P.L.C.*, 132 (my italics).
[2] *P.L.C.*, 246 (my italics).
[3] *P.L.C.*, 283 (my italics).
[4] Quoted in *P.C.*, page 287 (my italics).
[5] *C. on I.*, 83 (my italics).
[6] *P.R.*, 125 (my italics).
[7] *C. on I.*, 216 (my italics).

like an alien dark compulsion";[1] whether in his desire to abolish the teaching of traditional grammar in schools, putting the pedagogues who would control our language into the stocks instead; whether in his insistence upon our "freedom in definition" and general permissiveness concerning how we may logically analyse; or whether, in his describing "the logical use of words" as "no more like our usual ways of talking than the goose-step is like our strolling gait", inimical to "the fluidity, the incessant delicate variation in the meaning of our words", that characterises *free* discursive thinking"[2].

Last of all, in our consideration of Richards' use of freedom, we may note that, in discussing the problem of freewill, he defined freedom as "action according to its own laws",[3] and later wrote that when "most things most come together to determine our action", then we are "doing *naturally*".[4]

3. THE FREEDOM OF THE SELF IN PRACTICE

Let us now look at Richards' practice, that is, the way in which he wrote, to see what this can tell us about his attitude to individuality and to freedom.

There is, as we have already noted, abundant evidence in Richards' manner of writing and thinking of his hostility to norms, whether in the many different senses in which he used words, in the varieties of logical categories he employed them in, in the ambiguity and over-determination of meaning of his words, and in the lack of logical connection of his free-associational thinking. All this must have helped him to get into the swing of writing more easily than would have been possible if he had constantly been held up in order to make more precise the logical structure of his concepts, or than if he had been meticulous about the precise compatibility of one section of his argument with another. In other words, this would help him to *move* and to continue moving without constant effort, a quality that his vigorous style with its forward momentum certainly shows.

Richards' argument in his books does not however proceed in straight lines. He is very digressive, something which one suspects him of capitalising on in his later books in his constant breaking off to suggest a multiple definition or to analyse phrase by phrase a particular specimen of prose. This indulgence in digressing, which at times

---

[1] *I. in T.*, 18.
[2] *I. in T.*, 256-257 (my italics). The recommended "goose step" is referred to as "the militarist solution" in *Practical Criticism* (343) and as a "bullying assumption" in *The Philosophy of Rhetoric* (61).
[3] *C. on I.*, 62.
[4] *H.T.R.P.*, 179 (my italics).

makes things very difficult for the reader, may also be a manifestation of freedom. It is in defiance of the tyranny imposed by norms of sticking to the point, it acts like a fidget, indicating the degree to which concentration is suppressing desires to move. But though he has his digressions, Richards does not lose his forward momentum. His ellipticalness, his brief suggestions of his point, enable him to digress without losing speed.

Richards' writing has an exhilarating quality about it which is imparted to the reader. One feels his enthusiasm and can take pleasure in his self-display—in his unusual quotations, in his gorgeous academic coinages like "Utraquistic" and "neo-Mohist paradox". In conformity with his attitude, there is in contrast with the soft aerialness of Coleridge's tumescent prose, little imbuement with sensuous pleasure in Richards' own. He wants movement, and he wants power. Experience of the Imagination, Richards' mysticism, that first came from poetry and then from philosophy, cannot after all, especially in a book like *How to Read a Page*, be something that had no relationship to his own writing. In wanting to stimulate his readers, he must have come near to feeling it in himself, to experiencing those moments when "BEING and KNOWING are somehow one", when one is moving forward to self-realisation. I think therefore that Richards' hostility to norms acted unconsciously for him as a short-cut to this desired condition. Self-criticism is a form of attack on oneself; it involves force and restraint and can make the process of creation very painful. Though few would wish to go to the heroic extremes of a Wittgenstein, and though perfectionism of an individual or of a society may stultify, the evidence we have presented of the effects on Richards of his loose attitude to language and thinking, suggests some of the dangers of justifying philosophical activity in terms of benefit to the self. Similarly, there are dangers in Richards' approach of over-individualism, such that his definition of freedom, "action according to its own laws", sometimes comes suspiciously near to 'being a law unto oneself'. I do not think Richards always succeeded in avoiding this danger. There are two ways in which this can be illustrated.

Firstly, as his practice became more extreme in his later books, conforming to his theory of the Imagination, his writing became more and more difficult to understand, though it did not, as it should have done if his theory had been correct, produce better insights. Richards sheds some responsibility for the correctness of his views by suggesting that, even if they were wrong, the exercise they gave the reader's wits, on central issues, would have growth-value for the reader. Though he complained of being misunderstood, he wrote more rather than less obscurely, at the same time laying more and more stress on the need for the reader to improve his skills of interpretation. "It is the hard sentences and paragraphs which can do us good, as readers", he wrote in his last book, *à propos* a passage by Whitehead. It is difficult to avoid the suspicion that, however much this general view is welcome as against current notions, Richards made too much use of this licence for himself.

Secondly, Richards availed himself in his practice of what was perhaps the most extreme of the freedoms he demanded in theory, namely, that from the Law of Contradiction. This, with its parallel in the sphere of action of his view that the highest value lay in simultaneously satisfying contradictory impulses, has of course a prominent position in the history of ideas. Nevertheless there are indications in Richards' practice that he was attracted to these ideas by a certain tendency to have the best of both of two alternative worlds, whether they were those of art and science, of associationism and Gestalt, or of relativist and absolutist outlooks. Occasionally, we find him dropping remarks that suggest that this was a way of thinking that had some significance for him. For instance, at the beginning of the *Principles*, when comparing the relative merits of a "long life to a joyous one", he claimed that those most qualified to judge will say "that they find very satisfactory a life which is both".[1] And in *Interpretation in Teaching*, he described "this very irresolution between definition and statement" that characterises our ordinary, non-logical use of words, as a "way of making the best of both worlds, of eating your cake and yet having it", adding that it was "a proper and normal source of power in ordinary discourse".[2] In this way we may account for his love of having completely general meanings of words such that *all* symbols are metaphorical, or emotive (since we always use them for a purpose), and only some of them *are*, or *all* perception is projective and only *some* of it is. Even his tendency to commit the very mistakes he was always warning others against may be an example of this same tendency.

Now this wish to have the best of both worlds did sometimes, I think, lead to neglect of the interests of others, suggesting that Richards on occasion operated a double standard, one for himself and another for others. There can have been few glass houses in which so many stones have been cast as *The Meaning of Meaning*. The astonishing accusation he and Ogden made there that one of their opponents "constantly shifts his uses of 'meaning' without elucidating any of them",[3] which by implication they make against all their exhibits in

[1] *P.L.C.*, 59.
[2] *I. in T.*, 256.
[3] *M. of M.*, 6th edn., footnote to page 175.

the chapters, "The Meaning of Philosophers", is repeated even in later books.[1] Richards in his later books constantly warned against the adopting of controversial attitudes. Nevertheless he himself continued to be extremely critical, often indeed faulting a writer by interpreting him in one way when other interpretations were possible and Richards' own theory of interpretation allowed such latitude. This is all the more odd when, as sometimes happens, what the other writer really meant to say looks remarkably like Richards' own view, a tendency which gives the impression of Richards as a kind of Devil's Advocate on the side of the angels.

So far we have seen how Richards' practice conforms to his theory and some of the consequences of this. But Richards' practice also frequently reveals a rather paradoxical failure to individualise on his own part.

We will start our examination of this by noting how he loves to vary the words he uses. He does this particularly with abstract words, in whose deployment he shows great skill. He uses them as approximate synonyms so as to give a shimmering impression to what he describes, so that its appearance differs from one description to the next. Like Impressionist painting in its impact (though not in its theory), this livens what is described. Now this procedure may be all right for description of the Imagination's operation,[2] but it is less easy to see its point when some relatively technical term is in question as, for instance, in his taking as approximate synonyms the phrases, "the *sense* of words" and "the *symbolical*", "*referential*", "*logical*", "*scientific*", or "*structural use* of words", or in his reluctance to go on using the same key words, like "sincerity", "Word Magic", "symbol", "attitude", "impulse", "imagination", "Good Sense"[3] in successive books, though the concepts themselves are more or less continued. The consequence of Richards' method of writing—and we also have to take account here of the converse procedure, namely, constantly using the *same* words with different meanings[4]—is then to confuse, to blur boundaries in such a way that the reader is lost or gets by a sort of averaging process a cruder impression than that intended.

---

[1] For example: ". . . that so many writers are still content . . . to build up elaborate theories in terms so treacherous as this [viz. 'image'] suggests a need for more *discipline* in literary speculation" (*C. on I.*, 33, my italics).

[2] A good illustration of this is provided in the footnote to page 71 above. The examples there quoted are by no means a complete list of his resources for expressing the "fact of mind" to which they refer.

[3] *Any* of these words may occasionally occur in his last books, but with nothing like the frequency with which they happened in the books when they were favourites.

[4] Cf. Sect. 4, Chap. Ten.

A similar vagueness results from the combination of Richards' love of abstract words with his tendency to elliptical writing. Though he lays such stress on definition, his 'something-along-these-lines' way of doing it might indeed be more aptly named Multiple *In*definition. On a larger scale, we may note that though Richards often makes valuable criticisms of the theories of others or of the grounds on which they justify norms, he himself frequently fails to provide anything very positive in their place. A particularly striking illustration of this is provided by the contrast between the complex articulatedness of language-uses concretely demonstrated by certain Linguistic Philosophers and Richards' few categories, which remained more or less unchanged throughout his books.

Now it might be said that this indefiniteness with which we have charged Richards is simply a consequence of his emphasis upon freedom, whether in his refusal to abide by norms concerning our use of words, or in his not writing to present 'the answer' to his readers, desiring them to work it out for themselves. One might say, too, that he avoids a hierarchy of concepts out of concern for the freedom of the individual instance.

But these considerations do not seem likely to be effective. For example, presenting better answers than the ones criticised can be done in such a way as to stimulate readers to think for themselves; it *need* not threaten their liberty of thought. Wittgenstein's practice, for one, shows how this can be done with very specific and individual examples. Then again, not wanting to threaten the liberty of the individual instance by elaborating a complex conceptual structure is reminiscent of that kind of *laissez-faire* individualism which, by neglecting the organisation of individuals in groups of intermediate size, results in a society peculiarly vulnerable to totalitarian take-over. Richards' vigorous practice of approximate synonymy, together with his constant digressions, seems too to be more than a mere by-product of his wish not to be bound. It suggests rather the continued having of the sense of being free by a continuous changing, even perhaps a *tabu* against naming. Names after all fix things and hold them still, so that they can be seen, and even possessed. If we remember what we noted in the last section, and treated at length whilst considering *The Philosophy of Rhetoric*, namely, Richards' aversion to whatever is concrete, solid, or definite, then we may suggest that, despite all his assertions, Richards was in a sense *against* individuality.

This idea is supported by more direct evidence, namely, that derived from the way in which Richards in fact treats his notion of self-realisation, a key concept in his system of thought. The emphasis is almost entirely on *becoming* rather than on *being*, on aspiration

331

rather than fulfilment.[1] The main value of experiences of the Imagination seems to lie, as we pointed out before, not in the impulses satisfied at that moment but in our increased capacity to satisfy impulses in the future. Now an alternative conception would emphasise maturity, the recognising and enjoying of it, though by implication rather than directly and self-consciously, and necessarily within the context of a person's work, his relationships, and his social situation. Such a conception would also entail a degree of self-acceptance, which would include a recognition of what was possible and what was not possible. The contrasting conception of Richards is of course one common to many religions; it has its advantages, just as the other has its dangers. But it is essentially a magical view. I think too that Richards holds it because maturity for him means a fixing, a being such and such a person. He continually lays stress on the maintaining, indeed, the maximising of possibility. He must always have, as it were, the possibility of being something else. This is why for him the journeying is more important than *arriving*, the process (the writing) than the product (the articulate theory or concept). This is associated with life; stillness with what is dead, with mechanism rather than organisism. When he dealt with organic images, just as elsewhere, the emphasis again was only on growing, not on being grown with all the functions this fulfils. Surely if growing, developing, becoming are so important, what is more important is that at which we aim, the self-realisation itself. One would expect Richards to have written a great deal about this, but in fact there is scarcely anything and what there is is extremely vague. At times one gets the impression that what Richards wants is something that is unattainable. This is suggested partly by the high valuation that Richards puts on it, which suggests great rarity; and partly from the suggestion of logical impossibility, achieving a condition when the self and the object of its knowledge were one, attaining insight by watching oneself attaining insight (Confucius' axe-handle example). In the words that Richards sometimes quoted, "The reaching never reaches". We will remember too that when we asked how the increase in value due to poetic experience showed itself, we found we were only on a spiral; all we achieved was the capacity to have still better poetic experiences. The solutions to problems achieved by only implicit movements are never applied.

4. AUTHORITY AND THE SELF

In the first section of this chapter, we suggested that attitudes to the

---

[1] Cf., for instance, "[Man's] life is an increasing effort, usually mistaken, to become in fact what in design he already is: to realise his own nature." (*H.T.R.P.*, 179).

past such as Richards' might be explained by nostalgia for a time when we were part of a community, namely, the family. Since at that time we were also in a dependent position, the problem of our relation to authority arises. We noted that a very common religious way of solving this problem was by submission and identification. Richards, by way of contrast, seemed to adopt the opposite method, one much more characteristically political than religious. But now it appears that this method is not all it seems, and that the freedom which is demanded and exercised is won only at the price of the renunciation of individuality, whether we regard this absence of individuality as defensive anonymity, or a consequence of some deficiency in the process of internalising early models. Does what Richards writes or practises throw any light on this? The answer, I think, is that it does, and this may be shown by considering Richards' relationships with others, so far as his books reveal this.

Richards' relationships can be divided into three types: a relationship of very great respect with regard to poets and certain very distant almost mythical figures from the past, like Plato and Confucius; a highly critical relationship with older contemporaries or figures from the previous generation, when these were theorising or stating norms; and a relationship of leadership with regard to those younger than himself. The first two relationships are shown by what Richards says in his books about the others concerned. These relationships are almost entirely with people older than himself. Except for one or two poets, younger contemporaries are hardly ever mentioned, at least not by name, except for an occasional footnote. The third relationship is implied by the way in which he writes his books, many of which are derived from lectures delivered to students. This relationship is certainly not one merely of giving information for transfer to note-books.

We will dispose quickly of the second of these three relationships, which we have already referred to from time to time in the course of this book. With the exception of his comments on students' protocols, this relationship includes nearly all the personal criticism that Richards makes. It is notable for its absence of animosity and its well-controlled tone, but there is a very great deal of such criticism. It is indeed in his capacity to see an *objection* to a particular statement or theory, that Richards mainly manifests his acuteness in perceiving the individual.

The first relationship is also in general one that Richards has to his seniors, though not, in the case of poets, entirely. This relationship, unlike the first, involves little criticism. What mainly characterises it is its degree of passivity; for it is surely one thing to recommend highly appreciation of the arts and to draw attention to the amount of hard work this involves and to urge the reader to do this, and quite another to assert that this is the most valuable thing anybody could possibly do.

One would have thought that attempts to create things for oneself, to observe and to experience things true to one's own individuality rather than in a derivative way, to do writing as well as reading, to practice independent judgment and seek in expression the release of feeling, might also have been tackled, if there is to be talk of highest value.

It is true that all these things can only be achieved through a sort of apprenticeship system. We learn from others, we may for a time progress by partly being others. Great painters after all may extend themselves by copying paintings of masters who interest them. But this is a way of becoming a better painter, not a better anything else; it is not the only means of becoming this; and the important activity is not this but the new paintings that the painter now becomes capable of. Granted that identification is an important part of growing up, Richards' attitude is too rigid, too narrow, allowing scarcely any interaction, and not paying any attention to the development that should take place after such identification, whereby one attains to what mature individuality one can.

The relationship, as Richards describes it, is one in which, by hard work and the involvement of one's whole personality, one earns the right for the time being to be someone else, someone very powerful though not threatening. Richards, in illustrating the operation of the Imagination, quotes with approval Coleridge's remark about Shakespeare, "You feel him to be a poet inasmuch as for a time he has made you one—an active creative being".[1] In this condition of being someone else (rather than a poet in one's own right), no further effort is required—the continuous movement is self-generating. But the poet, though powerful, is also acceptable. He is not trying to force anything on to the reader. This is why it was so important for Richards to emphasise that the function of poetry was not to instruct. And an additional reassurance comes from the fact that poets, being privates, are not in reality powerful; they are not agents of society. We must remember too that the "submission" was only "experimental".

It is perhaps for this reason, too, that the most striking manifestation of individuality, other than in criticism, that Richards showed, was in his very frequent quotations of other people's words. The quotations are not by any means confined to the kind of language he himself most skilfully used; they have a rare and distinctive quality and are always a pleasure to read. But they imply a rather precise

[1] *C. on I.*, 84.

memory for, or at least interest in, the products of others, in marked contrast to Richards' own continuous imprecision of statement.

So far in considering this relationship we have kept to poetry. Have we anything different to say in the case of the philosophers? There are in fact differences, but I do not think they affect the main points we are making.

For similar reasons as with the poets, the philosophers are not threatening. There is perhaps additional safety in their remoteness in time, which goes with increasing ambiguity. Admittedly, there is no question of identification with them. Nevertheless, identification continues to be suggested by all the emphasis upon fusion and merging of things with one another, and to be specifically implied in the "coalescing of subject with object in the act of knowledge". This latter, as we have seen, leads to the identification of the self with "Nature (Sense I)", a very distant, mysterious Unknowable, with no personality, therefore hardly threatening though promising great power, because promising the maximum satisfaction of our impulses.

It is true that when Richards turns increasingly to philosophy, a more active role for the reader is contemplated. In his last two books, for instance, he does occasionally refer to writing, talking, and thinking, suggesting that a relaxation of linguistic norms might make us more creative. It is suggested too that the reader might *translate* passages of philosophy into Basic English, which means changing the original wording. Nevertheless, I think the difference with philosophers is still only one of degree. The emphasis is still upon reading and interpretation, as the titles of Richards' last two books suggest; hardly any attention is actually paid to the many interesting problems involved in writing, and no practical exercises in it are suggested. Intense thinking about philosophical problems is considered valuable for the same reason as was artistic experience, namely, that it is fully and extensively felt. The old theory about the transfer effects of poetic experience continued, as we saw, to be assumed in his later books. Furthermore, compared with the procedure of professional philosophers, Richards was almost entirely concerned with presenting and interpreting the views of others. In this connection, his Conservatism comes very much to the fore again. Though he criticised philosophers who were senior contemporaries of his or of a previous generation, he put forward instead, not views of his own, but views attributed to earlier figures, like Coleridge, and particularly patriarchal figures like Confucius, Mencius, Plato, and Aristotle. It is continually striking, for all his criticism of others' theories, how very, often oppressively, traditional Richards is. This suggests too that his attitude of not faulting things because any criteria by which we judged them

335

would be extrinsic and therefore not applicable, that we took as evidence of his concern for individuality and freedom, served another function too. It is a manifestation of Conservatism, a sort of 'letting sleeping dogs lie' philosophy. One must only interpret, never try to change, which would be interfering. This was an attitude that Richards showed very much with regard to language with all its wisdom waiting to be fathomed.[1] Hence his faith in etymology, his belief that metaphors never died and his trust in the illumination that multiple definition could bring.

Richards' third type of relationship differs from the other two in that it is predominantly concerned with those younger than himself. His main purpose after all is education, and many of his books aim directly at this. However passive Richards may have been in his second relationship, he is here very active. It is not just a matter of his speaking or writing to an audience that can take what he says or not, just as it pleases. What is implied is a getting of his audience together, as a conductor his orchestra, and causing them to work under his leadership at the various tasks set them. It is interesting to note here how much Richards uses the word 'we', not in a negative sense for avoiding the exposed position of the first person singular, but as a sort of rallying cry. Thus in talking about language, he constantly talks in terms of what *we* do with words, how much of *our* meaning *we* put into them, and so on. His use of 'we' is not relieved as it is, for example, in the writing of Eliot or Empson, by frequent use of the word 'you', suggesting an individualised reader interacting with the writer.

In many ways this relationship of Richards with his audience is the obverse of his second, but it is now he who is playing the role of an authority figure. As he grows older, he becomes less and less prone to present theories or, if he does, to be very specific in his presentation; thus he avoids the position of being criticised. Writing more and more in the mode of the Imagination, as he conceives it, he enjoys more and more freedom. But he does not do this on his own, but to an audience. He is, in other words, with regard to his audience slowly moving into the position the poets stood in with regard to himself. In *Principles of Literary Criticism*, Richards as a young man wrote of the mystic experience of the Imagination: ". . . for most men after their early years such experiences are infrequent, a time comes when they are incapable of them unaided and they receive them only through the arts."[2] But to Richards himself it has been given, long after his "early years", when himself approaching patriarchal status, to publish for

[1] See Sect. 4. Chap. Nine.
[2] *P.L.C.*, 244.

the first time his own poetry,[1] and thereafter to address and advise poets, young poets, themselves.[2]

But, whatever the merits of his poetry, so far as his prose writings are concerned Richards' choice as regards his relationship to his models—masculine vigour achieved through exercise of freedom from authority figures in one of their aspects, and through denial of individuality and rather liberal identification with them in another—limits the potentialities of his relationship with his readers. It limits them because, despite his high valuation of this, Richards markedly lacked the capacity to *form* or *shape* things. This is a further aspect of his failure to individualise. We will conclude our analysis of Richards' thought by examining this.

We have often remarked on Richards' deficiency in structuring, particularly with regard to his neglect of distinctions of logical category. Some light may be thrown on this if we compare the way in which Richards and his best protocolists commented on individual poems in *Practical Criticism*. The comments of Richards' good protocolists both here and in *Interpretation in Teaching*, make a significant contribution to the value of these books. It was a wise technique on Richards' part to include them. Nevertheless these very interesting brief analyses of poems contrast rather markedly with Richards' own writing. They are quieter in style and do not mind going into a lot of specific detail. Above all, they treat the poems as wholes, comparing alternative readings and showing the effect of these upon how one takes the metre, indicating where the climaxes take place, in short, making one very aware of the poem as an individual.

Richards, on the other hand, though he often has acute and enlightening remarks to make about aspects of a poem, never seems to do justice to its totality. Though he may in a very brief phrase indicate the theme of the poem, he tends to atomise it by considering in turn successive words or phrases, all of which is done with an impression of haste.[3] Also he generally (not always) confines himself to parts or poems rather than to whole poems.

A similar technique is practised with the philosophers, as shown particularly by Richards' translation of philosophical passages into Basic English. We do not find him trying to put into his own words, in a detailed and connected prose statement, the gist of the passage; what we get instead is a phrase by phrase translation. Similarly, too,

---

[1] *Goodbye Earth and Other Poems*, (1958); *The Screens and Other Poems*, (1961); *Tomorrow Morning*; *An Infernal Comedy*, (1962).

[2] See, for instance, his broadcast talk, *Poetry as an Instrument of Research*, published in *The Listener*, 17 September, 1959.

[3] For an example of this see his comments on the two lines from *Venus and Adonis* quoted on page 71 above.

with his treatment of philosophical systems. Largely this is limited to 'definitions' of single words. In so far as he does talk about these systems as a whole it is at such a level of generality as to rob them of all distinctiveness and much of their special interest. The two books of Richards where he makes an effort to describe the thought of a single thinker are *Mencius on the Mind* and *Coleridge on Imagination*. I don't think it would be unfair to characterise Richards' presentation of these thinkers as highly confused. All we get is a statement of some fairly macroscopic distinctions, a lot of refinement on these distinctions, a good deal of wobbling but little development.

Bearing in mind that functions condense on any one process, what sort of functional explanation can we give for this particular aspect of Richards' failure to realise individuality? In accordance with what we said earlier, we might take it as an example of Richards' fear of limiting an individual—in this case a part of a poem or of a philosophical system—by subordinating it to some larger whole, such as a category or class, which would be pejoratively described as an abstraction. I do not however think this does full justice to the feeling of rigidity we get from Richards' approach. What we clearly have here is also an incapacity to reproduce or to communicate the individuality of others. It is as though they are regarded as inviolable; not capable of being taken into oneself so that they may be *re*-shaped.

This shows itself too in Richards' habit of taking contrary theories and asserting that both are true, and of himself oscillating within dichotomies, instead of absorbing the theories into himself and building from their parts something new. It suggests that, just as he analyses passages, so does he himself read, in a *word-bound* manner. And with regard to his own observations too, as we saw in his treatment of comprehension, he does not seem able to bring them together so as to body forth a well-knit theory.

Richards is both too defensive, in his militant watchfulness, as bit by bit goes by, and too assertive, in the rallying 'Forward!' cry of his writing, to be able empathically to bend to the curve of things. Despite all he says, he keeps things at a distance, touches them but never joins with them. He is not totally devoid of a sense of structure, but it is one that is exceedingly simple. There is, for instance, his notion of unitary organisation, whose only dimension is that it can increase in amount; this is most of what he meant by his frequently used image of growth. There are, too, the many suggestions of duality, whether in Richards' balances of opposites, his notions of keeping two things separate from one another or fusing them with one another, his unilinear scale of comprehensiveness stretching between extremes, gaps which can close to nothing between observer and what is observed, or in his idea of a tendency towards increased order in the organism so as to match that of "the outer world". On the rare occasions on which he does attempt more complex models, as in his various attempts to portray the working of the attitudes (for one example, see page 190), they are mechanical and not I think very elucidating. Many of these structures evidence Richards' predominant concern with the self. But when they do come, like an emphatic grid between Richards and what he is looking at, they seem like nothing so much as manifestations of indifference. They make everything so much alike and so dull.

With his audience, that is, in his third relationship, Richards maintains a distance too. He maintains this in that he does not seem to work on them directly, by means of what he is writing about, but by what he says or implies concerning what he is writing about. His good protocolists by being absorbed in the object, not minding slowing down and going into detail, deepen our attention. There is something in common between them and us, and if what they are writing about is interesting and valuable, this is communicated. The means by which Richards makes us think that what he writes about is important is partly by direct assertion that it *is* important, partly by the excited quality of his writing,—as though he did not dare go slow with his audience—and partly by a variety of hints. Amongst the latter, there are his references to famous philosophers of the past and to high-sounding philosophical theories, his frequent quotations from the great, his mentions in a non-scientific topic of scientific method and practices, his mass attacks on all previous thinkers, and the constant implication that his approach is getting at fundamentals and yet in contrast to scholars whom he regards today as over-specialist, concerned, too, with issues of wide general interest for all. Richards' failure to trust in what he is writing about to work on us directly is like his neglect of the way in which concrete images may move us by their symbolising power.

The main means by which Richards claims that what he is doing is important is that of language. Whatever the considerable merits of what he does, by means of language he inflates it out of all reason. He wins with it victories that are phantom victories, won in a glass box. Virtually through language alone, we can pretty well win the full understanding of dramatic poetry like Shakespeare's tragedies.[1] Through this our value is increased, but the only use of this gain in value seems to be further experiences with language. Similarly, Richards claims we may mature politically through our insight into

---

[1] Richards does occasionally mention the necessity of having experienced what poems refer to, but his way of doing it, as in his references to the "immaturity" and "general" inexperience of life of his young subjects in *Practical Criticism*, suggests an underestimation of the experiencing that may be necessary.

339

GENESIS AND REVELATION (II)

language's choices, and all this without considering politics and its problems. Its actual difficulties and agonies are not *felt*.

Richards' 'language' is not language itself, for this, too, he keeps at a distance, looking not at its structure but at its individual words, all equals, as they pass by. And not even the words may stand on their own, but are dissolved into the flux of consciousness. Richards' 'language' is magical, as we might expect in the case of one who, in Word Magic, attributed to words so much power over people. Such language magic is one of the great superstitions of the day. Russell initiated this, accusing ordinary language of breeding mysticism, and calling on modest science to free us. The popular work of Richards, of Korzybski and his followers of the General Semantics Movement, and of that still fashionable linguistic relativist, product of Culture Pattern theory, Benjamin Lee Whorf, has spread the Word, though in the name now of a better mysticism.[1] This conception is magical because they attribute such great power to language, and write as though their mere insight had already given them that power. Partly they claim this because of now magical Science, which day by day brings us wonders which no men have had before, and partly it comes from their magical ideas of language. According to these, language can mirror the structure of reality; we can take it into ourselves, making its structure our structure and thus by sympathetic magic become one with Reality, and therefore all-sufficient. Language is a system, its components interdependent with one another; as a system it is something we can grasp the essence of in a sudden great insight. It is however a dynamic, not a static, system; therefore it may stand for movement, life, and fruitfulness. Everything changes, nothing is merely itself, we are not bound and fixed. Underlying appearances, there is a secret structure which manipulates things. The excitement of this is like the excitement of gossip about those in high places. In so far as this secret structure is manipulating us, within a moment we, on possessing the code, may transform ourselves.

Recognisably, these are the hidden and personal motives of science, of psycho-analysis, even perhaps of Linguistic Philosophy. But all of them, to achieve their ends, need close harnessing to the object, just as the individual to achieve his purposes in society has to commit himself to society. We cannot by climbing out into the air flee the destructive element.

[1] Cf. Korzybski's description of the beneficial effects of using the Structural Differential, which enables us to "learn 'silence' on the un-speakable objective levels" (*Science and Sanity* (1933), page 404). Cf. also Whorf's last published article, "Language, Mind and Reality," *Theosophist*, LXIII, 1942. In a negative way one might also include Wittgenstein, insofar as he aspired to dissipate philosophical worry and so accept silence.

340

INDEX OF SUBJECTS

INDEX OF NAMES

347

349